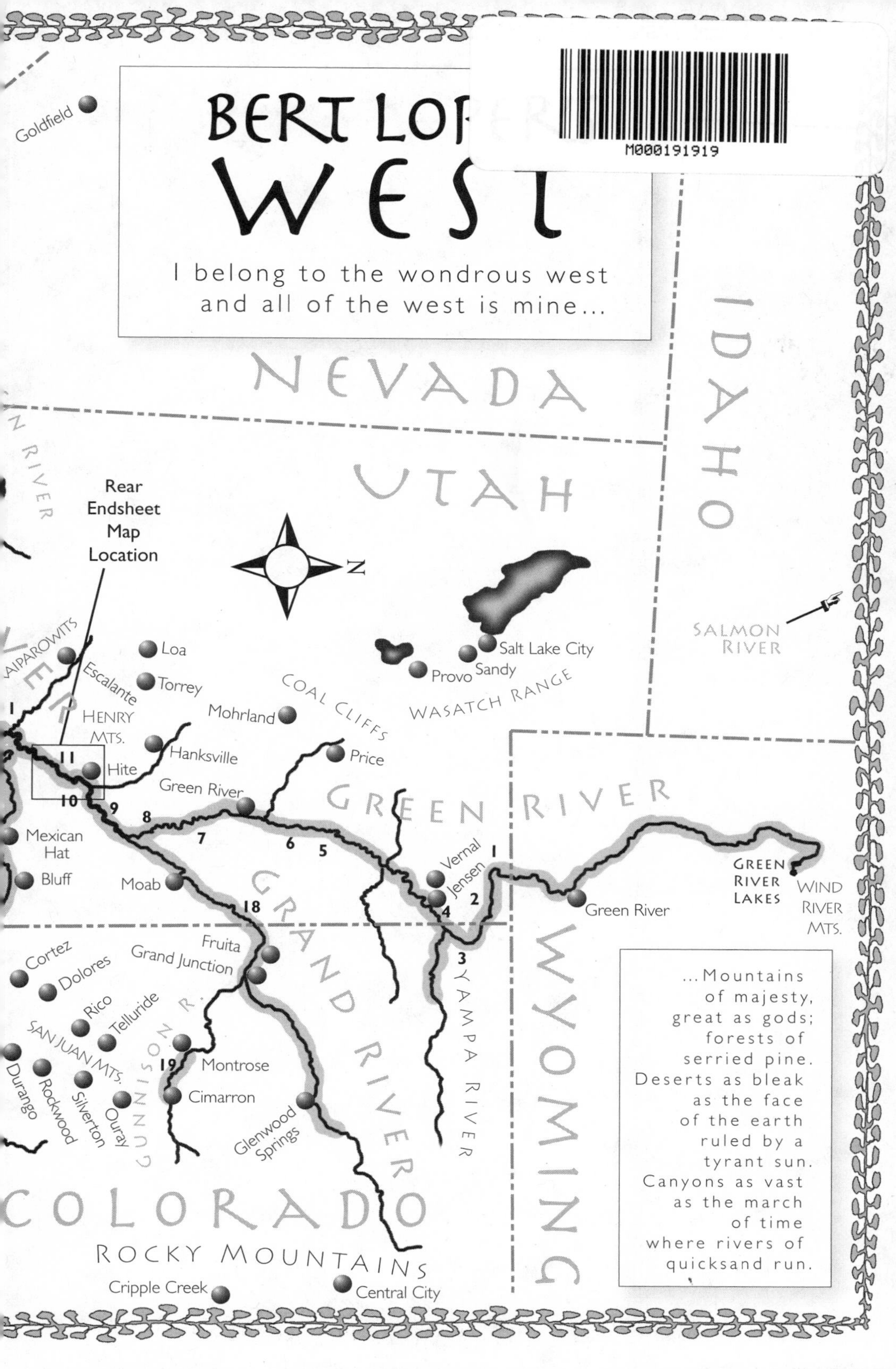
BERT LOF
WEST
M000191919
I belong to the wondrous west
and all of the west is mine...
Goldfield
NEVADA
UTAH
IDAHO
WYOMING
COLORADO
Rear
Endsheet
Map
Location
N
SALMON
RIVER
Salt Lake City
Sandy
Provo
WASATCH RANGE
COAL CLIFFS
Loa
Torrey
Mohrland
Escalante
HENRY
MTS.
Hanksville
Price
Hite
Green River
GREEN RIVER
Mexican
Hat
Bluff
Moab
GRAND RIVER
Vernal
Jensen
Green River
GREEN
RIVER
LAKES
WIND
RIVER
MTS.
YAMPA RIVER
Fruita
Grand Junction
Cortez
Dolores
Rico
Telluride
SAN JUAN MTS.
GUNNISON R.
Montrose
Cimarron
Durango
Rockwood
Silverton
Ouray
Glenwood
Springs
ROCKY MOUNTAINS
Cripple Creek
Central City
1
2
3
4
5
6
7
8
9
10
11
18
19
...Mountains
of majesty,
great as gods;
forests of
serried pine.
Deserts as bleak
as the face
of the earth
ruled by a
tyrant sun.
Canyons as vast
as the march
of time
where rivers of
quicksand run.

The Very Hard Way

The Very Hard Way

Bert Loper and the Colorado River

Brad Dimock

FLAGSTAFF
ARIZONA
· 2007 ·

Fretwater Press
1000 Grand Canyon Avenue
Flagstaff, Arizona 86001
www.fretwater.com

© Brad Dimock 2007
All rights reserved
Printed in the
United States of America
on permanent acid-free paper

First Edition

07 08 09 10 11 * 6 5 4 3 2 1

ISBN
(cloth) 978-1-892327-49-9
Limited edition of 700

(paper) 978-1-892327-69-7

Library of Congress Control Number
2006911324

This book was set in
Adobe Minion and P22 Typewriter
designed and typeset in Adobe InDesign
on a Macintosh G4
Cover and interior design by Fretwater Press

Front cover illustration:
Loper running Rapid 16, Cataract Canyon
by Henry Sandham
Wide World Magazine, England, 1908

to
Don Harris
Jack Watkins
and Bill Busenbark

for their enthusiastic
contributions to this book—
a story they were eager to read
but did not live long enough to see.

Glen Canyon 1939

Charles Hunt

The trail I have traversed has all been the very hard way and more than once I have gone up to a drift with a saw-hammer and a wrecking bar and come away with a boat and even in my mountain climbing I never belonged to an alpine club and the deserts I have plodded over was with blistered feet and a parched tongue and everything I have done in my 60 years in the west have been the very hard way but I still love it all.

– Bert Loper, 1947

introduction

THE STORIES of the Colorado River have long been my passion, from the time I first floated through Grand Canyon in 1971, and increasingly throughout three decades of whitewater expeditions. Those tales now permeate my career as a writer. The history of the men and women who were drawn to the River—long before it was fashionable—intrigue me, lure me to research just who these peculiar folk were, what brought them here, what they experienced, how the River affected them. For a third of a century I have inhaled facts, anecdotes, unattributed stories, and outright lies, trying to sort and sift through them in order to exhale the best tale, as truthfully as I can. There lies the snag. Truth.

History is at best a collective hunch: the rendition of past events that finds the most agreement. So, for that matter, is truth. We are informed and guided by facts, but "facts," when scrutinized, are often skewed, out of context, incomplete, biased, contradictory, transitory, and often exasperatingly far apart. And they may not be facts at all. And to quote my wise friend George Sibley, "Between any two facts lies a gap filled by an assumption." History, then, is largely up to the teller to define and shape, and the reader or listener to reshape as they understand it.

My style often frustrates the professional historian—a profession of which I am at best a self-taught poseur. Rather, I am a long-winded fireside storyteller with a penchant for accuracy and thoroughness, a weaver of threads with a weakness for seductive tangents and obscure anecdotes. Wafts of juniper smoke, fumes of bad whiskey, and the echoing gurgles of wild water often guide my thoughts in lieu of formal schooling in the science of history and art of prose.

In assembling historic tales I wrestle with contradictions and gaps. As often as not, they cannot be reconciled or filled except with a rather arbitrary assumption. In such cases I prefer to leave that assumption to the reader, for I believe there to be more than one valid conclusion.

I have come under fire in the past for not delving deep enough into the minds of my subjects, for not trying to guess their unspoken motives, their fears, their innermost secrets. But I believe such suppositions would far more likely tell you about me rather than my subject. So I will leave that up to you as well.

In this book I beg a bit of work from you—a bit of participation. In addition to asking you to supply many of your own assumptions and suppositions, I will often make you wade through the unique phrasings of original quotations rather than losing a generation of accuracy and authenticity by rephrasing it in my own, perhaps more fluid, prose. I have tried to spare you when possible, but may frustrate you here and there with more "voice" than you find altogether charming.

For the tale of Bert Loper I struggled to find one thread to follow. I failed. At best I could render Loper into two stories.

One storyline, the life of Loper, is a more-or-less conventional history and runs from Loper's birth to his final afternoon. It is a long and involved tale of hardship and poverty, perseverance and disappointment, joy and contentment.

The other storyline, the legend of Loper, is less linear. It begins with Loper's death and meanders through various reflections of his tale as told, interpreted, and perhaps misinterpreted, by those who knew him or knew *of* him. As well, Bert Loper was part of a far greater story: the birth and evolution of river running. Loper is part of most other rivermen's stories, much as they are part of his. You will meet many other river folk throughout the tale, and learn much about the growth of river running before, during, and after Loper's life. It is only in this context that Loper's place can truly be understood.

To weave these two threads, life and legend, I have chosen a structure that has delighted some of my colleagues and confounded others (comments range from *brilliant* to *ballsy, bothersome* to *bipolar*). The story runs in parallel tracks in alternating chapters throughout the book. Legend (odd chapters), life (even chapters), legend, life, and so on.

The tales of these two Lopers often compliment and inform each other, and at other times contradict. Truth, if such a thing exists, dances in the shadows. #

End of 1922 Green River survey

contents

life & legend

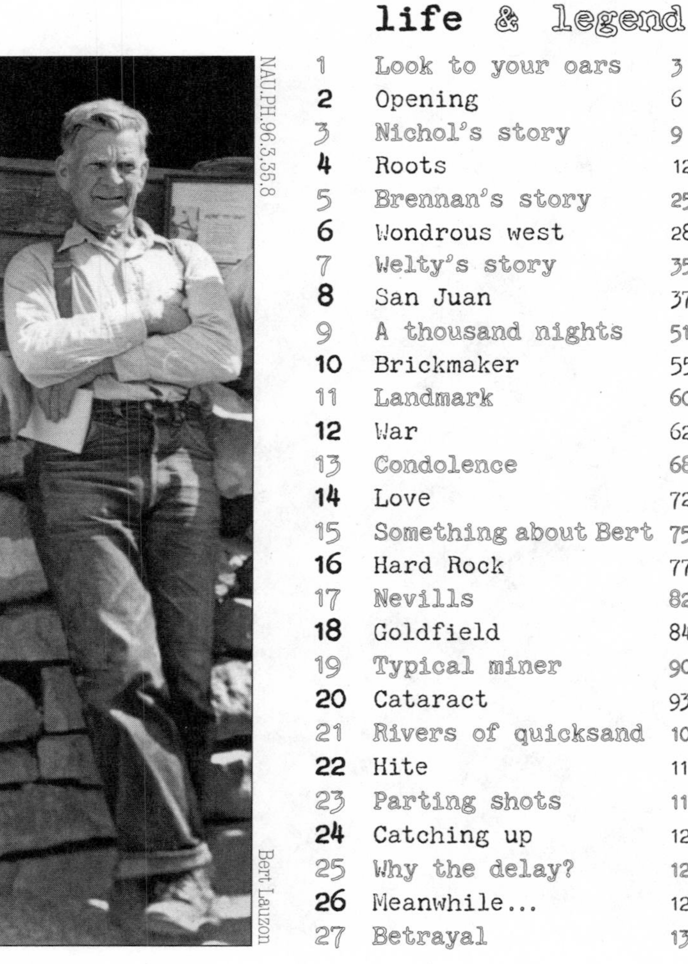

NAU.PH.96.3.35.8

Bert Lauzon

preface

Few "ordinary" lives are written. One supposes that readers do not want to read about the ordinary, but the extraordinary.

—Leon Edel, *Writing Lives*

Bert Loper was nothing if not ordinary. His writings, his occasional transcribed musings, his professional career, all reveal a man of modest goals and limited introspection. His education was spare, his ability to express himself equally so. His long marriage was devoid of sparks and flash, his abilities as a boatbuilder little more than adequate, and his skill in whitewater eclipsed by many contemporaries and understudies. Yet Bert Loper is a legend on the rivers of the West—an ordinary man with uncommon perseverance and an unusual drive to boat the muddy waters of the Colorado River.

If his life is extraordinary, it comes largely from circumstance and fate. A horrendous childhood of discord, abuse, parental loss, hunger, and little education is certainly not ordinary. If anything, in the value and class system of America his was "below" normal, a substandard childhood. His careers as cow-milker, ditch-digger, mule-skinner, coal miner, prospector, brick-maker, hard-rock miner, caretaker, duck-plucker, bridge-guard, and geyser-geezer are menial, mundane, mediocre. They call not to the imagination, nor give rise to fantasy.

It is his chance intersection with the Colorado River that draws him from the ordinary. From his first boating experience on the San Juan River in 1893, the West's brown rivers grabbed him, drew him back over and again for a lifetime, befriending him to extraordinary men: geologists Gregory, Miser, and Hunt; renown river men Kolb, Stanton, Galloway, Stone, Dellenbaugh, Marston, Aleson, Rust, Holmstrom, Frazier, and Hatch; protégés Blake, Harris, Lint, and Brennan.

Amid this panoply of western color, Loper was the straight man, the regular Joe who called it like he saw it, who quietly struggled to keep home and family together through the sweat of his brow, while returning again and again to the River—the River that increasingly dominated his life.

While many more colorful and eloquent men came to the river and moved on, Loper endured—the simple straight-shooter who was there before most arrived, and remained after many had followed other interests, drawn by fate to his fitting and inescapable end. #

Loper at end of Grand Canyon, 1939

NAU.PH.96.4.114.9

Bill Belknap

Legend

1 Look to your oars!

"LOOK TO YOUR OARS, BERT!" screamed Wayne Nichol, clutching the ropes on the foredeck. The rapid was coming quickly into view as they rounded the bend, waves exploding at random, the frail plywood boat sweeping toward the right shore, half-sideways. The other boats were nowhere in sight, Loper having cast off while the others were still packing lunch. Damned stubborn, cantankerous old fool. Eighty years old—you'd think he would've mellowed a bit by now. Now they were alone, dropping into a perfect maelstrom, out of control at the mercy of the river. Nichol was about to turn around and see what on earth Bert was doing, why he wasn't straightening the boat, when a mammoth wave billowed up on his right. Instinctively, for he had rowed boats of his own, Nichol threw his weight into the wave as it broke over him, hoping to keep the boat upright. But it was no use. It was early July and the Colorado was still in flood, the waves and holes far larger than normal, the river more undeniable.

By Loper standards, it was a brand new boat. He had built it for this trip out of donated plywood, straightened nails, used screws, old paint. He test-floated it near his home town of Green River, Utah, weeks earlier, rowing it a bit, then affixing his outboard motor to test it under power. It worked well either way. Loper named it *Grand Canyon*—for that was where he planned to row it. He motored it through Glen Canyon with a group of Boy Scouts in June. The craft was sound.

This trip was to be a celebration, a ten-year anniversary of Loper's first successful run of Grand Canyon in 1939 with Don Harris. That trip had made up for thirty years of Loper's foiled attempts and botched plans. They had run every rapid—quite a feat for that era—with Loper in the lead. That's how Loper wanted it this time, too. In the intervening years he and Harris had run rivers throughout the West, setting new records, covering new ground. Now, finally, they were back in Grand Canyon, and Loper, in spite of the deep concerns of some, was leading the pack.

The wave exploded. The *Grand Canyon* heaved up onto its left gunwale, wavered on its edge for a moment, then toppled over, upside-down, slamming Nichol deep into the turbulent roil. He grabbed a rope as he went under. All was dark and suddenly very silent—his hearing aid drowned in the dunking. Quickly, he hoisted himself onto the slick plywood bottom. Moments later he saw Loper a few yards upstream, floating motionless. Nichol screamed to him repeatedly, but Loper gave no indication he was conscious, or even alive. Nichol rode the inverted skiff through three more rapids, trying in vain to paddle it to shore. With another rapid approaching and no way to land the capsized boat, Nichol dove into the river and swam ashore. In an eddy downstream, the *Grand Canyon*, its stern compartment ballasted by Loper's outboard motor, spun eerily, the pointed bow protruding vertically from the river. Three revolutions and it was gone. Standing, Nichol saw Loper, eyes closed, heading straight down the tongue of the next rapid. Loper made a perfect entry, hit the exploding wave at the foot of the tongue, and disappeared.

✣ ✣ ✣

The evening before, Loper sat in the sand, having hauled out his typewriter. A man with less than half a dozen years of formal schooling, Loper loved to read, and loved to record his daily doings. He rolled in three sheets of paper, with carbons, and pecked:

> I would like to explain that there have been 4 Doctors told me that I would come down on the Colo. River and never return on acct of a bad heart so on that account I hesitated on coming on any further but there were several persuaded me to finish the day and it was a hard day considering the condition of my heart—but I was the first to pull out and after kissing Don's Wife Good-by I pushed off and in 6 miles we passed under the Navajo Bridge on our way to mead Lake and another 3 miles we came to—and passed Badger Rapids without looking them over....
>
> The personnel of the party is composed of the following: Ralph Badger who is a paid passenger next is Howard Welty who will accompany us as far as Bright Angle—Then two in a rubber boat—Harry Aleson who is the navigator and a lady whose name is Mrs. Lou Fetzner

> and Don Harris—super boatman—Jack Brennan also super, Wayne Nichol who is a friend of Don's and yours truly—Bert Loper who is taking this opportunity of celebrating his 80th year of my birth—having been born in the year 1869—ran every rapid of this turbulent stream the year I was 70 and at that time it was suggested that we do it in 49....

When Harris and the others caught up, they saw Nichol's arm-waving, and pulled ashore. They piled back into the three remaining boats to chase Loper. Harris, Brennan, Aleson and their passengers scanned both shores, squinting downriver and into the eddies. They did not find him. Although Loper wore a kapok life preserver, it may have been damaged or in poor repair—once waterlogged, they became what riverman Dave Rust called "burial insurance."

Seventeen miles later they spied the *Grand Canyon* snagged against the right bank, badly battered, upside down. They pulled it onto shore, righted it, bailed it out, and dragged it up the slope. The stern was smashed, the sidewalls shattered. Just a month into its existence as a whitewater craft, its career was irrevocably over. But it had done its job. *Grand Canyon* had delivered Bert Loper to his grave. #

2 Opening

On a blazing July afternoon in 1869, three battered wooden boats crept down the muddy Colorado River against a stiff headwind. Ahead on the left, a tributary joined the mainstream. The leader waved his signal flag; the sinewy oarsmen ruddered, backwatered, and brought the three craft ashore. Nine men scaled the mud promontory splitting the streams. "It has a very rappid tide and is quite muddy," noted George Bradley:

> There is not a tree at its mouth and the place is most desolate and uninviting.... The temperature seldom gets lower than 100° except just before sunrise when it falls a little.... [T]o find shade we have to crawl into the rocks, and the rocks are almost hissing hot.

"There is nothing growing at the junction but a few willows," grumbled Jack Sumner:

> Cañon walls from 300 to 800 ft. all sandstone, so steep and smooth that it is next to impossible to get out. Distance [downstream] from Grand River, 116 miles. General course, due southwest. Country worthless to anybody or anything.

Yet their leader, a small and energetic man, his right arm missing below the elbow, was oblivious to his men's dismal spirits. "Cool pleasant ride today through this part of Mound Cañon," he observed. "The large boats racing. Still more cones and rounded points." Major John Wesley Powell was exhilarated. Despite wrecking a boat, losing provisions to river and spoilage, and having one man leave, Powell's expedition had survived more than two months out of Green River, Wyoming, and was pressing ever farther into the unmapped expanse of the Great Unknown. No one had ever explored the length of the Green and Colorado Rivers of the

West, no one had ever described their stark, naked-rock scenery, no one had ever attempted to traverse this jagged landscape by boat. Although trappers had long been sluicing canoes down the brisk streams of the Northwest, the art and skill of "river running"—navigating whitewater rapids by rowboat—had yet to be born. Powell and his men were inventing it as they went along.

It was just four years since the Civil War ended at Appomattox—the war that wrenched the country inside-out against itself, the war that stole Powell's right arm. America was exhausted, sick from fighting. It was a great time to be in the West, to explore new terrain, to forget the horrors that soldiers like Powell and his men had endured. Although rations were as spare as hardships were plentiful, no one was shooting at them.

Contemporary maps of the West showed rivers entering and departing the region, but the true course of the streams and the extent of their navigability remained unknown. Still, Powell had studied enough charts and journals to know he had just discovered the confluence of the Colorado and San Juan Rivers. Native Americans had tramped this ground for millennia before Powell, and an unheralded trapper or two may have passed this way, but none left a record. This was the heart of canyon country, still one of the least known and least traveled parts of the continent. Powell's party planted no flag, claimed no dominion for their country, but this landscape was theirs to name, to describe, to invent—their prize to bring back to civilization.

Sextant in hand, Powell scrambled for altitude. He needed to determine the precise location of this confluence—another vital point to place on the unmarked map. But sheer cliffs and an overcast sky thwarted him. He returned to the boats. To his men's chagrin, Powell called for camp. It was Saturday, the thirty-first day of July, 1869.

That very day, as Powell and his men tramped along the desert shoreline, one thousand miles to the east in a dingy, red house near the Mississippi River, eighteen-year-old America Loper gave birth to her second child, a boy called Bert.

Powell's voyage thrilled the country and his descriptions came to define the arid Southwest and the rivers and canyons that incise it. Restless settlers pushed steadily west, staking their claims wherever their imagi-

Powell's Whitehall boats, 1871

nation deemed a new life possible. Prospectors, with their burros, gold pans, and dreams of bonanza, scoured this new terrain. Most came overland, but a few, following Powell's audacious example, attempted these streams by boat. In time, one man, the stubborn Missouri loner named Bert Loper, centered his life on the San Juan and the Colorado, seeking gold but finding a home; scratching for sustenance but discovering peace; learning to navigate the swirling rivers, only to be consumed by them. #

Legend

3 Nichol's story

DALLAS WAYNE NICHOL was born in Salt Lake City in 1910 to a devout Mormon family. Like three of his brothers and his grandmother, Wayne lost his hearing in his early twenties, and wore a hearing aid for the rest of his life. He was an early skiing enthusiast, and while trudging about in the snows of the Wasatch Range above Salt Lake, he befriended Alf Engen, whose exploits at the early ski mecca of Alta became skiing legend. Although he worked as a building contractor, skiing became Nichol's passion. When in 1944 Don and Berta Harris moved in next door to the Nichols, their talk soon drifted toward their hobbies. Mutually intrigued, they struck an informal deal: Harris would take Nichol boating if Nichol would teach Harris to ski. Afterward they were, in Nichol's words, "ski bums in the winter, river rats in the summer." In this they presaged a predominant theme in the embryonic river industry.

Nichol's first river trip was through the Canyon of Lodore with Harris in 1946. Nichol was smitten enough that he began building a boat, the *Laphene*, based on Harris's craft. (Don Harris's first name was Laphene.) As the 1949 trip with Bert Loper approached, Harris invited Nichol to go along as Loper's passenger, hoping that old Bert would relent and let Nichol, by now a competent oarsman, take over when he tired. But of course that was not to be. Three days after Loper vanished in the river, Nichol, by no means a writer, penned one of the few letters of his life:

> July 11, 1949
>
> Dear Leith and family,
>
> I've written a card, but you may not be able to read it. After leaving Berta at Lee's Ferry, we went under the bridge. About 30 min. later Berta came out on the bridge and waved to us as we went under it. Bert said we went through Badger Creek rapid without looking it over but

we didn't. [They did scout it.] We camped about ½ mile below Badger Creek rapid. Soap Creek was a wild looking rapid, but not too bad to run. I think, I got a good picture of it. Bert went through it alone. Bert wouldn't let me touch the oars even between the rapids, and he was so afraid he wasn't going to be the first one through a rapid that he would always pull out before anyone else was ready. We lunched at about mile 21½, and as usual, Bert and I pulled out about 10 min. ahead of the rest. He wouldn't stop rowing between the rapids or let me spell him. We went through 3 or 4 smaller rapids before we came to the mile 24½ rapid. I could see it was a big one from a long way up stream and that we would have to pull out on the left bank to look it over, and I told Bert in plenty of time to of made it in, but it was a long pull across the river. I tried to get him to let me pull it in, but he wouldn't let me. We got almost in but there was a few rocks there and he was afraid they would bump the boat and he pulled back out. I could see, then, we had to go through. We hit the rapid just right, but I think Bert was too tired, and I know from past experience he didn't have the strength to pull into the waves as he should have. It was not a hard rapid to run, but it did require some strength to pull it through. About the third big wave hit us sideways and over we went. I grabbed a rope and hung onto the boat. I climbed on top of the boat, and looked back. Bert was about 25 or 30 feet behind me, but I couldn't get to him. He didn't look like he was doing much struggling. I got the spare oars on the boat and started to try to get it to shore. I went through three rapids before I could get it into an eddy. I couldn't quite get it into shore, so I let it go and swam in. I got on the bank and about 5 or 10 min. later I saw Bert coming down. He was facing down stream and going into a rapid that had a big under current. His eyes were closed and they had that goeyish look that a drowned or dead person has when they're wet. He hit the rapid right down the center of the V and I thought then that there couldn't be a more fitting way for him to go out, and I figured that would be the last time we would see Bert Loper, and I still think so. I don't think that anybody should feel that it was a terrible thing. I think it's the way he wanted it. Don's probably told Berta about finding the boat 8 miles down stream, so I won't bother about that. It sure is a nice trip. The trouble hasn't spoiled the trip too much. I think everybody feels it was the way things were meant to be. I lost my watch, the camera and my ear

Nichol riding with Jack Brennan

Wayne Nichol 1980s

mould and the ear piece that fit on the mould so that I've got to make the rest of the trip without sound.

A few post scripts to Nichol's tale: His family recalls Wayne feeling that Loper's wife Rachel somehow blamed him for Bert's death. Conversely, Nichol's family felt Loper had no right to take Wayne on what appeared to them to be a suicide run. Nichol was also accused by some of changing his story. His family points out that much of what went on for the remainder of the trip was fraught with misunderstanding, as Nichol could not hear a word from the time of his inundation until the trip was over.

All small details in the big picture, but one lasting thing stuck with Nichol: he was known to muse that if Loper could die in his boat, doing what he loved, then he wanted to die on his skis. He nearly did a few times, blowing out a shoulder, shattering his knee, but always returning to the slopes. He taught skiing at Alta until he was 79, hollering advice even to those not in his class. (And his ski pal Don Harris loaded the chair lift there until well into his seventies.) At the end of the 1989 ski season, Nichol emptied his locker at Alta and brought his gear home—he'd never done such a thing before. He died peacefully a month later in his bathtub. #

4 Roots

I WAS BORN in Bowling Green, Pike County, Missouri July 31st 1869 in a house on the outskirts of the town and as I remember the house was painted red and had 4 rooms.... I had a stick horse named dolly varden and there was an old chair that I managed to drag around and called it my wagon.... I had an uncle named Winnie and he had a span of mules and the barn was on the back of the lot and there was a cistern at the barn and my brother and I nearly filled the well with about every thing we could carry and throw down in the well.... I do not remember my father for he and my mother parted when I was two years old ... and I was always taught that he was dead.... I still tell that my parents both died when I was three years old—that being the time my mother died and it was from there on that I was an orphan in every respect.

In the basement of the old Masonic Temple in Salt Lake City, Utah, Bert Loper pecked at his typewriter. Still robust in his seventies, he was proud of his long, difficult, and eventful life, and grateful for all he had achieved. He was not a wealthy man; he was childless with scant education and little to his name. But he was comfortable, living rent-free as a caretaker, and his wife of twenty-five years still adored him. Loper wanted to set his life down on paper, to share it with the world. He set about transcribing his journals, recalling river trips, writing autobiographical essays. He corresponded with many of those he had met along the way, often answering at length their questions about his origins and adventures. Of his youth in Pike County, he remembered much, but of his parents and heritage he had little accurate information. He wrote what he believed to be true. His renditions of who they were and how things came about told of a rough infancy, yet the true facts are tougher than Loper ever imagined.

Deep in the courthouses, libraries, archives, and attics of Missouri and Texas lie fragments that, woven together, hint at the roots of Bert

Loper. Censuses, genealogies, local histories, cemetery, military and probate records—all give clues to the story Loper never knew. It is a tale of an unsettled family adrift on the frontier, set in the harsh years surrounding the American Civil War.

Bert's father, Jehail P. Loper, was born in Lycoming County, Pennsylvania around 1830. His family had been in the country nearly two centuries by then. Sea captains and whalers, millwrights and farmers, they were practical, hardworking, and adventurous. When Jehail was two years old his father William, a New Jersey-born farmer with a westering itch, put down stakes near the headwaters of Big Raccoon Creek in Putnam County, Indiana. There, six years later in 1838, Jehail's mother, Frances Dominy Loper, died. The Lopers moved on, this time to Des Moines County, Iowa on the west bank of the Mississippi. By his mid-twenties, Jehail had drifted downriver 150 miles to Pike County, Missouri. There he met and married a Missourian named Ann and fathered three daughters, Florence (1856), Eugenia (1858), and Alice (1862). He worked as a brickmaker and in 1857 bought twenty acres east of the county seat at Bowling Green.

Jehail Loper's Civil War record is spotty and lackluster. He joined Captain Hardin's Company B, Pike County Regiment on July 20, 1861. And although he was not formally discharged until September 2 of that year, on August 7 Loper also enlisted in Company A of the First Regiment, Illinois Cavalry. After several assignments in central Missouri, Loper's company was surrounded by rebel forces in the Siege of Lexington, and surrendered on September 20. Loper was taken as prisoner but paroled the same day. The company reorganized and guarded supply trains and depots at Rolla, Missouri throughout the first half of 1862.

On April 24, 1862, Colonel Robert Lundhausen wrote to General John McAllister Schoffield:

> J.P. Loper was taken up day before yesterday as a deserter of the United States Army. He was mounted on a Government horse, armed with a navy revolver, and wears the United States Cavalry Uniform. The prisoner … pretends to have a leave of absence which he is trying to prove by enclosed permit.… The Prisoner is about 5 feet 8 inches high, light complexion, blue eyes, and apparently 24 or 25 years old.

The "permit," written in a hand strikingly similar to Loper's, granted him permission to pass between Rolla and Bowling Green. His last roll call notes that Jehail P. Loper, private, deserted on April 22. Loper's military record ends with no indication of court martial or further service. His company mustered out on July 14, 1862.

Loper returned to his young family in Bowling Green. Perhaps not coincidentally, the last indication of his wife Ann's existence came that same year with the birth of her third daughter, Alice. Perhaps she died in childbirth. Perhaps Alice's birth or Ann's death had something to do with Jehail's desertion. Divorce is possible although no records of it exist. Ann Loper simply vanishes from all records.

Then, on May 29, 1867, five years after Alice's birth, Jehail P. Loper, thirty-seven, father of three girls, married sixteen-year-old America Mettler.

America Mettler, the third of six children, was born in Franklin, Ohio, on October 6, 1850. Her parents, Philip A. Mettler and Teresa Lyon, had married there five years earlier. The family wandered west in the 1850s to Minnesota and central Missouri before settling in Pike County. Philip, a farmer, volunteered for the Missouri Infantry in 1862, and served the Union army as a musician. After fighting in several battles, his company was captured during skirmishes at Resaca, Georgia on October 12, 1864. In prison Mettler contracted a virulent strain of diarrhea. Although he was turned over to Union forces, he died in a Union hospital in Annapolis, Maryland on March 19, 1865, just three weeks before Lee's surrender at Appomattox.

Back in Bowling Green, Teresa Mettler struggled to feed her children. It was two years before she was granted Philip's back pay, and another year before her widow's pension of eight dollars a month was approved. Young America, fourteen and illiterate, was likely working alongside her brothers to help support the family. Perhaps America felt lucky when two years later Loper, old enough to be her father, married her. She immediately became step-mother to three daughters, though age-wise, at eleven, nine, and five, they were closer to being her sisters.

Not quite nine months after the wedding, on February 26, 1868, America gave birth to Andrew Jackson Loper. Seventeen months after that, on July 31, 1869, she bore her second and last son. No birth records exist, so the boy's given name remains in question. The family bible records him as Berta; the 1870 U.S. Census lists him as Albert A. The 1880 census is smudged but appears to read Berta. And an 1872 court record lists the children as Philip Andrew and Albertus. From an early age, the boy went by Bert.

> I was born of Northern parents and at that time Missouri was a border slave state and nearly all of the people were southern and all of the men folks that was old enough to go went off to war on the side of the Union and that left my Grand Mother at home with a house full of children and the insults and indignities that were heaped on her were plenty and while I was not born until 5 years after the end of the war the recollections of all my Grand Mother had endured were still very vivid in her mind and it was all transmitted to me, so in that way I learned the northern side of the story and I also had my disadvantages for my folks were called "Black Republicans" and there was very few children of northern people.

Although Missouri was a contested state in the Civil War, Pike County was, in spirit, part of the South, on the fringe of an area known as "Little Dixie." Slaves were common, tobacco was a chief crop, and those who sympathized with Lincoln's emancipation of the blacks—Black Republicans—were derided. The area is said to have supplied as many soldiers to the South as to the North. Pike County, however, was better known for other cultural traits.

By the time Bert Loper was born, Pike County was nationally maligned as the home of the uncouth yokels known as *pikes, pikers,* or to those who truly disdained them, *pukes.* Their language and behavior were imitated and mocked in literature throughout the country. Mark Twain immortalized the lingo in *The Adventures of Huckleberry Finn,* stating: "In this book a number of dialects are used, to wit: the Missouri Negro dialect; the extremist form of the backwoods Southwestern dialect; the ordinary 'Pike County' dialect; and four modified versions of the last." A Bret Harte character claims, "We ain't hankerin' much for grammar and dictionary hogwash, and we don't want no Boston parts o' speech rung in on us the first thing in the mo'nin. We ain't Boston—we're Pike County—we are." "A Pike," wrote Bayard Taylor:

> is the Anglo Saxon relapsed into semi-barbarism. He is long, lathy and sallow; he expectorates vehemently; he takes naturally to whisky; he has the shakes his life long at home, though he generally manages to get rid of them in California; he has little respect for the rights of others; he distrusts men in proper clothes, but venerates the memory of Andrew Jackson.

The Pikers disagreed, the 1872 *Pike County Pocket Gazetteer* claiming, "The society of the county is composed chiefly of, and receives its tone from the descendants of the original settlers of the country, the most of whom came from Virginia and Kentucky. Morality, intelligence and hospitality are distinguishing traits of citizens of the county." Eighty miles northwest of Saint Louis, with good rail, river, and road access; temperate climate, fertile soil, and ample rainfall; Pike County was and is ideal farming country.

✣ ✣ ✣

The new Loper family shifted around the county for the first few years. Jack, as the first son was called, was born in Ashley, seven miles south of Bert's birthplace in Bowling Green, and by 1870 they had moved eleven miles east to Louisiana, Missouri, Pike County's port town on the Mississippi. Their unrest was more than geographic. When Bert was two years old his father filed for divorce, hurling vitriolic accusations. In the probate records of *Jehail P. Loper vs. America Loper*, the complaint, after stating the day of their wedding and attesting to Jehail's faithfulness and character, reads, "the Deft. wholly disregarding her duties as a wife has demeaned herself wantonly, & lightly and lasciviously and disregarding her own and her husbands honor, did on the 1st day of May 1871 commit adultery with one Chat Leuk & at other times did act in bad faith to her marriage vows." Jehail went on to plead for divorce and custody of the two boys.

Counterfiling for America Loper, attorney A.C. Sheldon requested the descriptive language about her behavior (wantonly, lasciviously, disregarding honor, bad faith, etc.) be removed, on the grounds that such allegations were "irrelevant and redundant and facetious … and so indefinite that the precise nature of the charge is not apparent." Sheldon neither affirmed nor denied the charge of adultery. He subsequently filed on America's behalf to impose a lien against Jehail for legal expenses as the plaintiff "has no property goods chattels or effects whereof to levy said costs and that he—the said Plaintiff—is so unsettled in his business and property interests and affairs as to endanger the officers of the court with respect to their legal demands."

Court records fail to provide the reaction of the judge, but it seems the case was denied, or at least dropped for a year. In September, 1872, Jehail filed again. This time he made no mention of adultery, but claimed, after averring his faithfulness as a good husband, that "the defendant on the said 9th day of August 1871 without reasonable cause or just provocation deserted the bed and board of the plaintiff and ... has absented herself ... for more than one year." Loper asked for divorce once again, but this time did not request custody of the boys.

America's attorney counter-filed, this time all business. He stated that Loper's claims that he had treated her kindly and with affection were *not* true, and it was *not* true that she left without reasonable cause or just provocation, but that:

> said plaintiff during all that time disregarding his duties as the husband of this defendant did offer such indignities to this defendant as to render her condition intolerable. That on many different days ... said plaintiff beat, struck and kicked this defendant and that about two weeks prior to said day ... struck this defendant several blows with his fist and pulled defendant's hair and ... ordered this defendant out of his house and told her never to return. Thereafter this defendant did leave his house and has since that time in obedience to the express command of said plaintiff kept away therefrom.

The document goes on to describe two children now living with the defendant, and asks to be granted a divorce and custody. America, twenty-two years old, signed with an X, "her mark." Again, the court decisions do not survive, but history implies America won the case and was granted the divorce and custody of her sons.

Was the true story one of adultery? Abandonment? Abuse? Or perhaps a combination? We cannot know, but it is clear the loveless marriage ended none too soon. Regardless of how the relationship crumbled, Bert Loper's first three formative years could not have been pleasant.

Jehail, apparently taking his daughters with him, left Missouri that fall a bitter man, walking forever out of the lives of his sons.

America, Jack, and Bert moved in with Teresa Mettler, America's widowed mother. But before America could begin to get back on her feet, the family curse struck. Her sister Orpha Ann had been taken by tuberculosis as an infant in 1862. Now it came after America. A highly contagious "armored" bacteria that eats away at the lungs, tuberculosis brings progressively worse coughing, choking up of blood, and ultimate death by asphyxiation—a miserable way to go. In a few short years both America and her brother Winchester succumbed, leaving Bert and Jack essentially orphans. Although the exact date of America's death remains unclear, Bert later wrote:

> I was three years old at the time of my Mother's death but I can remember it very well and I can also remember standing at the grave and to my childish mind that was the most awful and deepest place in the whole world.
>
> ... and then it was that my brother and I were separated, he going with our aunt Waty Johnson and I remaining with Grandma, so my boyhood was spent in Bowling Green. My brother would be allowed to visit me a couple times a year but I now know that his babyhood was far worse than mine, for while Grand Ma never missed a chance to whip, that old inhuman Uncle (Allen Johnson) would not whip but he would beat, and there must be so much in the raising for it seemed that all the tenderness was beat out of him, and where I would cry to see something in pain he would call me chickenhearted, and where I would pick up a wet bedraggled kitten home and give it a saucer of milk and warm it, he would kill it.

America's oldest brother, Benjamin Lyon Mettler was a wagonmaker and set up shop seven miles west of Bowling Green in Curryville, a farming village of around two hundred. Teresa Mettler followed with her youngest son Marcellus "Pete," seventeen, and young Bert. Austere and deeply religious—"a consistent member of the Baptist Church, having made a profession of religion when quite young," according to her obituary—Teresa Mettler raised her grandson with little lenience. Within a few years Benjamin left for the West, settling in Durango,

America
Loper

Teresa Mettler

Marcellus "Pete" Mettler

Colorado, and Pete went to work as a rail hand, leaving Bert alone with his grandmother.

> I think about all the toys I ever had was a sled and a two wheel cart—both were made by my wagon maker uncle but they were about the best sled and cart in town.... We had an old milk cow named Lucy and it was on Lucy that I learned to milk which later stood me in good stead....
>
> When I was about nine years old I would get a job riding rake horse during hay time and would get 50¢ per day and I must have been about 11 years old when I got a job off bearing brick and that was about the toughest job a kid could have for it seemed that my back would brake....
>
> I was a very puny kid so it is natural that I always got cuffed around plenty in the winter time as I was always sick most of the time but in the summer I got along better and my mania was swimming and my Grandmother being of the old school where to spare the rod was to spoil the child and the whippings I got for that one thing alone was

Brad Dimock

Jack Loper

Mettler tombstones, crumbling in Bowling Green: Teresa, Winchester, America. Orpha Ann

plenty and many a time I would start out with the knowledge that I was going to get whipped but I always figured that it was worth it so I would go swimming and sometimes it would be two beatings a day for me....

About 3 miles north of Curryville there was a creek and it was sure a pleasure to me to get down on the creek especially on sundays.... Our religious services would start Saturday morning and again in the evening then sunday we would have preaching in the morning sunday-school in the afternoon then preaching again in the evening.... [I]t seems as though I always wanted to do the very things that I should not have done and many times on a sunday when I was all cleaned up and ready for church I would get in with a bunch of boys and to the creek we would go and as a rule we would make a day of it and when spring came it was the joy of my life to get out in the woods along the creek and just why it was necessary to be beat for doing such things is still beyond me to understand....

The creek was such a wonderful place with its clear pools and nice swimming holes and the little fishes and the old craw fish was something I could not get to see every day and there was no harm but I got my beatings just the same.

> My schooling was in an old red brick schoolhouse and the schools of that day were different to the schools to-day for a kid could be in the 5th reader and still doing addition and things like that and as I said before I would lose about half of my schooling each winter so therefore I never got to more than the 6th grade.... [I]t always seemed to be easy for me to do a good job of reading but mathematics and grammer kept me back and I find as I go on through life that that is what I need the most.
>
> I was always puny spindly and sickly ... and just how I managed to dodge the T.B. is more than I can understand for most all my Mothers folks passed on with that dread disease.

Loper's grandmother was the next to go, in 1882 when Bert was not quite twelve. With his uncle Benjamin gone to Colorado, the Curryville Mettler clan was down to his uncle Pete, twenty-six and soon to marry, and aunt and uncle, Waity and Allen Johnson, still guardians of Bert's brother Jack.

> I was housed up in an airtight room ... with a hot fire in it and every window shut tight ... the last winter of my Grand Mothers life ... her with one lung gone and the other on its way.... I slept in the same bed with her ... and she passed on the 17th of March and us being poor people that caused the breaking up of our home....
>
> So that put me with the brute of an uncle Johnson, that is I hired out on a farm for the summer but in the fall I went with Johnson ... and a bigger brute never lived and he just beat and would use his fist or anything that he happened to have....
>
> My uncle would put me to work uncovering corn—to uncover corn means that I would follow after him when he was cultivating the corn and all of the corn that got covered up I would have to stoop and uncover it and because I could not keep up with him I would get beaten....
>
> But that put my Brother and me together so it did not take long for us to plan it all out so in the fall or corn cutting time we departed and was gone for one and a half years.

Bert was thirteen and Jack fourteen when they ran away from Allen Johnson's farm, headed for Texas "as that was where the Cow Boys were located." They arose before dawn, walked five miles to the railroad, and hopped a freight west. There were few through-going trains, however, and between rides they begged food, "that is, my Brother did the begging for that was out of my line." At Booneville, Missouri they spent the night at Flournoy Snelling's dairy and the next morning Bert got a job milking. Jack was sent fifty miles upriver to work for Snelling's brother.

> I was not long in becoming the best milker of the dairy and the agreement was that I was to go to school during the winter but that part of the agreement was not carried out so I only got my board for my work for the winter and all the next summer too and in the fall the man ... sold out his dairy and moved to Clinton, Mo. and I went with him and I got about 4 months schooling and then returned to Boonville to the dairy and went to work for the new owner by the name of Sebe Hazel and I believe I got $8 per month and it was not long until my Brother quit his job up the river and came down and went to work for the dairy and in due time my brother and I got in a fight and both of us got fired and it was then that we started on our way home again and after some hungry days we reached home....
>
> My Brother was something of a man by now and he got a job with the fencing gang on the railroad and I got a home with a widow by the name of Bettie Rose and if a growing boy ever fell into a snap it was me for I went from the puny kid into a man in very short notice and I went from about 80 pounds to 145 in two years and I really believe Mrs. Rose got the enjoyment of her life in watching me eat and about all I wanted to do was eat and sleep for it was then that I began to come into my own and I got the schooling of my life during that time.... I had to walk a mile and a half to school but that was easy for me....

As Loper approached adolescence, an author born a stone's throw to the west in Florida, Missouri was blooming on the national scene. Samuel Clemens, now married, fifty, and ensconced in respectable Connecticut, was publishing some of his great works: *Life on the Mississippi* in 1883, and *The Adventures of Huckleberry Finn* in 1884. While *Life on the Mississippi* told of the wonders of running a river boat and learning rivers, *Huckleberry Finn* described the moral struggle of a young Missouri boy. Trapped between Miss Watson's overbearing Calvinism and his father's godless drunken brutality, young Huck ran away downriver with

Miss Watson's slave Jim. Huck's musings over right and wrong, religion and slavery, mirrored major issues of the day. When Huck decided he could not turn Jim in, saying, "All right, then, I'll *go* to hell," he summed up what many young men, such as Loper himself, came to think. Huck's conviction that true freedom was expressed only when adrift on the big river came to permeate Loper's life as well.

> I mentioned that it was such a treat for me to get out in the woods and along the creek and here I was living right where it was such a paradise to me and I think that there was never a boy that enjoyed the trees, birds, and flowers more than I did but in all that time that I lived with the widow Rose I was getting letters from my Uncle in Durango and in due time he sent for me to come out to Colo. and stay on the ranch that he had located in the Montezuma Valley so on the 8th day of June 1885 I reached Durango and on the 17th of June I reached the valley and the ranch. #

Spencer Creek, north of Curryville, Loper's escape

Brad Dimock

5 Brennan's story

JACK BRENNAN responded to a small ad in the *Salt Lake Tribune* in 1944, looking for participants in a river trip. He signed on with Loper and Harris as a passenger through Cataract Canyon that July, and soon found himself captivated by the river. He joined them on the Yampa in 1945 and in the spring of 1946 built his own whitewater boat, the *Loper*. When Loper's health threatened to keep him off the Yampa trip planned for that spring, Brennan wrote,

> A river trip would not seem the same without you, and I know Don feels the same way I do in that respect. I think we would both feel very queer going down the big creek without you. As for running the rapids you mention, if I am going to continue these trips, I will have to run them all sooner or later, and I would surely like to have your experience and know-how to get me off on the right track.

By the time the 1949 Grand Canyon trip launched, Brennan had logged over 2500 miles on the Colorado system. His log of Loper's last trip remains the most extensive of any written.

> The next day was Friday, July 8th, and we were up early, and had good shade from the east cliff of the canyon for our morning chores. We were on the river about eight o'clock, and about an hour later arrived at Soap Creek, and one of the largest rapids in Grand Canyon. It is much rougher than Badger, and although we decided we would run it easily enough, decided our passengers would have to walk. Most of them wanted to take pictures anyway. As usual, Bert merely glanced at the water from below, and then started up for his boat. I told Don I had better go on down, that is follow him thru. We intended, of course to pull out for our passengers, but Bert made no attempt to do so …
>
> Our next stop was at about Mile 21, and since it was about noon,

Jack Brennan

decided to eat lunch.... As usual, it was very hot, and we scattered out through some large boulders seeking shade, and after eating, loafed around for half an hour or so.... Bert was about the only one of us who did much more rowing, except for enough to stay in the best current, but until now, he had been pulling in to wait for us when he came to any thing very bad.

When someone said let's go, Bert simply walked down to his boat, and shoved off. Hardly waited for Wayne. The rest of us had the lunch things to stow, so when we finally got under way, Bert was out of sight, and since we were in rough water almost at once, I don't think any of us gave him a thought. It did not take long to run to Mile 24½, and we could see this was a rapid that demanded some respect. All we could see of it was some spray kicking high above the river, so as a matter of course we landed above. Don and I remarked about Bert not stopping, and it worried me a little, but knowing how that old boy often bulled through these places, was not too alarmed.

We found it was not hard to run, but felt repaid for stopping, since it had to be entered through a somewhat crooked channel above.... Don pulled out into the eddy to wait, and when I saw he was in position for pick-up man, I went on down. I don't know just why I did this, as I usually waited, but I could see there was nothing ahead, and I just wanted to see if the other boat was alright. I ran a couple of medium rapids, and was approaching a third, when I spotted Wayne on the right bank, and he was doing some mighty urgent waving. I was too close to the rapid to pull out above, so I ran through. This little rapid, Cave Spring Rapid, gave me the worst scare I had on the whole trip, and I think Welty just about had a mess of kittens.... When I got into the eddy, I looked back upstream, hoping to see the other boat, but of course it was not there, so I knew whatever had happened was very bad. When we landed, the first thing Wayne said was "Well, I guess we buried Bert at sea."

He told us, in part then, and the whole story later, that Bert had apparently become exhausted trying to land above the rapid at mile 24½, and though he entered the rapid, after failing to make a landing, in good position, he made no attempt to keep the boat straight, and about the third wave they hit rolled the boat over. [Wayne] grabbed for the side of the boat as it went over, and caught hold of a piece of rope, and pulled himself on to the bottom of the overturned boat. After he got on, he looked upstream, and saw Bert, but he said he was apparently making no effort to help himself, although he yelled at him. I might add an aside here for the benefit of anyone who might think that Wayne could have attempted to reach him, to read the description of what happened to my boat when I entered the rapid where we picked Wayne up, that this type of water was prevalent all through this section of river, and to attempt to pull anyone out would have amounted to virtual suicide. Bert was unquestionably dead when Wayne first saw him.

The first time the boat approached close enough to shore, Wayne jumped off and swam in, and when it got caught in the eddy in which I had so much trouble, he tried to get it to shore, but could not handle it with the one oar he had salvaged, and fearing it would pull him into the river again, let it go. He again saw the body after he had landed, and said he went right through the middle of the "V." That was the last time Bert was ever seen. #

6 Wondrous west

THE WESTWARD MIGRATION was old news when Benjamin Mettler left for Colorado. The days of wagon trains and stage coaches had drawn to a close. The first transcontinental railroad had busted across the continent a dozen years earlier and new lines were opening as fast as they could be built. Rich silver deposits in the San Juan Mountains in southwestern Colorado had encouraged General William Palmer to press his new Denver and Rio Grande Railroad into the mines at Creede, Silverton, Ouray, Telluride, Rico, and Ophir, crawling up canyoned rivers and zigzagging over passes. In 1880, on the south flank of the San Juans, where the Animas River—the River of Lost Souls—gushed down from Silverton, Palmer established the town of Durango. Surrounded by good farm land, the whistlestop grew quickly, with coal mines nearby and, soon, a smelter for the ore coming out of the mountains. All that activity meant ample employment, and Mettler signed on as a bridge builder for the railroad. He acquired land and soon established a ranch near Cortez, in the Montezuma Valley west of Durango. It was only when the workload on the ranch grew unmanageable, Bert Loper recalled sourly, that Mettler remembered his orphaned nephew.

> And now comes the Uncle in Durango. When my grandmother died she left me in the care of that uncle [Benjamin] so all he did for me was to put me with that brute of an uncle [Allen Johnson] and there was no one that knew him better than the uncle in Durango but I was off his hands so perhaps his mind was made easy on that score until he got his ranch so he became solicitous once again for my welfare so he sent for me.

Loper, not yet sixteen, was already an adult by most measures. He had no family to lean on and had spent two years on his own, working for scant wages and scrapping for an education. His years in the country's heartland had treated him none too kindly. He recalled his youthful excitement as he headed out into the mythic West in June 1885:

> The mountains always had a most wonderful fascination to me and I can remember how excited I was when some one awoke me just after we had entered Colorado and pointed out the Spanish Peaks still covered with snow which was some novelty to me but in due time we reached Pueblo and I remember that I bought an old cap and ball pistol there for I had to wait nearly 24 hours there before we continued on our way which was by way of Alamosa and the Cumbers pass and when I reached Chama I missed my Uncle there so I went on to Durango and my Uncle came in the next day.

The excitement was short-lived. Mettler took Loper out to his ranch in the Montezuma Valley for a summer of plain, old-fashioned, back-breaking labor:

> He told me to fence that quarter section and grub the sage brush and in the course of time I did that very thing and in less than a week after the job was finished he told me it was time to shift for myself so he gave me two old blankets and an old comfort and told me to beat it....
>
> So I got me a job with a ditch out fit and it was a sure enough job—the dirtiest, lousey, and filthy job in the world and I had for my companions Niggers, Mexicans, Wops, and a very low grade of whites—a nice place for a strip of a boy, with 11 and 12 hours per day....

No doubt his ditch-mates groused just as bitterly about the scrawny Missouri Puke with whom they shared the ditch. At least there was no shortage of work—as farmland opened up there were plenty of irrigation canals to dig. But it wasn't all drudgery. With his uncle still working for the railroad, Loper found time to develop his budding vices. He had learned to chew tobacco after his grandmother died, and discovered the joys of wine drinking while working in central Missouri. But once out west:

> All the associates I had was cowboys and they seemed to think it was fun to see me drink and they would pay for it so I drank plenty the first year

Mule teams arriving in Telluride

Ben Mettler

in Colo. but my Uncle came from his job on the R.R. and went over to the Dolores and told the store keeper to not let me have any more so I thought that was an imposition on my personal liberties so when Xmas came around I found another bar tender so the cowboys bought me all I could drink and it near killed me and there was about two years that I never touched the stuff.

Loper, as he had throughout his childhood and would continue to do, survived, but little more. From the beginning he had learned that he was nothing special, that he had little value in the world, and that life was tough. He kept digging.

But having experience with mules in Missouri it was not long until I was driving "PLOW TEAM" with 8 and 10 mules to the team and was I a swelled up kid—I can remember that I used to wish that the folks at home could see me. From the plow team I developed into a real mule skinner and was soon on the road with an 8 mule team driving a freight team up in the San Juan Mountains....

During my teaming days I was in and out of Durango Colo. and I

> worked for awhile in a dairy for Bob Shields and it was in Durango that I cast my first vote in 1888.
>
> But after putting in a winter driving through 12 and 14 feet of snow— … we would get a mule down and then we would have to work to get him back on the road and by that time our clothes would be wet and sometimes we would be until 10 oclock in getting in and our clothes all frozen stiff … —I called it a day and went from that to the mines—there is still a question in my mind if I made a good trade or not for while the hours in the mine was a little shorter the air was not near so good as the mule skinners had.

With dozens of coal mines surrounding Durango, producing tens of thousands of tons of coal per year, there were ample openings. Loper signed on at the Black Diamond coal mine, east of Durango in Horse Gulch and entered the dark, dank, risky, noxious, low-paying world of the underground miner. Uninspiring to be sure, but at least it didn't snow down there. The grass, of course, now seemed greener elsewhere—he returned to the Montezuma Valley and went back to digging ditches. And then back to freighting. And from there back to his childhood occupation for a year, milking cows at Bob Shields's dairy on Lightner Creek, five miles west of Durango. The thin, puny youngster became a strapping, husky, and handsome young man. He took a job freighting from Rockwood, just up the Animas River from Durango, up to the mines at Rico, and spent a summer working on a ranch near Rockwood. Loper's moral development took the next step here when he had what he termed his first "clandestine affair."

> I worked one summer there and the owner was Polk Adams and he had a wife many years younger than he and if there was ever a man raped by a woman that was me for at that time I had very exalted ideas about womanhood.… I had placed them on a pedestal high above man but this affair that I am speaking of started from our first kiss and at that time she asked me to be good and not to insult her so I still left her on her womanhood throne and in the course of time it was her that seduced me and not me her but from then on it was surely different for I always could be depended on to get mine wherever that I found it.

Well, almost wherever. He later related to Elwyn Blake that he did give it a break from time to time:

> That reminds me of a boarding house I had in Victor with an old scotch lady and she had several girls and all of them very beautiful and of their virtue I can say nothing but one day the old lady knowing I was overlooking very few chances, commented on the fact that I did not bother her girls so I told her that her son was as much a brother to me and it was my religion to let wimmen folks of my friends alone and it mattered not to me what course their girls pursued they were not for me.

Loper soon ended up back in the mines. Although his descriptions are vague about just where and when he mined, he mentioned working in Ouray, Silverton, Telluride, and Rico, as well as working with the legendary road-builder of the San Juans, Otto Mears. The histories of these mountain mining towns follow a similar pattern. Prospectors poaching on Ute Indian land made the first discoveries in the 1870s, and by the mid 1880s whites had swarmed in, settled, and displaced native claims to the land. A wild spirit of lawlessness prevailed, with saloons, gambling halls, and brothels springing from the chaos.

The wealth that poured forth from the mines built flashy Victorian downtowns, but the men who actually prospered from the mines were precious few. The vast throngs were little better than wage slaves, laboring in the dark for long shifts, spending what little they eked on nightly amusements. Each town had a spur of the Denver & Rio Grande bringing people in and ore out; each town had its famous outlaw tales; and each was poised to collapse should the high price of silver waver.

> For several years all of the society I had was miners—teamsters—gamblers—and dance hall girls and all the place I had to loaf was in a saloon and gambling hall.... It is a sure thing that I drank too much but I never became a habitual drunkard ... but [if] it so happened that I got on a spree I would be sick of it for some time....
>
> I have breathed enough gass and powder smoke and bad air to have killed a horse.

By 1889 Loper was mining in Rico, some fifty miles up the Dolores River valley from his uncle's ranch. There, in the 1880s, hard-rock miners blasted, shoveled, and hauled more than fifty million dollars worth of silver out of the mountainside. The work was primitive and mining accidents were all too common. Falls, cave-ins, floods, bad air, equipment failure, and miscalculations in blasting all took their toll. Health benefits were nonexistent. But mining was, like many other horrendous jobs, a lifestyle with its own code of honor.

Old photographs of haggard, filthy miners filing out at the end of a shift do little justice to the exacting nature of the job. One began not as a miner but as a mucker, a hauler, or any number of attendant jobs, moving heavy objects about until an opening appeared on a mining team. Miners usually worked in pairs, often a senior miner and a younger man picking up the trade. A typical shift began when the men arrived at their station and began shoveling out the blasted debris left by the opposite shift. They pried and flaked off any loose rock in the tunnel-end, and when the site was finally cleaned of rubble, they began drilling for the next blast. Drilling was done in one of two ways. Single-jack work consisted of one man with a four-pound sledge in one hand and a hardened-steel drill-bit in the other. Smash, twist, smash, twist, all day, drilling into solid rock as far as seven feet. A double-jack team had one man swinging a ten-pound sledge, trading duties with a second man who held and turned the drill bit. The holder required incredible faith in his partner's accuracy.

Perhaps the most exacting art was in the placing of the holes—six in the center of the wall to blast out a core, then a series of holes high and low to blow the remaining rock into the newly vacant core, and a final blast to lift the entire heap of rubble out into the tunnel. With a cry of "Fire in the hole!" the team would end their shift on a dead run. *Blam-bam-boom!*

Each hole, of course, had to be carefully packed with dynamite and tamped in properly, and each fuse cut to the exact proper length. If the holes and charges were right, and all the charges went off, the next shift had a perfect mountain of rubble to remove. If not, there might be unblown charges that could kill an unwary driller, or a blast that went so haywire that it blew out the mine supports, necessitating tremendous labor to make any progress for the day. With bonuses paid for extraordinary production, a good partner was the best prize a man could have, and a good team on your opposite shift was close behind. Slackers didn't last long. A skilled miner could easily find work at just about any mine in the West.

The silver market was on thin ice, however. For years the federal government had been buying tremendous amounts of silver, guaranteed by the Sherman Silver Purchase Act. But in 1893, with America's gold reserve dwindling, President Grover Cleveland, in spite of vigorous opposition from the western states, pushed through the repeal of the Sherman Act. Meanwhile the nervous market in the East collapsed and banks failed across the country. The silver-mining economy crumbled overnight. Loper explained the situation in Colorado:

> As the panic came on not only the mines at Rico were closed, but all the mines in Colorado and most of the other western states also ceased operation. Naturally, the business houses closed their doors due to the slump, excepting a very few, which were able to corner the meager trade which was left.
>
> Being broke was, and is, a chronic state with most miners. Without means of earning a living, want and suffering was acute within a very short while. It took some rustling to scrape up a meal now and then. I left the high country and drifted down the Dolores river to the Montezuma valley where I had spent some time when I first came to Colorado. I was young and naturally drifted to the ranch where I had eaten regularly for my first two years of my stay in the west.

By then Ben Mettler had sold his ranch to Nicholas Krone, a German, who was living there with his wife and two children. Loper he did what he could to help the family get by. Although they had a fine crop of wheat, there was no market for it. Loper took odd jobs baling hay, earning a sack of groceries here and there, but his main service was hunting rabbits for the Krones to eat. Loper was, above all else, a survivor.

> I should have learned a lesson in saving money from that experience, but I can't see that I did. I have made good money many times since and still don't seem to realize the value of a dollar. #

7 Welty's story

Howard Welty had run the Salmon and Snake Rivers with boatman Norman Nevills in 1946, then joined Nevills again for the lower two hundred miles of Grand Canyon in 1948. Welty, a high school principal from Oakland, California, was also an amateur filmmaker and gave lectures about his adventures. Feeling Nevills did not give enough consideration to his filmmaking activities, he looked for another guide to take him through the upper stretch of Grand Canyon. Friend Dock Marston recommended Don Harris, and Welty signed on. His journal gives one more perspective on the severity of the whitewater and circumstances of Loper's death:

> Turbulent rapids occurred near Miles 22, 23, 24 and 25. We got out to scan Rapid 24 where Bert was awaiting us. It looked rough and tricky. Bert pushed off first, as usual, and that was the last any of us except Wayne saw of him. Three or four minutes ahead of us, they ran 24, and half a mile below encountered a short, rough rapid that capsized the boat in the fourth trough. Wayne said he noticed the boat beginning to yaw across the current on the third trough, he looked over his shoulder and shouted "Bert, Look to your oars," but Bert was just sitting there, making no movement, and in the next drop the boat was across the current and rolled over.
>
> Looks like Bert's heart was failing him at this moment. Wayne grasped a trailing rope and managed to climb on top of the capsized "*Grand Canyon*." He saw Bert floating supported by his life vest but eyes closed and making no movement to swim. The river carried through two or three more rapids while Wayne was trying to unfasten one of the spare oars lashed to the submerged deck. Securing it he was able, luckily, to get the boat into a big eddy on the right hand side, of the river. As he left the main current he saw Bert, apparently dead, carried by in the racing flood and on down the river. The eddy was about a hundred yards

long and half as wide and running very swiftly. The boat was carried clear around it two or three times but Wayne could not get it close to shore to tie it up. He finally swam ashore with the one oar and awaited our arrival. The *Grand Canyon* soon re-entered the current and went on down stream.

The current passing this eddy ran along the left bank of the river and was the most powerful and unpredictable I have ever seen. "Holes" so large and deep as to hide us standing up from Wayne on the shore changed in a moment into twisting pools that spun us so fast we were almost tossed from the boat by centrifugal force. Waves rushing in from all sides once covered the boat and us up to our waists standing up, and a moment later we were on a great hilltop of water down which we coasted with enough impetus to carry us into the eddy. Don's boat had gotten into an eddy some distance up the river and we had passed him and become the leading boat. We saw Wayne standing alone on the right shore, with no sight of Bert or his boat. Once in the eddy we got back up stream to where he stood and called "Where is the boat, and Bert?" Pushing his hands palms down and outward he gestured "Finished" and we then knew tragedy had overtaken Bert. #

Howard Welty on Snake River, 1946; Dock Marston in back

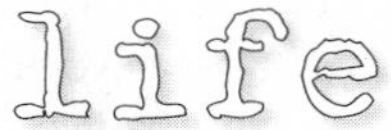

8 San Juan

NOT LONG AFTERWARD I met a Mr. Honaker in Cortez. He had some samples of rich placer dirt from the San Juan river. Fired with thoughts of riches, I started immediately for the San Juan, in company with several other Montezuma county men. As a starter we struck the upper reaches of the river. I began to putter around with a boat right away. Although there was no bad water, I learned to handle a boat and so was prepared for the rougher water in the lower canyon.

The river snared Bert Loper in the fall of 1893. Rumors of the "Bluff Gold Excitement" had reached the Montezuma Valley several months earlier. In December 1892, a story had leaked out that a large-scale "coal mining operation" headed north from Winslow, Arizona, was in fact a gold mining endeavor headed for the San Juan. With the silver market wavering, gold fever was in the air, and the rumor begat a stampede. By New Year's Day thousands of fortune seekers were reported to be flooding into the San Juan River. Railroads advertised bargain fares to the area, and newspapers throughout the West spouted ever greater hyperbole—"the richest gold fields ever found," "the new El Dorado," "excitement at a fever heat." Yet most prospectors, finding little but dust in their gold pans, soon turned away. A *Durango Herald* reporter described "coming up on a large flat rock upon which someone had printed this legend: '$100.000 reward for the son of a bitch who started this gold boom.'"

Yet gold there was. Most of it, to be sure, was "flour gold," too fine to collect by standard means. But in the high alluvial gravel banks some miners found granular gold and occasional nuggets—enough to keep die-hard miners looking for years. Henry and Augustus Honaker were there early, staking and working claims, but also sensed where the real gold was: in the eager gold miners' pockets. They offered stage transport from the Cortez area to the Mormon town of Bluff, Utah, on the San Juan, with business being equally good in both directions. Thirty miles west they pioneered a route into the deepest part of the San Juan canyon to work their own claims and supply other miners. It was no accident, then, that Honaker was showing off his gold-rich soils to the citizens of Cortez.

The San Juan River heads near Wolf Creek Pass in the San Juan Mountains and meanders westward, gathering waters from the mountains surrounding Silverton and Telluride to the north and the deserts of Chaco Canyon and Canyon de Chelly to the south. Somewhere in its vast headwaters it scours out gold and grinds, rolls, and tumbles it along the gritty river bottom as it winds westward across the desert. The river flows a scant mile north of Four Corners, where Colorado, New Mexico, Utah, and Arizona meet, then continues another forty-five miles to Bluff. Just west of Bluff the river enters a series of sandstone and limestone canyons, meandering another hundred and forty miles west to the Colorado. It is bleak terrain. A thousand years ago this was the heartland of the ancient Anasazi culture, but by the mid-1300s societal factors and the San Juan's fickle climate drove them elsewhere. Although their great cliff dwellings and expressive rock art remained, the area became home to the more nomadic Navajo, Ute, and Paiute.

Mormons attempted to colonize the San Juan area in the 1880s with minimal success. Throughout the ages, the San Juan has had a habit of defeating all those who sought to prosper in its barren bosom. Even today along its nearly four hundred miles the San Juan encounters few settlements of any size, excepting the mountain town of Pagosa Springs, Colorado and the oil-rich area surrounding Farmington, New Mexico. "The current is generally swift ... and there are numerous rapids," wrote Hugh Miser in his 1924 treatise on the river. "These features, together with the muddiness of the water, the quicksands, and the frequent and sudden rises, are well known to the Navajo Indians, whose name for the river is Pawhuska (mad water)."

As Loper wandered from the mountains to the San Juan River he was following in the tracks of perhaps the first person to float through Grand Canyon. Twenty-six years earlier in 1867, Captain Charles Baker left the San Juan Mountains to seek gold on the San Juan—Baker had earlier been among the first to explore the Silverton and Durango areas, leaving his name on Baker's Park and Baker's Bridge. Seeking further untrammeled ground, Baker set off with two prospectors, George Strole and a thirty-year-old New York native named James White.

The three men prospected their way down the San Juan to where canyons prevented further downstream travel. According to White, they proceeded overland, north and west, eventually hitting the Colorado River. There they were ambushed by Indians and Baker was killed. Strole and White fled to the river and, under cover of darkness, made a crude log raft and cast off. As the river turned violent Strole was washed overboard and drowned. Two weeks later Mormons at Callville, in what is now Nevada, pulled White from his raft, emaciated, burnt, blistered, and delirious. Those who believed his tale posited he had run the Colorado through Grand Canyon, predating Major Powell's famed expedition by a full two years. The debate endures today, some championing his voyage, others calling him a monumental prevaricator. Although Loper was likely unaware of White's tale, he too was beginning his slow march from the San Juans to the Colorado and controversies of his own.

> My start in boating was in the fall of 1893 and was a smooth water trip from the Colorado line down the San Juan to Bluff City, Utah and from my later experiences was a rather tame affair but it being my first it was sure pack with thrills and I sure enjoyed it very much. I did no more boating the balance of the winter but in the spring of 1894 I went down the river from Bluff and it was on this trip that I had my first rough water and it was then that I got sold on rough water boating.

Loper not only found his calling in the rapids of the San Juan, he also found his home. Although the lush forests and rolling hills of the Mississippi River basin were his birthplace, and he returned there for a time in the late 1890s, the Midwest never held him. It was the canyon country of the Colorado Plateau with its sere, stark mesas and roiling muddy rivers that cemented Bert Loper to the earth.

The Colorado Plateau is a remarkably stable chunk of the earth's crust, encompassing western Colorado, eastern and central Utah, northwestern New Mexico, and northern Arizona. For more than a half-billion years it has remained essentially flat, alternately sinking below sea level where it collected layer upon layer of sediments, and rising thousands of feet above the sea to expose these solidified sediments to erosion. Whereas most regions of the earth have been crumpled and torn asunder over the eons, the Colorado Plateau, other than a few minor folds here and there, has preserved these layers of rock strata intact, showcasing them in the canyonlands of the southwest as one of the world's greatest geologic displays. Moreover, the entire Plateau lies in what Major Powell termed "the arid region," leaving the rock strata naked, crisp, and harsh. Fed by distant mountain runoff, the muddy, erosive rivers buzz-saw straight down through the desert floor. The San Juan, the Green, the Yampa, and the Colorado: each carves its own series of multihued canyons as it incises ever deeper into the great deserts of the West.

It is a region so stark, so shockingly different from the pastoral scenes of Europe and the eastern United States that Castañeda's 1540 party—the first Western explorers to see Grand Canyon—recoiled in shock upon seeing it. Subsequent visitors saw little to do but leave. It was more than one hundred and thirty years before Major Powell's scientists described and attempted to explain the scenery—only then did it become something marvelous to the Western eye. "Great innovations, whether in art or literature, in science or in nature, seldom take the world by storm," wrote geologist Clarence Dutton. "They must be understood before they can be estimated, and must be cultivated before they can be understood."

Although Grand Canyon was becoming a tourist attraction by the early 1890s, the canyonlands of Utah were still terra incognita to the average American. It was desolate wilderness. It was not the scenery that drew Loper and his ilk—it was the lure of gold, that toxic drug that draws otherwise sensible men into the wilds, sure that they will be the ones to hit the jackpot. Like casino gamblers, they pour their time, energy, and resources into a losing proposition, knowing that eventually someone, somewhere, is going to strike it rich and it might as well be them. For many it is a life-long affliction. Prospecting is no trade for a pessimist—one must have a certainty that soon his luck will turn in a most spectacular fashion. It rarely did and rarely does.

It certainly didn't in 1893. Loper and his compatriots had little success that first season with what he called "an experimental placering process." There were nearly as many novel attempts to coax the San

Juan's reluctant gold from the gravels as there were broke miners along the shore. Loper's team worked the gravel bars between Four Corners and Bluff. On June 8 Loper and William Rogers filed a placer claim called the Missouri, to no financial avail. As summer and fall passed and winter set in, Loper returned to the Montezuma Valley. The following spring he returned to the river.

In March 1894, Loper launched from Bluff with four other men in two boats, bound for Honaker's claim in the second gorge of the San Juan. Most of the boats on the San Juan at that time were simple row-boats, about sixteen feet long, four or five feet wide, flat bottomed with a slight upturn at each end. Crude but functional, these craft were not designed for beauty or sport. They were built and run for the sole pragmatic purpose of transporting men and equipment through a difficult and hazardous environment.

On the upper stretches of river Loper had to learn to row, to move back and forth in flat current, and to make quick landings along rapid shorelines. The only obstacles were the occasional rock or overhanging branch, the shallows—sand bars and gravel bars—and an elusive channel that would, without warning, thin to nothing. The hazard was minimal: running aground and having to get out and drag to deeper water.

Twelve miles below Bluff, Chinle Creek flows in from the south, draining a vast expanse of the Navajo Indian Reservation. The San Juan makes an abrupt right turn and enters the first limestone gorge. Constrictions speed the current to form waves; current is often complex and mined with boulders; hazards increase. The gradient steepens to form riffles and rapids—the delineation between the two is subjective and poorly defined. To most folk, riffles have quick current and waves, perhaps a few obstacles, but pose no threat of wrecks or swamping. Rapids are serious business—the boatman must be cautious, alert and responsive, or suffer the consequences: damage or loss of boat, equipment, limb, or even life. The more serious the rapid, the graver the peril.

Consequently, early boaters developed their own protocols for dealing with rapids. Portaging the boat—removing the boat from the river and carrying it around the rapid—certainly removed all water-related danger from the operation, although the labor and strain supplied risks of their own. Sometimes only the cargo was portaged to make the boat lighter and more manageable.

Lining the boat was a second option. The boat was left in the river—with or without its cargo—and lowered with ropes along the shoreline currents. Often one person remained in the boat, fending off and working around rocks. Here again, the risks of running the rapid were eliminated, only to be traded for those of working a heavy boat through slippery boulders in strong current.

Loper also described a third option called "nosing" which involved working the boat through a rapid by holding onto its bow, or "nose," wading along the shallow shore, and maneuvering through without use of ropes.

The most obvious procedure, of course, was simply to take one's chances and run the rapid. The risks to life and limb (and boat and cargo) could be minimized with careful handling. Boaters often scouted from shore or by standing up in the boat before entering the rapid. Once they took into account the placement of dangerous rocks and waves, and analyzed deceptive currents, they could plot a course and attempt to run the rapid. As knowledge, skill, and nerve grew over time, running the rapid increasingly became the choice of river runners—it is easier, quicker, often safer, and most importantly, exciting and fun. But it took experience, which was in scant supply on the San Juan in the 1890s. Although the rapids of the San Juan pale in comparison to those of the Colorado, they could still sink a boat. And Loper and his colleagues were starting from scratch.

> My first boating down in the canyon was the taking of a boat from Bluff to our claim down in the canyon.... We had lots of difficulty, because down to the Chinle creek it was just a case of walk, that was all.
>
> We had little stretches there, we could ride a little ways, but with two men in one boat, with lots of provisions, and three men in the other boat, we didn't have enough water to do very much boating.
>
> They had their supplies. Bacon and beans and coffee and flour, just as few blankets as possible. They had their beds down at their camp, you know.
>
> At Soda Basin [now called Eight-foot Rapid] there is a rapid there you have to be very careful about. There at Gypsum creek is a big rapid; there is nothing to that but just get right out and nose your boat over the rapid.

Charles Goodman

Typical San Juan boats, 1890s

> We lined over [Soda Basin] and we nosed over Gypsum creek rapid, because whenever you have provisions freighted from Dolores or Thompson to Bluff and then boat from Bluff down to Soda Basin, you are not in a position to lose them, so we had to use caution and not lose anything.
>
> We had a very good bill of grub but when that was gone we had to do some tall russeling.

They went to work for Henry Honaker in the deepest part of the second gorge of the San Juan. There the three-hundred-million-year-old gray limestone rises jaggedly to the rim above—sixteen-hundred feet of crumbling slopes punctuated with sheer cliffs. On the north side of the river, on the inside of a long right bend, lies a massive sand and gravel bar containing alluvium from throughout the San Juan drainage. Honaker and company were betting their resources, time, and effort on the possibility it held gold. On April 28 Loper and several others filed on the Golden Star claim. They set to work but supplies soon ran short. They climbed out for more.

> We freighted our stuff in to what is now known as Honaker Trail; there

was no trail there at that time, and Mr. Honaker and some associates had located a claim.... I was employed in that company ... and there was two or three of us young fellows at that time carried the stuff down from ledge to ledge until we got to the last big ledge, was about one hundred and thirty or one hundred and forty feet, we had to let the stuff over with ropes, and then when we got our stuff let over the cliff we would go out to the point where the trail now goes over and climb down a rope ladder, and then came back to the ledge and went down to the river. I think it was March because it was pretty chilly there yet.

On our first trip into the canyon George Edmondson and I had to carry a four horse load of provisions down to the big ledge which at this place was about 120 feet thick then George went below and I let the stuff over and George would untie the rope and just about dark we had finished so our next job was to get Mr. Honaker over the crevice and it was sure some job for he was deathly afraid of any thing high and we tried to persuade him to try it but of no avail and it was growing late and all our stuff at the foot of the ledge including our beds—George and I in our desperation jumped on Mr. Honaker and tied him up and put him on the end of the rope and in that way got him into camp for the night....

[We hauled in] provisions and our beds and a few working tools, and one of our company was a kind of inventor, he had a machine and it went the way of all other placer machines I ever saw, didn't amount to anything, so we sluiced and we rocked and sent out for more money to buy some more grub with.

It was always a battle to get something to eat. I hiked many miles over the desert in quest of food and will never forget the strenuous rustling I had to do. Many a time we were down to just beans and sour-dough bread. One time I walked to Bluff ... and loaded down with 30 pounds of beans. I carried them back to camp ... with my feet blistered and my shoes just about worn out ... and never knew just how heavy that many beans could get until then.

There was Mr. Edmondson, Mr. Honaker, Mr. Hambleton, Mr. Goodman, and myself ... and there was two or three of us young fellows, George Edmondson, Mr. Edmondson's son, Jim Hambleton was Mr. Hambleton's son, and myself, were all about an age. We was younger—they was old men—so the burden of the business came mostly on us....

We would hunt up a spot that panned pretty well, we would sluice

Charles Goodman

Honaker works. Loper may be in photo

it or rock it.... [W]e made a tank about ten feet long, about three feet wide, and four foot deep; then we would make a hand rocker and we had a copper plate; we tried that a while; we tried pretty near every scheme we could figure out to save this gold; we got a little gold, but not much....

I think our outfit brought in two bunches of grub by wagon, and then we ceased operations, and Mr. Goodman and the two boys and me worked a while and that was a failure, so Mr. Goodman went to Bluff—Mr. Goodman was a photographer and he done the cooking for the outfit....

The placer proved to be a fizzle so that caused me to have to do a lot of moving up and down the river so the boating, and the more boating I had to do the better I liked boating but there was times that I had to do the boating in reverse and would have to pull the loaded boat up the river—I did not know it at the time but I was only getting my education for future use for it is many miles that I have had to do that very thing but the entire year of 1894 was put in on the river and there was very few days that I was not boating in some way....

I had about all kinds of boats mostly bad or indifferent—I also had many different companions on my boating trips, but about the most constant companion for nearly the entire year was George Edmondson—

> there was Jim Hambleton who was with George and on many of our short trips but he quit about the middle of the summer.
>
> I also had a rather nice experience in June of that year although a very strenuous one—in company with Bill Clark and John Clark we went to the very head of the canyon and made a raft of more than 1000 feet of lumber and took it to the mouth of Slick horn where Clark's Camp was, a distance of 58 miles and the educational end of that trip was worth the price for we became very proficient in the handleing that raft and the knowledge thus gained has stood me in good stead many times since.

Twenty-two miles below Honaker Trail, the men brought the raft into Slickhorn Canyon, a major sidecanyon entering from the north. Loper knew Bill Clark—no relation to John Clark—from his mining days at Rico. At Slickhorn he ran into another Rico friend, newspaperman Al Rogers. The Clarks and Rogers had a base camp here. What's more, they had a boat. Leaving the raft of lumber at Slickhorn, Loper, Edmondson, and John Clark took the boat and continued downriver. Seventeen miles below Slickhorn, the gray limestones of the second gorge of the San Juan plunge back below river level, exposing open terrain and offering easy access to the north and south. Here was Clay Hills Crossing—now buried beneath the silts of Lake Powell—and, a few miles farther, an oft-irrigated area called Paiute Farms. Beyond that, the third and final gorge of the San Juan—made of colorful sandstones and shales—continued another fifty miles to its confluence with the Colorado River in Glen Canyon. Every few miles was another placer camp—more holdouts from the gold excitement.

> We had a little sixteen foot rowboat, a very light boat, and we went down by boat.... August is quite a warm month; we had very little water, so it made no difference to us whether we was in the river or out of it. I know when we got to the Indian Farms we got out, we couldn't ride, because the river was so shallow, that we just had to drag the boat along. I imagine the bed of the river was probably three hundred feet wide, and so very little water that there was no channel that would float a boat; there was places the three of us actually drug the boat.
>
> I don't think we had a roll of beds for the three of us, and very lit-

tle grub; I know we had a pennyweight and a half of gold in a button [about 1/12 ounce—in 1894 worth about $1.70—roughly equivalent to $35 in modern dollars].

I got down there to some of the placer parties that was down there, and I gave this pennyweight and a half of gold for ten pounds of flour. We drug it back up the river; we didn't row it, because we didn't have water enough. We had to have the boat in order to carry what little grub we had, and our bedding.

We came back up the river on that ten pounds of flour—no meat or any thing just flour and when we got to the mouth of Slick Horn Canyon where Clarks camp was we found nothing there so George and I had to hike on up the river—we left the boat at slick horn—and it was on the first day from slick horn that we came to a placer camp where a Mr. Smith [probably O.A. "Crasy" Smith] was doing a little work and he told us that there was a pot of beans there and go up and help ourselves which we did and it so happened that the beans were just beginning to sour and the way we loaded up on those beans was no bodys business but the fortunate part of the whole thing was that we had time to reach our own camp before we became sick which we surely did good and plenty and if there is anything that is worse for that than sour beans is more sour beans and we surely took on more sour beans for we were nearly starved and we did not know just when to quit but there was a couple of sick boys in camp for several days.... But when we did get all right we proceeded to put on a pot of beans.

But our trip down the river was a very interesting one, in fact there have been very few uninteresting trips for me when taken on the rivers of the Colorado System. On our trip down we had some very interesting experiences—for instance at the mouth of Grand Gulch we had to take the boat out of the river and work it in around and between the huge boulders and it would have been impossible to have taken a boat through, and when we reached Clay Hills we had to get out and drag the boat and in so doing we encountered several holes and as we would be dragging the boat along we would go in all over, but we did not care for the water was warm and we were young and we would laugh it off and go on but on our return there was times that the laugh would be sadly lacking for when a person had to do a real he mans work on straight flour it became rather trying but our good nature among ourselves never

> vanished, in fact it held until George and I had to get well from our dose of sour beans and then I am afraid that we got a little grouchy....
>
> I placered with several different people during the summer but always with a very poor degree of success ... and in the fall I got in with another outfit and we worked what was known as the Mendenhall bar and the balance of the winter was so spent at what was known as the Mendenhall Cabin, in company with an old man by the name of Mulenix and his boy and another man.

Although the gold "excitement" had by and large died down, articles on the San Juan still appeared in the Salt Lake City newspapers, sometimes talking up its potential, other times talking it down. A particularly scathing piece ran in the October 10, 1894 Ogden *Standard Examiner* in the form of an interview with an investor named T.C. Chamberlain who had just returned from the canyons. "I would not make the same trip over," he said, "for all the gold in the San Juan river." After belaboring all the difficulties and hazards of the region he closed with, "The enormous expense attached to doing even a little development in the canyons makes the mining proposition in San Juan not one to be considered." So outraged were the San Juan miners that they drafted a lengthy rebuttal, ending with:

> Mr. Chamberlain has certainly been very unjust and very unkind in his exaggeration of the defects of the placer interests of this part of Utah and in his withering detraction of its merits. We do not want erroneous opinions either in favor or against this section to obtain, but we do desire that the truth be known, and the undersigned miners, as a matter of fairness, ask space of *The Standard* for the above expression of their opinion to resent and deny the harsh inferences of the interview in question.

Among the twelve miners who signed below were W.E. Mendenhall and Albert Loper.

At the beginning of the second gorge of the San Juan lies the small present-day town of Mexican Hat, originally known as Goodridge. Oil prospector E.L. Goodridge had stopped here in 1882, staked an oil claim, and boated on down the San Juan and Colorado to Lee's Ferry—becoming the first person to run the San Juan. About two miles below Mexican Hat, the San Juan loops back on itself, expending a mile to return within a hundred yards of where it just was. In the middle of this loop lies a peninsula connected to the north wall by a small flat-topped saddle paved with smooth limestone. It was on this natural plaza that Walter Mendenhall and his extended family built a cabin during the heyday of the gold excitement. From there they could climb down one hundred feet to the river off either side and work placers along the shore. Walter Mendenhall claimed to have pulled between four and five thousand dollars worth of gold out of this bar before moving on in the fall of 1894. He then wandered off downriver by boat to Lee's Ferry, probably the second man to run this stretch.

"I believe that I have mentioned elsewhere that Mr. Mendenhall was the first man that I did placer mining with," recalled Loper, "and he was also an inventor of a placer machine and it was this same machine that we tested out on the upper San Juan." Too, Loper had likely visited Mendenhall at his cabin during his 1894 river sojourns. But by late 1894, Mendenhall had moved on, his diggings unoccupied. The vacant cabin and promising placer claim were an open invitation to Loper and Mullenix.

Thirty-five years later Loper spoke of some of the remarkable things he saw on the river. Among them were sand waves, a phenomenon unique to fast muddy streams like the San Juan, formed when an overload of sediment begins washboarding the river bottom, throwing up a series of crashing waves where calm water flowed moments before.

> I have crossed every way you can think of. I have waded across, I have swum across, and I have boated across, and there have been times I wouldn't cross, not with an open boat. I have been working the rocker along the river banks and not a cloud in the sky, and have seen the river raise eight feet—across the river from Honaker Trail.
>
> The largest sand waves I ever saw in my life was above Mendenhall cabin; I think it was about February, 1895. Just before these sand waves there was an ice gorge at the head of the canyon, which stopped the flow of the river. I got out along in the bed of the river and went up and down panning, thinking probably I could find a pocket of gold in

> there. I crossed the river without getting my feet wet, because the river was dammed off. Finally, when this ice gorge broke, I know I moved my placer outfit twice, and then it carried part of it away, rose so high. After the ice got through I got up about, I imagine, a half mile above the Mendenhall cabin … and the waves, if they was an inch, they was ten feet high; I believe you could hear them a mile and a half or two miles away, when they would break. When a sand wave breaks, it makes a great roaring noise, and those were so big … Whenever you have a flood you have sand waves.

Loper and his companions spent a long cold winter and much of the spring at Mendenhall Loop. Hard work, slim pickings, scant rations, and tight quarters on a cold stone ledge all winter—Loper, at twenty-five, was a long hard row from easy street. Perhaps Mendenhall had been exaggerating with his claims of thousands in revenue, or perhaps he extracted the majority of the gold that was there, but by spring Loper and his companions had little to show. Each man's share, according to a later recollection by Loper, came to about one hundred dollars for the half-year's labor—most of which they spent on grub and supplies. In May they abandoned Mendenhall Bar, broke and hungry, and returned to Bluff.

> Young Mr. Mullenix was a brick maker so we talked the Mormons of Bluff to let us make some bricks for them so in the spring we quit the placer mining and so ends—for the time being my boating.
>
> I had done a whole lot of boating on the San Juan in 1894 and 1895; in fact, my boating experience was whenever I could get into a boat. I always liked it. That's the reason I got the experience. #

9 A thousand nights

LAST NIGHT was a thousand nights long. It seems I awakened with a start every few minutes. It didn't seem possible Bert was gone. It just couldn't be so.

Don Harris was haunted by the loss of his old friend and mentor. Harris was the trip leader and the responsibility for allowing Loper to participate rested on his shoulders. Sort of. But the fact was, Loper's stubborn side had reared high as the trip approached. No one was going to stop Bert Loper. Not Don Harris, not Wayne Nichol, not even Rachel. If Harris had refused, Harry Aleson might have offered in his stead. If Aleson balked, Loper may well have set out on his own. And had either of them refused Loper's company, the stress and anger might just as easily have set off the heart attack that Loper most likely succumbed to. As Harris explained to Frank Masland: "Since there was a tragedy on our trip, I have received a bit of criticism from the National Park Service at Grand Canyon for ever starting on such a trip with a man of Bert's age and condition. Really, knowing Bert as I did, I had no alternative."

In a mason jar they placed a signed "In Memoriam." It read:

> July 8, 1949
>
> Bert Loper, Grand Old Man of the Colorado, rowing his own boat, the *Grand Canyon*, was capsized in rapid at Mile 24 and lost his life. He was last seen by his passenger, Wayne Nichol, about one mile below the point of disaster, in very swift and turbulent water, eyes closed and apparently dead. His boat was found stranded and badly wrecked at this point, about sixteen miles below the point of capsizing, by the undersigned. His boat and its outboard motor are placed here in his memory by his friends and companions.

Signed:
Howard o. Welty—Oakland, Calif.
D. Wayne Nichol, 2512 E 148 St. So.
Ralph A. Badger Salt Lake City
Mrs. C.R. Fetzner, Pasadena
Harry Aleson, Richfield, Utah.
John B. Brennan, Salt Lake City
Don Harris S.L.C. Ut.

"We placed a cairn," continued Harris in his July 9 journal:

> headed by an oar given to Bert by Julius Stone, at the head of his boat and painted this epitaph on the front deck:
>
> BERT LOPER
> GRAND OLD MAN OF THE
> COLORADO
> BORN: JULY 31, 1869 DIED JULY 8, 1949
>
> Bert's motor was wrapped in a quilt from his bed roll and left in the cockpit of his boat. Due to overloaded boats already it was unwise to try

bringing it out. The rest of his things which were of no particular value or sentiment were cached under some brush about 200 feet upslope & to the R. from his boat, with the hope that souvenir hunters would not find and molest them.

It was indeed a depressed feeling which we all had as we shoved off from the site of this monument to Bert, knowing that we probably never would see it again, and that undoubtedly Bert's body would never be found, and how grief stricken Mrs. Loper would become upon learning of the death of her husband.

Jack Brennan wrote:

> After we had done all possible, we still loitered, hating to leave, it seemed like we were running out on something, but finally we pulled reluctantly away. At that time, if there had been any way out of the canyon, I think we'd all have taken it, and we all felt that way for some time. Bert had gone in the way he would probably have chosen if he could have done so, but knowing this didn't seem to help a bit. Don and I had both lost a friend of long standing, a figure full of color and the romance of the river, and it wasn't easy to leave that spot. I kept my feelings pretty well to myself, and didn't know the others felt pretty much the same until we had all loosened up a little.

"Another day of terror and misery for me," wrote Lou Fetzner that evening. "The water is so vicious, whirlpools so frightening & waves so huge." Her ride with Aleson had shaken her badly, even before the loss of Loper. Aleson, here on his first attempt at Grand Canyon, was pioneering the use of a military surplus inflatable raft. "Harry was thrown from the boat," she had written of Mile 22 Rapid, "I almost went in ... Harry lost an oar.... I am losing my courage in this big water. Hope I won't break down before going out at B[right] A[ngel] as I plan now to do." Morale had collapsed with Loper's death. Fetzner no longer wished to finish the trip, but to leave with Howard Welty, who had only signed on for the first part of the voyage. Ralph Badger was also considering leaving with Fetzner and Welty at Bright Angel, just one third of the way through Grand Canyon.

They cast off from Loper's memorial around 10:30 and almost immediately the calmer water, beautiful weather, and unparalleled scenery began to work their curative powers. At lunch a gas can of Loper's swirled by in the current and was gone. The next day at the first truly major rapid, Hance, Harris faltered. Without Loper's damn-the-torpedoes leadership, Harris and Brennan opted to line around the rapid. They spent two hours lowering the boats with ropes along the shore, Loper, no doubt, spinning in his watery grave. That evening they arrived at Bright Angel. Fetzner and Badger, by then, had relaxed enough to continue on with the journey. They made several calls from the water gager's telephone. Not wanting to deliver such horrific news to Rachel over the phone—or worse, have her read it in the newspaper—they looked for someone to relay the tragedy in person. Berta Harris was not around; Mae Brennan and Leith Nichol accepted the difficult task.

The next morning Welty hiked out; the rest continued downriver.

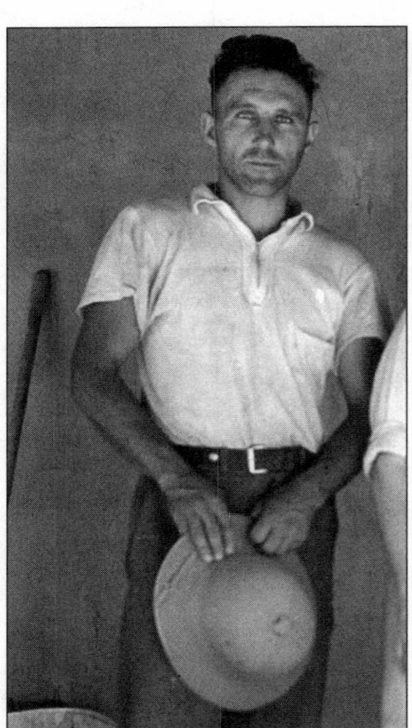

Don Harris 1939

The disaster had occurred, Harris later wrote to Dock Marston:

> As a result of my gamble to carry out an old man's wish—which old man had been a close friend to me for nearly 11 years. I hesitated in my mind when considering whether or not to take Bert thru in his 80th year. I decided to take a long chance—against many odds—and lost. #

Life

10 Brickmaker

BLUFF CITY, as it was then called, was just fifteen years old in 1895, and many residents had arrived on the founding trek. Called the Hole-in-the-Rock Expedition, it is among the more bizarre expeditions in the history of the West.

In 1879, the Mormon Church, in a preemptive strike against non-Mormon cattlemen encroaching from the southeast, issued a mission call for a group of the faithful to form a new settlement somewhere near the San Juan River. An initial exploring party set out from Cedar City, crossing the Colorado at Lee's Ferry and continuing across the desert highlands of Northern Arizona. Great distances between water and uneasy relations with the Navajos convinced them that this route was not viable for their planned migration. Once they reached the San Juan they selected Montezuma Creek as the site of the new settlement, and turned back to gather their mission. They headed north to Moab, crossed the Colorado, and followed established wagon roads back across Utah and south to Cedar City, their round trip forming a great circle. The return route they rejected as too far—four hundred and fifty miles to get to a point only two hundred miles away. Instead of either proven route, they chose to try a direct cross-country route for the settlement trek. With a minimum of information, they made a plan to pass through the settlement of Escalante, cross the Colorado, and head up the San Juan to Montezuma Creek in time for spring planting. They had no map. There was no route. No one had ever attempted it.

Amassing a group of more than 230 men, women and children, a fleet of wagons, and herds of livestock, they left Parowan in late October 1879. Their first major obstacle, a month and a half later, was a two-thousand-foot cliff towering above the Colorado, with but a narrow slit leading nearly straight down. They dynamited the crack wide enough for wagons to pass, lowered them by rope, and proceeded to cross the Colorado, only to find more cliffs, canyons, high country, and snow. Their short-

Kumen Jones home, Bluff

cut, in the end, transformed what could have been a relatively easy six-week pilgrimage into a grueling six-month marathon. When on April 6, 1880, they finally found open green bottom-lands by the San Juan, they were too exhausted to continue. They simply stopped, fifteen miles short of Montezuma Creek, and founded Bluff City.

Among the stalwarts of the expedition were Kumen and Mary Jones and her father, Bishop Jens Nielson. Loper, upon arrival in 1895, soon befriended them.

> During my sojourn in Bluff I lived with a Mormon family by the name of Jones—Kumen Jones—and his wife was the daughter of the Mormon Bishop and "Aunt Mary" was one of God's own people and during my time here on earth I have never met a finer woman and I believe that she took just as good care of us "Gentiles" as she did her own people.

In Bluff Loper took a few halting steps in the footsteps of the father he never knew—Jehail P. Loper, brickmaker. If placer mining seemed back-breaking work, it was just a warm-up for brickmaking. Although there were mechanized brick factories in the east by the 1890s, out on the frontier it was still done the hard way. First the clay had to be dug by hand from a river bank—tons upon tons of clay—and hauled to the brickyard. It was then dried, pulverized and screened to get the rocks and other impurities out. Next the clay was mixed with the right amount of water to form a pliable consistency. This was so arduous it

Kumen and Mary Jones

Jens Nielsen

was often done with a horse-powered pug mill.

The making of the bricks took two or three men. The first was a clot-molder, who formed up melon-sized gobs of clay and rolled them in sand so they would not stick to the mold. The second, usually the boss of the operation, was the brickmolder, who mashed the clay into the steel-rimmed beechwood mold, then struck off and discarded the excess. A third person, the off-bearer—a position Loper held when he was eleven, back in Missouri—carried the full molds to a flat sandy area, ejected the bricks from the mold, then dampened the mold, dusted it with sand, and hustled it back to the brickmolder, who had the next batch ready. A good team might be able to knock out three or four thousand bricks in a long day.

The bricks, drying on the sand, were turned over every few days until firm enough to stack, then built into giant kilns. Back in the deciduous forests of the East, collecting enough firewood or coal to fire a kiln was a project, but nowhere near the undertaking it was in barren Bluff—scrounging driftwood, hauling cottonwood logs, maybe freighting in coal. They fired the kiln at low heat for a few days until it quit billowing steam. Then they hurled in wood, keeping a raging fire going for a week or more, until the bricks approached eighteen hundred degrees. At this point the team bricked up the ports and chimneys and let the kiln cool for another week or so. Last, they sorted out the passable bricks from the clinkers.

It took all of May and June to make and fire the kiln of bricks. But as hard as the work was, Loper seems to have had time for socializing and perhaps a bit of mischief. Elwyn Blake, a longtime friend, associated Loper with a Bluff legend wherein a few local lads discovered a keg of whiskey locked in a tithing shed. One of the men crawled under the shed with a brace and bit and bored through the floor, directly into the keg. The others formed a bucket brigade and sent jug after jug under the shed to be filled and consumed.

Whether or not that really happened, a rough and tumble man like Loper could not help but run afoul of the strictures of the Mormon Church—or any other church for that matter. Although his pious grandmother had him baptized when young, it didn't take. Like many who never witness firsthand any grace of God, Loper threw religion off as excess baggage, sorting out his values with blood, sweat, and more than a few tears. "I became an avowed atheist in my early twenties," he wrote, "and that frame of mind continued for several years ..." Blake recalled Loper saying, "When I was at Bluff I would rather argue against the Bible than eat a Thanksgiving dinner." Loper somehow avoided banishment.

> There were many nice times for me while I was in Bluff for.... I was not in sympathy with their religion but the people treated me very nice and there was never any one that did more arguing against their religion than I did but "Aunt Mary Jones" was a sure sister to me also Uncle Kumen and many more was awful nice to me....
>
> I still believe that the old Bishop Nielson was one of the best men that I ever met.... I really believe that he died without an enemy—loved by all ... and Aunt Mary was his daughter so that may be the reason that she was so nice to me.

Kind and generous, Hole-in-the-Rock Mormons were also very old-school. Among other things, some were still practicing plural marriage. In addition to "Aunt" Mary Nielson, thirty-seven, Kumen Jones was married to Lydia May Lyman, thirty. Between the two wives they had had seven children by 1895, with more on the way. Aunt Mary's father, Bishop Jens Nielson, had three wives and eleven children. It was Annetta Nielson, born of Nielson's third wife, that caught Bert's eye.

> And of course there was a little love affair and I must have had my gall with me for it was the Bishops daughter but she would not have me with out me joining the church and as I had not reached the point of burying my identity as a man I had to refuse her and there were a few tears on my leaving Bluff.
>
> In June our kiln of brick was all burned so we got a contract to make brick in Moab so about the last of June we went to Moab.... I went out on horseback; the rest of the boys went with the wagon.... I remember that I left Bluff and Net Nielson stopped [Aunt Mary] on the way to Sunday School and on learning that I was leaving it was then that the little cry came off and I was begged to join the church but I could not see it that way so she finally married Zeke Johnson so that was that.... [T]he affair hurt neither of us for it was soon forgotten.

That was that. They rode north one hundred miles to the small ranching community of Moab on the Grand River (now called the Colorado) and went back to mucking clay. They set up shop north of town, about a mile from the river, and over the next few months burned two more kilns of bricks. That took them well into autumn.

By then Loper had been in the West ten years. He had grown from a scrawny sixteen-year-old into a strapping self-reliant man. He was a coal miner, a mule skinner, a prospector, a ditch digger, a hard-rock miner, a brickmaker, a freethinking, freewheeling roustabout, and a very big fan of the ladies. Perhaps it was time to go back home now—what little home he had—and see how things looked.

There was no bridge at Moab then, just a wooden ferry for crossing wagons, teams, and livestock. On October 1, the day that Loper left Moab, they ferried three thousand sheep, headed for the railroad thirty miles north. Loper followed the sheep.

> At the conclusion of the job I took what little money and, getting a ride to Chicago with a train load of sheep, I took my leave of Utah for a while. #

11 Landmark

On July 12, Howard Welty reached the South Rim of Grand Canyon, notified Superintendent Harold Bryant of Loper's death and gave the National Park Service (NPS) an extensive interview. That same day, Norman Nevills was at Lee's Ferry readying a Grand Canyon trip. Nevills had essentially invented commercial boating in Grand Canyon back in 1938, and was now beginning his seventh Grand Canyon voyage.

The NPS, knowing Nevills was due to launch, had opted not to form any sort of search party of their own, feeling Nevills was far better equipped to do the job. Besides, Loper had died far upstream of the National Park, in the limbo land of Marble Canyon, under the vague authority of the General Land Office. Really, Loper was not the Park's problem at all.

Two days later the Nevills party spotted Loper's boat high on the bank. They pulled ashore. Nevills had his two main boatmen along, J. Frank Wright and Jim Rigg. Dock Marston, another of Nevills's regular crew had either quit or been fired, accounts vary. In his place rowing the *Joan*, Nevills had a new man: an aircraft toolmaker who had signed up for a San Juan trip a year earlier and impressed Nevills with his rowing skills. His name, although few ever knew him by it, was Plez Talmadge Reilly. He went by P.T. or simply Pat. It is oddly fitting that he should inherit the boat of the blunt and occasionally caustic historian Marston, for Reilly was already on his way to being another from the same mold. Reilly's critical notes on Loper's boat that day hint at his budding matter-of-fact style:

> Boat poorly designed, some screws used but mainly shingle nails; oars too light and oarlocks misplaced. Plywood only ¼" thick, tho double in places. Gunwale too high.

NAU.PH.97.46.121.76

P.T. Reilly

Nevills left of center in white shirt.

Reilly was a fastidious taker of notes and became a meticulous researcher of history. He carried on an edgy lifelong correspondence with Marston, jabbing, sparring, and becoming another of the many voices who painted Loper's—and many others'—legacies.

The party read the Memoriam, took a few photographs, and drifted on downriver. Although they, too, looked for Loper's body along the way, they saw no further sign. #

12 War

FROM CHICAGO I went back to my old home in Missouri and after a brief visit there I went down into the Indian Territory where my brother was, to the town of Ardmore.

Bert Loper never wrote of his visit to Chicago, but Alden Lewis, a Boy Scout who accompanied Loper on a 1949 Glen Canyon trip, recalls Loper saying he hit the town hard and blew his entire wad. That could not have taken very long. Loper had never seen a big city before, still had a youthful hunger for the wilder side of life, and doubtless had a very small wad to blow. He moved on.

Loper's visit to Missouri was understandably short. He had little love for his uncle Allen Johnson, leaving only his other uncle, Pete, now married to Emma Steele. He soon headed south to find his brother Jack.

Some time after Bert went west in 1885, Jack Loper left Missouri. His next twenty years are poorly documented. His grandson Jack Watkins recalled tales of his grandfather swamping in saloons and cowboying. On Watkins's wall is a mounted Colt 45 six-shooter, said to have been given to Jack Loper by the infamous Tom Horn. Rough company.

Horn was involved in the capture of Geronimo, and the Rough Riders' assault on San Juan Hill, but his greatest infamy comes from the 1890s when he worked as a hired killer for cattle barons, dispatching alleged rustlers, usually from a distance, with a high-powered buffalo gun. "Killing men is my specialty," Horn is said to have stated. "I look at it as a business proposition, and I think I have a corner on the market." Before that Horn followed a similar line of work for the Pinkerton Detective Agency and the Wyoming Cattle Association. Horn's association with Jack Loper was likely around this time, as Loper is said to have been shot in the knees in the 1892 Wyoming range massacre known as the Johnson County War.

Perhaps that cured Loper's itch for gunplay. His obituary states that in September, 1893, he joined the Cherokee Land Rush into what became Oklahoma, and settled for a time in Guthrie. The first solid information of Jack Loper's whereabouts comes when Bert arrived in Ardmore in the fall of 1895. Even then, Jack's occupation is unknown.

Ardmore in 1895 was the largest town in Indian Territory and was, in the words of historian Paul Nelson Frame, "an anarchist's dream." Although there were several thousand people living there, there were no police, no courts, no public schools, and no sanitation. Whites outnumbered the Indians and lease laws to limit white occupation had become unenforceable. To make matters even more chaotic, eighty-two downtown businesses were razed by fire that summer.

Jack Loper appears in no Ardmore records. Cleda Loper, Jack's granddaughter, believes he was working as a teamster at the time, running mules and wagons. He may well have been hauling loads for the booming cotton business. Just what Bert did that winter is unknown as well. Whatever it was, he didn't like it.

> My stay in that country was not very agreeable to me so … I started to look for other places so I started out and my money supply was very meger so I had to travel easy that is I had to hook my rides so I would have money to buy food.… I left there in the spring of 1896.

In early July 1896, Bert Loper, apparently by pure chance, hopped out of a boxcar in Mulvane, Kansas, a small railroad town south of Wichita. "I happened to run into some of my relatives in Mulvane," wrote Bert, "for the town is nearly made up of Lopers. My Uncle John and my Uncle Dan with all their off spring lived there."

John and Daniel Loper were older brothers of Bert's father Jehail. John and his wife Charlotte had homesteaded in Mulvane in 1871, about the time Jehail was filing for divorce in Missouri. Daniel came a few years later, and in 1879 John donated a portion of his land for the Mulvane townsite.

It may well have been here that Bert found out that his father had not died in Missouri, as he had always been told, but had left. Jehail Loper had moved to Whitesboro, Texas, and established another brickyard in the fall of 1872. The tiny town was incorporated the following year, and

Loper brothers:

Top: Lorenzo(?) Jehail(?) Uriah

Bottom: William(?) John & Charlotte, Daniel

(Guesses based on apparent ages)

Jehail Loper made it his home. He remarried on Valentines Day, three years later, to Sarah Jane Smith Truly, a widow with three boys. It seems he left his unsettled past behind him, as an 1888 *Whitesboro News* story stated:

> J.P. Loper, our brickmaker and bricklayer, is one of Whitesboro's old settlers. He came to this town in 1872 and by his skill and honest dealing he has successfully run the brick business ever since, and is well established with a brickyard one mile and a half north of town and has brick enough on hand to supply the demand for the next two years.

Jehail P. Loper is buried in Whitesboro. Sarah, his wife of eighteen years, commissioned a headstone to read: In memory of my dear Husband J.P. Loper, Died Feb. 4 1893, Aged 63 years. Bert and Jack had come just two years and fifty miles from meeting their father when they were in Ardmore in 1895.

Perhaps Bert learned some of these details from his uncles in Mulvane. But probably not the whole story. Bert never expressed ill will when he mentioned his father. He stated that the reason his parents separated was that Jehail's three daughters were older than America (they weren't) and that friction caused the breakup. Perhaps Bert's grandmother had told him that. He never knew of the accusations of adultery, of abandonment, of corporal abuse. He never knew his father held a grudge, not only against his mother, but against Bert and Jack. He never knew that Clause 4 in J.P. Loper's last will and testament, written and signed just hours before he died, stated:

> I desire that our said property after the death of my wife be equally divided among our children hereafter described. Florence Saw Tilhe, Eugenia Ebert, Allice Hedrick, R.B. Truly, P.E. Truly, that said children shall share alike.

Loper listed his three daughters by his first wife, and Sarah's two living sons. But there is not a mention of Loper's two sons. They no longer existed in his world.

Bert never mentioned just how much of Jehail's story he learned from the Mulvane Lopers. Perhaps some of Jehail's ill-will toward his sons had been passed to his brothers, as Bert did not stay long, and never mentioned his uncles again.

> I stayed with them for a week or two and hoed corn for 50¢ per day and made $10-00 so I had another grubstake and that was the money that took me to Nebraska.
>
> I think that the climate of Nebraska is the most disagreeable in the world, but Nebraska had, I think, the very nicest people I ever met.... in due time I landed in [the] Town of Kennard [and] got a job on a farm with a man by the name of Bob Schaffer, and my pay was 75¢ per day, but even at that it was better than Ardmore and by cold weather I had enough to go to Omaha and buy myself a very nice winter outfit of clothes.
>
> The most time I spent in Nebraska was with the Arlington Nurseries—The Marshall Brothers was the proprietors and the very nicest people to work for it was ever my lot to work for. I was working for them when war was declared against Spain so it was the army for me so I went to Omaha and tried to enlist but the City was full of people in the same mood so I

> returned to Arlington and started back to work but the opportunity to enlist soon came so I hiked to Lincoln and joined.

For three years Cuban revolutionaries had been hammering their Spanish rulers, and the overlords in turn were imposing increasingly draconian retribution on the citizenry. In January 1898, President William McKinley sent the warship *U.S.S. Maine* to Havana harbor to protect American lives and interests. On the evening of February 15, the *Maine* exploded and sank with the loss of 260 Americans. Two possibilities for the explosion were put forth. It could have been caused by spontaneous combustion of coal in a chamber adjacent to the ammunition magazine. Many analyses—and modern forensics—support this. Or it could have been caused by a mine exploding just outside the ammo magazine. This, in turn, offered three possibilities. The Cuban rebels, who had the technology, could have done it to provoke war with Spain. Or rogue Spanish officers, impatient with their leadership's inaction toward American aggression could have attacked the ship. Lastly and least likely, the Spanish government, who had the least to gain and most to lose by provoking the Americans, could have ordered it.

But back in the States, William Randolph Hearst was waging war with his newspaper rivals for domination of the American press. The more sensational the stories, the better the sales. When Hearst sent artist Frederick Remington to Cuba to cover the conflict, Remington complained there was nothing newsworthy and asked to return to the States. Hearst allegedly wrote back, "You supply the pictures, I'll supply the war."

Indeed, the Spanish American War is often called Mr. Hearst's War, as it was the press that whipped the nation into a frenzy, screaming "Remember the *Maine*! To Hell with Spain!" Patriotism soared and on April 25th, the United States declared war on Spain.

Bert Loper was nothing if not patriotic, and walked the fifty-plus miles to Lincoln, enlisting on May 4. Along with thousands of others he was shipped back East to training camps to prepare for war. Unfortunately for most of the patriots, the United States was thoroughly unprepared for the military build-up, and training camps throughout the southeastern states quickly filled to overflowing with men. Housing was minimal, overcrowding was rife, and sanitation was horrendous. The camps could be smelled for miles.

The conflict in Cuba was, in the words of Teddy Roosevelt, a "splendid little war." His famous charge up San Juan Hill made him a national hero and eventual president. On July 3, American forces sank the entire Spanish Fleet. The Spanish soldiers were outnumbered and cut off from any help. It was only a matter of time. Yet America's most formidable foes were just beginning their assault: acute diarrhea, typhoid, malaria, and the most lethal, yellow fever—also known by its final symptom, "the black vomit." Casualties from disease soared, not only in Cuba and Puerto Rico, but back in the States at the camps. Loper was stationed on the Georgia-Tennessee border at the old Civil War battleground of Chickamauga, which had been hastily converted for troop training.

> That which I [enlisted] for was denied me for all we got out of that enlistment was a nice sojourn in that fever infested hole—Chickamauga, and while I did not get the typhoid I very narrowly escaped the Hospital and there was very few that escaped disentary, and the southern malaria—I went in at 150 and came out at 128 and there was others that fared worse than me.

It is no exaggeration to say that Loper fought in the deadliest battle of the war: more men died at Chickamauga from yellow fever and typhoid than died in combat in the entire war. In fact, nearly ninety percent of the U.S. fatalities of the Spanish American War were due to disease (the number two killer: contaminated meat). Loper reported sick ten times, and was in the infirmary for two stays with acute diarrhea. On their healthy days the men marched around camp on maneuvers. Sick soldiers were often sent on furlough to recover rather than subjecting them to camp conditions.

With the hostilities over in Cuba the armed forces began downsizing. Even though the struggle continued in the Philippines for several more years, the military was eager to depopulate the disease-ridden camps. Loper's company returned to Omaha and was mustered out on October 24. Of his 164 days of service, Loper was sick twenty-nine and on furlough thirty-two.

> But outside that it was a very good step in my education for I learned things there that I could learn no where else. #

13 Condolence

Death is a shock to us yet we must know that it came the way that Bert wanted it. He had lived his life and said so frequently. If he wanted the end that way, why should he not have it?

Dock Marston to Dave Rust July 13, 1949

Rachel Loper took the news hard. Berta Harris said she had to talk Rachel out of leaving immediately for Lee's Ferry to join the Nevills party to search for Bert. That he might really be gone was, to her, unacceptable. "I would like to have Bert," she wrote to Margaret Marston:

> but I would not call Bert back for I love him so—he was my life and what I lived for.... We both loved each other so much, that is why I miss Bert so much, if he was not doing for me I was for Bert, so these things you just can't forget. I will always love Bert's Memory as much as I loved him.... [I]n my heart Bert knew the river and I am to Blame for trusting Bert in someone else care when I knew how he was and may God and Bert forgive me.

Although Millie Biddlecome urged her to return to Green River, Utah, and live rent-free, Rachel could not bear it. She stayed on at her nephew's in Salt Lake.

Condolences rolled in. Loper was, for many, an institution—his loss was deeply felt.

> I have always thought that I could stand anything that could come up—but that telegram set me back on my heels—while I anticipated something of the kind never the less it hit me very hard—if he was in a nice grave it would not be so bad. O why did he go on that trip if he had first been satisfied but what is the use to regret it is done.... I don't know

what to do. I am the last of five children. Of course I am the next to go. And if I could take Edna with me I would like to go to Bert tonight.

JACK LOPER

If you hadnt taken such good care of him that winter he would never have been here these last three years, and think of the good times he has enjoyed, he just loved the river, and he has had a number of trips that he sure had a good time on, he never could have done it without your help, you have been good to him and think of the times you have done nice things for him, like helping him make the boat, you tried to talk him out of it, and when you saw it made him unhappy, you let him have his own way and helped him, pounded nails and every thing, coaxed him in the house to rest when he got tired, and so many things, they may seem small now, but they helped a lot, Rachel, and I hope you can get some comfort out of them.

MILLIE BIDDLECOME

I don't need to tell you how much Bert meant to me. You already know that he has been Romance and Glamour to me since I was a little girl and that wasn't the day before yesterday, either! …

But the thing I can't face for you is The River. Don't hate it. Let Bert's deep love of it somehow enter your heart and maybe you can be the one to carry on in his name the romance of it.

PEARL BAKER

Almost the last thing he said to me while we were alone in your front room, was "Rachel! Rachel! I don't know what I would have done without Rachel all these years."

MARGARET MARSTON

He knew when he went down there that he was asking for the call and he accepted the challenge with a high head.

I hope they do not find his body. I know he would want it left there.

We know you have lost a gallant and devoted partner and you have our heartfelt sympathies.

OTIS MARSTON

We all appreciate the fine qualities that Bert showed all his life, and I certainly know his love of the river was a very real part of his life and was a fine example to all river travellers.

NORMAN D. NEVILLS

Although Bert may be gone he will live in our hearts the rest of our lives. I will remember always his sayings and stories. I'm sure glad that I'm one of his boys.

NOEL BAKER

In my life I have known few men who are so much a part of the land. There is satisfaction to be found in the mark left in both the country and the hearts of men with whom he associated for we all loved him for his fine spirit, his interest in youth and his desire to do. He was a man who did the most with what the Lord had endowed him.

JOHN L. CROSS

Bert became my friend shortly after he became your husband.... It seemed to me that Bert looked upon me as a son during the close years of our association.... Only one slightly comforting thought comes to me and that is: Bert would have wanted it that way, rather than from a lingering illness which would have been burdensome to others.

ELWYN BLAKE

He was a good friend of mine. He was a wonderful man filled with wise counsel, an unbounded knowledge of the west & world affairs—and also filled with the spirit of adventure in the Canyons of the Snake & Colorado Rivers

HUGH MISER

I know of no man who was so much a part of the Colorado as Bert. He was a pioneer in that he pointed the way to the irresistible adventure of the River to so many. Those of us who were so fortunate are grateful and mindful of this great loss. Yet he will always be a part of the story of the Colorado and I am sure his memory will be as enduring as the River itself.

C. GREGORY CRAMPTON

> What bothers me most is Mrs. Loper who is so grief-stricken. For Bert it is O.K. as he is where he wanted to be when he died, but for Mrs. Loper—she cannot, as yet, see it that way.
>
> Don Harris to Marston

"I don't suppose you saw anything of Bert," Rachel wrote to Marston after his 1950 Grand Canyon trip:

> Had I known you were going I surely would have asked you to look along for Bert. I just can't help but think he is coming back while yet I know he can't but I really wish I was down there with Bert....
>
> P.S. if you hear of anyone going down the Grand see if they will keep a look out for Bert I still want Bert.

Rachel felt the loss for years. She made Salt Lake City her permanent home, her marital status: widow. In 1952 she wrote to Dock and Margaret Marston, "I am well but life is now over for me, nothing is interesting any more, I just go about from day to day waiting for my day." #

Rachel Loper

14 Love

October 15, 1940

Dear Elwyn;-

I WILL BE STARTING to work and my job may last two months and I do not know how much time I will have to do any writing but will try to do some....

After the war was over I returned to Arlington and worked that winter and in the spring I got a job with the Nye Schnieder elevator Co.... and it was my duty to go from place to place and repair the different elevators but before the summer was over I got a job with the Furgeson Co. on the Burlington System and it was while employed that I had my real love affair and it would be hard to try to tell you just what that meant to me for ... you will never know how I would like to tell you all but I will do the very best I can.

It was while repairing an elevator that I got to board with a farmer family and the farmer family consisted of a Father, Brother and a sister and the sister was a housekeeper and in due time the sister and I fell in love and I want to say this that while I have since married and been so for many years I do not believe that I will ever lay awake nights thinking of the one that I love like I did the girl of that family but Elwyn it is so hard to tell even you of that affair but to make a long story short we went the way of so many before us and perhaps did that which we should not have done but I do wish I could tell you instead of write it but I will say that there were many nights that I would lay awake and build castles of how we would go on through life for I really loved her—

it is so hard to write—but we finally decided that I would return to Colorado and in due time send for her but after I had reached Telluride her letters stopped for some time but after a period she wrote me again and told me that we had got in a mix up but at the same time she called our engagement off so there was no more letters until later when she wrote and said that her first fears were true and as I well knew her father that would be no home for her when he learned the fact but said that if she had the money she would go to her sister in Central City Colo. so I sent her $50.00 and told her to let me know and I would come up and we would be married but I heard nothing from her after sending the money but on the first day of April I quit my job at Telluride and went to Denver and from there to Central City and when I went to the door of her sisters house and told them who I was they told me that the girl had gone home in Nebraska the day before so the conclusion I came to was that all she had told me was lies for I could not think that she was in a fix and would return home but after visiting with her sister for a day or two I went to Cripple Creek and went to work

but in the mean time I subscribed for her home paper and it was not long until I saw an item in the paper saying this girl had returned to her sister in Colo. so, I think it was in Aug that the mine that I was working in had an accident so I got a lay off and went to Central City and I arrived there at noon and as I stepped in the front door they were at their noon day meal and the girl had a chair drawn up to the table and as I stepped in the door she reached down and gathered up the baby and went out of the room but I came in and it was then that I had a talk with her sister and Brother-in-law and in the course of time the girl came back in the room and it was then that she said she wanted nothing to do with me

so I returned to Cripple Creek and in due time I wrote her that in order to give the baby a name I was willing to marry her—in name only and give the baby a name and that I would provide for her and the baby if that met her views but she would have nothing to do with it and it was not long until she married a man by the name of Smith and that is the last I have ever heard from them

but even until now I sometimes lay awake in the nights and wonder if it was my boy that was born there or not but I will say that I have never had another love affair the same as that one and of all the dreams of happiness I have had there was never a dream like this one—there is so much that I cannot write and if I was with you I could explain it all—and even until this very moment I have never had another like this one for in my thoughts I had this one placed on a pedastal above the common herd and was trying to make an angel out of her for all of the sacrid things the most sacrid was, to me, a mother and to think that she had given to me a son was, to me, the most wonderful thing in the world but after accepting my money to come west and then turning me down was beyond my comprehension for the hours I had lain awake thinking of her and the happiness in store for us to-gether and after I had complied with all her requests and then to be turned down was something of a blow and after all these years it is hard to cease thinking of the heaven I had contemplated with her.

She was not a young thing but was 27 years old and had taught school and the indiscretion was mutual and there is much I could tell you …

Love to all

Bert #

15 Something about Bert

Bert Loper, Intrepid Boatman, Makes Final Voyage Down Turbulent Colorado River

The *Salt Lake Tribune* ran a quarter-page editorial on July 12 devoted to Loper's passing. He had gotten quite a bit of press leading up to his expedition. Many newsmen knew him well.

> It was time to retire from the rapids of life and nature, time to float on an eddy of ease and security. But the "call of the wild" could not be ignored by this lover of adventure who felt more at home in the swirl of turbulent waters rushing seaward between towering walls....
>
> Mr. Loper was a kindly gentleman, an interesting conversationalist and a lover of the great outdoors in the wide-open west. It was a privilege to have known him and to feel that he was prepared for his final voyage across the river that flows between here and hereafter.

An uncredited clipping from Rachel Loper's files carried this obituary by Stan Anderson of Logan, Utah:

> If he had made it through this time, he might have tried it again at 90. He was that kind of guy. He had glory in his eyes.
>
> But he didn't have any trips lined up after this big one clear to Lake Mead, he said, and didn't want to "just sit down the rest of the summer." So he thought maybe he'd take his wife on a leisurely little river trip—down the Green from Greenriver, their home, to Moab. They would have taken about a month to do it, he figured....
>
> There was nothing wrong with the boat. Standing by it in Salt Lake City last week before leaving for Lee's Ferry, Bert Loper looked like no river would ever get him, no less old age. One of the reasons he gave for trying the Colorado again at 80 was that he wanted to "get some fresh

memories to carry into my old age." …

There was something about Bert that was so big you couldn't see it all, something like there is about the desert, which he loved passionately. He had great sweeps of open land in him, and long stretches of river. Talking with him was somehow like talking firsthand with history. #

life

16 Hard rock

BERT LOPER returned to the West for good in late 1899. He went to Telluride in the San Juan Mountains, where he had worked ten years earlier. He was a strong, fit thirty years old. He took a job in the Bessie Mine, high in the mountain valley overlooking town.

Although modern technology was making the job of hard rock mining easier with compressed-air drilling, electric lighting, and more sophisticated hoisting machinery, the increased complications of such technology brought their own risks, and the ever deepening mines made the inevitable disasters ever more horrendous. Injuries and deaths were still commonplace. Wages for a hard rock miner ran between two-and-a-half and three dollars a day for eight to ten hours of work. For a dollar a day a miner could get board and room. Work ran seven days a week with Christmas and the Fourth of July off.

Miners who worked near town had the disadvantage of local enticements to siphon their paltry wages. But those who worked at the high, distant mines near Alta, such as the Bessie Mine, were often stuck there for months at a time during winter—an unpleasant but effective way to save money. Loper, for once, had a serious incentive for thrift: he hoped to bring the woman he loved to Colorado and marry her. When Loper sent fifty dollars to her in Nebraska, it was close to a month's net wages (equivalent to over a thousand modern dollars)—no small commitment. Sadly, that relationship was not to be.

By the end of March he had still not heard back from her. He quit his job and went to Central City, only to confirm what he already suspected—even though she may have borne his child, she no longer wanted anything to do with Loper. He went back to the mines, this time heading for the Cripple Creek Mining District, one of the world's largest gold producers. He landed in Victor, the "City of Mines" adjacent to the goldfields, where most of the eight thousand mine workers resided.

The downtown had burned several months earlier and was undergoing massive reconstruction in brick, stone, and steel. Loper took a room in Nick Boyle's house on the hill overlooking town, along with Boyle's family of seven and twelve other boarders. Two years later he was living downtown in Ida Cree's Victoria Hotel and working in Stratton's Independence Mine.

W.S. Stratton, one of the most famous millionaires to come out of the Cripple Creek, had started the boom when he staked his claim on a granite outcrop of Battle Mountain in 1891. After reaping more than four million dollars from the Independence Mine, he sold it in 1899 for eleven million. The mine was just a few hundred yards above town and a miner could step into a saloon in the morning for a good stiff eye-opener, then descend directly through a staircase in the bar into the tunnels and walk to the mine underground. The next daylight he saw might be twelve hours later, through the swinging doors of the same saloon.

Cripple Creek was a rich gold mining district and had boomed when the 1893 Panic had busted the silver mines of the West. In 1894 the Western Federation of Miners (WFM) won a strike for fair wages—three dollars for an eight-hour day. For a hard rock miner, Cripple Creek could not be beat.

In 1903 the WFM's Executive Director, Big Bill Haywood, moved to unionize the mill workers in the surrounding area. When several mills refused the Union's demands for hours and wages similar to those of the miners, the battle lines were drawn. On August 10, 1903, Haywood called a general strike, shutting down the mills and mines of the entire district. The protracted crisis soon involved martial law, murder, hundreds of miners run out of town, and the irreversible decline of the once great Cripple Creek district.

Although some accounts claim Bert Loper was escorted unequivocally out of town by the union busters, he shows up on none of the lists of those imprisoned or deported. Pearl Baker, in an early draft of *Trail on the Water*, described a confrontation with a company tough named Blackie Smith, who, with two other thugs, gave Loper a good roughing up and sent him down the road. Just what Baker may have heard from Loper in this regard is unclear. A set of hand-written notes in her file reads, "Run out for being a Union man. Wes Fed Miners," indicating that Loper may well have joined the WFM. Charles Hunt wrote that Loper

Headworks of Independence Mine in Cripple Creek

Single-jack drilling in Copper Queen, Bisbee

was fired for his union activities. "In his words, he had a military escort on his way out of town, and was given a special car on the train—a flat car near the caboose." Yet it seems Loper, if indeed he had been run out of town, would have mentioned it in one of his many autobiographical essays. Instead, his own account shows a more canny decision based on the writing on the walls:

> I worked in the mines until the 10th of Aug. 1903 when we became tied up in a strike so I started on my way again and after traversing Wyoming, Utah, Nevada, California, and Arizona, I landed in Bisbee Arizona....

Loper never elaborated on his great circular wander through the West. Baker's handwritten notes read, "Hoboed for 3,000. Ogden, Sacramento, Frisco, L.A., Yuma, Tucson, Bisbee." Loper had mined silver, coal, and gold. Now, in Southern Arizona, he tried his hand at copper. The great open-pit mines had not yet been invented, however, and Loper the hardrock miner went back underground.

Bert Loper, thirty-five, registered to vote in Bisbee on October 17,

1904, and the 1904 city directory records an A.L. Loper working in the Copper Queen Mine. The Copper Queen at the time was the fifth largest copper producer in the world and, when combined with the adjacent Calumet Mine, out-produced them all. Bisbee, approaching a population of 20,000, claimed to be the largest town in the Southwest. But the mining was as primitive as anything Loper had experienced. Compressed air had not made it to Bisbee, and it was back to single-jack hand-drilling. Depending on where in the mine one worked, a miner could be groveling in a cold, dripping muckhole, or sweltering in a furnace over one hundred degrees. The good news was that shifts were only eight hours and paid an unheard-of four dollars. Of course there were plenty of establishments ready to absorb that pay along the steep winding street called Brewery Gulch.

At some point Loper ventured south about fifty miles to Cananea, Mexico, where copper had been mined since the 1760s. American interests bought the mines in the 1880s, and by the time Loper arrived, owner Colonel William Greene was paying an outrageous five dollars for an eight-hour shift to lure American miners to Sonora. Mexican miners, on the other hand, were paid just one third of that for a ten-hour day—which was still six times what they could earn elsewhere in the region. Greene, under pressure from Mexican miners for equity, but under equal pressure from surrounding Sonoran employers to stop luring workers away from other industry, cut Mexican wages. The murderous breaking of the Cananea strikes June 1, 1906, by the Mexican government and Arizona rangers is often credited as the spark that led to the 1910 Mexican Revolution. But once again Loper, perhaps smelling trouble as he had in Cripple Creek, had already moved on.

> You know that I spent about 5 years down in that country—4 years in Bisbee and one year in old Mexico and the barrels of sweat that I have given up in those hot boxes is beyond reckoning and La Cananea was no better.

It probably have seemed like five years, but arithmetic demands the duration of his southern sojourn be shortened to no more than three years, as he left Colorado in 1903, toured the West on his way to Bisbee, and by late 1906 had moved on to Nevada. Suffice it to say he found con-

Postcard of Cananea

ditions there unpleasant. Not only did he find the work disagreeable, his racial prejudice flared. Such intolerance may be no less common today, but admitting to it is far less acceptable than when, in 1940, he wrote of his Mexican tour, "my trip to that country cured me of wanting the U.S. to go down and annex that to this country—it is a fine country all right but it is populated with the wrong kind of people and New Mexico and Texas and Arizona has plenty of that same breed."

Loper returned to Bisbee after his Mexican sojourn, and soon departed for the mines of Goldfield, Nevada. He went there with a good friend—and their tempestuous and sporadic relationship would shape both their lives for the next decade. #

17 Nevills

On September 15, 1949, Norman Nevills wrote Rachel Loper, apologizing for not getting up to see her since his July river trip. Nevills knew Bert Loper well, but there was no love lost between the two. Loper felt Nevills too much the boastful showman; Nevills considered Loper an amateur. To Marston, Nevills had written:

> Loper. No ability at leading or mixing, upset innumerable times, and in my opinion his greatest claim to distinction lies in the number of years he has and still is boating.... He's of the Frank Swain school of pull like hell on the oars and hope you make it.

In spite of the fact that the two men were members of the same small Masonic lodge in Green River, Utah, they seem not to have shared any bond.

The day he was to launch from Lee's Ferry, Nevills received word from the National Park Service, notifying him of Loper's death four days earlier, and asking him to search for the body. He had found nothing, and summarized his efforts to Rachel:

> We investigated the Canyon quite thoroly for any sign of Bert, and it seems quite certain that he did not reach shore.
>
> I feel quite certain that you can feel assured that his passing was from a heart attack—and the heart attack was sure to occur sooner or later, whether on the river or at home. You have much to admire in Bert's courage, in that despite failing health he carried on in the tradition of his sport of running rivers.
>
> I know it is hard for those left behind, but I assure you that if I have my choice, the way Bert went will be the way I will go too.

It was not to be. Four days later Norm and Doris Nevills boarded Norm's plane for a routine flight to Grand Junction. The *Cherry II*'s engine sputtered on take-off, then quit entirely. Nevills banked around to land. He was too low. The plane exploded against a low cliff near the runway's base.

Harry Aleson, who had been on Loper's final trip, came to Mexican Hat to console Norman's mother and daughters. Aleson, once a friend of Nevills, had split with him in the mid-1940s and gone into competition. Joining him in business was Charles Larabee, a former Nevills passenger who for reasons poorly defined, came to despise Nevills. When Aleson went to Mexican Hat, Larabee accused him of hypocrisy, saying simply, "I'm sorry about Doris." Aleson, though, seemed genuinely bereaved, as if his rivalry with his former friend had been just some sort of bad game, and now it was horribly over. Regaining his business sense, he made an offer to buy the company. The survivors would not hear of it, and soon accepted an offer from the Rigg brothers—old friends and boatmen of Nevills. The name was changed to Mexican Hat Expeditions.

Having lost two of the biggest names in river running in less than three months, Grand Canyon Superintendent Harold C. Bryant began to talk about closing the river to boating, as he felt the only folks who knew how to do it—Loper and Nevills—were now dead. Not a chance. Aleson howled in protest, and the Rigg brothers and partner Frank Wright were soon back on their feet, running regular trips through Grand Canyon. Don Harris and Jack Brennan formed Harris-Brennan Expeditions and began offering trips as well. The momentum built by the pioneers could no longer be dampened.

Aleson made a few more Grand Canyon trips, but never was able to make himself well-known on the national scene. But one of his hiking clients, a diminutive woman named Georgie White, soon turned the budding river business on its head. #

18 Goldfield

I WOULD LIKE TO BACK UP and tell about a pal or friend I made in Telluride—one who was a real pal to me and I to him—everything we had was held in common and the one that needed it was the one to get it—at that time I was, very frequently, telling about my experience on the San Juan River and my desire to go through the Grand Canyon, but when I left and went to Cripple Creek we became separated and for awhile lost track of each other but during my sojourn in Bisbee I made a trip over to Tombstone Arizona and who should accost me but My pal—Charlie Russell—we kept track of each other and when I went to Goldfield we got to-gether and made our plans for a trip through the Canyon....

Charles Silver Russell's roots both echo and contrast Loper's. On March 28, 1877—when seven-year-old Loper was getting whipped by his grandmother in Bowling Green, Missouri—Russell was born on a farm near Bunker Hill, Illinois, just seventy miles to the southeast. Like Loper, Russell eventually wandered west and was working in the Colorado mines by the time he was twenty-one. Russell, too, was drawn to the rivers of the Southwest.

But here the similarities stop. Russell was not content to labor year upon year in the same low position. Russell had drive. He took correspondence courses in mine engineering and rose high into management during his mining career. He wrote, and wrote well; he edited a newspaper. He conceived grand and daring schemes to bring riches and glory. Meanwhile, Loper hammered, drilled, picked, and shoveled—and day-dreamed of getting back on the river.

Why the difference? Why does one man strive for power, position, and wealth, while the other putters about at the bottom? Native intelligence could play a factor, but it is hard to measure at this late date. Certainly neither man was short on persistence. The most revealing clues come from looking at their families. From the beginning, the Loper brothers were limited in education and pounded down by all who held sway over them. What meager jobs they snagged they felt lucky to get. Although they loathed their beatings, they seemed to accept them as part of life. Perhaps the Lopers' lesson, ever-so-early in life, was that they belonged at the bottom.

The Russell clan, on the other hand, had the benefits of a good home, a solid family, and a full education. Their parents' marriage held strong. Charles's elder brother, John E. Russell, became a lawyer; his other brother Frank, an electrician. His sister Nellie was the assistant to the Executive Secretary of the Lutheran Orphans' Home in Saint Louis.

Charles attended a country school and later a military academy in Bunker Hill, completing his education at Stratten Business College in Saint Louis. His brother John remembers Charles as "a powerful man," about 180 pounds, and around five-foot-nine or -ten:

> My brother was a man who said little, feared nothing, and usually accomplished anything he made his mind up to do. While not a large man he had a powerful physique and was able to withstand most any hardship that came his way, his eyesight was unusually keen as were his perceptive powers, he could analyze a situation and have his results in a very few moments. While well educated he never boasted of the same, on the other hand rather gave off the impression that his education was limited.

"We considered him our smartest brother," recalled Nellie, "and he had a beautiful handwriting that was the envy of us all."

Charlie Russell wandered west and in 1897 began placer mining in Placerville, California. Two years later he was working in Telluride, where he met Loper. "Charlie Russell was one of the very best pals I ever had when we were working in the mines to-gether," recalled Loper after the ups and downs of the decades that followed, "that is the part of Russell I like to remember." Loper added, "Russell was an accomplished Spanish scholar and a Damn good Miner." Both Loper and Russell referred to their Telluride friendship, and to discussions of running the Colorado.

For a while they were "chums and bunk mates together," but Loper quit work on the first day of April, chasing his lost love, landing in Cripple Creek. After that, he recalled, "there was only an occasional letter passed between us and in the course of time we stopped writing."

The June 1900 census of Telluride lists Russell as a gold miner, boarding with a dozen or more men, but out of work for the previous two months. Russell moved on. In 1904 he was mine foreman at the Octave mine, northeast of Wickenburg, Arizona. Within a year or so he was shaft foreman at the mine in Tombstone.

> So the next time I saw Russell I was in Tombstone, Arizona and then we only had a talk and we did not mention the Grand Canyon trip at all but it so happened that I was located at Bisbee Arizona and in a short time I got a letter from Russell reminding me of our previous talks about the Grand Canyon, so the issue was revived and in 1906 we both left Arizona and went to Goldfield Nevada and it was then that we began to lay plans to make the trip.

Russell must have left Tombstone shortly after encountering Loper there, as he shows up in the 1906 City Directory for Prescott, Arizona. Like many of the settlements in Arizona at that time, Prescott was a mining town, and the news in the papers was primarily about the mines. Prescott became a hub for Russell around then, and his brother John established his law practice there, focussing on mining law. Just what Charles was doing at that moment remains unclear, but he could well have been looking for the next place to go. The *Prescott Journal Miner* carried a story in early May 1907, detailing Loper and Russell's plan to prospect the Colorado and stating that Russell "left yesterday for Goldfield, Nev., where he has mining interests."

In the summer of 1906 Goldfield, Nevada, a squalid mining camp south of Tonopah, was found to overlie one of the richest gold veins of all time. It was not long before miners throughout the West heard of the quality of ore and flocked to Goldfield—Russell and Loper among them. Few expected to prospect their own lucky strike. Nor was it the paltry miner's wage that brought them, of course, even though it had risen to four or five dollars a day. It was the "benefits."

In rich veins around the country an art form had evolved called high-grading. A miner working a particularly pure bit of ore would tuck a few of the primest chunks in his pocket and sell them on the sly later on. In this manner, miners learned to double or triple their wages. In the best veins, a miner could sneak out with fifty dollars' worth on a good day. Miners described two types of ore—the very best was "family ore," the rest "company ore." And it was not just the men in the shafts that high-graded—trammers, hoist operators, virtually everyone had their crack at the riches, or worked in partnership with someone who did.

In the lower grade mines, the pilfering was not a problem and mine owners often looked the other way. But in Goldfield, the high-graders had access to small fortunes. One favorite system was to wear two shirts, sewn together along the bottom. At the end of the day the miner would load his little pile of select ore into his "waistbelt" and waddle back to town. The mining companies' threats to institute clothes changes at the end of shifts were met with counter threats of strikes. The mining unions fought fiercely to protect this "right" of miners and, since many of the mining companies operated on short-term leases, a prolonged strike could ruin them. For a while, the high-grading continued. And in spite of minor labor squabbles, production ground on.

The three mines where Loper worked—the Mohawk, the Little Florence, and the Hayes-Monette—were among the three highest producers of Goldfield. Loper and Russell were surrounded by high-grade ore in a city bursting its seams and giddy with wealth. By 1907 Goldfield had become, by far, Nevada's largest city, with indoor plumbing, electricity, motor-cars, and, according to the papers, an inexhaustible supply of gold.

> I was at that time hoisting Engineer on the Little Florence Mine and Ed Monett was top man—commonly called a trammer so, as I was still talking Colorado River he too became interested and he joined with Russell and myself. I know nothing of where he came from before that only that he had worked as a boiler maker helper on some railroad.

Edwin Regan Monett's background was far closer to Loper's than to Russell's. Monett, a fellow Missourian, was born near Joplin on June 20, 1885. Like Loper, he had left home young, running away when he was fifteen and wandering west. He landed briefly near Grand Junction,

Bert Loper at Goldfield, 1906-07. Earliest known photograph of Loper

Charles Russell

Colorado, where he worked for a dairy, for a farm, and for the railroad. By 1902 he was working for the Santa Fe Railroad in California as a boilermaker's helper. Then, again like Loper, he drifted throughout the West, to Colorado, California again, Arizona, Mexico City, and the wheat fields of Palouse Country near Spokane, Washington, before finding his way to the mines of Goldfield at the age of twenty-two. In 1949 Monett wrote:

> I was working at the Little Florence Mine as a top man. Dumping cars that were sent up and sending down Steel, Powder, Timber and other things the miners might need.
>
> A Hoist man quit and Loper took his place and began telling me about the trip that Russell and him were planning to prospect the Grand Canyon. The rest was easy. Very little talking was needed. I did not meet Russell till I arrived at Green River. Loper was the Promoter all the way.

These were the hurly-burly boom days of Goldfield, with thousands upon thousands of eager men surging through. It was by chance and not design that Loper met Monett. And equally by chance he did not meet someone else.

During 1906 and 1907 two men ran a produce store in Goldfield: John King and Arthur Sanger. These two, along with a third man, Elias Benjamin "Hum" Woolley—who was in Goldfield or nearby Tonopah around 1906-7—had recently completed the least-known traverse of Grand Canyon that has yet come to light. Under Woolley's direction, the three men built a boat in Los Angeles, then transported their disassembled craft by rail to Arizona and by horse cart to Lee's Ferry, where the Colorado River enters Grand Canyon. They launched September 1, 1903 and spent the next three weeks with Woolley at the oars running rapids, lining their boat along the shore, panning for gold, and drying out. They continued on through the Mojave Desert to Yuma before leaving the river and returning to Los Angeles. How Woolley (like Loper and Monett, another wandering Missourian) came to know boatbuilding or river running is unknown. In fact, their entire trip remained unnoticed until P.T. Reilly stumbled across Sanger in 1951.

Yet for perhaps a year in Goldfield, the two groups of river men coexisted—Loper, Monett, and Russell in one contingent, Woolley, Sanger, and King in the other—but failed to connect. Goldfield's boom was peaking around 1906–7, however, and with a population of over thirty thousand, it is not surprising the two groups missed one another.

During the first half of 1907, Loper, Monett, and Russell completed their river plans, ordering three steel boats from the Michigan Steel Boat Company. Just how much, if any, of the river expedition was financed by high-grading is anyone's guess. Although neither Loper, Russell, nor Monett admit to it, reports at the time say the practice was nearly universal. But as far as capital contributions, most recollections, including Loper's, agree that Russell was the sort who earned and saved more than the average miner, and most likely did the lion's share of financing the trip. In mid-August they departed Goldfield for the Green and Colorado Rivers. Once again Loper managed to slide away just ahead of major trouble. That winter labor strikes shut down Goldfield and federal troops were brought in to establish order. #

19 Typical miner

I KNOW THAT I am getting old and perhaps something of a crank but I sure get burned up over some one that waits for a man to die before they start to fight him—I might hate a man but if I could not fight him during his life I would try to let it go at that.

So wrote Loper to Dock Marston in 1947. At the time Loper was referring to his own ire against Robert Brewster Stanton, who had spent great effort on a post-mortem defamation campaign against John Wesley Powell. But it could well have been an admonition to Marston not to do that very thing to Loper himself.

The history of river running was dutifully scribed by a few early historians, all of them boaters. Frederick Dellenbaugh from Powell's 1871–72 voyages wrote two books: *Romance of the Colorado River,* detailing the full history of the Colorado; and *A Canyon Voyage,* devoted to the expedition Dellenbaugh had been a member of. Robert Brewster Stanton wrote an exhaustive history of the river, in part devoted to diminishing the character of James White and Major Powell—but so vast it remained unpublished during his lifetime. Ellsworth Kolb summarized the exploits of river explorers in the appendices of his 1914 *Through the Grand Canyon From Wyoming to Mexico.* And Lewis Freeman, in his 1923 *The Colorado River: Yesterday, To-day and To-morrow,* brought that history up to date. Each of these authors was careful to look at whatever records they could find before setting them to paper—albeit sometimes with a healthy peppering of opinion.

Yet all these efforts pale before those of Otis "Dock" Marston—river passenger, turned boatman, turned river historian. His quest to unearth the details of Colorado River history went from an offhand interest in 1947 to—within months—an obsession that devoured the last three decades of his life. He found all earlier histories to be spotty, inaccurate, even fictitious in places. "Hokum!" he cried, whenever he detected another inaccuracy.

Marston's obsession with history soon developed a sub-obsession. Whenever he could find any dirt on someone, he reveled in it. When he found a weak side of a personality, he showcased it. Norm Nevills felt such a reversal of affections from Marston even before he died.

Loper had not been gone long before Marston began painting a darkening picture of him. It is revealing to watch the slow change in tone as Loper disappears from the scene.

Ed Monett's interchanges with Marston also began to show a less favorable side of Loper. Perhaps it was out of politeness that Monett had little ill to say of Loper during his life. Perhaps he did not know Marston well enough to say it. Or perhaps Marston was doing some convincing of his own. Memories evolve over the years, events gain and lose emphasis. Hindsight carries its own distortion, and attitudes fall prey to the power of suggestion.

In 1948 Marston had tracked down Ed Monett, then an old man working as a plumber in the Mojave Desert. Marston interviewed Monett, but no tape or transcription of the conversation exists—only Marston's terse notes remain, giving a few glimpses of Monett's recollections prior to the trip.

> Loper was fellow most anyone would like—do not remember his being quick tempered.... Loper was kind of a ladies man.... Think Russell thot Loper was playing around with girls in Goldfield.... Loper was promoter of trip—thot gold would deposit at lower end of rapids—had found that pattern on San Juan.... I never had any boat experience & don't think Russell had but Loper had some experience.... Don't think Loper had much boat experience before trip.

Marston struck up a friendship with Monett after his initial interview, and in 1950 got a more detailed picture of Monett and Loper's time in Goldfield. But Marston had a way of asking leading questions, and could often prejudice an interview. By 1950, Marston had adopted a decidedly dim view of Loper, and the notes from this second interview portray a considerably less honorable fellow:

> Monett met Loper at the Little Florence.

Loper went to work for Hays Monett mine.

Loper was blowing money around dance halls in Goldfield.

Monett would go to dance halls very little but saw Loper there.

Bert would stay at dance halls late—reported by other miners.

Little Florence did not want men who drank—may be reason he left Little Florence.

Loper had been working on a lease—then went to work on the Mohawk Mine—anticipated high grading enuf to pay his share—he took 20# of ore to Salt Lake & got less than $1 per pound & then he had no money for his share.

He told Monett he would get some of their high grade but foreman apparently sized him up and didn't let him near the real high grade.

Loper left—decidedly cool. When he got to Salt Lake he had a couple suit cases of ore.

Some ore that could be stolen would run $15–20.

He had anticipated more.

When I got to Green River the boats were in the water—put up my share.

I may have paid money to Russell.

Russell put trip together.

Loper could not be trusted.

I knew little of Loper at Goldfield. I knew enuf about him.

After reading the above, one might well believe Loper was little more than a hard-drinking, high-grading, womanizing ne'er-do-well. And perhaps there is an element of truth in that. Loper readily admitted "I drank too much"; that with regards to the opposite sex, "I always could be depended on to get mine wherever that I found it"; and as far as being fiscally responsible, "still don't seem to realize the value of a dollar."

Loper, in short, was a very typical miner. The history of mining towns are replete with the tales of those few mine owners who made it big, but rarely mention the name of a single man who worked down in the hole. Nor did the miners write their own tales. Mostly they staggered from one shift to the next, squandering their scant wages in the saloons, dance halls, and brothels. #

20 Cataract

IN THE THIRTY-EIGHT years since John Wesley Powell's voyage of exploration passed Green River, Utah, few had followed. River running had not caught on. Powell, in fact, barely finished his own voyage. Just a few dozen miles from the end of Grand Canyon, out of food and shaken by the river's unending violence, three of his men abandoned the trip and hiked out, never to be seen again. Powell and his remaining five men floundered through two more major rapids and drifted out into the Mojave Desert.

With the notoriety Powell gained from his trip, he garnered federal financing and clout, soon becoming the Colorado Plateau's preeminent explorer. He retraced portions of his river route in 1871 and 1872, moving far slower, mapping and documenting the terrain in much greater detail than his hurried and calamitous 1869 voyage. After halting his second voyage halfway through Grand Canyon, he led a series of overland surveys, synthesizing much of his work in his 1875 *Exploration of the Colorado River of the West.* With that work and subsequent geological and geographical treatises published by Powell and his colleagues, the Colorado Plateau lost much of its mystery, but retained its reputation as formidable and unforgiving terrain.

In 1889 Frank Mason Brown organized the Denver, Colorado Cañon and Pacific Railroad Company, with the intent of pushing a rail line along the Grand and Colorado Rivers, from Colorado to Southern California. His theory was that a river-grade route would avoid the mountain passes and be spectacular besides. To direct the survey he hired Robert Brewster Stanton, an accomplished railroad engineer. After surveying the upper Grand River, Brown and Stanton launched from Green River, Utah for the main assault on the Colorado. For boats they chose a hull design much like Major Powell's—a narrow, round-bellied boat with a full-length keel.

Powell's and Brown's craft were modeled after the New York Harbor

"Whitehall" boat, built for fast and sure handling in choppy flat water. Although they did go fast, Powell's men found them cumbersome and tough to steer in rapids, even when using a long sweep oar as a rudder. Knowing no different boat, Powell used the same style on his second voyage. So it is no surprise that Brown and Stanton went with what was known to work, even though it did not work all that well. The Brown-Stanton expedition had bad luck in the rapids of Cataract, losing much of their gear and provisions. Then, a day after entering Grand Canyon, Frank Brown's boat rolled over in a small rapid and he was drowned. Thinking they would portage the roughest water, Brown had ordered no life preservers.

After two more drownings a few days later, Stanton, who had taken over leadership of the expedition, stashed the boats and gear and retreated. Back in Denver he regrouped. After raising more funds and contributing much of his own, he returned with life jackets and stouter boats, although still of the Whitehall hull style. With much difficulty and significant boat damage, the men struggled through. In 1891 a group of his men joined James Best to prospect through Cataract Canyon, again in Whitehalls. After sinking one boat in Cataract, the men left the river at Lee's Ferry, never to return. Fortunately for posterity and the environment, Stanton was never able to raise capital to build the railroad.

Although Stanton published no books on his river experiences, he did write articles for *Scribner's* and other magazines, so his exploits were widely known and available, along with Powell's reports, for men like Loper, Russell, and Monett to study.

During the winter of 1896–97 two teams of trappers ran the Green and Colorado: George Flavell and Ramon Montez and, a few months later, Nathaniel Galloway and William Richmond. Neither party reported excessive difficulty, nor did they find much in the way of fur to trap. Their success on the river, however, was due in large part to the boats they chose. But since these men's trips were poorly publicized at the time, the knowledge and skills they gained were not available to Loper. Likewise, Hum Woolley, whose 1903 trip went unreported, had no influence on those who followed. Of the three, the only surviving concrete descriptions of boat style and technique came from Galloway. He had abandoned the keeled boat of Powell and built lightweight flat-bottomed boats for shallow draft, upturned at the end for ease of pivoting.

Stanton boats: full-length keel

Galloway's 1897 boat prior to decking: flat bottom, raised ends

And unlike Powell, Galloway turned to face the rapid, pulling upstream to slow his boat and pull diagonally upstream away from obstacles. As word spread, Galloway's boat and technique revolutionized whitewater boating. Unfortunately for Loper's group, descriptions of Galloway's techniques would not become commonplace for several more years.

> In the starting of our 1907 trip Russell and I met in Salt Lake City, and proceeded from there to-gether to the town of Greenriver where we found the groceries that we had shipped to that point and we immediately made camp down on the bank of the river at the Ferry landing—(there being no wagon bridge at that time) and started to get our outfit ready—The little country bank pulled a bone head and sent our funds to the Michigan Steel Boat Co. when they should not have done any thing of the kind and it cost us more than 30 days delay and the delays were long and exasperating.

It would be inaccurate to say there was no river knowledge in Green River in 1907. Many locals had run small boats on the Green, rowing down 120 miles to its confluence with the Grand River where the Colorado River began. (The name of the Grand was later changed to the Colorado, thereby moving the Colorado River's beginning from its confluence with the Green to its headwaters high in the Colorado Rockies.) A few men had been up the Grand sixty miles to Moab. As early as 1891 steamboats began attempting the round trip journeys to the confluence from both Moab and Green River, but low water, sandbars, and techno-

Russell's boat after the expedition

logical and economical limitations inevitably shut down all attempts at continued motor navigation.

So when Russell, Monett, and Loper arrived, there was ample knowledge of the flatwater Green and Grand, but little save rumor about the whitewater of Cataract Canyon. Although launching a boat from Green River was commonplace, only a handful of trips had ever continued into the rapid stretches of the Colorado, the most recent being a full decade earlier.

With no literature about any trips other than Powell's and Stanton's on which to model their expedition, the three men had chosen a modern version of the same style craft, the Whitehall. They were steel-skinned instead of wood-planked. Their maker, the Michigan Steel Boat Company, claimed to be the largest manufacturer of "pleasure boats" in the world. "All our boats built with our celebrated lock seam making them NON-LEAKABLE. Every boat fitted with air-tight compartments making them NON-SINKABLE." Russell described them:

> We are equipped with three steel boats, each 16 feet long and decked over, fore and aft, with sheet steel covers, which are bolted down by means of a row of small bolts along each gunwale; these covers or decks reach from each end to two transverse bulkheads placed 3½ feet apart near the center of the boats, thus leaving only an open compartment 3½ feet long for the oarsman; all of the load is placed under cover and lashed securely to prevent shifting. The boats are also provided with airtight compartments in each end and under the seat, containing sufficient air to float both boat and load should all other compartments be full of water.

But there were problems. First off, the boats were built for puttering about on lakes. They were in no way designed for the rough usage they were about to get. Second, they were, like Powell's boats, keeled Whitehall boats and difficult to pivot. Had they ordered boats twenty-two feet long, like Powell's main fleet, they would have had difficulty maneuvering at all. But since they were only sixteen feet long, the men were at least able to turn them, albeit with difficulty.

The three miners assembled in Green River to begin preparations on August 27, but were stuck in town for three weeks waiting for supplies and funds. Russell:

> In the mean time we were busy getting our outfit ready—as I have said before, the expedition was for the purpose of prospecting so we made our perforated screens for our rocker and got other things ready. We had our gold pans—picks—shovells—Quicksilver—retorts and many other things making a rather big load for the three boats—we had a shotgun and I nearly kept the camp in meat during our forced stay on the banks of the river—we were equipped with a 5x7-film pack camera but were rather handicapped for the want of funds but we had a small supply of material but in view of the equipment that others have taken we had a very megar supply—we had to put in the bulk heads and put on the covers and it was quite some job.

The *Emery County Progress*, in the county seat of Castle Dale, made note of their preparations, inadvertently beginning a long streak of Loper faring ill with the press:

> Daring Navigators Go Down Green River
>
> Bert Poper and Ed Monett of Goldfield Nevada and Chas Russell of Prescott Ariz have had some special boats and other equipment constructed for a voyage from the town of Green River by water to The Needles Arizona a distance of 217 miles [nearly 800 miles actually]. They expect to consume several months along the route thoroughly exploring the country for its mineral wealth it being known that there are big copper deposits there. A great deal of time will be spent about the Grand Canyon of the Colorado.
>
> The partys equipment will consist of three steel boats a first class

placer outfit mining tools and chemicals for assaying. Each of the boats will have five compartments four air tight and one open. They will be covered with sheet steel. In their placer mining they will use an amalgamating rocker with silver plated copper plates for the gold in the Colorado is said to be so fine that the amalgamation process is the only practical method.

At last they were ready. Loper wrote:

Sept- 19th. 1907

Got every thing ready for our trip down the Colorado River, launched our boats, and partly loaded the *Utah.*

We named the three boats after the three states that we were supposed to traverse—*Arizona* being my boat was called the flag ship, the *Utah* was Russells boat while the *Nevada* was manned by Monett.

Sept-20- 1907

Arose at 3.00 A.M. took the *Arizona* up the river about mile to a watermelon patch, got 10 nice ones, returned to camp got breakfast, finished loading our boats, and pushed out into the river on our voyage at 7-35 A.M. stopped at 10 oclock at little valley and ate one of our watermelons, then we journeyed untill 12-M. when we ate lunch—Then we continued on our way, killed six ducks, and went into camp at 6-P.M. about 12 miles below the mouth of the San Rafel River.

Sept. 21-1907

We arose from our slumbers by starlight, got breakfast, loaded our boats, and at 7-15 pushed off feeling a little sore from the hard rowing we did the day before. We had gone about two miles when I ran on to a bar and had to pull my shoes off and get out and push my boat off, when the boys had the laugh on me.... The stream has a very slow current and requires continual rowing, and my hands are covered with blisters and I can hardly close them—they being that sore. Charlie Russell ran the *Utah* on bar this afternoon and had to pull and we got the laugh on him—it being his first time—later Ed Monett did the same thing.

For seventy miles the boatmen wound through the meanders of Labyrinth Canyon, the rusty sandstone walls rising hundreds of feet above them, higher with each bend. They found ranchers and settlers here and there on the wide bottomlands, trying to make a living in the harsh and remote landscape. They stopped to explore an Indian ruin atop a hill at Fort Bottom, where Labyrinth Canyon breaks away to a wide, weird, open landscape spiked with buttes and spires that Powell called Tower Park. Twenty miles later the Green cuts into Stillwater Canyon, its steep limestone cliffs quickly rising to great height. The river creeps along, its placid surface giving little clue of what is to come.

> Sept. 24-1907
>
> We took an exploring trip to the top of rim rock after breakfast and could see where the Grand River came in—Returned to camp and pushed into the stream and was soon to the Grand and now comes the Colorado and with it Cataract Canyon and also our troubles.... We soon returned to our boats and again drifted down to the last piece of bottom land.... Here we made Camp at 1-Oclock and ate our lunch and after lunch went on a trip of investigation down the river about three miles viewing the first five of the seventy five rapids which we will have to pass over before we will be through the Cataract Canyon—The rapids are not as bad as I expected to find them.

They were camped at Spanish Bottom, at the head of the notorious Cataract Canyon, "the Graveyard of the Colorado." There is no complete count of fatalities in Cataract Canyon. Historian P.T. Reilly enumerated a modest twelve in the first hundred years after Powell's voyage. But with over a hundred miles of flatwater both above and below, the rapids of Cataract are a violent anomaly. An unknown number of prospectors may have been lulled into the rapids during the gold excitement in the 1890s, leaving no record of their attempt, nor of their demise.

Although Loper, Monett, and Russell were getting their hands and backs used to rowing, the flatwater since Green River had given them no sense of what they would be up against in Cataract. Only Loper had seen whitewater before, and then only on the relatively modest rapids of the San Juan more than a dozen years prior. The learning curve steepened abruptly the next day. Russell wrote of their initiation:

The next day we carefully divided our cargoes, so that an accident to one boat would not lose everything of one kind, especially our eatables. We did not push off for the rapids until 3:30 P.M., the *Arizona* in the lead, the *Utah* second and the *Nevada* last. It was our intention to run all the rapids we had seen thus far. As the *Arizona* went over the brink we could see her rear and plunge as she took the first waves, sometimes going completely out of sight as she dropped into the troughs, but she got through safely. It was now my turn, and to be my first experience in shooting rapids. I rowed out, taking the center or tongue of the current. I seemed to go very slowly until very near the brink, when my speed was suddenly greatly accelerated and over I plunged, the boat taking a stiff angle downward as she went over, only to rise abruptly as she climbed the next one, then another pitch downward for the next, but this she did not climb. This wave combed back fiercely and the stern end of the boat plunged under and the huge wave deluged the boat, almost taking my breath away as it swept clear across the boat, but she rode nicely and was out on top of the next one easily and we were soon through the worst part and I pulled into the eddy where the *Arizona* was waiting, and found the open compartment almost full of water, but no harm done. We had neglected to provide ourselves with bailing cans and I was compelled to use my hat to empty the surplus water.

Our experience in the second and third rapids were much the same, although No. 3 was much worse than either 1 or 2.

Rapid No. 4 is a long one, almost one-third mile, and making a reverse curve in its course, and in the last stretch a large rock protruded three feet above the water and crossways against it was lodged a large cottonwood tree, obstructing about thirty feet of the river. The *Arizona* and *Utah* succeeded in running this rapid easily, but the *Nevada* captain, being so busy with his oars, forgot about the tree until too close to save himself, and the boat was carried against it by the swift current. It quickly swung broadside against the log, and, as the point of contact was near the gunwales, the boat simply turned turtle backwards. Monett came up alongside of the capsized boat, his cork jacket holding him high in the water. He reached for the keel with the intention of righting her, but the demons of the river would not thus easily give up their prey, and a vicious wave came over the boat, striking him squarely in the face and knocking him back. A second attempt was unsuccessful; but

> a third was, and with a hand on the keel and his knee on the gunwale, he righted her and climbed in. The oars were still in their places, and he was able to grasp them and pull the waterlogged craft to safety. We then concluded to camp. We had run four rapids in one hour. Almost everything in the *Nevada* was wet, so the next day we put in prospecting while the stuff was drying.

Russell described the wave combing back, and the stern of his boat plunging beneath it as the huge wave deluged the boat. Sitting in the traditional oarsman's position, the pointy bow end of the boat would be behind him and the blunt stern out in front of him. By this description, he is entering the rapid looking downstream, but prepared to row upstream. He elaborated:

> I will here explain our method of running rapids, as it has a bearing in this case, but I do so with fear and trepidation that President Roosevelt may see this and brand us as fakirs, as we shot rapids exactly the opposite to most boatmen. We start in stern first, that is, with the stern downstream, thus the oarsman is facing his course. When a rock is to be missed, the oarsman simply turns his bow away from it and pulls upstream, and, the current now traveling much faster than the boat, whips it quickly away from the rock or obstruction to be missed. In this manner a boat can be jockeyed back and forth across the current, going much slower than the water itself, and rocks can be easily dodged.

This "stern-first" technique was first popularized by Nathaniel Galloway, who came through Cataract Canyon ten years prior to Russell and Loper. It is, in fact, the foundation of modern rowing technique, and most attribute its development to Galloway. Prior to Galloway, both Powell's and Stanton's crews rowed with their backs downstream, pulling hard to gain maneuverability by exceeding the speed of the current. Instead, they often hit the obstacles with tremendous velocity.

Yet Galloway had written little of his experiences by 1907, and nothing of his technique. Loper would not meet him for another two years. And here are Russell, Loper, and Monett, entering Cataract Canyon using the stern-first technique in their very first rapid. Obviously they had prior knowledge, but from where? Both Russell and Monett admit this was their first whitewater experience and that they were learning from Loper. And since Loper had spent the previous twelve years far from the river either mining or bouncing around back east, we must assume that he was using the techniques he had learned on the San Juan River back in 1893 and 1894. If so, this indicates that the stern-first technique predates Galloway's invention of it in Northern Utah. In fact, it is highly probable that this logical method for maneuvering a boat in shallow rocky streams—where maneuverability is critical and velocity a handicap—evolved on many separate streams around that time. If indeed Loper was using the stern-first technique on the San Juan, it puts him among the first whitewater practitioners to adopt the technique.

In an undated response to a question about boating technique from Pearl Baker, Loper wrote: "We always went over a rapid stern first—that made the boatman facing the direction that he was going and it was in that way that we were able to dodge the rocks." Loper does not, however, state where or when he first used the technique, whether he learned it from someone else, or devised it himself. But most modern boaters who have rowed the fast, shallow, rocky San Juan would agree that no boatman would have lasted long there in a wooden boat if they did not learn, adopt, or invent, the stern-first technique.

> Sept-28-1907
>
> Finished loading our boats at 8-30 and made our start with No. 5 before us the worst to be encountered so far, the *Arizona* being the first through—We each struck three rocks but no damage. The *Nevada* came near capsizing but was finally brought safely through We had no trouble untill we came to rapid No. 16 which was a bad one Russell decided not to run it but I thought it could be run so I took the *Arizona* through then walked back up the river and brought each of the other boats through, after 16 we ran 5 more making in all 17 rapids for this days work here we camp at head of rapid No. 22 which does not look good the channel being split by an Island.... We are camped above two roarers....They are awful rough but we think we can run them all right.

They were in the heart of Cataract Canyon, in a stretch of back-to-back rapids, numbers 13 through 20, nowadays grouped as Mile Long Rapid. Along this stretch of river unstable subsurface sediments have shifted,

"She turned almost on end." Loper running Rapid 16

shattering and tilting the cliff strata above. The walls are chaotic, boulders tumble willy nilly into the river, and rain-moistened Halgaito shale loosens mud into tremendous debris flows. The chaos of these processes is expressed in Cataract's rapids. It is an intimidating stretch of river for the experienced modern boatman. Loper's "number 16" is, according to the official map charted in 1921, actually number 15, also known as Capsize, or Hell To Pay. The latter name comes from a mournful inscription left on a boulder by the 1891 Best Expedition: "Camp #7, Hell to Pay, No. 1 Sunk & Down." Considering Russell and Monett were novices rowing tippy, recalcitrant steel boats, it is no surprise they balked. Russell's impressions give a stronger sense of the dynamic that day:

> So rocky is No. 16 it looks impossible to get through it at all. After viewing it a while, Loper proposed to try to run it with the *Arizona*, we to wait below. Accordingly, he went back to where we had landed, and soon we saw his boat coming. He handled her very dextrously, being an excellent oarsman and a past master in the art of running rapids. He was entirely successful in striking the only place in rapid 16 that a boat could pass through, but here the current dashed hard against the right hand oar [shore?] and rolled over a huge rock and took a vertical drop of four or five feet over it, or rather off one side. It was impossible to keep the boat away from it, and she was swept against it, but the amount of water covering it and the rebound of the waves prevented the boat from being injured, but she turned almost upend and plunged off the rock, but luckily the water was deep and she came up like a fish, and the worst was over. Monett and myself were fearful of our ability to do the trick, and Loper bravely volunteered to bring our boats through, which he was entirely successful in doing, the *Utah* taking the wildest plunge off the rock, striking an angle that was near the vertical in going off and taking both boat and man entirely out of sight as he dove off the rock.

Loper had struck a few rocks in Rapid 5 and opened up a seam in the *Arizona.* The next day they laid over in camp, doing repair work, drying supplies, fishing and prospecting. "It will have been noticed before now," Loper ruefully wrote, "that as far as finding any gold we were doomed to disappointment."

On September 30 they encountered the series of rapids now known as the Big Drops. In higher flows these rapids become some of the most formidable on the continent. But with the lower flows of late fall, they present only rock-dodging and a few good waves. Of Big Drop One, also called Rapid 21, Loper wrote, "A keen wind blowing and a hazy sky so when we got our wetting, our teeth chattered very freely—next came 23-Skidoo—and skidoo it was the fall being all of 12 feet and the waves was the highest we have found so far they were easily 10 feet high but our boats were built expressly for them for they could not do better." In Big Drop Three, Russell hung up briefly on a rock:

> In running 25 the keel of the *Utah* struck a submerged rock, and as it stuck a moment, the boat turned broadside, and thus it went over the brink, but so easily do our boats ride the waves that it made no attempt to capsize, and by a few strokes I soon had her in her course again.

The weather had turned most foul and after a few more rapids they pulled in to camp.

"We were making a trip that should have been taken at least two months earlier," observed Loper decades later, "for it is no hardship to be wet in warm water but when a person gets soaked in ice cold water it is bound to take the heart out of him." Indeed, from the 1890s through 1937, a majority of trips were launched in the fall, presumably to avoid the high, dangerous flood flows of summer. But as Loper later realized, they had gone a bit overboard in shunning the floods. By mid-July the highest flows invariably subside, but enough water—warm water—remains to cover the worst of the boulders and make for an enjoyable trip. But hindsight is cheap, and so often useless. Chilled, they laid over again to warm up, work on the boats, scout downstream, and prospect.

> When we camped at this place we thought we would surely find some Gold but was disappointed and have about come to the conclusion that we will be made no richer in Cataract Canyon—The day was very nice in the forenoon but a very strong wind came up in afternoon and covered every thing with sand.

On October 2 they ran another eleven rapids that, as long as Glen Canyon Dam stands, modern boatmen will never see. The river from here to Glen Canyon Dam, a distance of over one hundred and eighty miles, now lies deep beneath the reservoir and silts of Lake Powell. But in 1907, problems still lurked downstream. The day was cloudy, windy, cold, and generally disagreeable. At Rapid 36 Monett ran afoul of the rocks again. Russell described the show:

> Monett, with the *Nevada*, misjudged the current and approached the rock too closely, and was thrown against it. Another just under the water caught the keel of the boat, and there she stuck. By his gesticulations I understood something had floated away, and I rowed out into the current and caught one of his oars as it floated by. He finally succeeded in using an oar for a pry and getting the boat over the lower rock, and she swung around and came down gracefully, striking another rock and turning on the way down. We met him as he came down, and I gave him his oar, and he was able to get into the eddy before the next rapid was reached.

The next day it was Loper's turn, at what they called Rapid 49. For many years each river trip through Cataract Canyon wrote of the rapids by number, and everyone kept their own count. The count varied with water levels and the discretion of the counter. Of the many rapids now drowned beneath the Powell reservoir, this could be any of a number of them. Charlie Russell gave a blow by blow account of what happened:

> The worst accident of the trip occurred at Rapid 49. Our plan of battle was for the *Arizona* to take the lead, the *Utah* following closely and the *Nevada* slightly behind. The *Arizona* ran too close to a rock at the head, and was caught by the eccentric current and hurled against it, where she stuck in much the same manner as the *Nevada* had in 36, but in a far worse predicament. She was careened to one side and the water was pouring over her and filling the covered compartments, which are not absolutely water tight. I could only give her a momentary glance as I shot by. I made a good run and pulled in the eddy, ready to give assistance as soon as he succeeded in loosing it, but he had a poor footing to work from, and there was great danger of his being left on the rock, as when the boat started it would go quickly. He finally succeeded in getting her loose, and by a scratch jumped astride of the rapidly receding bow and came through right side up, where I caught his tie chain and

> towed him ashore. By the time we reached land the boat was entirely full of water. The *Arizona* contained the photographing outfit, and it was found that every picture film and plate had been ruined, together with most of the supplies. The camera, however, was not injured, but it has cost us every picture between Green River and Hite.

The pressed on. Loper wrote:

> Oct. 4.1907.
>
> Loaded up and got a very good start and had a nice long run
>
> We ran six rapids with ease when we came to 55 which we had to pay our respects to by making a portage which took us all afternoon and was very tiresom but it being our first we should not complain
>
> [Loper later added:] I am not just sure why we portaged this perticular rapid because I have ran scores of worse rapids since and some times I think we were loosing our nip but the work attached to making a portage is rather severe.

Disappointed but far from defeated, the trio continued. The following day they stopped to scout Rapid 58—very likely Dark Canyon Rapid. At low water this rapid was considered one of the worst, if not the worst, in Cataract, with a total fall of twenty-five feet.

> Oct 5
>
> started out rather late this morning and after runing 56-57- we came to No. 58 at 11 oclock and it was a fierce one too but after looking it over very carefully decided to run it but was opposed by Russell but I ran it and out side taking lots of water there was no mishap Then Russell and Monett ran it then came lunch then we ran on down to the end of Cataract Canyon and passed over the last rapid which according to our count is No.63—Here we had a very miserable camp for it rained all night—The *Nevada* capsized in rapid 63. [Loper later added:] Just why the *Nevada* had to capsize in a fourth rate rapid has never been solved by me and I cannot see how he could have done it for the rapid did not even need a looking over.

Cataract Canyon had taken its toll on the expedition. Monett had been pinned to the rocks once and flipped twice. Loper had been pinned and virtually sunk, at the expense of their photographic record, but had taken all three boats through Capsize when the others balked. Russell, although he hit a few rocks here and there, had come through unscathed. For his first whitewater trip anywhere, he had done remarkably well. Dock Marston's notes on his 1948 interview with Monett contain the simple phrase, "Bert was leader—he knew river but Russell had brains." Indeed, Russell was a quick study, and already rivaling Loper for prowess at the oars.

The mining angle had been a complete bust, however. The theory that Cataract Canyon should be nature's great sluicebox had proven, for one reason or another, a fallacy. "The San Juan was just the opposite for the San Juan Canyon acted as a precipitator," puzzled Loper, " while the Cataract did nothing of the kind."

They had survived. In spite of their economic bust, they'd had an incredible adventure, and Glen Canyon, downstream, was known to have gold. They had made it through Cataract, with several miles of flatwater before the next settlement at Hite, where they could send letters and perhaps get a few supplies. Russell was pleased with what they had accomplished as he summarized their trip thus far:

> We camped that night with easier minds, as we were now safely over the cataracts, forty-one miles of river, the equal of which would be hard to find, and through which very few trips have been made.
>
> In its deepest parts the walls of the canyon were nearly 3000 feet high, and in some places nearly vertical. We had the unique experience one evening of seeing it pitch dark in the canyon, while at the top the walls were bathed with the sunset glow. A large sulphur spring bubbled out near our camp at the end of Cataract canyon, and several more were passed the next morning as we pulled down the quiet quarters of Narrow canyon toward Hite, which we reached shortly after noon. The first stage of our eventful journey is done, but 400 miles yet remain, and 283 of that is the mighty gorge of the Grand canyon, which may far exceed our experiences in the notorious Cataract canyon, of whose sixty-three rapids we ran, all but one. #

Legend

21 Rivers of quicksand

BERT LOPER loved the land, plain and simple. But he was frustrated by his inability to adequately express those feelings in his own words. So when he heard a song or read a poem that echoed his sentiments, he learned it, reciting it whenever the situation dictated. According to many, his favorite and most often recited poem—the opening line of which grace his cenotaphs in both Grand Canyon and Green River, Utah—was *West.*

WEST

I belong to the wondrous west and the west belongs to me,
Border to border, north and south, from Wichita to the sea,
The land is mine by inheritance, by my father's fathers' blood
That spilled on the earth of the frontier roads, when like a living flood
The immigrants came in their ox-drawn trains, lured by the call of soil
And claimed the kingdom of wilderness by courage and faith and toil.
The country is mine by the right of love, its timber is bone of my flesh,
Its blue horizons are in my soul, its roads weave a magic mesh,
A web invisible, yet as strong as the links of an iron chain
To draw my heart from the world's far ends back to the west again.

I belong to the wondrous west and all of the west is mine,
Mountains of majesty, great as gods; forests of serried pine,
Deserts as bleak as the face of death ruled by a tyrant sun,
Canyons as vast as the march of time where rivers of quicksand run.
All of the trails that my feet have walked, all of the land I've known,
Prairie and mesa, lake and brook, valley and cliff I own.
All of the people are kin of mine by the bond we understand ...
Clan of the West, a brotherhood, through love for this splendid land.

—DON BLANDING #

22 Hite

Charles Russell, Bert Draper and party, who left Green River September 20th with boats for a trip through the canyons of the Green river and the Colorado, arrived at Hite on the 7th of October without having had any accidents of any consequence. They made but one portage in Cataract Canyon, successfully shooting all the other rapids.

Eastern Utah Advocate (Price, Utah) October 17, 1907

Throughout the canyoned stretches of the Colorado River there are few places where one can get to the river from the surrounding country, and fewer yet where one can find access on both sides. For the better part of a thousand miles the river is surrounded by deeply dissected canyons and sheer cliffs. Although Native Americans knew many crossings for millennia, the white men were slow in discovering them. Lee's Ferry was the first crossing noted when Fathers Escalante and Dominguez found it in 1776. They had attempted to find an overland route from Santa Fe to the coastal mission at Monterey. They went far north, then turned west across northern Utah. But as winter approached, they turned back and were funneled to the Colorado by the cliffs surrounding Lee's Ferry. Finding the river too deep and swift to cross, they called the place Salsipuedes—*get out if you can.* After much scouting they found an easier crossing forty miles upstream, later known as Crossing of the Fathers. Yet few Anglos retraced either of these trails for nearly a century, until John D. Lee established Lee's Ferry for the Mormon Church in 1871.

Farther north, around the 1820s, New Mexican traders began using an old Indian crossing at the foot of Utah's Book Cliffs. In 1853, railroad surveyors Beale, Gunnison, and Fremont crossed here. With the coming of the Denver & Rio Grande Railroad thirty years later, the town of Green River sprang up at this important crossing. Green River and Lee's Ferry became the only two established crossings of the river between

Monett and Russell

the Uinta Basin in northern Utah, and the Mojave Desert, some eight hundred miles down river.

It was in an effort to find a more convenient crossing that, in 1880, the hapless Hole-in-the-Rock Expedition blasted their unlikely route through the heart of Glen Canyon, eighty-four miles upriver from Lee's Ferry. That route was so desperate that the Mormons located Hall's Crossing another thirty-five miles upstream. Yet neither of these routes were passable enough to warrant much use. So in 1883, when the Navajo headman Hoskaninni led prospector Cass Hite to an ideal ferry spot fifty miles up river from Hall's Crossing, roughly halfway between Green River and Lee's Ferry, Hite pronounced it a "Dandy Crossing," and settled in. The placer mining was good enough on some bars that a small gold rush ensued, bringing many of those who had shown up for the Bluff Gold Excitement a few years earlier. Hite was soon joined by his two brothers, Ben and John, and nephew Homer. By the time Loper arrived, the small settlement of miners had been renamed Hite.

Oct. 6-1907.

Arose this morning to find every thing wet as well as our selves.

After crossing the river and finding nothing we loaded our boats and started out at 10 A.M. and after rowing very hard for about three hours we passed the mouth of the Fremont (Dirty Devil) river and took lunch—Shortly after lunch we came to a camp which belonged to Mr. Harshberger Mr. Harshberger was putting in a Ferry—four miles on

> down the river we came to Hite (Dandy Crossing) here we received some mail and Camera supplies—We met Mr. Frank Bennett, Mr John Nubia and Mr John P. Hite. We passed a very pleasant evening with them.

The settlement of Hite was situated at the mouth of Trachyte Creek on the west shore of the Colorado, and consisted of a cabin, a store, and a few outbuildings. Most prospectors entered Glen Canyon here, coming in via White Canyon on the east, or via Crescent Creek (later renamed North Wash) on the west. By 1889 the community, although widely dispersed along the canyon, was substantial enough to warrant a post office. Homer Hite became the first postmaster.

Loper, Russell, and Monett felt immediately at home among the local miners. They settled in for a few days of resupplying, resting, drying out, visiting, and writing letters. Russell sent out the first installment of his trip story to the *Salt Lake Tribune,* and Loper made friends.

> Oct. 9-1907.
>
> Packed our outfit this morning and started down the river at 11-A.M. and about three miles down the river we met Mr. Cass Hite—one of the most widely known pioneers in the western country having prospected and fought Indians British Columbia to Old Mexico and from the Rockies to the Pacific coast 40 years ago and having spent the last 25 years in this section of the country and is the best posted man in the state or elswhere on this section of the country.... Mr. Hite is now located on what is known as the Tickaboo Bar about 15 miles below the Post Office of Hite. Tickaboo Bar is at the mouth of Tickaboo Canyon which has a fine spring and Mr. Hite has a little home at the head of the flat and is very comfortably located—Tickaboo derived its name from an old Ute Indian Chief who inhabited the Henry Mountains about 50 years ago Tickaboo in Ute means "Friend"—Mr. Hite is with out comparison the most genial host it was ever my lot to meet and I think I could go and finish filling this book about him.

Cass Hite is truly a book unto himself. But in brief, he was one of the most famous, or infamous, miners of his day in the Canyonlands region. Like Loper, he came from the Midwest and prospected around Colorado and adjoining areas before coming to the San Juan in 1881. He took up

Cass Hite

The *Hoskaninni*

the search for the fabled Pish-La-Kai mine south of the river, alleged to be the source of silver from which the Navajos made their jewelry. Two miners, Mitchell and Merritt, had been slain in Monument Valley for a similar quest. But Hite was somehow able to win the friendship of the Navajo headman Hoskaninni. Hoskaninni allowed Hite to prospect the Navajo territory for two years before the rest of the tribe grew restive and pressured Hoskaninni. The chief then escorted Hite out of Navajo land to the Colorado River, telling him he would find his riches there. He did. Hoskaninni and Hite remained lifelong friends. Because of Hite's infatuation with the silver mine, they named him Hosteen Pish-La-Kai—the Esteemed Mr. Silver Peso.

Cass Hite placer mined extensively from Dandy Crossing down into Glen Canyon. As the settlement grew to over one hundred people by the turn of the century, Cass Hite migrated downriver to the mouth of Tickaboo Creek, where he staked a lucrative claim. He called it the Bank of Tickaboo, always joking that he had plenty of gold on deposit there. He did well enough to import heavy machinery to work both Tickaboo and Good Hope Bars. Some say Hite may actually have made a fair portion of his money, however, from mining the pockets of investors.

Hite was a tall, good-looking man, popular with the ladies, a good fiddle player, and a crack shot. Things went awry when another miner across the river, Adolph F. Kohler, began competing with Hite for investors. Kohler tried to run Hite off, threatening to kill him. When the two met in Green River in 1891, the argument turned to gunfire and Kohler lay dead. Although Hite claimed self-defense, witnesses' accounts varied. Hite was convicted of second degree murder and sentenced to twelve years. After a year he was pardoned. He was ill with tuberculosis when released, and went from that to alcoholism. By the turn of the century, however, he had quit the bottle and returned to Tickaboo. A set of handwritten notes in Pearl Baker's Loper file describes Hite, possibly in Loper's words: "Tall—wore goatee—clean shaved—very immaculate. Hands long. Hair medium. Rider instead of walking."

When Loper's group encountered him, Cass Hite was on his way to check his mail, but insisted that the three men stop at his home at Tickaboo for the night.

> We stopped at Mr. Adams little ranch which he has fixed up in a very nice shape then we ran on down untill we came to Mr. Hites place and proceeded to get supper Mr. Hite not having returned from the Post Office Just as we were over with supper he came along and had us to come up to his little ranch where we spent a most delightful evening talking of frontier days he having known lots of people that I knew in Colorado 22 years ago. In the course of the evening I made an examination of my camera and found, to my dismay, that the shutter was rusted so it would not work and I will have to send it to the factory to have it repaired—We are intending to stop at least one month before take our final plunge in the Grand Canyon—11-30 and to bed.

The men ended up spending two nights with Hite, listening to stories and reading from Hite's collection of books, magazines, and scrapbook. Loper went so far as to copy down an epic poem that railroad poet Cy Warman had written about Hosteen Pish-La-Kai. They packaged Loper's camera lens and shutter and sent them in for repairs before departing the following day.

> Oct.-11. 1907.
>
> Ate breakfast with Mr. Hite and then loaded our boats and drifted down to the bar where Mr. Hite is working and watched him work his sluice for awhile and then bade him farewell and entered our boats and pushed into the stream and at 4-P.M. we arrived at what is known as the Dredge which was erected by Robert Brewster Stanton about 7 years ago

and which has proven a failure—It is now owned by Mr. John Newby—here we camped.

The Dredge. The largest relic of mining in Glen Canyon was—by far—the *Hoskaninni*, a gigantic 115' floating Bucyrus dredge conceived and built by riverman Robert Brewster Stanton. When Stanton passed through Glen Canyon in 1889, he had seen Cass Hite and others placering on the bars. The thought struck him that there might be a way to mine the gold of Glen Canyon on a grand scale. Before finishing his railroad survey of the Colorado in 1890 he had already begun staking claims in Glen Canyon. For several years his mining ideas languished while he pushed, unsuccessfully, to finance the trans-canyon railroad. When that idea died, he turned back to Glen Canyon. He envisioned a series of gigantic dredges churning up the sediments of the Colorado and running them through an on-board series of sluices. Like Loper, he saw the river as nature's own sluice-box and envisioned tremendous wealth along the river bottom. In 1897 he began raising funds and formed the Hoskaninni Mining Company, primarily with moneys from Eastern investors. Meanwhile he staked or bought out contiguous mining claims the entire length of Glen Canyon, from Hite to Lee's Ferry. Once he had sufficient capital he brought in lumber and heavy machinery via overland roads blasted into bedrock, and floated them to a central spot to build his pilot dredge.

The great dredge was completed in 1901 and began operations. Within weeks it became apparent that Stanton was receiving the second great blow of his river career. His great dream of a railroad had died on the drawing board. Now his dredge was producing little but smoke, noise, and mud. By the end of 1901 the operation was not making enough to pay its own expenses. The gold was there, and is still there today, but was and is far too fine to be collected by the technology Stanton had. The company fell into receivership and Stanton sold the remaining equipment for two hundred dollars. When Loper, Russell, and Monett arrived, the dredge was in ruins.

Oct. 13-14-15-16

Moved down the river to Mr. Newby's camp and are here located intending to do some placer mining for our funds are very low We over-

> hauled the enjine—fixed a new battery. Prospected the ground and are now ready to begin sluicing.
>
> Oct. 21 to 29. 1907.
>
> For the last 9 days we have been placer mining and have made three clean ups and have not done very much good and have come to the conclusion that we had better quit.

The three miners returned to New Year Bar, adjacent to the old Stanton Dredge and made preparations to continue their voyage. Their plan was for Loper to return to Hite for the repaired camera, then to head downstream to Lee's Ferry and rendezvous with Russell and Monett, thence to begin the final push through Grand Canyon.

Historical accounts of all three men seem to agree up to this moment of their lives. But from that final evening on New Year Bar, accounts, impressions, and memories diverge radically.

At the time, the men recorded nothing out of the ordinary. In describing the events for the *Salt Lake Tribune* three weeks later, Russell wrote:

> About November 1 we returned to the dredge and proceeded to make some needed repairs on our boats, while Mr. Loper returned to Hite to get the camera lens and shutter which we had sent away to be put in working order once more.
>
> After completing our repairs, Monett and I once more headed downstream.

Loper's journal adds details without shedding any light on the dynamics of the trio:

> Nov. 1-1907.
>
> After breakfast this morning I loaded my outfit in the *Arizona* for my trip up the river to Hite 45 miles away got started at 9-30 and had some very hard work working against the current and wind—I have a sail on my boat but the wind blows the wrong way and I am not sailor enough to go against the wind—I continued on untill dark and had a very poor place to camp and worse wood—very miserable night. #

23 Parting shots

CHARLES RUSSELL and Bert Loper's friendship ended badly. The indefatigable Dock Marston, of course, wanted to know just how and when the relationship began to sour. Even before Loper's death he had written Loper to ask about his 1907 parting with Russell. On September 16, 1948, Loper had written Marston:

> You know that the number of three is called a devils bunch and one night after I had gone to bed Russell and Monett were both still up and thinking I was asleep Russell did lots of talking and the long and short of it was that Russell was trying to wean Monett over to his side—On our trip through the Cataract I took all 3 boats through and when we got to Dark canyon Russell wanted me to do the same but in the mean time he was getting to the point that he wanted to be the leader so when I refused the Dark canyon and he ran it he was a different companion so the talk that he made to Monett after I had gone to bed....
>
> Russell told me that I was over sensative—perhaps I am but the morning he told me that was when we had it out over his talk with Monett while I was asleep.

Loper's reasoning: When Loper refused to take Russell's boat through Dark Canyon Rapid, Russell found he was capable of running it himself—and quickly grew cocky. Cocky enough to want to lead the trip. But to do that he needed Monett's vote. Just how much air was cleared the following morning—or how much things began to fester—is unsaid.

Monett, however, remembered a *different* argument. During a November 1948 interview with him, Marston scribbled the following notes:

> Was argument at placer bar over amount Bert had put up.
>
> Russell and Bert never had any words until night when Bert was

going back to Hite.

Loper was fellow most anyone would like—do not remember him as being quick tempered—some coolness that night.

On December 20, 1949, Marston sent Monett a long series of statements to respond to. They seemed to be a combination of what Marston had gathered along with a healthy helping of conjecture. Most questions were about Russell and Monett's Grand Canyon adventure. But two were about Loper. Unfortunately, they are not really questions, but rather suppositions put forward for Monett's comments. In a court of law, this is called leading the witness:

Marston:

The argument he had with Russell at the placer bar was the key to all this funny business. The argument was over the matter of the money that Loper had put into the deal. It seems Russell had saved his money from working and had to put up all the money. Loper blew his money and had none to finance the trip....

Monett:

Russell and myself compared notes and found we had financed the trip.

Marston:

Careful study of the record indicates to me that Loper thought you fellows could not go on without him. He was sore over the argument he had with Russell when you quit the placer work at New Year Bar and moved over to the dredge the next day. Loper was also sold on Cass Hite and thought he would like to settle in that section. He took a lot of extra time loafing around thinking he would teach Russell and you a lesson. He thought he would come drifting in to Lee's Ferry and find you waiting there for him. He didn't think you would dare the rapids without his superior skill and experience.

Monett:

I think that is the reason nothing else.

On the edge of the questionnaire, Monett scribbled:

> I had put up 1/3 at least had turned it over to Loper, I think 150 or $175. the boats cost $100 F.O.B. Green River (I think) Russell wanted Loper to agree to a less than a 1/3 of anything we found after leaving the Dredge
>
> But Loper refused so the Parting was not a very warm affair.

On January 6, 1950, Marston interviewed Monett. His notes give some clue as to Monett's response:

> At the camp at New Year Bar Russell told Monett about Loper's plan to finance with high-grade....
>
> Russell put trip together.
>
> Loper could not be trusted....
>
> Russell wanted him to give up share of discoveries until the two had been repaid. Loper thought that was unfair. He had taken too many chances—he had too much at stake. It was pinching pennies that we didn't have. If we had found anything we would not have cared. It was an expression of the irritations of the trip.

Loper remembers having it out with Russell about the leadership of the trip. Monett remembered a disagreement about Loper's share (or lack thereof) of the trip grubstake, and its relationship to Loper's share of the earnings—but wrote it off as "an expression of the irritations of the trip." Was this the same argument, remembered differently? Or did both arguments happen? Did either?

Marston did not get a chance to check with Loper about the monetary argument before Loper died. But Marston *could* have checked with Monett to see if he recalled the late-night gossiping with Russell, or Loper and Russell's subsequent argument about trip leadership. But for some reason, Marston never mentioned it in the following two decades of correspondence with Monett. And so we are left to wonder.

The more Marston cross-examined Monett, the less flattering his comments about Loper became. But as early as December 4, 1949 Ed Monett admitted, "The more I try to give you a little light on the Subject, the Darker it gets and the more confused I am." #

24 Catching up

Nov-2-1907.

The same old thing as yesterday only a worse place to camp it being on the sloping side of a rock but better wood—had a couple bad rapids to pull the boat over camped at dark.

Nov. 3-1907.

Another hard days rowing and my hands are very sore and it is weary work—Arrived at the Bank of Tickaboo and spent the night with the Hosten Pes-La-Ki.

Loper had learned the dreary art of rowing, poling, dragging, and rowing up a rapid river on the San Juan in the 1890s. It was not out of desire but necessity—there was no overland transport to haul boats back upriver, few trails to trudge back on foot, and the value and carrying capacity of the craft demanded that the boat be kept and used. It took Loper three days to make the twenty-seven miles from the dredge back upstream to Cass Hite's, and another day to make it above Tickaboo Rapid to A.P. Adams's cabin at Red Canyon. After two nights with Adams, Loper continued to Hite.

The lens was not back yet, and Loper eased into the rhythm of upper Glen Canyon, a society of lone men working their claims, visiting, farming, checking their mail, caring for livestock, boating, and when four or more men congregated, playing solo—a complex German card game with bidding, trump suits, tricks, and often played for small amounts of money. Loper fit right in. While he waited for the lens he helped where he could and took odd jobs. He had a decent boat so ferried gear for miners and freighted items up and down river. On November 20 Loper sent $10 to Cap Yokey, a steamboat captain in Green River, for whiskey. (That's a lot of whiskey: Hayner, the most popular whiskey of the day, was sold mail-order, four quarts for $3.20 postpaid.)

Nov. 27-1907.

Started out this morning by loading my boat and started down the river and as I started into Trachyte rapid I broke an oarlock and drifted on a rock and punctured my boat and lost my mess box and a sack of flour and a sack of sugar—walked back up to Hite.

Loper later elaborated: "On going into Trachyte Rapid at that time I was loaded very heavy—within 3 inches of the water so it can be seen that I was rather handicapped going into rough water with an overloaded boat with only one oar."

Thursday-Nov 28-1907.

Thanksgiving; went down the river and loaded some of the wreck and started down river with Bill Pohlman and he took boat and went on down to Mr. Adams place and I returned to my submerged boat and raised it and pulled it up to Dandy Crossing.

On November 30 Loper's lens and shutter arrived in the mail. It was time to hoof it down to Lee's Ferry and rendezvous with Russell and Monett. He was already nine days late for their agreed meeting. But first he had to fix the boat. For three days he finished his work with Bill Pohlman and hauled freight for Adams. Then he sought repair materials.

Dec 4-1907.

Took Mr. Adams horse and went down to Goodhope after some soldering fluid but could not find any but some nitric acid so I got some of that. Got to Mr. Adams place about 11-30 and stayed to dinner left at 2-30 and got to Hite by 4-30 found two packages for me one a package of gloves and another a package of hypo both from H.T. Yokey. Wrote three letters one to J.E. Russell and one to H.T. Yokey and one to L.S.

Dec-5-1907.

Helped Cass Hite pack up started to fix my boat but it being in a worse fix than I thought it will require some material which I hope to get down the river.

Loper made another trip downriver thirty miles to Smith Fork to retrieve a stove for Adams, arriving back in Hite on December 12. On the 14th and 15th he worked on his boat. The fine fall weather was drawing to a close as the thermometer dipped to 23 degrees. On the 17th he received a letter from John Russell, Charlie's brother, stating the men were at Lee's Ferry. The whiskey arrived. But still his boat was not satisfactorily repaired.

For the next week he waited for more gear to come in by mail and worked cutting willows for Fred Gibbons's irrigation dam at Trachyte Creek. On the 23rd, Loper got up at 3:30, walked twelve miles downriver to Adams's cabin looking for some acid for soldering. Adams had none. He walked back up past Hite another four miles to Schock's cabin. Two prospectors there gave him some that Frank Bennett had sent in from Hanksville.

> Wednesday, Christmas Day, Dec.25-1907.
>
> Christmas did nothing to-day but solder my boat had a nice chicken dinner.

Loper spent five more days cutting willows. The mail on the 28th contained a final parcel from Sears Roebuck.

> Dec 31-1907.
>
> Cut willows in forenoon and got ready to go on my trip long deferred to Lee's Ferry which I should have made at least 5 weeks before, but circumstances have been such that it has been impossible to have gone sooner. I spent afternoon getting some grub together which it has been impossible to get sooner and in the collecting of my belongings.

To say Loper was late is certainly an understatement. To say things came up that delayed him is certainly true. His December 31 entry—which may have been edited later—seems defensive, twice stating it would have been "impossible" to leave sooner. Could he have headed downriver earlier? Probably. The lens arrived November 30, three days after Loper had gashed the steel hull of his boat. He does not elaborate on just how hard he searched for the needed repair materials during the next three weeks, but it was not until the 23rd that he had the acid and solder. He then spent a week finishing the willow-cutting job before departing.

✣ ✣ ✣

Wednesday-Jan.-1-1908.

New Year. It is just two months since I left my companions and although I have written to them at Lee's Ferry I have never heard a word and if they have not received my letters I am afraid that they will be gone for they will think I am not coming for I was due there Nov-21 but circumstances have arisen which has made it impossible for me to leave a day sooner and if they are gone it will mean an up hill pull for me back to Hite a distance of 135 miles [actually 162]. At 10-30 A.M. I finished loading and started down the river arriving at Cass Hites 3-P.M. camping with him for the night I stopped at Mr. Adams and got my bed and some other things I had left there.

Loper made good progress. Twenty-seven miles to the Dredge on January 2nd. He rowed another forty-three miles to the San Juan River by the morning of the sixth, the water so low and icy he occasionally had to get out and drag the boat through shallows.

Jan-8-1908.

Got started at 10 A.M. and after nothing but hard rowing I arrived at Lee's Ferry at 3 P.M. Went up to Mr. Emmetts and found that my two companions had been gone two weeks so I will have to turn around and drag my boat up the river for 135 [162] miles and will have to be in the river every day and it is icey cold too but such is fate. I expect to complete the trip next fall. I received a letter from Charles Russell which he left here for me and he is going on down to Bright Angle and there sto[w] untill next fall—I spent evening writing letters—six in all.

As Loper feared, Russell and Monett had moved on. Russell's letter explained:

Lee's Ferry Dec 13 '07

Dear Friend Bert,

Monett and I have been here since Nov 21 and we have heard nothing from you. We have watched the weather turn from reasonably pleasant to unpleasantly cold till nearly ½ inch of ice is found in our water buckets of a morning and the water in the river has become so cold it almost takes the skin off to wash in it. It has completely taken the heart out of us. We have concluded something serious must have happened to you, and we think that it would be far better to complete the trip next fall, say Sept, Oct, Nov, than to continue on at present. We seriously debated storing our boats here and going out, but finally concluded to go on to Bright Angel.

Now if you should leave your boat here 2 of us could come here next Sept bringing only enough supplies to carry us to Bright Angel, take pictures along the way, and we ought to go from here to Bright Angel in warm weather in 15 days.

These people here are not very friendly to prospectors, that is one reason we decided to try to reach Bright Angel, that would be a better place to outfit from next year.

From all the information we can get, the rapids to the Little Colorado are not very bad, and we will take it slow from there, prospecting & building fires at the bottom of each rapid.

I am sorry conditions have caused the trip to turn out as it has so far, but we are still as strong as ever in our determination to finish the trip if it does take another year.

As ever your friend
Chas Russell #

Lees Ferry. Dec 13.07

Dear Friend Bert Monett and I have
been here since Nov 21. and we have heard
nothing from you. We have watched the
weather turn from reasonably pleasant to
unpleasantly cold till nearly ½ inch of ice
is found in our water buckets of a morning
and the water in the river has become so
cold it almost takes off the skin to wash
in it. It has completely taken the heart
out of us. We have concluded something ser
must ha

25 Why the delay?

I AM AFRAID some of the study was disturbing to Bert since he had a few skeletons in his memory closet which were more formidable than most.

I gained much River lore from Bert but his frustrations thru his early experience with Russell and Monett aroused some violent feelings.

MARSTON to SARAH FRASER ROBBINS, May 15, 1953

For the last two years of Bert Loper's life, Marston had riddled him with questions. He borrowed Loper's journals and letters to examine and copy. He cross-examined Loper, digging for facts, questioning motives. Among the topics that Marston probed Loper about was the precise cause of his delay in getting to Lee's Ferry in 1907. He pored through Loper's diaries and began firing questions. On January 3, 1949, he wrote:

> The damage to the boat occurred in Trachyte Rapid the 27th of November but obviously the repairs would not have consumed the time until the 1st of January. Therefore it was not the boat damage that was responsible for the delay.

Loper responded immediately:

> You will note that on Dec. 25th I was still working on boat but I was under the impression that I had recorded the arrival of a freight team between the 25 and 30th of Dec which was why. I had to have food before starting on my trip—you spoke of it being obvious that it would not take that long to fix the boat there are things that have to be taken into consideration and that is a walk from Hite to Good-Hope and return would call for a 36 mile walk and on another occasion I walked to red canyon and back and after noon walked 8 miles more and another time

> went down the river for more than 30 miles and another thing was that we had mail twice a week and if on sending out and something on the other end it would cause another week delay and about the time that I made the trip up from the dredge all the money that I had was in a check and during the 1907 depression all payments were stopped so I had to send the check out and in the course of time Yokey got the money so I could send for the camera so you can see that being 150 miles from the R.R. and mail twice a week and on top of that it was horse and wagon days so things did move but rather slow.

Marston was unconvinced. On January 12 he wrote again:

> It does not seem to me the check clearance trouble accounts for the delay. The camera was received Nov. 30th and used for taking a picture of Cass Hite on Dec. 3rd. It would appear to me that the damage to the boat must have been quite serious to require all that repair....
>
> You mention the freight team which arrived between the 25th and 30th of December. There are mentioned in your notes the arrival of several teams. Why was the supply problem delayed so long that it was the team of the 25-30 of December which took care of the grub problem?

Loper, exasperated, wrote back:

> Now I will try to enlighten you about the conditions that you do not understand—in the first place we will have to disassociate our minds from an Automobile and truck down to a 4 horse freight team.... I am telling you all this to show you just how fast we did move in those days more than 40 years ago and I believe if you will read my diary of Dec-31 and ponder a little you will know that there was a cause for my long delay and the boat that I was plowing up and down the river was by no means one that I would care to start in the Grand with.... now about the repairs on that boat they were never as good as they were before the accident but the boat was the best I had and another thing was that the willows I cut went to pay for the food I got on the last days of Dec, and as my record for the 31st of Dec says it was the best I could do—Now if we were to-gether with the diary we could talk with more enlightenment but I will say that it was the easiest thing to do was to spoil a day

> and if there was something to take a day and we had two hours to put in before we started it would spoil the day that is if we had to make a trip to Red Canyon and back so I am telling you all this to impress on your mind that we moved fast awful slow.

Loper could also have pointed out the shortness of days surrounding winter solstice, and the difficulty of climbing from a bedroll on those bitter cold mornings—but it would not likely have swayed Marston.

"It does not seem to me that there was sufficient justification for Loper's long delay at Hite," Marston wrote to Ed Monett on February 25. "I do not understand just what happened."

Did the alleged argument at New Year Bar have anything to do with it? Probably not. Monett never attributed the argument to Loper's failure to make haste to Lee's Ferry. About the delay, only a couple lines from the interviews even refer to it: "I don't think Loper was scared," he said in 1948. (Russell's brother John concurred: "Charles never indicated any belief that Loper was scared. What little [I know] about Loper, nothing would scare him.") But in 1950 Monett cryptically added, "We were not surprised when Loper did not show."

By 1950 Marston retained little respect for Loper. To Dave Rust he wrote, "It is logical to doubt this information as I have found that Bert liked to pose as an authority on the river with nothing that he did not know. I have found that he freely expressed opinions which were not backed by anything more than hearsay."

Unwilling to swallow Loper's explanations of one delay leading to the next in a remote setting, Marston began rooting for ulterior motives. And like a dog in search of a buried bone, he would not be deterred. #

26 Meanwhile...

On Friday, the 13th of December, while the entire population of Lee's Ferry watched our fortunes, Monett and I started out running through the two small rapids at the mouth of the Paria and heading down into the Grand Canyon of the Colorado, or rather Marble Canyon, as the first sixty-six miles is called.

Right off the bat Russell and Monett came to rapids larger than they chose to run, and began portaging. Somewhere in the stretch of rapids called the "Roaring Twenties," from twenty to thirty miles downriver from Lee's Ferry, Monett ran afoul of a boulder:

> Considerable water was pouring over the rock, forming a very vertical fall of five or six feet below it. As the boat struck the rock she turned sideways and the water piled against her until she was pushed over the rock, to drop down over the fall, where the pent-up waters struck the up-stream gunwale, capsizing her upstream and throwing Monett back under the very fall itself, where he was washed under, and when he reached the surface, after clawing water for what seemed to him like fifteen minutes, he had been carried away below the boat.

Russell was able to snag the boat before the next rapid and the men continued on. Fifty miles later, Monett ran into worse trouble, possibly in the foot of Hance Rapid:

> In trying to run the next rapid Monett struck a rock near the shore in such a manner that though the water poured over her, she stuck fast, the whole side almost being torn out. Having gotten through safely I was able to return along the shore and by throwing a rope to Monett we were able to pull ashore most of the cargo, but darkness found us unable to budge the boat, and we were compelled to give her up. During the night

> the river raised nearly a foot, and in the morning the boat was gone.

They continued on, Monett clinging to Russell's boat, and arrived at the foot of the Bright Angel Trail. There they climbed to the South Rim of Grand Canyon and met with the press. One man in particular was credited with much of the coverage of Russell and Monett's trip—a reporter named Hayden Talbot, whose accuracy often took a back seat to sensationalism. Much of Talbot's breathless retelling of the excitement of the trip Monett later described as "fertilizer." But that is what was printed, and that is how the story was told and retold for years. Russell and Monett returned to the river, determined to make it through in their remaining boat. Talbot wrote of their departure and had this to say of Loper's absence:

> BRIGHT ANGEL, GRAND CANYON, ARIZ. JAN 18
>
> ... Up to the time they left here no word had come from their former comrade, and whether he lost his life in attempting to catch up with them, or whether he concluded at the last moment that the trip held too many dangers in store, and deserted, they have no means of knowing....
>
> In describing this stage of the journey, Russell did not mention the remarkable nerve both men showed in starting down through what is admittedly the wildest part of the river without the third companion, who at the outset had seemed absolutely indispensable. Instead, he expressed the belief that Loper had chosen not to face the greater danger and had voluntarily stayed behind at Hite—and that therefore he and his companion were not quietly deserting a comrade. That they might be held so accountable seemed to concern him much more than that their daring might be commended.

In short, Talbot asserted that rather than be thought of as having deserted a friend, Russell felt it important for the world to know that the friend had deserted him. Did Russell really feel that way? Or was this more fertilizer? We will never know for sure. We do know, however, that Russell and Monett were lucky to make it much farther. Just six miles below the Bright Angel Trail the men came to Hermit Rapid. Leaving their gear piled on the left shore, they rowed to the opposite side of the river where it looked easier to line the boat past the drop at the head of the rapid. Midway through the slippery, awkward operation, the boat tore away from them, running the rapid empty and quickly drifting out of sight down the sheer-walled gorge. Russell and Monett had to hike upstream far enough to swim across the river in order to get to their gear. From there they had two choices: give up and hike out the Hermit Trail, or try to find their boat in the most inaccessible fast-water stretch of the entire Grand Canyon. They chose the latter.

To Russell's credit, he had done his homework while on the Rim. He knew that he was indeed at Hermit Rapid, that there was a trail out, and furthermore, that he could climb up above the inner gorge and traverse downriver on the Boucher Trail. This they did. They then had the good fortune to meet trailbuilder Louis Boucher himself, who suggested that the boat might be found at the foot of Boucher Canyon where, he claimed, the only eddy for miles collected a fair amount of driftwood. By the most astonishing good luck, Boucher was right. They found the boat, damaged but repairable. Boucher loaned them a canvas canoe, which they used to work their way upriver to their pile of gear at Hermit Rapid and retrieve it. Four days later they continued on, running some rapids, portaging or lining others. Monett often hiked around the worst rapids carrying their photographic gear while Russell braved the whitewater. They arrived at Needles on February 8.

NAU.PH.568.3466

Kolb Brothers

Monett and Russell at foot of Bright Angel Trail

Apparently Hayden Talbot was there to meet them, fabricating a crowd of hundreds to welcome the brave explorers. Again, according to Monett, this was manure. Russell, in his *Salt Lake Tribune* article quoted above, added his own fertilizer:

> It has been suggested that we continue our trip later, on down the river to the gulf of California, thence down the Mexican coast to the Isthmus, across and up the Gulf of Mexico coast to the Mississippi river, up that to the Illinois, thence to Chicago, over the great lakes and St. Lawrence to the coast, then down the Atlantic coast to New York, after equipping our boat with motor, of course. This is at present under consideration.

Monett and Russell instead took their boat by rail back to the South Rim of Grand Canyon and put it on display. Monett then vanished for more than four decades. Russell returned to Prescott, where he quickly changed occupations, appearing on February 22 as the editor and manager of the *Arizona Mining Review*. On page one of that issue he featured a five-paragraph story on the expedition, written in third person—perhaps the entire story is Talbot's. The first two paragraphs reiterated Talbot's tales of five hundred people welcoming them to Needles. The rest was devoted to Loper:

Russell and Monett at trip's end

> In the bunch of mail awaiting the men was a letter from Albert T. Loper who remained behind at Hite, Utah, 120 miles from the starting place, and who had been left behind as a deserter by Russell and Monett. Loper declares in the letter that the financial panic existing throughout the country was responsible for his failure to continue down the river to Lee's Ferry, where his companions waited on him for forty-three days. He wrote that he had no idea of deserting, but was unable to buy provisions because of the financial depression. As the boat which he had at Hite contained a full quota of provisions for the three months' trip the excuse seems hardly plausible to Russell and Monett.
>
> A letter written by John Hite, the postmaster at Hite, states that Loper finally started after his companions on January 1st, two months after they had gone on before him. He struck a rock before he had left Hite behind a half mile, in Trachyte rapids, a stretch of water described by Russell as a riffle. After securing help from Hite and repairing his boat Loper continued on to Lee's Ferry. He wrote Russell that he could not go further than this point if his two companions had left there, as his provisions were insufficient. No word of his arrival at Lee's Ferry has been received. Probably he arrived there on January 6th, the day which Russell and Monett were starting away from Bright Angel, 100 miles farther on.
>
> "I am sure Loper did not attempt to continue on from Lee's Ferry," said Russell today, "besides his letter I know that no man alone in his right senses would ever try to tackle the rapids through Marble Canyon. It is tough for two men. I suppose Loper is still at Lee's Ferry. How he could have expected us to wait for him more than two months, when our agreement was that he should rejoin us within three weeks at the very outside, is beyond me. If we had waited that long for him our grub would never have lasted through the trip."

Oddly, no part of the article told of the voyage itself. Clearly Russell felt it of utmost import to defend his own honor regarding his separation from Loper. Regarding his river adventures, Russell urged readers to subscribe to the *Arizona Mining Review* by March in order not to miss a single chapter of the serialized story he planned to publish. Unfortunately, by April Russell was no longer with the *Review*, and his full story, other than the *Salt Lake Tribune* version, was never told. #

27 Betrayal

WHEN [BERT] PULLED IN at Lee's Ferry, there were no boats tied up at the ferry and he was sure he had missed them somewhere. He was puzzled, annoyed, and viewed returning up the river to locate them with some irritation. Walking up the road to the house where the Emmett family lived, he reviewed in his mind what he would say to Charley for not meeting him as planned.

The Emmetts were surprised to see him but hospitable as was the custom. They showed him newspapers that passing travelers had left, and he learned why Charley and Ed were not at the ferry. Charley had let no moss grow on his oars at Lee's Ferry while he waited for Bert. He saw his chance to pay off his imagined grudge and made the most of it by declaring that Bert was afraid of the river and would never follow them to Lee's Ferry. He hadn't waited a day there but had overruled the protesting Ed and, taking all the ropes and other equipment, had gone on down the Grand. They had made it through, and Charley let the world know that it was due to the fact that they were not hampered by Bert's overly cautious methods.

Bert was angry—betrayed—sick at heart....

PEARL BAKER, *TRAIL ON THE WATER*, chapter "Charley Betrays Bert"

✣ ✣ ✣

The history of navigating the Colorado River is short but has its share of controversies. James White's raft journey of 1867 remains contentious: did he or did he not float through Grand Canyon in 1867? The departure of three of Major Powell's men two years later forms the basis of another riverine quandary: did they desert Powell in his time of need? Or did Powell, the martinet, drive them from the trip to their untimely deaths? And what became of Glen and Bessie Hyde in 1928? Did they drown? Starve? Or was it murder?

Bert Loper's late arrival at Lee's Ferry—as insignificant as it may seem—is the basis of another such debate. Loper maintained until he died that he had made all possible haste to Lee's Ferry. The popular press chose to brand Loper as a coward, the insinuation leaving a lasting sting on Loper's hide. Pearl Baker rewrote history to make Russell the culprit. Marston insisted Loper was trying to teach Russell a lesson—in later years he maintained that Baker's chapter should have been titled, "Bert Betrays Charley." Opinions cover the entire gamut of possibility. And then some:

> *Emery County Progress*
> January 18, 1908
> The three men Chas S. Russell of Prescott Ariz, E R Monett of Goldfield Nev, and Elbert Roper who left Green River three months ago to explore the Colorado river have been heard from at Bright Angel Ariz. The two first named are now making their way through the Grand canyon in a 16 foot row boat, Lopez having disappeared.

✣ ✣ ✣

The record is clear on a few points.

Russell and Monett did wait twenty-two days for Loper before moving on. Russell's letter clearly expressed his exasperation at Loper's unexplained delay, his distress in leaving Loper behind, and an intent to reconcile the situation. It is hard to find a villain here.

Loper clearly did not have the camera parts until the 30th of November, at which point he still had to repair his boat, which he had wrecked and sunk three days prior. Had all the necessary repair materials been at hand, he probably could have fixed it in less than a week, departed, and made haste to Lee's Ferry prior to Russell's launch on the 13th. The materials weren't there, however, and with even modest delays, Loper would not have been able to catch Russell. The fact Loper missed them by twenty-six days instead of just a few quickly becomes irrelevant. It seems events conspired to make Loper miss the trip. It is hard to find ill intent here either.

What remains unclear is how much either of the alleged arguments between Russell and Loper—the one Loper recalled about leadership, or the one Monett remembered about money—may have affected Russell's departure or Loper's delay. Conjecture is rife, but poorly substantiated.

Loper inscription across river from Hite

Russell's farewell letter shows no malice, and Loper's hunch—as written in his journal—that he might be too late, and his lack of surprise or anger at finding that to be so, bear no signs of grudge.

With all facts weighed, no one seems to be at fault. It appears to be a simple case of things simply happening. The men did what they had to do: Russell and Monett finally continued on and achieved brief fame for their descent of the Colorado; Loper turned back and began what he would always remember as the most miserable winter of his life. #

28 Up the creek

THE DAY AFTER Loper arrived at Lee's Ferry, he accepted an invitation to travel to Kanab with Bill Emmett, the ferryman's son. The eighty-five mile trip, that today takes an hour and a half, took them four days by horse and wagon. The following day they rode seven miles south to Fredonia, just across the Arizona border, for much the same reasons wayward Kanabites do today:

> Jan. 13-1908.
>
> Loaded our wagons to-day-Then in company with a Mr. Johnson, a cousin of Bill Emmetts, we drove to Fredonia—I came back the worse for the trip—Bill too.
>
> Jan-15-1908.
>
> More storm to-day
>
> Bill and his cousin put in the past two days finishing what we started at Fredonia but the once was enough for me so I stayed away from them and let them finish what we got in the shoe box at Fredonia.

They arrived back at Lee's Ferry on the 19th and Loper spent the next ten days puttering, doing laundry, fixing gear, having lunch with the Emmetts, helping them with ferry work, taking pictures, socializing, singing, and dreading his return trip to Hite.

With Russell and Monett gone, Loper faced a major decision: what now? Lee's Ferry did not tempt him, even though ferryman Emmett offered him a job digging ditch. He could hit out cross-country, abandoning or perhaps selling his boat, but to where? Back to the mines? Everything he owned was in that boat, and the boat was worth more than everything else put together. In the past two months he had lived out of the *Arizona*, making a few dollars here and there by hauling freight up and down the river. Although he had made no money to

E.C. La Rue NAU.PH.568-5204

Lee's Ferry

speak of on the San Juan, his time living along its shore, working with his boat, had intrigued him. Then at Hite he had fallen in with a loose-knit group of individualists and prospectors. The thought of joining their world sounded better than anything else. For years he had hoped to escape the wage-slave world of mining, and perhaps this was the way to do it. The problem was the vast length of river he would have to fight in the dead of winter. But his years on the San Juan and his time around Hite assured him that upriver travel, even if grueling, was entirely feasible. Too, at Hite he may have learned of others who had made the upstream haul—Galloway in the 1890s, Lon Turner in 1903. It was only a matter of persistence, and Loper had plenty of that. The choice was not difficult—he had made it even before leaving Hite. If his partners were not at Lee's Ferry, he would return.

> I took a look at the river to-day and it looks very swift and cold and to have to go up stream for one hundred and thirty five [162] miles but there is no other course for me to persue for my boat is the only home I have so must take it with me but I have enough grub to last me a month or six weeks which should be ample to last me through.

As disagreeable as the river appeared, it did not look any worse than the 1600 feet of ditch that Emmett wanted him do dig. He declined the job and at 10:00 on the morning on January 29 cast off:

> on my lonely journey and in all probility it will be three weeks before I see a soul. The river is in a miserable condition it is so low that it is

full of sand bars which are partly submerged and they cause me lots of trouble and hard work but I expect better conditions after I pass the San Juan and Escalanta rivers.

Four miserable days of rain, wind, headache, toothache, and wet feet got Loper to Wright Bar, where he laid over three nights in a cave out of the weather—a cave that, until it was submerged by Lake Powell in the 1960s, was thenceforth called Loper's Cave.

Feb-7-1908.

Had a very hard days work to-day the river being so full of sand and the channel crossing from side to side—The current is so swift that I cannot row so therefore I have to tow my boat by the roap and have to be in the water most of the time and my boots leak and that means I am wet the entire day.

Feb. 8.1908.

Got in camp to-night good and wet both boots being full of water—Have a pot of beans on cooking.

Feb. 9-1908.

Sunday and the most miserable one of them all …

Much of the work was not overly difficult. In eddies and calm current he could row. In straight current with passable shorelines, he could rig a kite-like bridle on the boat and it would hold itself offshore as Loper walked the gravel. The trouble came with shoals, which were aplenty. Here the water was shallow and swift far into the river. Loper had to wade to a depth where the boat would float, struggling against strong current. If he lost the boat here, or the rope failed, he would quickly be boatless and cliff-bound on a freezing river.

Monday-Feb-10-1908.

Cold—stormy and disagreeable but I did very well—After I had gone about 1 mile a stiff wind sprang up from the south and I stopped and prepared to hoist my sail but just as I had every thing ready the wind stopped blowing but I have my mast up so if it does start to blow I can soon put the sail on—It snowed very hard for a little while but I think the storm is over for to-night any way. Have a fine camp fire to-night.

Feb-13-1908.

It seems as though each day was trying to be more disagreeable than the last. The weather was very nice to-day but water was the coldest it has been yet. I had no feeling in my limbs from my knees down and it seemed as though my feet would freeze. I had to stop two or three times and build a fire and warm. I reached the San Juan about 4-P.M.

Saturday-Feb-15-1908.

When I awakened this morning I was filled with dismay for the river was full of mush ice and I knew it would be very hard work pulling against it but after I had pulled out I found out that the ice was coming from the Escalanta River. I got a fairly early start and had the best day I have had yet—nice still water and I must have made 15 miles any way and I stopped early to cook some more beans.

If my calculations prove true I should be at my journeys end by a week from next Tuesday making 10 days more and if I do not meet any one on the road before I get there I will be out of grub for I am runing very low at present.

Monday Feb-17-1908.

Had a very hard day of it to-day. The worst of the bad water was passed over to-day. Was wet to the waist all day—The first thing after starting out was to plunge into the icy cold water to my waist and there remain untill noon.

Tuesday-Feb-18-1908.

Got along fine to-day had some bad water but more good—I arrived at the dredge before sundown and found a party working the same plant that Russell, Monett and I worked....

With his arrival at the dredge and the group of men working there, the worst of the journey was over. Loper had been upriver from here to Hite before, and the men at the dredge supplemented his food. Many years later Loper tried to explain why the trip had been particularly tough:

It is rather hard to try to explain the condition I was in when I reached this place. In the first place my grub was runing very low and the strenuousness of the trip was such that I was under a mentel strain but the fact of the whole thing was that I had developed an appetite that could not be satisfied—when a meal was called I would go with the rest and eat all I could as long as they ate and then still be ravenously hungry—it was to say the least very embarrassing. I mentioned the mental strain—The strain was that I had no idea of meeting any one for many miles and my provisions was runing very low and the uncertainty was the mental part of it and if I had not have met the party at the dredge I would have had to have left my outfit and walked on in but meeting those men made it so I could go on in.

Loper rested a day at the dredge, then continued upriver.

Saturday-Feb-22-1908.

Celebrated Washington's birthday by having the worst day of my trip. In roping over Tickaboo Rapid and in the worst place my foot slipped and the boat pulled me back over the rapid completely submerged and when I reached Mr. Adams place I was completely chilled. I saw Cass Hite and he gave me the news that my two companions had completed the trip through Grand Canyon—I expect to hear more when I reach Hite.

Feb-23-1908.

Left my boat at Mr. Adams and walked to Hite where I arrived by noon received five letters two from J.E. Russell one from Charles Russell and one from my little Sweetheart and one from L.S.

(Note) My little Sweetheart is a little girl about 6 years old and is the daughter of some people that I boarded with in Goldfield Nev.

I answered Chas. Russells letter—I am getting some severe roastings in the papers for not being with Russell and Monett but I am not to blame and I surely expect to show the world that I have the nerve to finish the trip. #

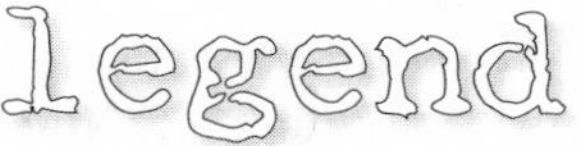

29 Monument

In December 1949 Moki Mac Ellingson headed a committee to honor Loper:

> A number of Bert's friends, including Veterans of the Spanish American War, Boy Scouts, members of the Masonic Fraternity, and just plain friends, have decided to erect a monument in Bert's memory. In addition to those mentioned above, the City of Green River, Bert's home town and also the starting point of many of his River Trips, has donated the ground and promised perpetual care of the site.

The Walker Monument Company of Salt Lake City crafted the five-foot granite slab, while Ellingson set about raising $750 to pay for it. They received just one letter of dissent:

> If Bert's spirit is with us today, and I choose to think it is, it will scorn a monument in a park. Bert had experiences in his life that made him wish for a better life but he ended up with a great happiness which came from doing things. It seems inappropriate to me that any memorial to him should not be something that does things. Bert sought education. Might it not be more suitable to put a good shelf of river history in the school at Green River and elsewhere with his name connected with it?
>
> Otis "Dock" Marston

Marston detested monuments to people and routinely campaigned against renaming rapids or other features in honor of fallen boatmen. Perhaps he was sincere in his feelings, but the story is often clouded, as those memorials he railed loudest against were to honor men Marston no longer cared for. In the end, his objections had little effect.

The monument was dedicated on Sunday, July 30, 1950, the day before Loper's eighty-first birthday. Tom Busenbark presided, Rachel unveiled the stone, Don Harris spoke, and members of the sponsoring organizations made presentations. "It was a beautiful service," Rachel wrote to Marston, "and there were over 600 people."

"Lost," reads the monument, "in the vastness of the Grand Canyon. The land of the blue horizons and the silent desert mesas that he loved so well. 'I belong to the wondrous west, and the west belongs to me.'"

The stone stands facing the main highway through town today, now flanked by tall shade trees and two rocket ships—one pointed up, one pointed down—monuments to Green River's later involvement in the White Sands missile testing program. #

Rachel Loper at Bert's new monument

30 Hermitage

LOPER RESTED one day at Hite before going back to cutting willows. For three weeks he did odd jobs for the local miners before getting a lease on the Olympia Bar from Frank Bennett, "to try to work an old dump over—it was about the only thing I had in sight at the time." By this Loper meant to rework an abandoned placer operation and run some of the remaining gravel through, in hopes of finding enough gold to make the shoveling worth his while. He got to Olympia Bar, about twenty-seven miles below Hite, on March 19, and began rebuilding the works. He ran his first gravel through the chute on April 14. For nearly four months he worked the bar, taking time out for occasional forays to Hite for mail and supplies. The rare encouraging days were inevitably followed by disappointment.

Friday-June-19-1908.

Made a run of one yard and did exceedingly well the wind was blowing too hard to do any shovelling—found a part of a sack of tobacco so I had a smoke—Things have been very discouraging but are looking better now and I believe I will make a go of it.

Saturday-June-20-1908.

Shovelled all day and it was in yesterdays writing that I said things looked better and to-day things look very blue but I am going to try to hold out untill the first of July any way—I have a headache to night and that may be the reason that things look so blue.

Tuesday-June-23-1908.

Did a little shovelling in the forenoon and made a run in afternoon. I have concluded to abandon the dump for there is nothing in it but I will give the bar above a trial and that will call for about four days work to get to it but I will try it any way for I do detest the idea of going out and looking for work—I have concluded to abandon my Grand Canyon trip for this fall unless I do better on the bar than I expect to but if I live and keep my health with a reasonable amount of good luck I hope to make it next fall if not next spring.

Wednesday-June-24-1908.

Made a part of a clean up also was very busy fighting the blues.

Tuesday-July-28-1908.

Did a very hard days work putting up the schute—I never thought it possible for one man to do that which I have done to-day all alone but a man does not know his own capabilities untill he tries him self—had a nice gentle rain last night.

Tuesday–Aug-4-1908

Shovelled in fore noon but did not do very well on account of the dirt being wet and would not run in the shute so I only got 1 yard which I run through in afternoon and I also run my slimes and things look very much more encouraging than before and I do so hope that I will make a go of it for I do so hate to go back to wages.

Saturday-Aug-8-1908.

Finished retorting my gold and found that I did not have enough to justify me in going back to Olympia.

Loper's first try at solo placer mining had gone bust. On August 11 he went back to work laboring for the local miners—Adams, Hite, Gibbons, Bennett, and others. At the end of October he left the river for the first time since February, making the trip out to Hanksville—a ranching community some forty-five miles northwest of Hite—and began hauling gear and mail.

Monday-Nov-16-1908 to Dec-31-1908

Between the above days I was in Hanksville driving team for D.B. Meacham and while in Hanksville I enjoyed myself very much—going to parties and dances. On Dec-30-1908 I left Hanksville for Hite arriving at Hite Dec-31-1908. and this ends another year and I do hope that the ensuing year is better for me than the last one.

The laconic Loper failed to mention one notable occurrence during his stay in Hanksville—his engagement to twenty-two-year-old Jennie McDougall.

✣ ✣ ✣

January-1-1909

The first day of the year and I do believe that the prospects are a little brighter than they were one year ago today.

Loper had leased A.P. Adams's claim at Red Canyon and ensconced himself in Adams's cabin, which he called "The Hermitage." In addition to the cabin, Red Canyon had a series of ditches branching from a dam high on the delta, distributing the perennial flow of Red Canyon to agricultural fields and the placer works. The dam failed regularly, giving Loper a few days' work—or in bad cases, a few weeks' work—rebuilding it from willow branches, boulders, hay, and mud. The ditches alternately filled with mud and weeds, or burst—either way dictating hard labor. For his farming work, Loper had the help of his two horses, Old Bill and Brownie, to pull the plows, mowers, and rakes. For the placer work, he had simply a shovel and a strong back. Occasionally he hired a helper, but they rarely stayed long. Most days were filled with repair and maintenance of dam, ditches, equipment, clothing, and self. Some days he actually made progress in expanding his fields or running gravel through the placer works. His journal lists the daily chores with little mention of his thoughts or emotions. Nor does he have much to say about his engagement, chronicling it in terse, uninformative notes.

Public records add a little: Jennie McDougall was born in April, 1887, the second of five children, to Ebeneezer and Almira McDougall, pioneer Hanksville farmers. Jennie married Wylie Mecham on June 9, 1905, but apparently that marriage ended with her reclaiming her maiden name.

They wrote each other once or twice a week, Loper noting Jennie's letter of February 1 was "the best yet." He kept busy in the meantime, plowing the fields, hauling wood, and working on the dam.

Thursday-Feb-4-1909.

On arising from my slumbers I found it raining and the dam being in no condition for a flood I came to the conclusion I had better make it as safe as I could so after breakfast I started to hauling rock and putting them on the willows. I took the load of hay up however and spread a thin layer of hay next to the willows then a layer of rocks to hold the willows down when the flood comes. I put in a very hard days work and feel the effects a little. I had to repair my shoes to-night—the storm had cleared away and it is nice and clear to-night. Wrote two letters one to Birdie Brewster and one to Jennie.

A week later he took time out from ranch labor and headed upcountry to see his fiancée.

Thursday-Feb-11-1909.

Arose at 4-A.M. and got ready to start to Hanksville with the mail got started at 5-20 and arrived by 5-P.M. there I saw my promised wife and spent the evening with her.

Friday-Feb-12-1909.

Spent day enjoying my sweethearts company and various other things I got a sack of potatoes and spoke for a sack of corn—up till 12 with J.

Loper went back to Hite on the thirteenth and worked on the ranch for another two weeks. Then:

Friday-Mar-5-1909.

Started to Hite by boat this morning and took boat up as far as cape horn and tied up and finished on foot. I arrived by noon I received one letter from my promised wife and I am afraid the answer may cause a change in our relations to each other for I was a little angry and said just what I thought or part of it any way but things will have to be right or no go—did nothing in P.M.

Loper did not elaborate on what ticked him off. The two continued corresponding for another month, while he shoveled ditches and planted fields. Finally:

Don Fowler

Hermitage at Red Canyon, 1950s

Sunday-April-4-1909

Started to Hite by boat but the wind was so spasmodic so after traveling about a mile I tied up the boat and proceeded a foot—in due time I arrived and found several letters among them was one from my promised wife calling it all off—I answered and acknowledged the same. In P.M. I returned to the ranch and am suffering from a very severe tooth ache and head ache and am feeling very bad.

With that ended another of Loper's ill-fated romances. The Nebraska woman—the presumed mother of his child, whose name Loper never mentioned—had faded from his life nine years earlier. Now, for reasons unmentioned, his engagement to Jennie collapsed. Pearl Baker, in *Trail on the Water*, gave an explanation—possibly based on conversations with Loper: "He met and courted the lovely Jenny McDougall, and they set their wedding date for the next fall ... until the letter on March 6. He read that she had gone to a dance with another fellow, but she was sure he would not mind. He minded."

Loper's isolation increased. He worked his fields, complaining bitterly of toothache for the next two weeks. He made occasional forays upriver to Hite, on July 25 mentioning seeing two women there—"the first I have seen since Feb." The change in lifestyle from rowdy miner to prospecting hermit cannot be overstated. For years Loper had been the rabble-rousing womanizer in mining camps. Now he was mostly alone, his female companionship restricted to his rare forays into Hanksville. Six days later on his birthday he wrote:

> Saturday-July-31-1909
> After breakfast Mr. Stoddard and John Hite started up the river by boat—I took my saddle across the river for the Seaboldt outfit. Raked hay and broke my rake and had to repair it—had peaches and cream for supper the first of the season—I am 40 years old to-day and all alone and I was all alone this time last year and if I live 365 days more I am surely going to try to not be alone for I am getting tired of being alone.

In mid-August Loper hired Bill Law. Law had come into the area as Loper had—by boat—the previous October. Law, an Irishman, and Karl Keller had wrecked in Cataract Canyon. Keller drowned. Law climbed the west cliffs and by luck stumbled into a sheep camp. When Loper met him he was still earning a grubstake to move on. After six weeks working with Loper, Law headed upriver to get new shoes and did not return. He wrote a week later that he was carrying mail. Loper wrote to John Noyes of Hanksville, hoping to get a replacement for Law. Meanwhile, he worked the ranch.

> Wednesday-Oct-20-1909
> I have been very sick to-day but kept going finished amalgamating then burnt some old carpet and will have to amalgamate it to-morrow. I expected John Noys to come and go to work for me but was disappointed and from now on I will be very much surprised if things come out as I try to make them but I will win.

> Thursday-Oct-21-1909
> Did a little pan work in fore noon John Noys came in at noon. In P.M. I retorted and had 2 ½ oz. Gold not as much as I expected but still enough to make me keep on.

Two days later Loper got a strong reminder of his thwarted desire to run Grand Canyon:

NAU.PH.568.6002
Ellsworth Kolb

Nathaniel Galloway

Julius Stone

Saturday-Oct-23-1909

At 7-A.M. I started on my way to Hite and as I neared Cape Horn I met three boats and four men—it proved to be Messers Galloway, Stone and two other men on a trip through the canyons and they report a fine trip.... [A]fter talking to them for about half hour we each continued on our way.

Although history would eventually herald Nathaniel Galloway as the progenitor of modern river running, he was little known in 1909. His 1896–7 transit of the Green and Colorado Rivers made brief news and earned him a chapter in George Wharton James's 1900 *In and Around the Grand Canyon,* wherein Galloway rowed James upriver from Lee's Ferry into Glen Canyon, and downriver through Badger Creek Rapid. Galloway continued prospecting and trapping in Glen Canyon, where he went to work for another old riverman, Robert Brewster Stanton on his great dredge, the *Hoskaninni.* When one of the *Hoskaninni's* main investors, Julius F. Stone, arrived on the scene to see where his money was going, his meeting with Galloway formed one of the better known teams in river running.

The *Hoskaninni* soon entered bankruptcy, its ruins remaining as a landmark and occasional home base for later rivermen and prospectors such as Loper. Although Stone lost his investment, he gained a valuable friendship with Galloway that soon changed his life. Galloway's tales of river running so excited Stone's imagination that he offered a bold proposition: if Galloway would oversee the design and building of boats and lead an expedition down the Green and Colorado Rivers, Stone would foot the bill. The catch? Stone, at fifty-four, wished to row his own boat.

Galloway agreed. The party launched from Green River, Wyoming on September 12, 1909, with four boats—Galloway in the lead boat, followed by Stone, Charles Sharp, and Galloway's friend Seymour Sylvester Dubendorff. Accompanying them was Stone's brother-in-law, photographer Raymond Coggswell. In the rapids of Lodore Canyon, Galloway often took all the boats through. "He is so dextrous," wrote Stone, "that one would not be surprised to see him run a boat on heavy dew if it were necessary."

By the time the men reached Cataract Canyon, both Stone and Dubendorff had gained enough mastery of the oars to run many of the rapids. Dubendorff upset in Rapid Eighteen, but they ran the rest of the rapids or lined them successfully. At Hite, Sharp returned home. Stone gave Sharp's boat to Fred Gibbons as repayment for his hospitality. The remaining four men—six weeks into their ten week expedition—continued on in three boats.

Stone was nothing if not fastidious. He had researched river history extensively. Of the few river runners who preceded him, he was well acquainted with Stanton and was in the company of Galloway. Stone knew of Powell's journeys and tribulations, and had read of Russell and Monett's 1907 journey—sans Loper.

But of their meeting with Loper, Stone (whose prose often rivals Loper's for opacity) had little to say. His published journal reads:

> We met Bert Loper yesterday forenoon as he was making his way up the river. From his statements, which seemed straightforward, we gained the impression that he did not desert Russell and Monet on their trip down the canyons last year, as they claimed, but that instead *they* deserted *him.*

An unedited version of the same journal added two more sentences: "His opinion of Russell isn't of the highest order. He has about the same regard for him that a tom cat has for a marriage license."

Indeed, the "roastings" Loper had gotten in the press had largely accused him of cowardice. Yet as mentioned before, nearly all of the accusations came not from Russell or Monett, but from the sensational press. Stone now stated it was the opposite, that Loper was deserted by his friends—which is not quite true either. Loper's own journal is explicit about how late he was in arriving at Lee's Ferry, and how he half expected Russell and Monett to have moved on, which indeed they had. And Loper recorded correspondence with Russell on a regular basis as recently as a month before meeting Stone. Would Loper counter-slander Russell just for revenge? Did it make a better story? Or did Stone read more into what Loper said? We cannot know. Just how Loper portrayed it is unclear. But what would become the great controversy of Loper's life was hereby given a healthy shot in the arm.

Stone and Galloway continued on. Although Loper did not likely have time to discuss rowing or boatbuilding technique, he undoubtedly had time to examine Galloway's unique boat design. And lest he forget the details, he could look at Fred Gibbons's new boat that Stone had left at Hite.

✣ ✣ ✣

John Noyes stayed just two and a half weeks but during that time he and Loper made an encouraging sluicing of placer gravel: "Finished fixing the sluice and ran 25 cars—I had an excellent day and it begins to look as if I might accomplish something."

Noyes departed on November 9. Loper cleaned up what was left of the sluicing operation, amalgamated the residue, and shipped it off to the mint. His total take for the fall run had been close to $150—nearly $3,000 in today's dollars. That certainly helped, but Loper had little other income to supplement it. The Scorup brothers of Moab, whose free-range horses Loper looked after, occasionally slipped him ten dollars. He also worked a little for other claim holders in Glen Canyon, although he never described the pay arrangement. He certainly bartered a great deal with his labor and the fruits of his farming. Still, Loper needed cash for equipment and staple foods not produced locally. Altogether Loper's was a meager existence with little margin for error. And errors happened.

Wednesday-Dec-15-1909

Helped Mr. Turner take his boat up to the landing then started to take the small boat when I fell and run a stick in my left eye and came near losing it—did not do much in P.M. on account of my eye.

The eye survived, as did his aching teeth, at least for that year. On December 19 Loper packed up for his holiday visit to Hanksville. He spent a few days visiting before running into Jennie McDougall. "I met my last years sweetheart but we do not love each other now." After a week of visiting and going to dances, Loper returned to the Hermitage.

Saturday-Dec-30-1909.

Walked up from Tickaboo and found my boat badly frozen up and a hell of a time getting it loose and in so doing cut a hole in it—in P.M. I walked down and posted a notice on the Hosten claim for Seaboldt.

Friday-Dec-31-1909

The last of the year and a bad day for me—it was raining when I got out of bed and continued most of the day and me with an all days walk and in snow 6 inches deep with a crust of ice and I had wet feet all day—and did not get home untill dark but I finished posting the notices for Seaboldt. and so ends the year—and as I look back I don't think the year was as misspent as many others I have passed—it might be deemed a failure from a financial standpoint, still I hope to profit in the coming year by the experience of the year just passed—

Sat Jan 1, 1910

So begins another year and with it a new book. I have no new resolutions to make, no pledges to record, but will do the best I can in all things. I rested up from my trip yesterday. Mr. Law came up and brought my saddle home and took his back with him. There is an awful big flood down Red Canyon today, the largest I ever saw. Snow is going fast with this heavy chinook wind from the south.

Mon Jan 3.

Very stormy all day. My boat is under water and I am without a boat now.

> Tues Jan 4.
>
> The river raised about 4 feet last night and the boat is completely out of sight.

The new year was not starting off too well. When he finally extracted the *Arizona*—the last vestige of his aborted trip through Grand Canyon—it was "very badly wrecked." He spent much of the first two months of the year with a wicked toothache. In an effort to make the ranch work, he made a deal with another miner:

> Sun Jan 16
>
> I have sold ½ interest in my lease to Mr. Joe Riley for ½ interest in his team and harness and I am to get $250 besides. Mr. Riley has gone to Tory after his team and should be back by Feb. 1.
>
> Wed. Feb 2
>
> Mr. Riley came up on opposite side and told me one of his horses had died.... I am wondering if it was his horse or mine.

Finally, on February 9, Loper could stand the pain in his teeth no longer. He borrowed fifteen dollars from Cass Hite and made the five day journey to Salt Lake City.

> Went to see a dentist about my teeth then to an occulist about my eye. Was told that I would have to undergo an operation for my eye. Had three teeth pulled.... expect to leave for Greenriver tomorrow. Guess I will not have my eye operated on until I am better fixed financially.

Loper returned to Red Canyon, passing through Hanksville on the way. Pearl Baker, who was a young child there at the time, recalled, "he brought back to every child in Hanksville a string of beads for the girls and a pocket knife for the boys. My sister and I had our beads for years and how we loved them!"

Loper spent the spring placering with Joe Riley. The addition of another man seemed to provide the necessary momentum, or morale boost, to engage in such backbreaking labor. They made a good spring run, bringing in $142. But as Halley's Comet peaked in the sky that

May (Loper never mentioned it) Riley had his fill of Red Canyon—or Loper—and terminated the partnership. "So I am alone once more. But I am equal to the occasion so I started to cut hay and broke the machine. Had to stop and repair it some for the bal of the day."

Solitary life. Time passed. Loper made note of the days and activities, but little else. He engaged himself in a debate as to whether it was easier to travel the twelve miles upstream to Hite and back by boat, as he did, or by foot or horse, as did nearly everyone else.

> Sat Mar 5.
>
> Started to Hite by boat today and after a hard day's work, I tied the dam boat up at 4 mile canyon and walked on in. About to think the overland trail is easier in the long run.
>
> Tues May 26
>
> Scorups and other stockmen never seem to understand why I don't use horses to go back and forth to Hite. The river is a good enough trail for me and the boat a good enough "cayuse."
>
> Sat July 2
>
> Raked hay all day and a hard day's work too. Looks like I'll either have to quit raising hay or get some better way to rake. I have a mowing machine but this rake I pull by hand is too much hard work. Another advantage of the "trail on the water"—the boat don't have to be fed when it isn't working.

Throughout his years at Red Canyon, Loper was repeatedly laid low by bad headaches and general malaise. He does not describe it well, however, at one point saying, "Have had a very bad headache all day. I have come to the conclusion that the catarrh what is bothering me." Catarrh is an inflammation of the mucus membranes of the nose and throat, sometimes associated with sinusitis, which can indeed bring nasty headaches. Another cause was his lifelong work with dynamite, well known for giving "powder headaches" which Loper did indeed suffer from. More often he just complained of being "sick."

Summer passed, working in the fields, fighting with the dam and ditches, puttering about the cabin, boating back and forth to Hite and downriver to visit Cass Hite.

> Thurs Oct 13.
>
> Was not feeling very well today. Done some irrigating and puttering. Moved my bed in, its getting a little too cold to sleep outside these nights. I always enjoy sleeping under the stars in the summer and hate to move in for the winter. It looked very stormy for a while but passed.

On Christmas Loper went up to Hite and ended up doing some mining claim location work with Thomas Humphry. They rode east for a week into the high country of Cedar Mesa, spending New Year on the trail.

> So ends the year.
>
> In looking back over 1910, I find on the whole that it was a better year than 1909. I made a trip to Salt Lake and got my teeth fixed and that added lots to my comfort. I lost the *Arizona* but have another boat altho not as good a boat as my own. I made more money this year and if I could have got a man to help me this fall so I could have got around to make a fall run, would have done a lot better.

One thing Loper did not mention that year—perhaps he did not know of it—was the publication of George Wharton James's *The Grand Canyon of Arizona: How to See It.* In it, James included a chapter called, "The Story of a Boat." It was a reworking (a plagiarizing, actually) of David Allen's "A Daring Voyage Down the Grand Canyon," originally published in the British *Wide World Magazine* in November, 1908. It recounted the voyage of Russell and Monett. When speaking of Loper's absence in Grand Canyon James claimed that Russell " … emphasized rather his belief that Loper had elected to face no more dangers, and had voluntarily remained behind at Hite." So there it was, between hard covers, for all of America to read: Loper chickened out. #

31 Hates

"ONE OF THE amazing things about Bert was the terrible hates he had of people," Marston wrote Pearl Baker a month after Loper's passing. "He quite frequently assured me that he disliked only one man yet the hating seems to have been quite widespread. I could name Nevills, Frazier and Kelly without stopping to think. I wonder why his feelings were so intense?"

"It doesn't seem out of character to me that he was so intense about things," responded Baker.

> Remember, too, that when you were there he was stimulated to a degree and his emotions might have been a little higher because of his being impressed by you. At least, that is the idea I got when I saw him talking to you. I asked Mama about it and she said that Bert's lodge work was entirely against hate and he was wrapped up in it so tried to do right by it. But he hated plenty of people.

"I suppose I should not be surprised at Bert's hates," wrote Marston. "It wasn't only when I was there, that I found expression to such violent hatred. I run into it in other places."

The "one man" Marston refers to in his first missive is undoubtedly Robert Brewster Stanton, whose post-mortem assaults on Major Powell's character so offended Bert Loper. The others he names have a common theme: men who came to the river long after Loper did and worked hard at making a name for themselves, sometimes to the point of overstating the significance of their deeds. Although Loper never seemed to exaggerate, he believed his accomplishments worthy and resented being overshadowed by newcomers with questionable claims.

It was as if a man, having had a quick vacation frolic with a woman, claimed to know her. Hell, Loper had moved in with her! He lived with her on and off for decades, endured her moods and tantrums, made his living with her. These fair-weather cads knew nothing of her!

It was probably that simple.

More complex is Marston's use of the phrases "terrible hates," and "such violent hatred." The written record certainly supports the notion that Loper took a dim view of the folks mentioned above, but he never seems to rise to the level of hatred, be it terrible or violent. More accurately, Loper was expressing disapproval, disagreement, sometimes disgust. Perhaps Marston was privy to some undocumented outbursts of rage, but it seems atypical of Loper. #

32 Solitaire

Tom and I located some ground then started for Bluff where we arrived in due time. There I met some of my old time friends who I knew 16 years ago when I lived in Bluff. We staid there for a week and had a nice time. Then we bade adieu to the people and started west.

Loper began 1911 like years previous, splitting his time between working the ranch and placering. He hired two different men, firing each of them within a week—"We started to repair sand chute when my hired man and I had a row and I fired him.... So I am alone again and as far as for the man I had, I am glad of it." Spring brought bad luck.

Mar 27

Started to scrape in forenoon when Bill Bow Legs balked and reared over backwards and rolled over cliff into the river. So he is no more and I am one horse short.

Friday Apr 28

Started to run car and got along fine until the 15th car when the dam bronco knocked brownie over and crippled him.

May 19—11

Started up to the sluice and fell off a cliff and nearly killed myself but I put in most of the day cleaning up around works. Went down to Cass's in PM and took him some turnip seed. I didn't feel too good after my fall so Cass wanted me to stay all night. I did but didn't think it was necessary.

Day by day, week by week, Loper trudged on. A flash flood on June 20 blew his dam so totally away that he did not even attempt to repair it until August. He began reworking his mammoth gravel bin to improve his sluice operation.

Oct 25.

My old dog Jack is just about dead and I spent most of the day with him. He is still alive but do not expect him to live until morning. I surely hate to lose him for he has been a good old pal to me.

Oct 26.

Old Jack died last night at 11:45 PM and I sure miss him. I unloaded the boat then sewed Old Jack up in a sack and consigned him to a watery grave. I repaired pasture fence then chopped some wood.

It was a rare expression of emotion of any sort—stronger, even, than the loss of his fiancée. A week later, after cutting more willows to rebuild his dam, he spotted two boats heading downriver. He ran to the shore and hailed them in.

Nov 2

Two men, Kolb Brothers, came along on their way from Greenriver Wyoming to the Needles California and I met them below Red Canyon and went down to Cass's with them and stayed all night. We passed a very enjoyable evening.

Ellsworth and Emery Kolb were midway through their trip from Wyoming to the Mojave Desert. They had come to the South Rim of Grand Canyon nine years earlier with the idea of becoming photographers. They'd bought a small studio, moved it to the South Rim and begun photographing tourists and scenery, bringing in a modest income, all the while looking for ways to expand their business. They photographed Russell and Monett at Bright Angel Trail on their 1907 journey, and could not have missed Stone and Galloway's visit in 1909. They began corresponding with Russell as early as 1908, and Stone some time later about the idea of running the river. Stone shared with them the plans for the Galloway-style boats they had used, and the Kolbs ordered two such craft custom-built in Wisconsin and shipped to Wyoming. Since neither brother really knew much about boating, it was an audacious plan. Compounding it was their further scheme of using the latest technology—a moving picture camera—to make the first films of the Colorado. There was much to learn on both fronts, as their shaky

Loper plowing near placer bin

NAU.PH.568.5715 Kolb Brothers

films of boat wrecks conveyed, but they persevered. Their hired man left in tears early in the trip, and by the time Loper met them, they were becoming seasoned boatmen, having just survived Cataract Canyon.

Like Stone and Galloway before them, the Kolbs knew who Loper was before they met him, but also like Stone, their journals reveal little of their meeting. The men spent a night of conversation at Cass Hite's before the Kolbs moved on downriver. Loper began a friendship with the brothers, however, that grew for decades. And as the Kolbs began to publicize their feat with photographs, movies, lectures, and a book over the following years, river running slowly began to infiltrate the American consciousness. For Loper, it brought another resurgence of his longing to finish boating the Colorado.

> Nov 3.
>
> After breakfast the Kolb Brothers and I returned to the boats and I crossed the river where I bade them adieu then returned home not feeling very well. But after dinner I went down and cut willows and I am feeling very bum this evening.

Just over a month later Loper took a step toward working on the river for pay. On December 11, John Hite came downriver to ask Loper if he

Don Fowler

Looking downstream across Red Canyon ranch, 1950s

would take Bert Seaboldt to Lee's Ferry and back by boat. Although the last time Loper did this, in February 1908, the upriver trip had been the low point of his life, Loper did not hesitate a moment. "He and I hitched the team up and went to the dam and hauled down the tools I had been using." The next morning the two men returned to Hite and Loper began preparations for the trip. On the morning of December 14, Loper, Seaboldt, and Seaboldt's colleague George Meiss, a shoe salesman, mechanic, and all-around handyman from Price, Utah, headed downriver.

Bert Seaboldt was a regular around Hite. He had made good money years earlier when he and Samuel Gilson had discovered deposits of a gray hydrocarbonate mineral on the Ute Reservation in northern Utah. They named it Gilsonite and founded an entire industry on the rare deposit.

By 1905 Seaboldt had begun focusing on Glen Canyon. The Price newspapers stated that Seaboldt, owner of the Good Hope Placer Company, would soon have financing for an electric power plant at the coal deposits at the head of Hansen Creek to produce power for a massive new dredge and the soon-to-arrive thousands of miners. In 1909 a story ran in the same paper, calling Seaboldt "well and favorably known

Hite, 1914

E.C. La Rue

throughout Eastern Utah as one who does things"—in this case, proposing a dam and reclamation project on the San Rafael River. By 1910 he was back to promoting a road into Glen Canyon to haul in machinery for a $200,000 dredge. A July 1911 article had Seaboldt claiming "one of the richest placer propositions in the West.... There is plenty of water and fuel and enough gold to keep twenty dredges working the whole year round for a hundred years." Clearly Seaboldt was dreaming big, in the wake of Stanton's profound dredging failure a decade earlier.

Seaboldt had staked claims up and down the river and hired local miners, like Loper, to do the assessment work. By the time Seaboldt hired Loper for the river trip, the two men had known each other for three years.

On the second day of their voyage they awoke to find the river running full of ice. Alarmed that they might get frozen in, they began retreating upriver to Hite. But the following morning the river was clear again. They about-faced once more and headed for Lee's Ferry. On December 17 a snow storm drove them ashore for a day and a half at Hole-in-the-Rock.

The next day they burrowed ashore into a "Very bleak camp.... Nothing to burn but Rabbit Brush and it is green. Smokes awful and

NAU.PH.568.3361
Kolb Brothers

The *Charles H. Spencer,* Spencer front and center

the smoke is so acrid we can't get close enough to the fire to get warm." Three miles downstream the next day they met a group of men at the mouth of Warm Creek:

> building a boat to haul coal from Warm Creek to Lee's Ferry for a dredge outfit. We arrived at Lee's Ferry at 4:15 PM and met the Dredge crew. Mr. Watson, the foreman visited our camp and stayed untill bed time. We travelled about 33 m.

They had run across the crew of Charles H. Spencer, one of the more notorious mining promoters of Glen Canyon. Spencer, to give him the benefit of the doubt, seems to have started out an honest man, working large claims on the San Juan River. But as the ore failed him, he became increasingly adept at getting funding from investors, sometimes taking liberties with the facts. His project at Lee's Ferry revolved around mining the Chinle Formation. He believed there would be gold in the gray and purple shales, and had set up a hydraulic mining operation to recover the precious metal. To power the operation he built a gigantic coal-fired boiler. The coal was some twenty miles up Warm Creek, which in turn lay a good twenty-five miles upriver from the mining operation. Spencer's first boat proved too weak to pull an empty coal barge upriver from Lee's Ferry to Warm Creek. He then ordered a 92-foot steamboat built in San Francisco, disassembled and shipped by rail to Marysvale, Utah. From there the ship was hauled overland some two hundred miles by wagon to the mouth of Warm Creek. The steamboat, to be christened the *Charles H. Spencer,* was now under construction.

Such big dreams and schemes must have impressed a fellow idea-man like Seaboldt. Indeed, it may have been rumors of Spencer's activities that lured Seaboldt on this exploratory voyage. In the end, however, the *Charles H. Spencer* not only rivaled the *Hoskaninni* for size, but for magnitude of failure—it could not haul enough coal to fuel its own round trip. Its ruins lie sunken at Lee's Ferry.

Loper, Meiss, and Seaboldt set up camp at Lee's Ferry for a few days, celebrating Christmas with Spencer's crew, and visiting with ferryman Jerry Johnson's family. The next day, however, brought decidedly bad news: the river began filling with ice, worsening day by day until it was frozen solid.

Dec 31

Spent entire day playing solo with the boys. So ends 1911—and I didn't get down the Grand Canyon again this year. I haven't given up hopes, I looked down toward Badger rapid today and wished I could go on down right now. In checking back over this year, I find a number of things have happened, some good and some bad.

I made a trip the first of the year to Bluff and that was good. I enjoyed seeing old friends. Had two hired men, Pierce and Hinkley which was not all to good. Billy Bow Legs fell in river and drowned—very bad! Fell off a cliff and hurt my shoulder in the spring. Lost my dam in July and didn't get the new one done until the tenth of Dec. If the willows don't grow faster next year than they did these last three, I am going to be out of dam material.

Old Jack died in October and I sure did miss him. Kolb brothers came through the canyon. Made several trips to stake claims including this last one which finds me at the end of the year just about where I was in 1907, at Lee's Ferry and wanting to go on through the Grand Canyon. But I have a nice little home, my crops were good this year and while my gold take wasn't so large I hope to do much better in 1912.

Days soon turned to weeks and still the river remained frozen. Daily journal entries bespoke the monotony:

> Very cold and ice is still gorged and no signs of our going home soon.... No change in the river.... River still froze up and no prospect of going home soon.... Did nothing but loaf and wait for ice to move.... Mr. Watson returned from Warm Creek and reported the River frozen solid so it still looks bad for us.... It is becoming very monotonous laying around.... The cook went up the trail so I helped in the cook house. Shaved off about four month's crop of whiskers and got a new shirt.... I went over to Johnson's ranch and returned his shoe last night and got some envelopes. Nice day. I played poker and lost $18.00.... Put in day loafing. Played poker in evening and win $10.00.... I poled the boat up to the Ferry and the men and I had a little sail to camp. I played poker in the eve and lost $4.50, making in all $12.50.... Four years ago today I started up to Hite after my big disappointment....

The weeks became a month. Finally, on January 31, the river thawed enough to attempt their upriver trek: "We spent most of the day in getting ready for our trip up the River and I was never more eager for a trip for I want to get home." They departed, making five miles against the icy current. It was familiar work to Loper this time, unlike his miserable upriver trip of 1908. That time he was out of food, out of friends, and alone with no prospects of a future. This time he knew the work, knew the way, had help with the labor, and was on payroll. Still, it was not much fun, rowing against the current, dragging along the shore, occasionally sailing, and now and then falling in:

> Feb 9
>
> We broke camp at 7:25 and had very good water until we came to Aztec Rapid where I proceeded to get wet so we went about one mile farther and passed another small rapid then we stopped and built a fire so I could dry my feet at 10 AM. Got a big drink of whiskey so I think I will fall in the River some more. We started on at 12:10 and had some very hard work. We hoisted sail and sailed about half a mile when the wind quit. Then we had to buck sand the bal of the day. Camped about 3 miles below the San juan.

Feb 13

At 7:40 we started and we rambled right along until noon when we camped at the lower end of the Boston Bar. Saw a bunch of cattle and the Boss looked them over and decided not to kill any on account of being too large. We broke camp at 1:20 and was getting along nicely when the boss happened to think that he had left the rifle at our noon camp so we made camp at the mouth of Hall Creek and he went back after the gun.

Feb 19

Got started by 7:25 and got along very good. The Boss did some staking and at the Swirl Rapid we met Womack who helped me the bal of the day. The Boss came on to Hite. We had lunch at 2 mile and at 3:30 we finished our trip and it seems good to be at home once more. I sure had a big bunch of mail. The trip took 123 hours and 23 minutes traveling time.

Loper returned to Red Canyon to find Alva Womack caretaking the ranch. The dam and irrigation works were in good order, but his pet cat had been eaten by coyotes. Womack went to work on the placer operation with Loper, at least for a while.

Mar 1.

We both worked on the Bin today. We turned some weeds at noon. Looks very stormy tonight. Alva came to the conclusion to go to Hanksville next Wednesday so I will be alone after he is gone but I am used to that and suppose I can hold out another year.

In April Loper went up to Hite to pick up Seaboldt for a four-day river trip down to the Stanton dredge and back. On the way, " I had the misfortune to fall in the River and got soaked.... Mr. Seaboldt gave me a quart of whiskey." Other than that the seasons passed uneventfully, Loper maintaining his irrigation, repairing the dam, traveling up to Hite and back, entertaining fellow prospectors, visiting Cass Hite, and suffering sick spells and toothaches.

Sun June 30

I made a new hoe and used it all day in the corn patch. I hoed and replanted the sweet corn and irrigated some more. Cass went to Hite this AM and I crossed over and sent up for some rice for I am completely out of grub and things look worse for me right now than they ever have since I have been on the Colo River but I will survive and stick to it some way.

Sun Sept 15

I cleaned cabin then went up and looked the dam over for the water is off. I had a shave in pm, the first since the fourth of July. Hardly knew myself, like talking to a stranger again.

Fri Oct 11

Mr. Turner went on down the River and I went home. Sure hate to see anyone going down the river. I wonder if I will ever get below Lee's Ferry. The years go by, five of them now, and I still don't get down the Grand Canyon. Oh well—Finished husking corn and pulled and piled my squash. Daubed the cabin for winter.

Sun Oct 27

Stormed all day and my Friday and Saturdays work is all shot to hell and more too.

Sat Nov 23.

My visitors left this morning and in just about an hour Mr. Smith came. Mr. Smith is a man I got acquainted with at Lee's Ferry last winter. He is trapping. Mr. Galloway also paid me a short visit. He is on his way to Lee's Ferry. Cass Hite passed on his way to Hite in PM. Mr. Smith and I went up to the dam and set six traps.

One-eyed Charles Smith was a wandering trapper and prospector that the Kolb brothers first met on their 1911 trip through Cataract Canyon. Ellsworth Kolb described him:

> About medium size but looked tough and wiry; he had a sandy complexion with light hair and moustache. He had lost one eye, the other

> was that light gray colour usually associated with indomitable nerve. He had a shrewd, rather humorous expression of being very capable. Dressed in a neat whipcord suit, wearing light shoes and a carefully tied tie, neatly shaved … he was certainly an interesting character to meet in this out of the way place.

The Kolbs left him there in the middle of the rapid-filled canyon, but received a letter from him that winter saying he had made it through the rapids with his share of tribulations. He met Loper at Lee's Ferry that winter and was now on his way downriver again. In 1913, Smith launched once more from Green River, never to be seen again.

> Wednesday Dec 18, 1912
>
> I saddled Old Bill and came up as far as Red Canyon and tied up and crossed the River and fed my chickens and horses then continued on my way to Hite where I arrived by 1:30 PM. Put in bal of PM reading. I renewed my subscriptions to Bryan's Commoner, New York World and the Cosmopolitan magazine—$1.75 for the three.

> Tues Dec 31
>
> Got started on my way by 11 AM and after a hard ride I made a dry camp the other side of Blue Notch being unable to find the copper claim before dark. In thinking back over 1912, I find it hasn't been too profitable a year. I not only will not be able to make the trip down the canyon at the rate I have made money this year but I won't go anywhere else—I'll starve to death. If it wasn't for the fact that I have the Bin in good shape for spring and feel I have a lot better gravel to wash next year, I would go back to wages if I do hate the thought of it.

Loper hunkered in for the winter, doing the requisite chores to tide him through until spring. He made frequent trips to Hite to socialize, provision, and write to acquaintances, among them Robert Brewster Stanton and the Kolbs. As spring arrived so did a new bother—the Scorup livestock found his garden and ditches and repeatedly destroyed them.

> The cattle came last night at midnight and tore the fence down and got in alfalfa so I got up and fired the shot gun a couple of times and they stampeded back up the canyon....
>
> The cattle came about bedtime so I had another siege chasing them away....
>
> Found no water in ditch first thing so after breakfast I saddled Old Brownie and drove some more cattle off....

He managed to keep the beasts at bay and spent most of the summer working his crops, never getting around to placering that year. Then, on September 2, his world shifted. His journal stated simply, "I worked with grapes in forenoon and in PM took some things down to Cass' and we had a row over politics so I came home and repaired some fence."

Over the past twelve months, Loper had visited Hite at Tickaboo more than seventy times, spending the night there in nearly four dozen cases. No more. Six weeks later he noted, "John Hite passed going up the River. He never stopped." Another two weeks passed, then, "John P. Hite came along about 2:30 so I crossed the River and took Cass' mail to him." Still another two weeks passed before he wrote on November 16, "There was a man passed here yesterday who looked like Cass but I was not sure. Haven't been down since we had that argument. Have sure missed going down but still think I was right."

Loper never elaborated on the substance of the September 2 tiff, but it must have been a zinger. What we know of their politics comes tangentially. In his journal Loper cheered the nomination and election of Woodrow Wilson, and in writing of his early wanderings made note of just where he was when William Jennings Bryan made his famous "Cross of Gold" speech. Charles Hunt, who once tried to write Loper's biography, said Loper was a big fan of Bryan's, whereas Hite was a "Hearst man," subscribing to the beliefs of William Randolph Hearst. In 1913, Bryan was Wilson's Secretary of State, and was at odds with Hearst.

Both Hite and Loper were avid readers, subscribing to a wide variety of periodicals including Hearst and Bryan publications, as well as those of Hearst's rival, Pulitzer. Both Hearst and Pulitzer were guilty of increasing sensationalism in their coverage, for the simple motive of selling more papers. Those who depended on those newspapers for news, then, were basing opinions on increasingly polarized sources.

During the long years of isolation, Hite and Loper, hard-headed men both, had ample time to calcify in their beliefs. Loper, fond of Wilson and Bryan, had also had dismal experience in the world of wages and had flirted with organized labor. From a century away it seems Loper was by far the more liberal in his politics. Hite, who made much of his livelihood selling interest to investors, may well have held the more conservative beliefs. Beyond that, the gist of their battle can only be guessed at.

Tues Nov 23

Cass passed on his way to Hite but he did not speak, neither did I.

In early December a prolonged toothache sent Loper to Green River for an extraction. Arriving back in Hanksville on a Friday evening he wrote, "Had a nice dance in evening and I took Ethel Gibbons home." A week later he was back in Hanksville, for the funeral of Ethel Gibbons's grandmother. "I sat up all night last night with Grandma in company with Mrs. Biddlecome, Miss Jessie McDougall and Miss Ethel Gibbons." Pearl Baker recalled, "Mrs. Biddlecome is my mother and she remembers this very distinctly. Bert was a fine reader, had a musical voice and read easily and expressively. He spent the night reading *The Winning of Barbara Worth* to them." [a best-selling novel set on the lower Colorado.]

Back on the river, the glacial relations with Cass Hite began a slow thaw.

Wed Dec 17

Cass passed on his way to Hite. I crossed over and sent for some soap and salt.

Fri Dec 19

Cass returned from Hite and brought my soap and salt.

Wed Dec 31

This is the first time I have written in my diary since the 22nd inst. and since that time I have done nothing but hold down the cabin only on xmas day I went up to Hite in a snow storm, in fact it has been very stormy and cold ever since. I brought down 12# of oats and a big batch of mail. I sent a package of grapes to Ethel Gibbons and wrote her a letter....

So ends another year. I have no kick to make, although I made neither a spring nor a fall run at the placer. Have things ready to hum this spring. I have hopes for which I am very thankful, for without hope, life would be a failure. So to the year 1913 I bid farewell.

✣ ✣ ✣

Thurs Jan 8 1914

Saddled Old Dan and went to Hite where I arrived by 2 PM. Cass Hite was up. I rec'd my mail, including a letter from Ethel also a package of cake from her. Very cold.

On January 23, Loper arrived in Hanksville, ostensibly to buy some pigs, but certainly Ethel Gibbons was in the equation: "I stopped with Mr. B.S. Gibbons (Ethel's folks). Was just in time for a dance in the evening."

Sun Jan 25.

I hitched up my team and went down to Joe Biddlecome's and put in am shoing old Dan and stayed for dinner. Ethel Gibbons went with me. Mrs. Biddlecome went into the other room for something and I thought that was a fine opportunity to kiss Ethel which I proceeded to do. Either time passed considerably faster than it does on the Colorado or Mrs. Biddlecome came back sooner than there was any urgent need to for I was caught in the act. Promised her some dried grapes as hush money.

In the afternoon, Mrs. B. and her children, Ethel and I all went up to Mr. Ekker's to listen to the new Edison cylinder phonograph. Ethel and I took Martha Mac and Mrs. Biddlecome home and arrived back at dark.

Loper finally pried himself out of Hanksville and was back at Red Canyon by February 2. Two of his four new pigs died on the way. Back at the ranch he settled into a routine of woodcutting, horse wrangling and general chores.

✣ ✣ ✣

Sun Feb 22

I chopped wood all day. Was sitting in the evening writing in my diary at 7:45 when I heard a shot fired on the other side of the river. I knew in a flash that there was something wrong.

The night was pitch black, without a bit of starlight even. I went down and got into the boat and pulled across the river, guided by the voice of Lon Turner. I had barely grounded the boat when I asked what was the matter.

"Cass is dead," he said.

I don't remember answering him, such a feeling of desolation swept over me. He seemed pretty well done in so I put him across the river and got my walking shoes to go on up to Hite and tell John.

Never to my dying day, do I expect to have to make my way over such a trail in such Stygian darkness. There seemed to be a twilight along the rim of the canyon that pressed the gloom down to the very bottom of the chasm. It was 12 miles to Hite and the very worst trail in the state. Strange as it may seem my eyes never did become used to the darkness. The only way that I could tell if I was on the trail across the bottoms was when I stepped off to the side I would sink ankle deep into the thawed ground.... There was one place where the trail ran within about 4 feet of the edge and if I had gone off there I would have landed in the river about 400 feet below, so naturally, I was fighting the upper side of the trail. I thought I would choke to death. It seemed farther than I thought possible and I seemed to make very little progress....

Sometimes it seemed like I was standing still or walking a treadmill, and when I thought of the news I was to bear to Cass' brother, John, I seemed to be flying. I do so hate to be the bearer of bad tidings, so I tried as I walked along, and slipped and fell at times, to figure out a way to break the news without a shock.

I finally arrived and wakened Fred Gibbons who was sleeping in a tent, the cabin being too small to accommodate two beds. I told him what had happened and asked how we should break the news to John. He jerked on his pants and said, "Why just tell him, we all have to die some time." We went into the cabin and Fred shook John and said, "John, Cass is dead."

John put in the bal of the night writing letters to their folks. In the morning (Mon Feb 23) John, Mr. Hale and I went by boat down to Tickaboo, picking up Turner at Red Canyon.

Cass was lying on the floor on his face at the foot of his bed. It appeared that he had been trying to get outside to get his breath when he felt sick. By his diary he had been dead just a week....

Turner made a box and I dug the grave. We rolled him in a blanket and so he was buried where he so happily lived.

Tues Feb 24.

... I can't tell what this means to me. For the last two years Cass and I grew to depend more and more on each other. If I had new potatoes first or he got a piece of bacon we shared with the other. We read and discussed everything that came out in the papers and magazines we both took. I seem to be caught between the devil and the sea, if I go out and buck the wage system again, I know what it means and yet I don't know if I can stand the lonliness since Cass is gone. Feeling very blue tonight.

Loper's journal from February 25 through March 4 no longer exists. A pity, for it would be interesting to see what, if anything, Loper had to say in the week following Cass Hite's death. A month later Loper received letters from John Hite's brother and niece, thanking him for his "truly unselfish and fraternal care for the dead and sympathy for the living. Without your truly philanthropic and Christian assistance, brother John says he could not have performed the last said rights for brother Cass."

Whether Loper and Cass Hite were on speaking terms at the time of Hite's passing may be irrelevant. Loper had lost a long-time friend and his only neighbor, and life at Red Canyon was fast growing intolerable. Ethel Gibbons disappeared from his thoughts as well. Perhaps she had found someone else to kiss, as she married Andrew Ekker in April 1915.

Sat Mar 7

Burned a lot of trash then in PM I saddled Old brownie and drove a bunch of cattle up Red Canyon. Hate to face another season fighting these cows off my dam and ditch.

Sat Mar 28

Bennett and I found the remains of the boat belonging to C.L. Smith who started through Cataract Canyon last fall so that makes another victim for the Canyon. Mr. Smith made 2 trips through the canyon and his last trip was made in fall of 1912. He stayed two or three days with me at that time.

Fri Apr 3.

Worked at dam in forenoon and finished the shovell work and in afternoon I cleaned ditch from the house to dam. When I returned I found Frank Lawler at cabin and he is with me tonight. We have made an agreement to go it together until the first of May. I am to furnish everything and he is to get 2/5 of the gold taken out up to and including April 30.

Sun Apr 19

Frank and I went to work and about 11 AM Jas. A. Scorup came along and Frank went with him so I am alone once more.

Tues Apr 28

I surely woke to a hell of a day! A damned old badger killed 35 chickens for me last night and everything seemed to go wrong. I put in forenoon trying to trail the badger and found where he had buried 11 of the chickens. I poisoned some of them and placed them in Red Canyon. Last night I had 70 chickens and tonight I have 34, and have just about made up my mind to cut the chicken business out.

During this same hard winter, however, another old friendship that had fallen on rocky times began to revive. From a mine in the mountains of Mexico, Charles Russell began writing, imploring Loper to join him on a new expedition. #

33 Analysis

I AM MUCH TROUBLED with the patterns of emotions which become quite apparent in the study of records of the various river trips. These I have checked out and double checked with an expert in the field. Eddy's book is one of the outstanding cases of printed disclosure of emotional disturbance....

I have said that Nevills' death was suicide. That might need correction for definition. I do not say his destruction was premeditated as was Holmstrom's. We can start with a reasonable question asking just what Nevills was doing in the Canyon when he was frightened of the river.

Just how much of these things to say in a book is a point which gives me much concern. This job of writing does not end with the determination of facts. The next question is how much to say.

Dock Marston was writing to Grand Canyon Superintendent Harold C. Bryant in 1950, exploring an angle of river history that had begun to intrigue him. Psychoanalysis had come into popular culture in the first half of the twentieth century, and although Freud had died in 1939, his field was just entering its heyday. Marston was an enthusiast and began, in his own way, to psychoanalyze past and present river runners.

Bryant tried to dissuade him: "My advice would be to move with great caution in this particular field, which is slowly getting a kind of depreciatory attitude from many educated people." Marston bristled in defense:

> I would not give the impression that I am new in the psychological field. I found that it was half my problem in the giving of investment advice and I gave much study to it.... It is impossible to be completely objective on judging any situation. I have struggled to maintain an objective viewpoint.... But some of the topics studied by the psychologist are the only means to an understanding of some of the violent conditions which arise in the river parties.

Otis "Dock" Marston

Marston's expert was a neighbor named Dr. Thaddeus Ames, a retired psychoanalyst who had studied under both Freud and Jung, and an important figure in early American psychology. He would often sit in Marston's living room, the two constructing theories about river runners. Marston, in fact, attributed his own retirement from the Nevills operation to Ames's advice: that Nevills was dangerous and would try to kill Marston for showing him up as an oarsman. In early 1949, (according to Marston) he and Ames predicted that if Marston ran Grand Canyon by motorboat, Nevills would kill himself in his airplane.

What does this have to do with Bert Loper? A lot. A great deal of primary material on Loper was collected by Marston—material that can neither be confirmed nor contradicted. Often this material resides in the Marston Collection without full context as to what questions were asked, or what line of interrogation Marston may have been pursuing. It is important, therefore, to get an idea of the avenues of thinking Marston engaged in as he tried to define the historical characters of the Colorado River. In a 1976 interview, Marston expounded on his theories:

> In looking at the various early river travelers, fast water sections of the river, you will find with a considerable frequency the fact that the boy child has been raised under the dominance of the female parent. Apparently ... one of the grave concerns that this type of early life develops in a child was the concern over his masculinity. Now if we start to examine a few of the people that we know, where we do know the background, it becomes amazing the number to which this applies. We can start with Powell ... the dominance of a parent in his particular case came from the fact that his mother was controlling most of his growing phases, and this would lead normally to a concern over his masculinity. There isn't much question about it, that this is the major force that drove him to the river.
>
> Stanton ... had infantile paralysis.... His mother, again, over-mothered him in order to compensate for this.
>
> [Regarding the Kolbs] obviously again, suspicion of mother dominance.
>
> There was no question about it; Nevills was one of the more violent cases. It is painfully obvious if you look at it and ask the question, "Was he dominated by his mother?" the answer just comes, "yes, yes, yes."
>
> Dellenbaugh ... pretty much of a pantywaist. Little fellow.
>
> Now Loper is one that again had what one might call a certain feminine impact, particularly in his very young years.... The mother, and her mother, struggled along with the youngsters. Here again was Bert under female dominance. A little tragedy that occurred there, because of the limited funds and so forth, he slept with his grandmother and she died while he was in bed with her. These are obviously things that would give a considerable impact, you see. So all through Bert's life you'll find little indications of that. Bert decidedly was not an admirable character. One of the great things that happened in his life, he married a marvelous woman, Rachel. From that time on he was a pretty nice guy.

Psychoanalysis certainly has its place in both society and history; it also has pitfalls. Historical characters are not patients, and are not available to consult, nor are they in need of psychoanalytical treatment. True treatment involves the lengthy and participatory drawing out of a patient's innermost feelings, dreams, and fears—something that cannot be done from afar.

A second great pitfall is that the analyst's own ego may find its way into the process, thereby inflating itself and diminishing the reality of the "patient." The analyst then ascribes products of his own personal neuroses to the patient.

P.T. Reilly, who occasionally sided with Marston's analyses, in the end distanced himself:

> Dock constantly appeared eager to question the masculinity of anyone he didn't like. He was so concerned with this phase that I had the impression he questioned his own masculinity. He frequently tried to get attention by attacking a figure such as Powell, Kolb, Holmstrom, Nevills. He and I had lengthy discussions on this. I maintained that Powell was motivated by ambition and politics rather than by his sex drive or insecurity.

Of course, once Reilly got his pump primed, he couldn't help but take a swipe at Marston's character:

> It is significant that Marston presents himself as someone who knows the detail he does but never explains how he came by that knowledge.... Dock, in my opinion, was a master at getting others to cooperate with him, to do field investigation.... He collected the data at his spider's nest in Berkeley and dispensed little tidbits to keep other investigators going but seldom revealed his sources. He was the Oracle of Delphi and he manipulated the outflow to suit himself. It is a shame that he was not exposed as the rascal he was because by not crediting his sources, he reveals his character to be as small as his stature. #

34 Proposition

I DO NOT BLAME Russell and Monett so much for going off and leaving me but I sure did resent the implication, by Russell, at Grand Canyon, that I had shown fear and deserted them, but I mentioned before that Russell was beginning to get "Cocky" so I am of the opinion that there was a "Method in Russell's madness" about my being a deserter for that placed him very much in the spot light so he was the big IT.

Loper and Russell had written several times after their parting in November 1907, but by the end of 1909 correspondence had ended. And while Loper could understand Russell and Monett's motives for leaving without him, the insinuation of cowardice still stung. Although Dock Marston's later research shows the accusations came largely from overzealous reporting, Loper fixed the blame squarely on Russell.

Around 1909 Russell had taken a job in the administration of the San Luis Mining Company, 750 miles south of the border in the Sierra Madre of Mexico. There, some sixty miles northeast of Mazatlan on the Piaxtla River, he began squirreling away funding for his next expedition.

Meanwhile, the Kolb brothers had completed their 1911-12 voyage through Grand Canyon. Whereas Russell and Monett had been searching for mineral wealth, the Kolbs were out to mine scenery. In this they followed a widespread trend in the appreciation of canyon country. What the earliest explorers had considered a horrid obstacle was now being viewed as marketable splendor. The Kolbs succeeded, assembling a lecture show to accompany their still photographs and shaky movie images. Ellsworth was writing a book about their adventures and Emery was lecturing. The Kolbs presented their show in Prescott, where Charlie Russell's brother John lived. Corresponding from Mexico, Charlie heard poor reviews of the film. He thought he could do better.

On June 28, 1913, Russell wrote the Kolbs, proposing a joint venture to get better images and movies, offering to supply his services for a mere ten thousand dollars. He could not help but slip in a prideful stab:

> As I understand you were not making any money out of your other pictures, but that is easily explained. You made too many portages and did not run the worst rapids which would have made the best pictures, and you were not properly equipped anyway for that kind of trip. In our other trip we made only 8 portages.

Ellsworth Kolb wrote back, "We are hardly interested in your … proposition.…" He explained how uneconomical Russell's ambitious plans were, boasted of how well he and his brother had fared on their trip and how few portages they made, and slid in his own dagger:

> In speaking of your trip we always gave you credit for having unlimited nerve for attempting it in such a boat. We believe you have a record of starting with three boats and losing them all before you had covered half the rapids, and only recovered the last one by chance.

Kolb suggested Russell contact Galloway, who was offering his services for a similar trip for three thousand dollars.

Nathaniel Galloway's era had ended, however. The man who had popularized the flat-bottomed, upturned river boat and the stern-first method of rowing died shortly after Kolb's letter. After his 1909 trip with Julius Stone, Galloway had moved to Richfield, Utah, and gone back to the life of a trapper. On December 22, 1913, he suffered an epileptic seizure, fell from his camp wagon and, his head wedged between a grain sack and the wagon wheel, suffocated. In spite of the great place he holds in modern river-running, his techniques had received little notice in his day outside his hometown of Vernal. George Wharton James had described him in his Grand Canyon books as a competent boatman and guide, but failed to expand upon his wizardry at the oars.

"If your statements are true as you say they are I was certainly misinformed about your pictures," Russell wrote the Kolbs. "I was told you had made nearly 150 portages.… I was also told your moving pictures were no good.… So I have decided to abandon my project."

Russell, in fact, had no intention of giving up. He believed Kolb to be a bald-faced liar. "Every one who saw their moving pictures pronounced them rotten," Russell had written Loper back in October:

> As they didn't know how to run rapids and they only had about 1500 ft of moving pictures altogether as they made about 150 portages. All this I have on good authority.... I just rec'd a letter from them saying they only made 14 portages on the whole trip but this I know is not true.... [T]hey are evidently so afraid that someone else will do this thing in good shape and put their effort in the shade that they came back at me with a fearful string of lies.

Russell proposed to make thousands of still images, recording every bend of the river, and show them in succession, interspersing them with moving pictures of the boats running the most dramatic rapids. The full exhibition, he admitted, could take days to show, but contrary to Kolb's assessment, Russell was sure it would sell. He was so sure, in fact, that he decided not to let any film companies in on the project (none were interested at his price) but to finance it himself lest someone try to take the profits. He proposed to Loper that they launch in the latter part of July and be finished well before Christmas in time to have their show in order for the 1915 expositions in San Diego and San Francisco.

Russell's letters rambled on at length weighing the various options for the film, boats, finances, etc. with occasional tangents about his favorite Mexican fruit, the chirimoya. He sent Loper 50 seeds, urging him to plant them at Red Canyon, and waxed enthusiastic about his plans for a chirimoya plantation on his ranch on the Sandy River in Arizona (he had imported 20,000 seeds for it the previous year). "If we can make a success of this business I shall retire to the ranch and leave this land of revolutions for good."

The Mexican Revolution was now in full swing. Russell rode to Nogales guarding a trainload of gold bullion in February, taking the opportunity to write Loper and send the chirimoya seeds. He had settled on a plan.

> I really believe the best thing we can do is to go alone just you and I take our own camera and moving picture machine and take our own pictures and then we will have the whole thing ourselves.... [I]f I think

> I can raise the money to finance the expedition we will do it that way if you are agreeable.... You see if we go alone it will cut down the expense and we won't be bothered with any idiots that might be a bother to us.

And the fruit?

> If I could get a good chirimoya on the way up I would send it to you so you could tell what one tasted like, but as they will only keep about a week even when picked green, it would probably be in the last stages of decomposition when it reached you and if you eat it then it would make you sick as a dog.

Russell returned south and began raising capital for the trip, in March writing, "It can be done for about $2000 and I can raise the money.... Now if this is agreeable to you, and you are willing to go, let me know at once...." Ten days later he wrote again, fine tuning ideas for supplies and schedules, adding, "As you say we will have to have accidents to make our films interesting. If we don't have any we can easily invent some." Russell needn't have worried on that account.

Initially Loper agreed to go. When Russell announced he had chosen Mullins steel boats—a one-sheet molded boat similar to the boats they had used in 1907 but without the troublesome seams, Loper wrote back suggesting something different. It may have been that after seeing Galloway and Stone in the newer style flat-bottomed boats, followed by the Kolbs in the same sort of boats, and hearing both trips had fared well, that Loper was ready to abandon the keeled Whitehall hulls of the Powell era. Russell was confused. "I don't understand what you mean by designing your own boat," he wrote, expanding on the virtues of the Mullins craft. He offered to let Loper design his own decking.

"I am sorry to hear Cass Hite is dead," he continued:

> I had hoped to have another talk with him on our way down, but of course that can't happen now. And Nat Galloway is dead also. So then if we get through alright, I will be the only man alive who has been through the Grand Canyon twice.
>
> I had a letter from Monette the other day also.... He was no good whatsoever on the other trip so we don't want him along.

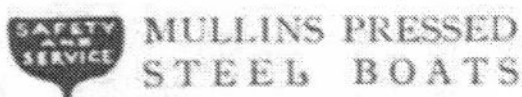

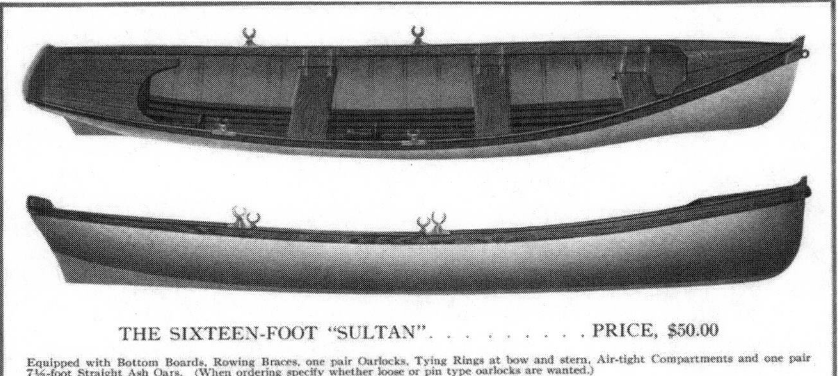

THE SIXTEEN-FOOT "SULTAN". . . . . PRICE, $50.00

Equipped with Bottom Boards, Rowing Braces, one pair Oarlocks, Tying Rings at bow and stern, Air-tight Compartments and one pair 7½-foot Straight Ash Oars. (When ordering specify whether loose or pin type oarlocks are wanted.)

See Price List of Equipment, Page 44.

The SULTAN is modeled on perfect lines, and will make an admirable boat for family use where a good capacity is required; the best boat for children, as it is roomy and very steady and with ordinary care should last a lifetime. It is easy to row. It will appeal to summer resorters on account of its durability, comfort and safety. Over one hundred used by the Star Boat Co., Kansas City, Mo., all of which have been used constantly for many years.

DIMENSIONS — Length, 16 ft.; beam, 50 in.; height, bow, 25 in.; stern, 23¼ in.; amidship, 15 in.; weight, about 225 lbs.; crated, 275 lbs.; crated for export, 350 lbs.; cubic measurement for export, 180 cu. ft. Code word, RUM. Finished in aluminum outside, light blue inside; natural wood trimmings; large air chambers under decks like a life boat.

As to reimbursing me for the money I can take that out of the profits on the pictures until it is all paid back.

By May Russell was back in the States, heading to Illinois to visit family before meeting Loper in Green River for the launch in July. But Loper, writing from Hite, was beginning to have cold feet. He never explained his indecision. Perhaps he could not quite get past his feelings over the outcome of the previous trip. Maybe Russell's exuberant wandering prose was giving of a hint of lunacy. Or possibly Loper was broke, had little faith in Russell's optimism, and felt he had to stay and work the ranch. We do not know. All we have to illuminate the situation are Russell's apoplectic letters from Illinois.

Gillespie, Ill. June 3, 1914

Dear Friend,

I can't quite understand your various letters you first say you will go, then you say you won't, then you say you will and then again that you won't. Haven't I told you that I could furnish all the money necessary and that the total cost would not exceed $2700.... I am sure that we can make at least 25 or $30000 dollars if we make a success of it.

Now on the strength of the last letter you wrote me I have everything ordered to be shipped to Green River, Utah, so I think this is a bad trick for you to back out now, I might get someone else but getting some one you don't know anything about is a poor scheme.

I am sure we can make a complete success of it and make a small fortune for the both of us. So I think you had better think the matter over and decide to go....

So I guess you will have to go whether you want to or not....

My furnishing the money is alright all I ask is that after what I have spent is repaid we will then divide evenly on the rest of the profit, and if we make a success I am sure we can clear up at least $10000 apiece after paying me back my money. So you better think the matter over and decide to go. We will not be at the mercy of anyone else as I can raise as much as $5000 if necessary.

Your friend,

Chas. Russell.

P.S. If you don't care to be in on a small fortune let me know at once and I will try to get some one else but I hope I don't have to as I do not like the idea of taking someone I know nothing about and who probably knows nothing of running rapids.

I will consider this a mean trick on your part after saying you would go and then backing out at the last minute when I have no time to find another suitable man.

C.R.

... So for Gods sake don't desert me now I know of no one else who would be as satisfactory as you would be, and I am positive if we make a success of it we will make a bunch of money.

You need have no fear but what I shall treat you square on all the business end of it. So for goodness sake make up your mind to go. You should know how hard it will be to get another man that would be any good.

Chas Russell

Reading between the lines it appears Loper's reason for backing out must have been monetary. Loper's reply may have played on Russell's desperation, as Russell made a better offer in the following letter.

Gillespie, Ill. June 17, 1914

Dear friend,—

Your letter rec'd yesterday and will answer at once. I read your last letter about six times but the last letter I had rec'd from you just before leaving Mex. you had said you would go and I was certainly surprised when I got your last one.

So I will tell you what I will do. I will loan you the $550.00 if you will go. I calculate we should be through by the first part of November so it will only require a little over four months of your time. I neglected to tell you that I had about $6000 in Prescott that I have saved in the 5 years I have been in Mex. Now as the trip will cost about $2700, I can loan you $550, and still have enough left to keep my ranch going on....

Now as your reply can not reach me before about the 1st of July, I probably shall not leave here until after the 4th of July. So I might arrange to meet you in Green River about the 9th or 10th of July ...

I know you have always wanted to go so I think it would be a shame if you should lose out this time as you may never have another opportunity.

When I arrive there I shall have a check for the $550 and shall turn it over to you at once.

Now for Gods sake make up your mind to go and meet me in Green River on the 9th or 10th of July.

Hoping this will be satisfactory and that you will be sure to go

Your friend.

Chas Russell

P.S. I know you would be a satisfactory partner and if I have to get some dam fool that I don't know anything about and who probably knows nothing about handling a boat I shall have a Hell of a time. So for Gods sake be sure to go.

C.R.

There is little indication of what Loper was thinking throughout these protracted negotiations. He may have jotted thoughts that no longer exist, as his 1914 journal entries from February 25 through March 4, and May 16 through June 23 are missing. But in what does exist—in spite of the fact he received the first of ten letters from Russell back in November—Loper made no mention in his journal of Russell or a river trip until June. We are left to wonder whether Loper was ever really planning to join Russell, or just never thought to write about it. Finally, on June 24, he journaled:

> Worked Water in A-M- and got an early start for Hite where I arrived in due time and I recd. a letter from Chas. Russell which caused me to decide to make the trip through Grand Canyon so I made arrangements with F.E. Butler to take care of my place untill I could go out and get a man to stay and take care of the place untill fall.

Loper finally made his decision—he would go with Russell. In the following week, Loper rode out toward Hanksville and hired Clifford McCall to run the ranch for a few months. Returning to Red Canyon he finished staking claims, retorting his gold, and left Red Canyon for Green River on July 2. He rode C.A. Gibbons's horse as far as Hanksville, where he had borrowed it the week before, then walked the remaining sixty miles across the San Rafael Desert to Green River—a god-awful walk any time of year, but utterly brutal in July.

Meanwhile Russell's machinations were rippling into the broader river community, as Loper leaked word to Ellsworth Kolb. On July 21 Kolb wrote river pioneer Julius Stone.

> It looks as if Loper and Russell will make the trip again to get motion pictures. Loper sent me some highly edifying correspondence from R (rather amusing letters they are) in which he pays his respect to us in no unstinted terms. L asked us not to give the snap away but thought we should know something about it.
>
> Among other things he says that any man who states he ran the Hance Rapid … was a liar. It couldn't be done. Also he has it on good authority that we portaged 150 rapids and of course failed to get pictures.…
>
> Meanwhile we have to keep our shirt on but perhaps we will show him a trick or two on the pictures.

Stone responded by return post:

> I met Loper below Trachyte Creek in Glen Canyon and from what he had to say about Russell at that time I did not suppose that he would

> ever wish to hitch up with him for another trip. I haven't had the luck to run across Russell anywhere but judging from the information that has reached me from several sources I would imagine that he is a good deal of an egotist as well as a sore head and a little bit of the same complexion as Stanton, that is, ready to question the accuracy or resent the achievement of anyone in connection with the Colorado River.

Stone could speak with knowledge of Stanton, having lost thousands of dollars in Stanton's ill-fated Glen Canyon dredging scheme. The two men knew one another well. Stanton, licking the wounds of his second great defeat—the first being the railroad he hoped to build through Grand Canyon—returned to the East and was engaged in a third great work. He was writing his masterpiece—a voluminous account of the history of the Colorado River. He had tracked down survivors of Powell's 1869 expedition, and interviewed James White, alleged to have floated through Grand Canyon two years prior to Powell. Stanton worked his material into a shrill dismissal of both White and Powell—making Stanton himself the first respectable person to traverse the Colorado. As yet though, he had not found a publisher.

History is told by the survivors, and Stanton, Stone, Russell, Kolb, and Loper were, even at this early date, bandying their own opinions and renditions of the Colorado's long saga. But first Loper and Russell had some more history to make. #

35 Surrender

"BERT CUSSED Russell all over the place," Marston wrote Frank Dodge in October 1949:

> I finally dug up Monett in Bakersfield and proved that Loper's stories were false. I never gave this to the public but I questioned Loper enuf so he knew that I knew and that he'd better not give me any more hokum. But he dug up another story and I just laughed.

Of the many tales told about Bert Loper, this one, repeated often by Dock Marston in one form or another, is worth investigating. According to Marston, Loper had for years been hurling vitriol at Russell for leaving him behind, and Marston's finding of Monett to straighten out the story drove Loper to surrender. In reality, the story unfolded this way:

"I am sure it will interest you to know," wrote Marston to Loper in September 1948, "that I have found your old friend Ed Monett." Monett had vanished from history after he and Russell reached Needles forty years earlier. Now the indefatigable Marston had tracked him down on a naval base in the middle of the Mojave Desert. Marston planned to visit him, and asked Loper if he had any questions. With Russell long dead, Loper had been, up until this point, the only eyewitness to the 1907 expedition. Marston was eager for another man's recollection. "I am most anxious to get his story ..." In terms of primary sources for early river trips, Marston felt he'd struck gold again. "Did I tell you I found Monett?" Marston asked Loper, six days after the previous query. Twelve days later he wrote, "I am planning to go see Monett soon."

Loper was not as thrilled about Monett as Marston was, having had a disagreeable ending to their previous relationship. In a 1940 essay, Loper had written of Monett, "While I never liked him much, I never disliked him." On September 16 Loper responded, telling Marston of the argument between him and Russell in Glen Canyon, and adding, "I do not know what Monett's attitude to-ward me is but I will say that I always found him a nice clean boy."

In the same letter, Loper offered up another bit of information: "I have a package of old letters from Russell but they are locked up in a safety box in walkers bank but they only pertained to our 1914 trip."

Marston immediately jumped on the offer of new material: "I'm going to ask a special favor of you and that is to have the opportunity to study the batch of letters you have locked up in Salt Lake and pertaining to the Russell 1914 trip."

That would have to wait until Loper made a trip to Salt Lake. Meanwhile he wrote back, "As I told you in my last letter I do not know just how Monett rates me but ... if he has an adverse feeling towards me that will be O.K. too but he was always a nice boy as far as our acquaintance went."

In early November Loper made a trip north: "I was in the Lake last week and got those letters out of the safety and am sending them on to you but you will have to separate them but you—if you are an expert on hand writing—make something out of them."

Marston responded: "I am delighted to have the chance to study the Russell letters which you so kindly sent me. I return them to you together with carbon copies which it may help you to have available in your files."

A week later Marston had his long anticipated interview with Monett. Although the interview focused primarily on rapids and adventures, Monett did hint at the argument between Loper and Russell in Glen Canyon. But about Loper, Monett had little ill to say. Marston soon reported to Loper:

> We had a very interesting session with Monett.... He had nothing but the highest praise for you. Since I know you are a human being and not a god, I can hardly believe that you are quite up to what he says about you.

All seemed well, then, between Loper and Monett. In February 1949 Marston wrote Monett: "It may interest you to know that [Loper] is now 80 years of age and is planning to run a boat thru the Grand Canyon this year."

Monett responded amiably, "I would like to see Bert Loper and have a talk with him. Tell him I wish him luck but don't envy him the trip.... I expect to do some Prospecting this Spring in Butte County.... Tell Bert he is welcome to go along."

The next correspondence between any of the three men was in August, a month after Loper had sunk beneath the Colorado's waves. Marston wrote Monett: "Bert Loper is gone. He went the way he wanted to go. He wanted to take one last crack at the Grand Canyon."

And Monett responded, "No one likes to admit he is growing old and Bert Loper was no exception."

The story, as portrayed in correspondence, shows Marston informing Loper that he had located Monett. Loper was not too sure if Monett would have favorable memories of him, but sent good tidings and received them in return. It also indicates Loper voluntarily told Marston of the 1914 Russell letters after he had heard of Monett's resurfacing—but there seems to be no connection between the two topics. No cause, no effect. Loper was more than happy to send the letters.

Yet somehow, by Marston's reasoning, there was indeed a connection. A big one. There had been a battle of wills between Loper and Marston. Marston's finding of Monett was the death blow, Loper's release of the Russell letters his surrender. If so, it was an odd victory—Monett never really said anything all that incriminating about Loper, especially before Loper died. And an odd surrender: the letters from Russell reveal little more than Russell's frustration with Loper's indecision on whether or not to join the 1914 trip. But as the years passed and Marston's impressions of Loper continued to decline, the Russell Letters Incident grew in magnitude. Even a quarter century later Marston still clung to his victory. In 1973 he wrote to Barbara Ekker:

> The life story of Bert shows an amazing louse and it is one of the great credits to the institution of marriage that his tie with Rachel made a rather decent man of him. He continued to be very dramatic in his charges against Russell but surrendered completely when he learned that the record was in my hands. #

36 Ross Wheeler

If you want to lose a man, let him think he is better than that river.
BERT LOPER, May 1949, Marston notes.

RUSSELL WAS AN accomplished scholar in the Spanish language also a good miner so after he finished his trip through the Grand Canyon he secured a position with the Hearst-Hagin Mining Co. in old Mexico and put in 5 years there and he had a great knack of saving money so he came out with about all that he had made during those years and it was then that he conceived the idea of photographing the Canyon with moving pictures—he told me he could get Monett but that Monett would never be a rough water boatman so he got me to go with him.

So he and I met in Greenriver the first part of July and proceeded to get our outfit arranged and it was then that I soon found that I had a different Russell to contend with for he absolutely would not help in any way and as a matter of course there were quarrels between us—I am mentioning this at this time in view of what is to follow.

The equipment was of Russell's choosing and was a very incomplete one—the boats were Mullins steel pleasure boats and only 12 inches deep and I predicted failure before we started, and besides the cover had to be put on by us and as I said before Russell would not help so therefore the job of covering was a very incomplete one.

Russell had two movie cameras and 20,000 feet of standard film and I think we lost about a mile of it in Cataract Canyon and outside the boats he had a very good outfit but as the boats should have been the foundation of the expedition that is where the equipment was not what it should have been.

Mullins was a leader in the boat business. Their sixteen-foot Sultan, which appears to be the model Russell selected, "is modeled on perfect lines and will make an admirable boat for family use where a good capacity is required; the best boat for children as it is roomy and very steady and with ordinary care it should last a lifetime. It is easy to row. It will appeal to summer resorters on account of its durability, comfort and safety." The Mullins boat was molded in one piece, avoiding the troublesome seams the Michigan Steel Boats had so plagued them with in 1907. But just as with the earlier boats, Russell was reading hyperbole meant for pleasure boating on a placid lake and projecting it into the rapids of the Colorado.

> We finally got started and so did the summer rains for by the time we reached the head of Cataract Canyon we had water galore and soon found out that our boats were inadequate—but I started out to tell about Russell more than the outfit or our trip through the Cataract.
>
> I have spoken of the change in Russell—as we were coming down the river and I might have been about 75 yards in advance I thought I heard someone talking so I eased down on my rowing and it was Russell and while I could not hear all that he said I could tell by what I did understand and by the tone of his voice that he was fighting someone so in the P.M. I again heard him going over the same talk that he made in the forenoon and this time I could hear most of the words he used and the next day it was the same both in the morning and again in the afternoon so in the course of time I memorized the entire talk and while my name was not mentioned I was quite positive that it was me that he was fighting and our first night in the Cataract we made our camp on the left bank of the river and the camp fire was between us and in the night I was awakened and Russell was sitting up in bed and going at it again and when one takes into consideration that we were 120 miles from a human being it was just a little creepy but the worst was still to come.

The men had little trouble making the first 120 miles of flatwater from Green River to the confluence of the Green and Grand. But the Grand was also full with summer rain, mud and driftwood—river gage records at Green River and Cisco indicate a combined level around 25–30,000 CFS (cubic feet per second)—a very challenging flow for a small rigid boat with almost no freeboard, and more than twice what Loper recalled seeing in 1907.

When we entered the Cataracts, of course, naturally we thought we knew the river, to a certain extent; but we didn't.... There was rapids that was mild affairs in 1907 that was ragers in 1914. Other rapids that was bad in 1907 that had entirely disappeared in 1914. In No. 4 I really believe that the waves was twenty feet high. I made this calculation because my boat was sixteen feet long; I had that to go by; my boat would be clear down in the troughs....

No. 4 had the very biggest waves I ever ran and all a man had to do was to take the -V- and ride those big waves and there was no trouble, but it was here that I began to think that Russell was losing his "NIP" for instead of taking the big water he pulled out to one side and took what we call short water—that is instead of riding 20 foot waves he took six or seven foot ones and in doing so he would invariably water log for our hatch cover would not keep the water out so therefore we would waterlog and as the containers were not water tight either we lost plenty film.

To explain a rapid, as a rule a rapid draws down in a long smooth stretch of water in the form of a -V-. At the end of that -V- is where the wave starts; they are the biggest at the end of the -V-. You can cut across the line of the -V-, probably, and get into short waves four or five feet high.

If your boat is sixteen feet long and your waves five feet high and ten feet apart, your boat is up on one wave when you hit another wave, so being up on this wave will naturally make you get under in the next wave; that is what smothers you. If you have got waves eight feet high and sixteen feet apart, your boat will ride them all without taking any water. Those waves twenty feet high in No. 4, I never took a quart of water.

Mr. Russell got in the habit of cutting across those -V- lines and getting into the five-foot waves, which smothered his boat; it got so he was water logged in pretty near every rapid he went over. Russell's boat was logged because he was afraid of the big waves. I don't mean to say he didn't have as much nerve as I did; just poor judgment, maybe, something like that. We lost five thousand feet of picture film, anyway, by him doing that.

We continued on down some twenty miles, and one day at noon he was water logged good while getting his boat out of the current; when he did his boat was absolutely full of water, so we took all of his stuff out and spread it on the bank to dry, and that was at noon. After noon we took a walk down the river, and between a quarter and a half a mile below where we was camped there was a jog in the river, and right there is where the big drop starts; that is where the real water was.

The next morning when we loaded up and started out, my boat was down maybe fifty yards below his; I set the camera at the edge of the water, a long rapid; he started through; I caught his picture as he came through.

There was a little point down here I could see he was trying to pull out of the current when he passed the camera; when he passed this point I became anxious about him; I saw him try to pull out, and he couldn't; and of course the bank of the river was a jumbled mass of huge boulders, anywhere from five foot square up to twenty foot square; it was hard getting over there.

When I got up and could look down the river I could see no Russell, boat, or anything.

I used all the speed I could, and went down that river and passed this jog and in going along there was a little spit of sand; when I started across there I seen fresh tracks, with water drops all around the footprints.

I looked ahead and there was Russell, going down the river. I hurried up.

I caught up with him. I said "What has happened?"

He said, "My boat went out from under me."

We spent two days going up and down the river trying to get some clue or sight of his boat—there was so much in the boat. We couldn't. Then, on the third day I cooked quite a sack of biscuits, and we took a pair of oars and a hammer, and started up the river. We was on the east side; we had to cross to the west side.

By the way, my boat was tied along that rapid. There is a side wash to those big rapids; every time the wash would come up, it would throw a little water in my boat. Incidentally, it would carry a little sand along with it, so my boat became full of sand, and sunk, and I tried to get Russell to help me get it out.

He wouldn't turn his hand.

Loper later described the sudden sinking of Russell's boat, explaining that the tie chain caught in the rocks, and dragged the boat to the bottom. Although Russell's brother years later claimed dragging a chain was Loper's idea to slow the boat down, there is never any factual indication that Loper or Russell conceived such an insane idea. Loper indicated Russell used a chain for a bowline, and that it washed overboard in the rapids, causing the accident. He added that upon returning to his own sunken boat, he bailed it out and salvaged the gear. When Russell refused to help extract the boat, Loper abandoned it and it swamped again.

> You know, when we started back up the river we stopped at the big drift and carried lumber down out of the drift and made a raft. He was to use an oar on one end and I was to use an oar on the other end, and we could go across nicely.
>
> When I pushed off into that river he turned white as a piece of paper. He had his camera with him, and this sack of biscuits. He sat there. I had to do the best I could.
>
> The reason we had to cross—one reason was because we became lodged on this side and had to walk out. You can walk out on one side or the other of the river clear through Cataract Canyon with one exception, that is just below the mouth of Dark Canyon.
>
> Anyway, I finally got the raft within about six feet of the bank, and Mr. Russell gave a mighty jump and landed all right, but in doing that he kicked that raft, started it back out in the river again. I had to pile off and get to the shore as best I could.
>
> We got up to Spanish Bottom that night about dark. We had no bed, and all the food we had was a sack of biscuits; it didn't rain, it poured all night.
>
> The next morning we started to climb out. I didn't know it at the time but Mr. Russell was becoming mentally deranged. It was quite a problem to get out of there. When we started to climb out—there was a place near the top there were trails kind of forked—I told Mr. Russell, "You go this way, I will go this way." I says, "Don't go far, we don't want to lose sight of each other."
>
> I went up my trail until I came to where there was no more trail, and I went back; I began to shout for Russell; I spent quite a while trying to locate him. No answer.
>
> Two people out that way, one hundred miles from a living soul, naturally becomes a little anxious in a case of that kind.

> I walked around a big rock, and there sat Mr. Russell. It was aggravating.
>
> When we climbed out, we didn't know where we were going; I had never been over there. We looked up towards Greenriver, which we knew was one hundred and twenty miles away; we could see it was box canyons; we knew we would have to head for one of them; didn't know anything about the water. I had heard the sheepmen talk about "under the ledge [a rimrock route paralleling the river]," so I told Russell it ought not to be over sixty or seventy miles to Hite, and I had two horses there. "If we can get there, we can ride out."
>
> So we made the trip in two days, got there at eleven o'clock at night of the second day, waded the Dirty Devil and got there at eleven o'clock.

Elwyn Blake, in a later account of Loper and Russell's ordeal, added, "When the two finally staggered into Hite, their feet were in ribbons of bloody pulp. The miners put them to bed and fed them, after cutting away their useless shoe uppers."

That would be enough to end the proposition for most folks. But Loper and Russell decided to continue. After a short recovery, Loper went down to Red Canyon to check on his ranch and get his horses. He returned to Hite, and the two men rode out to Green River.

✣ ✣ ✣

"Emery has just sent me a clipping from the *Green River Dispatch* telling of Russell's and Loper's loss of boats," wrote Ellsworth Kolb to Julius Stone in August, 1914:

> I'm sorry for Loper's discouragements but can't say that I sympathize with his partner after his bombastic remarks about their boats, etc. I would dislike being in Loper's place, making a trip with a man that I had no respect for and no use for. Loper says he is engaged at present in building new boats. He stated before that he would use a flat-bottomed steel boat.... Between the European War and the fighting on the Colorado it is a merry world.

"You and I agree exactly about Loper," replied Stone:

> I met him in Glen Canyon and we had quite a little visit which resulted in my forming a rather favorable opinion of him and not so favorable of Russell. This together with his insufferable egotism has only accentuated my poor opinion. He and Stanton seem to have been bitten with the same bug.

Loper, justified in his dim opinion of Russell's Mullins boats, now got his chance to design his own craft. On August 10 he arrived in Price, Utah, and hired George Meiss, with whom he had worked on the Colorado during the icy winter of 1911-12, to help construct two steel boats of the Galloway style. Loper continued on to Salt Lake City to purchase the steel, agreeing to meet Meiss in Green River to assemble the craft.

> WILL FACE DEATH TO SECURE FILMS
>
> Bert Loper with "Movie" Outfit Will Shoot Rapids of Colorado River. Many Dangers Ahead. Loses Equipment on First Attempt, but, Undaunted, Will Try Again.

While in Salt Lake, Loper was interviewed for an extensive newspaper story. He told of their grand plan to make more than a thousand still pictures and four miles of movie film, much of which had already been sold to the Santa Fe and Rio Grande Railroads. He recounted Russell's wreck as well, with no mention of a chain sinking the boat, nor of Russell's increasing madness:

> [He] had to enter the last section of the rapid with his boat more than half filled with water. In the very middle of it his boat capsized and it looked to me as if I would have to make the rest of the trip alone, for I saw little chance of Russell getting out of the river alive. He managed, however, to cling to the boat, which did not immediately sink because of the air chambers, until he had passed through the most dangerous part of the water.
>
> The boat had struck a rock which stove in the fore air chamber and it sank just as Russell reached the outer water.... The boat contained some films and nearly all of our food supply, making it impossible to proceed down the river without replenishing our stock....
>
> While the loss of part of our outfit is quite an inconvenience to us, it

really means nothing more than a loss of time. The money value of the lost outfit was about $800.

On September 16, Ellsworth Kolb passed through Green River and wrote Stone once more:

> I was very much surprised to find Loper and Russell still here. I was warmly welcomed by the former and have derived considerable amusement out of the embarrassment and nervousness of the latter. There is so much antipathy between the two for each other that I can't see how one can predict a successful expedition. Loper is very anxious, naturally, to make the trip and is putting up with a lot to make it. He is running the building of the boat. It is designed much on the style you furnished, a little less than 16 ft long, 48 in. wide, a wider stern with a sharp slope underneath instead of square, and with a four-inch rake from the center to the ends. It is constructed of 18 gauge iron sheet, galvanized, with 1 in. angle iron ribs, riveted thoroughly from end to end.... It looks strong enough to go to sea.

George Meiss returned to Price on September 27, the *Eastern Utah Advocate* reporting, "The new boat is made of steel sheeting and there are four thousand rivets in it. Owing to a shortage of funds, however, the trip planned by Loper and Russell has been deferred to a future date."

The rancor that had been building between Loper and Russell had finally overflowed. In 1949, less than a week before his death, Loper told it this way:

> I had gotten a bad deal in 1907 so I insisted on having the money in 1914. Russell advanced me the $550 which was my share ... I told him I could not leave Glen Canyon without it. The first proceeds from the picture was to go to Russell to pay back the $550 he advanced.
>
> When we cracked up in Cataract I agreed to get the stuff from ZCMI [Zions Cooperative Mercantile Institution—the Mormon department store] and build a new boat, keep a record of costs, and Russell would pay. I bought material and paid a man four dollars per day to help build the boat. When it was finished, Russell wanted the costs to come out of the $550.

It was an argument that both men had a good case for, and neither chose to lose. Russell, who had bankrolled the trip, felt the new boat was his. Loper, on the other hand, felt the $550 advance was his to keep. After all, it was Russell who had chosen the low-sided, frail Mullins boats, and it was Russell who had sunk his own boat and refused to help rescue Loper's. And without Loper to guide him out of the canyonlands, Russell might well have perished. So until Russell paid for the new boat, it was Loper's. Plans for a second new boat evaporated amid the bile.

With the trip on hold, Loper accepted an offer from the Reclamation Bureau, working on a drill rig at the confluence of the Green and Grand. He put "his" new boat under lock and key, only to be released if Russell deposited its cost in the bank. Russell apparently headed to Salt Lake City, perhaps to raise additional funds. Before he left he asked Loper if he was still going on the river trip. Loper told him he would be at the confluence, "ready and waiting."

In early July, John F. Richardson of the United States Reclamation Service had come to Green River to "commence the survey of the Green, Grand, and Colorado rivers with a view to determining the feasibility of building detaining dams ... to control the floodwaters ... that said waters may be distributed for irrigation and navigation.... Then if ... the plan is feasible, locks will be installed throughout the cataracts of the Colorado, in order that boats may pass them in safety." Locks!

By mid-September Richardson had an eight-man crew working a Sullivan Diamond drill, afloat on a barge at the confluence, drilling for bedrock to determine the feasibility of a dam. When a vacancy opened on the crew, Loper signed on. To get there, Loper caught a freight wagon to Tom Wimmer's ranch, twenty-three miles downriver, and boarded Wimmer's launch *Marguerite* for the hundred-mile trip to the confluence.

Wimmer had one of the few viable motorized boats for traveling the Green. The *Marguerite*, built by his neighbor Edwin T. Wolverton, was thirty-three feet long and powered at that time by a sternwheel. It drafted little water and carried most of its load by towing a barge downstream, then pushing it back up. Wimmer had been downriver to the confluence many times and occasionally up the Grand to Moab. This job was one of the few times he was able to do it for pay. Wimmer had learned his boating from the boatright Wolverton, and from another local pilot, Roswell "Ross" Wheeler.

Wheeler plays a significant but mysterious role in the Loper/Russell saga: the new metal boat Loper and Meiss had just finished constructing, was at some point named the *Ross Wheeler.* Little is known of Wheeler's role in Loper's life, however, Loper saying in later years, "While I was acquainted with him I am rather hazy on his history."

But Wheeler did have a long history on the Green River. Ross Wheeler and his brothers Arthur and Wallace, all bachelors from New York, squatted and began farming in 1884 at what would later be the Wimmer Ranch. When his two brothers headed north to the Yukon around 1898, Ross moved up to Little Valley, about eight miles below Green River. He was a civil engineer by training, worked as a railroad engineer, a stream gager, and achieved modest acclaim as a river pilot, a 1910 issue of *Recreation* magazine saying:

> A picturesque character of the Green river region is Captain Ross Wheeler, citizen of the prairie. He has piloted various parties down the river, and has navigated it alone on many occasions. He promises to become as widely famed as Captain Hance of the Bright Angel trail, who claims to have 'dug out' the Grand Canyon of Arizona. Captain Wheeler knows every foot of the Green river region and holds that it is the greatest of all hunting grounds.

Wheeler's life ended on a suspect note, when his charred body was found in the burnt ruins of his cabin in September, 1920. "Although preferring to be alone most of the time & strangely discountenancing the presence of a single living thing in the way of a dog or other pet," wrote the *Emery County Progress,* "he was not supposed to have an enemy in the world and it is hard to account for the murder, if this theory is correct."

Russell, meanwhile, was fed up with Loper and decided to replace him. In Salt Lake City he hired August Tadje, an actor with some history of film work. In Green River, Russell added William Reeder, a prospector and oilman who had spent a good deal of time on the river, having made the trip to the confluence and back, and up the Grand River to Moab with Ross Wheeler a decade earlier.

Russell was determined to get the *Ross Wheeler* out of hock. According to Loper, Russell tried "every trick of an insane mind to get the boat without paying for it but he had to come through with the money." Russell, Tadje, and Reeder piled into the small craft with all their duffel and camera gear and headed downriver for Cataract Canyon. On the way, they camped a day or two with Ross Wheeler himself—perhaps it was then that the boat was named.

Loper wrote to Ellsworth Kolb on December 2:

> Dear friend,
>
> I have just returned to Hite and after my sojourn out in the world it does not look very good to me.
>
> I suppose you heard about Russell and I having a split. I went down to the junction of the Grand and Green and worked a little over a month for the Government and while I was there Russell came along and we got in a fight and I had the satisfaction of giving him a good beating.

NAU.PH.97.46.114.179

Martin Litton

Ross Wheeler

The *Ross Wheeler* in Grand Canyon, 1955

> He got two men to take my place one an Expert Photographer by the name of Tadje from The Youths Photo Play Co. of Salt Lake and the other man is W.H. Reeder & they went on down with the boat I made in Greenriver, and when they came to where I had left the boat I started with, they raised it and fixed it up and started on and lost it in the very next Rapid, so they had to come on through with the one Boat and when they reached Hite Tadje and Reeder went back to Salt Lake after another Boat and Russell is waiting here at Hite for them. They have been gone over a month now and no word of them yet. It looks like a very late trip for them and that means lots of ice cold water and very poor light.

The scene at the confluence had been bad. Loper, on seeing three men crowded aboard the *Ross Wheeler*, knew he had been replaced. Russell had brought a promissory note for Loper to sign pledging to repay the $550 Russell fronted him. Loper refused, perhaps figuring the work he'd done thus far was worth all that and more. Russell called him an S.O.B. " … in the mix up he called me a name that meant fight so that is what we done."

"Bert was never a gunman," recalled Elwyn Blake. "He used his fists, although I have known him to even the odds with a billiard cue." It was quite a fight, by most accounts, Tadje recalling that, "They had to be separated by men in the surveying party." Russell, Tadje, and Reeder reboarded the *Ross Wheeler* and headed downriver into Cataract Canyon and thence to Hite.

An eight-foot rise in the river tore loose the drill rig in early November, and Richardson elected to halt operations for the year. Although they had sunk the casing 125 feet into the riverbed, they had yet to hit bedrock. Piling the equipment on the barges they spent five days pushing the entire operation back up the Green with the launch *Marguerite* and another motorboat. "We was on sandbars quite frequently," recalled Loper. "I remember one time I was on the pilot wheel, and I pretty near stood everything on their heads; I run on to a sandbar where the channel crossed, and made a right-angle turn."

They plowed on upriver to Wimmer's ranch, offloaded the barges and gear to be hauled overland, then chugged the remaining twenty miles upstream to Green River in the *Marguerite*. From there Loper caught a freight team to Hanksville, where he picked up his horse team and returned to Hite.

Launch *Marguerite* September 1914

"Things are very dull here and if I can dispose of my holdings here I will try something else," Loper continued in his letter to Kolb. "We have had no bad weather yet but it is getting the time now for it to come any time."

Hite must have seemed an especially small place with both Loper and Russell there, though neither mentioned it. After a month or so in Salt Lake City, Tadje returned in early December with a wretched new boat. "I remember how disappointed I was when the boat was ready," recalled Tadje. "It was altogether the wrong construction, I do not know what a boat builder would call it. It was built perfectly flat instead of either stern or bow being raised somewhat from the water level. It made it extremely difficult to maneuver this boat in the water." They christened the thing the *Titanic II*. Reeder had jumped ship during the interim—"He was crazy," recalled Reeder of Russell, "Was walking around at night." Tadje replaced Reeder with his own brother-in-law, Goddard Quist.

No one recorded any parting shots between Loper and Russell's crew as they left Hite. The men drifted into Glen Canyon, headed for Needles.

Loper had once again lost his chance to go through Grand Canyon. The first time may have been no fault of either party. This time both parties contributed their cantankerousness to the separation. Loper's infuriating indecision and insistence on pay at the beginning gave Russell fuel for bitterness. Russell's bizarre and combative behavior and final firing of Loper fostered aggravation in return.

After separating with Loper on the first trip, Russell and Monett had gone on to national acclaim. This time, however, it was not to be. Russell's 1907 trip was calamitous; the 1914 trip was catastrophic. If the first trip was like a Laurel and Hardy show, the latter was Keystone Cops. They had sunk both Mullins boats before they reached Hite. Then it got worse. The rest of the voyage warrants summarizing before returning to Loper.

After an uneventful voyage through Glen Canyon, Russell, Tadje, and Quist spent several days at Lee's Ferry re-outfitting before entering Marble Canyon. Camped at the foot of the first major rapid, Badger Creek, they found themselves frozen into an icy river. They hiked out and waited three months for the river to thaw. They returned around March and continued to Bright Angel Creek, running some rapids, lining others, getting stuck on rocks midriver, but surviving. "There was something wrong with Russell," recalled Quist. "He would always sing, 'Put on your Old Grey Bonnet'—just the first line. Made me nervous."

At Bright Angel they climbed to the rim and spent three weeks drumming up publicity before returning to the river. By this time Quist had quit the trip, to be replaced by another friend of Tadje's, Jake Jeffs. Russell put Jeffs in charge of the *Titanic II* for the shortest career of a boatman on record. Jeffs pulled into the river, got caught in an eddy, and became hysterical. Tadje and Russell rescued him and they climbed back to the rim. Jeffs left, to be replaced by a cameraman named Leslie Clement.

Back at the river, their first move was to line the *Titanic II* down to a better spot for loading, but a miscommunication between Tadje and Russell ended up with the boat escaping and vanishing around the bend. They chased it in the *Ross Wheeler* for a mile or two but gave up. They parked and pulled the boat high on shore, then climbed back to the rim to order another boat from St. Louis. Russell by this time had exhausted his bank accounts to the tune of six thousand dollars, recalled his brother John, who then loaned him another two thousand.

Weeks later the new boat, about which little is known, arrived at the South Rim. The men fashioned a cradle and axle for it and spent two days working it down the Bright Angel Trail to the river. Upon floating down to the *Ross Wheeler* they found a falling rock had blasted through its bow, leaving melon-sized holes. It was back to the rim for tin and rivets, and back to the river for extensive repairs. Finally they departed once more.

"We hadn't gone but two or three rapids when this boat we had just added to our equipment was lodged in the river," recalled Tadje of their arrival at Crystal Creek. "Mr. Clement being at the oars, swam to shore." Back to the rim. This time, however, they were far from a trail. They climbed up to the Tonto Platform, about 1500 feet above the river, where a faint trail runs up and down river. Clement wanted to continue straight up the Slate Creek drainage to the rim; Russell insisted on traversing upriver on the Tonto to the Boucher Trail and climbing out from there. Neither could be dissuaded and each set off in his own direction, leaving Tadje in the middle. He chose to follow Clement. The two climbed, scraped, scrambled, and chimneyed to the rim, dehydrated and half starved, and wandered through the forest until they found, late at night, a ranger's cabin. The following day they went on to W.W. Bass's cabin where they waited for Russell to appear, Bass all the while insinuating Russell was the victim of foul play. But finally, late that evening, recalled Tadje, "Russell walked in with his coat buttoned tightly around him and his right hand in the bosom of the coat and exclaimed, 'I have been lost.' It was difficult to get another word out of him and it was clearly discernible that his mind was affected."

They returned to the South Rim for supplies, then back down the Boucher Trail and across the Tonto. They fashioned a Spanish windlass out of driftwood and rope and after several attempts, "were able to finally rescue the boat by rolling it over and over side ways, and by this action we lost or ruined all our cameras and the biggest portion of our film, which were soaked and consequently destroyed." Apparently the boat was not salvageable. Another account has the boat bailed out, reloaded, relaunched, and instantaneously and irretrievably sunk again in the very same spot.

The dispirited men continued downriver in the *Ross Wheeler*. At the foot of the Bass Trail, huddled in a tent in the pouring rain, they "decided to unpack our boat of what little food was left to take with us up the trail." They abandoned the *Ross Wheeler*, the sole survivor of five otherwise sunken boats, and climbed out. Russell's great film expedition was finished. What few clips remain are almost slapstick in the portrayal of their calamitous trip.

Charles Russell's tale ends on a sad note. His ranch house burned, taking with it all of his journals and writings, and most of his film. The chirimoya plantation was a bust. Around 1919 Russell was institutionalized, and died in 1926. His brother attributed the mental disorder to a blow on the head, "in the mines." His sister had a more dramatic, if less supported view of the cause:

> When he made, or tried to make, the second trip … the man with him became so angry because he would not abandon the trip that he hit him over the head and left him for dead. How long he lay there he does not know but he finally came to and got help. From that time on he began to lose his mental faculties and became worse from year to year.

With his neighbor and intermittent friend Cass Hite gone, and with his prospects at Red Canyon hovering near subsistence level, Loper's interest in Glen Canyon continued to wane. Having missed another chance to run Grand Canyon could not have helped his morale. Loper found someone to caretake the ranch that winter and went out to work in Hanksville.

The following spring Bert Seaboldt and a man named Evans hired Loper to run a boat back and forth between Hite and Seaboldt's holdings at Good Hope Bar seventeen miles downriver. That lasted until May, at which point Loper went out to Green River, bought supplies, and returned to Red Canyon. He worked the placer there well into August but his heart was no longer in it. So when Lon Turner, who had been working California Bar nineteen miles downriver, offered to trade claims, Loper jumped at it. "Bert Loper came up from the Colorado river after supplies," reported the *Eastern Utah Advocate* on September 17, "returning with a load yesterday morning. Bert has traded for other placer properties down there and has splendid prospects."

Not that splendid. The change in river scenery held little immediate lure. Rather than move downstream that fall, Loper returned to

Hanksville to run freight. His grand experiment in self-sufficiency had run its course. Loper could no longer deny it.

> The reason I held on as long as I did was the hopes that in some way I could forever get away from the wage system but after all the years and when Cass passed on I felt so much more alone and I had made up my mind that my efforts to forever dodge the wage system was futile so I was ready to move so when Lon Turner came along and made an offer I immediately took it and started out on another venture. #

37 Brother John

In 1947, Dock Marston tracked down Charlie Russell's brother John in Phoenix, Arizona, and set about querying him.

> Before your brother made the trip with Bert Loper in 1914, your brother was required to put up all the money—his share and Bert's share. After their difficulty in Cataract Canyon, Bert refused to make any restitution. Did your brother ever discuss this with you?

After Loper's death, Marston intensified his interrogation. John Russell responded in suit:

> Bert Loper had no money to pay his portion of the expense of the river trip and brother Charles advanced Bert's portion and was never repaid. My brother advised me of this shortly after the trip and tried to get in touch with Loper without success.
>
> In addition to one of the boats, Loper got away with quite a little equipment my brother had paid for including a six-shooter my brother prized very highly.

John Russell seems to have been a bit muddled on which trip was which. Certainly Loper did not get away with a boat on the 1914 trip, nor any equipment, unless they carried it on their backs during their overland escape from Cataract Canyon. What Russell-funded boat or equipment Loper ended up with would more likely have come from the 1907 adventure—Loper used the *Arizona* for years.

Another confusing detail is that John Russell said Charles advanced Loper's share of the *expenses.* Certainly Russell advanced *all* the expenses, buying the boats, camera gear, film, food and so forth. But the $550 he advanced Loper seems not to have been for a "trip expense"—those Russell had paid directly—but more of a salary advance. All of Loper's share and salary, of course, was supposed to be amply repaid to Russell by the film proceeds—proceeds that would never come. Whether Loper earned his advance on the aborted Cataract trip remains a matter of opinion.

John Russell weighed in on the 1907 "Loper's delay" debate as well, adding some new grist:

> Brother Charles had provided him with expense money to wait for the shipment which was then over-due, and as it afterwards developed he spent the expense money and had to acquire other moneys to take out the shipment, which was the chief cause of delay. Not only my brother but old man Bass told me of Loper's spending moneys he was entrusted with and having to work to earn moneys to take out the shipment. I don't suppose Loper told this to you.

Curiouser and curiouser. Loper did take what little gold the men had accumulated back to Hite to sell to the mint, but no other funds were mentioned. The camera repairs were paid for, eventually, by check. Just what the "overdue shipment" was is hard to say. And Old Man Bass? William Wallace Bass lived on the South Rim of Grand Canyon and encountered Russell, Clement, and Tadje as they hiked out in 1914. But Bass never met Loper. In all, these sound like mixed and metamorphosed details of two thirty-year-old misadventures, with little in the way of factual grit. What shines through the confusion is Loper, once again, not pulling his fair share of financing. About that there seems little controversy. But about Bill Reeder, Russell was quite clear:

> Reeder made an agreement with my brother relative to the river trip and Charles advanced him the full amount. At Hite, Utah, he deserted my brother and refused to pay one single cent. I tried to have some correspondence with him but without success, he apparently was just a coward and a gyper. From all I was able to learn of Reeder he was afraid to make the river trip, and did not have the honesty to be fair with the man who had advanced him moneys.

According to Reeder, who freely admitted to welching, John Russell threatened to litigate. Reeder's response: "Go ahead and sue!" #

38 Sundry things

SUNDAY DEC 31-1916

After a lapse of two years and six months I again start to record events in this old Book and since the first day of July 1914 much has happened for on leaving the Red Canyon Ranch for Green River to go on an expedition down the Colo River which I never completed sundry things have happened. I traded the Red Canyon property for the California Bar (summer 1915) then went to Hanksville and put in the Winter of 1915 & 1916 freighting from Loa and I also found me a wife....

Bert Loper was forty-six years old when he quit Glen Canyon. He had spent the better part of eight years living on the Colorado River, trying to wrest a living from her shores. He had given it his damnedest, but it was not to be. It was time to try something else, even if it meant working for wages.

With no future plans he put in at Hanksville for the winter. He found work with his team of horses, hauling freight to Loa, the county seat, sixty-five miles to the west. The route followed the Fremont River much of the way, making one notable detour as it reached what is now Capitol Reef National Park. Instead of following the river through the gorge, which was prone to floods and quicksand, the route veered south up a sidestream called Capitol Gorge. This narrow sandstone slot was barely wide enough for a wagon—scrapes and scratches from the hubs and signatures of travelers are still visible—but at least it had a solid bottom and only flooded during storms. Once out of Capitol Gorge the route veered back north to rejoin the Fremont at Fruita, and follow it up to the settlement of Torrey—another in a string of Mormon settlements, its residents engaged in farming, ranching, and subduing the wilderness.

In those days, before the advent of radio, movies, or television, entertainment was self-created. Storytelling and singing were extremely popular. Loper was more than ready to reenter society and found his rich baritone in demand. Loper's nephew Bill Busenbark remembers one lovesick song that Bert used to sing—in fact he wondered if Loper himself wrote it. Although the song seemed to capture Bert's lonely life at Red Canyon, it was actually a popular tune around the turn of the century. Busenbark recalls the refrain:

There's a sigh of every breeze, and a sigh comes from the trees
And the meadowlark now croons a sadder lay
For the sunlight plays no more 'round my cheerless cabin door
Where the silv'ry Colorado wends its way

Pure Loper. The best time to sing, of course, was when the local fiddlers and dance callers would get together for a dance at a local schoolhouse or church. Folks would walk or ride into town from miles around and the festivities often ran well into the morning hours. Loper was always up for a party or a dance.

Whether Bert was singing or dancing one evening with the local Torrey folk cannot be known, but sometime that winter he met the love of his life, a twenty-two-year-old Scottish woman named Rachel Jamieson. How she came to be there is a bit of a story.

The Mormon Church had been actively shedding its more radical doctrines (polygamy, for example) since 1890, becoming a more mainstream religion. They continued to grow and expand rapidly. In addition to colonizing as much of the intermountain West as they could—enlarging the Kingdom of Zion with hundreds of small outposts like Torrey—they had begun sending missionaries around the world to convert gentiles to their faith. One such missionary, a Scottish miner named Robert Peden, returned to Torrey from his mission to Scotland and befriended John Busenbark.

Busenbark, whose father had crossed the Plains with Brigham Young and colonized some seven settlements in Zion, had recently moved to Torrey from the failed settlement of Giles, or Blue Valley, a few miles down the Fremont. Busenbark's wife had left the family for reasons no longer remembered, and John was struggling to raise his three children.

Peden, assessing Busenbark's situation, told him of a young widow he had met in Scotland, Maggie Jamieson. Maggie, her mother, her husband and siblings had converted to Mormonism. But before they could immigrate to Utah, Maggie's husband died, leaving her with two young children. Peden suggested that Busenbark sponsor Maggie's immigration, marry her, and combine families. After corresponding with her for some time, Busenbark did just that. Leaving her children with her mother in Scotland for the time being, Maggie sailed, railed, and horse-coached her way to Utah. She married John Busenbark in 1911. Fifty-two-year-old Busenbark was twice Maggie's age. Three years later the family had enough money to send for Maggie's children, mother, brother Scotty, and little sister Rachel. As Bill Busenbark tells it,

> And now Grandmother and Rachel and the rest of them start their migration into the United States in 1914 during the height of World War One, relegated to an old wooden ship, and to try to avoid the German submarines they went to the far North Sea and came down through the icebergs—more apt to get wiped out by an iceberg than they were a submarine, but both of 'em were high danger. And they came to Canada. World War One was still on, and Scotty would've been eligible for service, 'cause as soon as he hit the shore, they asked him, "What country do you pledge allegiance to?" And he said "This is my new country." So they gave him a uniform and sent him back to Europe.

The remainder of the family arrived in Torrey in December of 1914. John and Maggie Busenbark formally adopted each other's children and had already begun to have children of their own.

The contrast could not have been much sharper had the Jamiesons moved to the Kalahari Desert. In Scotland they had a fine home in Aberdeen, had servants, and were active in Scottish society. In Torrey they lived in rustic cabins, grew their own food, washed their own clothes, even made their own soap. Life was hand to mouth. The cowboys and ranchers of Torrey that comprised their new "society" spoke an English barely comprehensible to their thick Scottish brogue. That Maggie, or any of the rest of her family, did not bolt back to Scotland is a testament to their faith and commitment. The Busenbark family established a ranch in Grover, about seven miles south of town, while

Jamiesons arriving in Montreal: Mother Jamieson in black dress, lower right. Rachel adjacent

Rachel and her mother moved into the Busenbark's old cabin in Torrey. Bill Busenbark recalls the family legend of Rachel's courtship:

> Here's Bert down in Red Canyon you know, probably nostrils full of mine dust, and he picks up the scent of this Scotch lass and he makes his way up into the valley.... Bert was no slouch at singing. He could sing a beautiful ballad. And the people in those days liked to get together 'cause all they'd do is talk and then for entertainment they'd sing.
>
> Well so he's got up there and he's come to one of their town parties, and I don't know what he mighta looked like, if he had a beard or what, I don't know. I never heard Rachel say and I never heard mother say, but they prevailed upon him to sing. And I guess that something came together there, cause it wasn't too long after then until Bert and Rachel were singing love songs. Bert and Rachel really hit it off. And Bert is making preparations ... they're going to get married, and gonna take Rachel back down with him.
>
> Now I don't know which came first, the announcement or the event, but I think it was the announcement ... and the townspeople were quite protective of each other and they're pretty upset at this rascal. He had some kind of a reputation anyway, you know. And he's not gonna take one of these fair maidens and run off to the deep canyons with her. They

Wedding picture 1916

were ready to deal right and properly with Bert if it was hangin'. So I guess Bert and Rachel musta had a pretty convincing presentation on their part, 'cause she was permitted to go with him. But not after a lot of 'em weeping and wailing.

There was a lot more romance in there. Jeez, I'll tell you, they were really in love, right from day one, I guess. Right to the end.

Long-time Torrey rancher Gary George recalls many old-time Mormons having a dim view of Loper. He was a man with few possessions, little stability, and no allegiance to the Church. Not a man to be trusted. But Loper would not be denied. After what Rachel said was a four-month whirlwind romance, Bert and Rachel Loper were married in the county seat of Loa on April 29, 1916. Like her sister Maggie, Rachel had chosen a man twice her age—she was twenty-four, Bert nearly forty-seven. They soon headed back down to the Colorado to work placer claims.

> The summer of 1916 was put in on North Wash where we lived in a tent and put in untill about the last of Aug. then we went to Torrey and I rec'd a letter from E.L. Kolb wanting me to go on an expedition down the Grand and Gunnison Rivers and was gone nearly two months....

Loper had first met the Kolb brothers five years earlier when they stopped at Red Canyon on their great river expedition, and later visited with Ellsworth in Green River while building the *Ross Wheeler*. Since then Ellsworth had published his matter-of-fact account of the voyage, *Through the Grand Canyon from Wyoming to Mexico*. With their photographic business running strong, his book selling well, and the river in his blood, Ellsworth was ready for the next adventure. Having run the Green and Colorado Rivers with his brother, he now wished to run the other main fork of the Colorado, the Grand [upper Colorado] River. In addition Kolb planned to run the spectacular Black Canyon of the Gunnison, one of the Grand's tributaries. After a calamitous first attempt, Kolb's helper, cattleman John W. Shields, decided he preferred cattle to boats and left the expedition. Kolb decided he needed a real riverman and wrote Loper.

Kolb offered Loper a healthy wage for three weeks of boating. Although just four months married, Loper could not help but chose his first love, the river. He left in early September and Rachel began the first of a lifetime of vigils at home, while Bert went down the river. #

39 The spot where Bert is

"I JUST WANT to satisfy myself," Rachel Loper told the newspapers. With help from Don Harris, Rachel arranged to visit Bert's boat where it lay beneath a gnarled mesquite tree along the Colorado. In November of 1951, together with Tom and Blaine Busenbark and Bert's trip-mate Ralph Badger, Rachel drove south to the rim of Marble Canyon where a dam site survey camp was based. Alex Toth loaded them aboard the small cage and winched them a breath-taking 2,900 feet down to the river's edge. There project manager Bert Lucas met them in a small motorboat and drove them the mile-and-a-half downstream to where the *Grand Canyon* lay settling into the slope.

A year earlier Harry Aleson had come in by cable and removed Loper's oars, to be preserved for posterity, and his outboard motor, to recondition and sell for Rachel's benefit.

Rachel made plans to return. Back in Salt Lake City she had a bronze plaque cast. The following May, with Tom, Blaine, and Tom's wife Willmer, they returned to the river. Using mortar and native stone they built a small monument above the boat, capping it with the plaque:

IN MEMORY OF
BERT LOPER
BORN JULY 31, 1869
LOST IN MARBLE CANYON
JULY 8, 1949
THE GRAND OLD MAN OF THE COLORADO RIVER
"I BELONG TO THE WONDROUS WEST
AND THE WEST BELONGS TO ME."

And he did. Loper, the consummate Westerner, had become a permanent part of the landscape he loved.

As for herself, "I wish I knew the spot where Bert is," Rachel wrote to Margaret Marston, "there is where I would be." #

40 Bad water

MONTROSE, COLO., OCT. 27.—In a Montrose hospital today lie Ellsworth L. Kolb and Bert Loper, painfully injured after a second attempt to explore the unknown reaches of the Black canon of the Gunnison river. The two men spent ten days of almost unbelievable hardships in traversing eleven miles of the gorge and then, their boats demolished and their food and bedding swept away, they escaped starvation only by a climb, which took six hours, up a 3,200-foot granite wall in a blinding snowstorm.

For slapstick boating, Charlie Russell had nothing on Ellsworth Kolb. Kolb had begun his new venture with high hopes, allotting six weeks to boat the upper stretches of the Colorado basin. He had invited Julius Stone to join him along with a New York businessman named N.B. Stern. He had hired local cowboy John Shields to assist. On the morning of July 26, 1916, the men had assembled on the banks of the Gunnison River with two canvas canoes and a small rubber raft with an Indestructo trunk to float along supplies rather than portage.

Within minutes of their launch, the Indestructo had torn loose and careened out of sight. Kolb and Stone gave chase in their canvas boats, Kolb wrapping his boat around a boulder with a horrific crunch: "My craft had gone to pieces; canvass, boards and cargo were being spewed up on all sides." Stone floated coolly along behind his inverted boat. "He calmly surveyed both shores as he sped past; his spectacles were riding serenely on his nose." Stern leapt into the rapid to chase the trunk while Shields sprinted down the far shore—both in vain. They returned to town and rested a day, waiting for rain to pass.

They tried again, more cautious this time, lining the remaining canoe around rapids, but by the second night, with a badly mangled boat and failing spirits, they elected to quit for the time being, climb the 3,500 foot ridge out to cattle country, return to town, and order

NAU.PH.568.5859

Kolb Brothers

Team Indestructo: Left to right: Kolb, Stone and assistants

better boats. Stone and Stern returned to the East. Shields and Kolb, however, heard their Indestructo had been salvaged at the mouth of the Gunnison Tunnel. They hiked into the canyon to retrieve it. From there, Kolb clambered a few miles up the shore to their stashed gear, spent a day repairing the boat, and launched again. After working the boat off another midstream boulder, wrote Kolb:

> I leaped on top of the wreck, a canvass rag and a board kept afloat by four air-bags. Duffel bags, held by ropes, streamed out from the sides. The end on which I kneeled was two feet under water, the other end floated on top. I held to the gunwales, swinging my weight from side to side when threatened with a spill. Twice again I was marooned on rocks.... It rained in torrents.... I was chilled to the bone.

Kolb made it to the tunnel where Shields awaited, and they returned to town, bent on trying another stretch while the upper river dropped to a more conducive level. By this time, a Peterborough freight canoe had arrived. They decked it out with hatches at either end and installed a set of oarlocks. They put in below Black Canyon at Delta, Colorado, and rowed to the Grand River, then on downstream to the beginning of Westwater Canyon. Ranchmen convinced the two to portage the boat around to the foot of Westwater, telling them the water was so rough that, "the fish's brains are spattered on the walls." After hiking along the rim of Westwater, they reboarded the canoe and rowed to Moab.

On the hike through Westwater, however, Kolb had examined the rapids, the largest two being named "Double Pitch" and "Whirlpool," (now called "Funnel Falls" and "Skull.") "I imagined it could be run at a lower stage and expressed a determination to try it at some later time. Shortly after this trip Shields returned to his old employment."

It was now quite apparent to Kolb that he needed a real riverman as a helper, and he contacted Loper. He offered him one hundred dollars for three weeks' work, and five dollars a day after that. If his contract looked anything like the one Kolb wrote for Shields, it probably said something like, "I will not expect you to do impossible things, but will expect you to enlist for the entire trip the same as a soldier. I will not ask you to do anything I will not do myself and where I think you can follow.... I do not accept anybody's statement regarding impassable places...." On September 8 Loper telegrammed, "WILL START TOMORROW MORNING."

The stretch of river Kolb chose to assault this time was the upper Grand, just above Shoshone Falls. Loper wrote postcards home to Rachel—sometimes two a day—mostly stating that they were having a hard time getting downriver.

> 9-12-16 Dearie—just a card to let you know that we worked all day and got a few pictures, movies I mean. We did not cover very much of the River but hope to reach Glenwood tomorrow—
>
> 9-13-16 Little Wife—Just a note to let you know I am still alive.... I had a very hard day today.
>
> 9-14-16 Dear Rachel—I may be on the river about 3 weeks longer than we first thought.... We may be here for two or 3 days yet.
>
> 9-17-16 Dear Rachel—This is Sunday but we are going to work anyway—this is 9 days I have been here and we have not made over 5 miles on the River—it is awful slow taking moving pictures and I may come home with $200 instead of $100. We are living in the hotel and go up every morning in the Auto.
>
> 9-17-16 Dear Rachel—We worked hard today and did real well and should be to Glenwood to-morrow.... We had a fine day today and we are over the rough water and will have clear sailing to town.
>
> 9-18-16 Dear Rachel—We finished the River above here today and now

NAU.PH.568.5977

Kolb Brothers

Kolb at Shoshone Falls

will not take any more pictures untill we get to what is called West Water canyon which is in Utah then we will come back to Colorado and go thru the Black Canyon and I expect to be gone over a month yet and I surely do want to see my sweetheart—Lovingly Bert

A fair amount of Kolb's great boating adventure had turned into more of a land-based process of moving boats and gear down along the shore. Their work near Shoshone Falls is unrecorded, Kolb simply calling it "some bad water above Glenwood Springs." He later assembled some of the film, however, and his screenplay offers a few details.

Scene 4. At Shoshone Falls. Equipped with a life jacket, filled with Kapo[k], and a helmet of the same material. A novel use for an ice-cap—protection of exposed films, matches, and a notebook.
Scene 5. (cut back.) Canoe overturned in a rapid 150 feet above Shoshone Falls. Kolb saves himself by holding to the life line.
Scene 6. Turning the canoe upright.
Scene 7. Climbing board—Land quickly, bail out and proceed …
Scene 8. Portaging Shoshone Falls.
Scene 9. Some rapids by the way. Loper wants to run them all.
Scene 11. Loper explains how he will negotiate a rapid.

NAU.PH.568.6004
Kolb Brothers

Kolb and Loper portaging Shoshone Falls

Ellsworth Kolb was a handsome and outgoing bachelor. He was often photographed back at Grand Canyon nattily dressed in the company of young women. Even here, he could not resist one bite of cheesecake:

> Scene 14. … Hanging Lake—A gem in the Rockies; an emerald in a perfect setting. A mountain fairy-land—and lo the nymph appears on the scene. Glenwood Springs is proud of her expert swimmers. Miss Zelma Aultman is the peer of them all. She poses for a portrait photographer, and for the movies as well. Swimming in a mountain spring is cold work.

Loper and Kolb were based at a hotel at Glenwood Hot Springs for nearly two weeks. With their upstream work finally done they rowed down the relatively calm 130 miles of river to Westwater. In the more than 250 miles of river between Shoshone Falls and the confluence of the Green, only the twelve miles of Westwater Canyon—also known as Granite Canyon or Death Canyon—posed any serious navigational threat. But that threat remained severe enough that until the arrival of Kolb and Loper, no one was known to have passed through it. Although rumors persist of at least one earlier transit—Miller and Babcock, two dentists, claimed passage through in 1897—none are yet documented.

NAU.PH.568.5856

Kolb Brothers

Kolb and Loper, Grand Junction

Stanton and Brown's 1889 Railroad Survey portaged around it.

Westwater is a perfect miniature of Grand Canyon—high sedimentary rock cliffs, in this case the reddish Wingate Sandstone, rise five hundred feet above the black Precambrian metamorphic rocks that form the core of the Canyon and give rise to the rapids of Westwater. Kolb had hiked along the rim of the granite with Shields, and now orchestrated a support crew: photographer Frank E. Dean of Grand Junction, cattleman William Stubbs, and the deputy of the small settlement of Westwater, Ed Herbert. The crew was to work their way along the rim trail while Kolb and Loper took turns rowing the rapids in the Peterborough canoe. Loper was to row first, while Kolb filmed.

"The death grapple with the river began," frothed the *Grand Junction Daily Sentinel:*

> Kolb shouted orders to Loper in the river below, from where he was situated on the rocky walls of the canon. He saw Loper run the first two, then the third and fourth. Each one got worse and the boat leaped, tossed, rocked and bucked but Loper held on and let 'er lope. Kolb called to Loper after he had crossed the last rapids before the terrible Double Pitch which he had planned to attempt the next day, recognizing it as the demon of all demons between the start and the whirlpool. He had not told Loper of this especially as he had not thot of making a try at it the first day. He saw the danger and shouted to Loper to come out of

NAU.PH.568.5968

Kolb Brothers

Kolb Brothers

NAU.PH.568.5929

Loper entering Westwater

Film crew overlooking Whirlpool (Skull Rapid)

the river. Loper could not see the terrible double pitch, a sheer drop of 10 feet with a succession of falls following which made a fearful cataract. Kolb could see it and yelled hoarsely to Loper, who mistook the frantic signals as a 'go ahead' and go ahead he did, his steady eye and strong arms tuned for the next rapids. Little did he know its power.

Kolb Believes Loper Lost.

Powerless to yell louder or to make himself understood in the din filled gorge of mighty waters, Kolb saw the boat take a nip at the awful plunge which had cracked many a man's skull on the rocks below. The canoe leaped into the air and crashed down, down, down, out of sight in the gnashing, grinding, murderous water which boiled and tangled in the veritable maelstrom of fury, a fury so deadly that the foam stood out in clouds on the water surface.

Kolb, heart sick, watched for the reappearance of the small craft and his friend. He could see nothing of it. For an hour he clambered back and forth almost beside himself with apprehension. He thot how he had failed to warn Loper of the awful place, how he had not wanted him to try it. He imagined the worst had happened to his comrade. He had never had a fatality on any of his expeditions and he grew faint as he

Loper in the canoe, Westwater

thot of the possibility that at last one had happened.

Finds the Truth

Finally he gave up looking as the sun sank behind the cliffs to the west and climbed up to the trail to go to camp, which he knew was a few miles further on. He had made arrangement to have the other three men meet himself and Loper on this trail and return to camp together. He met Dean and asked quickly if anything had been seen of the wreckage of a boat or of Loper. "Why he's in camp," was Mr. Dean's rejoinder. Kolb almost discredited his own ears and soon reached camp and grasped Loper's hand with a mighty handshake and the first thing Loper said was that he had had a frightful time and had had enough of rapids for a while. Then he asked if the pictures would be good. "Pictures," said Kolb, "why man you got way beyond camera range and would not come back, you were so wild to run more rapids." Loper was crestfallen to think he had mastered a king of rapids and no movie had been possible. How he went over the drop and kept the boat upright, water-filled as it was, and finally was able to get away from the maw of the river monster, only he knows.

Kolb Runs Death Traps

The next morning a new start was made with Kolb in the boat and Loper helping Dean and the other two men who were to throw life lines if needed. Loper was to run part of the rapids later on and did so. Kolb got away under ideal picture conditions and started for the Little Niagara Whirlpool section, the most demonical on the entire river. He had not been gone long when his boat got into a place where the waves were running many feet high, tangoing back and forth between granite cliffs and making slaps at his boat that sent it hither and thither like a chip. Kolb clung on with his masterly skill and rode the bronco.

Suddenly he struck a place that would have made a whirling dervish seasick and the boat shot over and he "got out and got under" good and plenty. He reached the life line and keel of the good ship and finally by might and main turned the craft right side up and crawled aloft. The watchful picture men, perched like magpies on the skyline above, did not see the upset. He had inhaled water and choked and gasped for some minutes.

Then came the whirlpool. The picture men who had gone down stream a ways saw his hat floating down the river and all of them had a terrible scare, fearing he was lost. Then came the worst place of all. Straight down the stream Kolb could see the water spouting many feet in the air as it shot with tremendous force against a boulder the size of a house in the whirlpool rapid. To the left was a "nigger head" rock which was covered with water about half the time. He saw that by making a corkscrew curve with a back action kick and a swipe at the scenery he might get thru, if he could dodge all the 100-ton pebbles and avoid the geysers of idiotic water that spit at the sky and found a target far below in the chugging foam under the rocks. He made it not. A wave slapped him a half-ton lick on the face and picked him up, gunboat and all and rammed him over five feet, right up on top of the nigger head. The boat skidded off upside down, full of water, in the insane foam.

Here Kolb made the movie man above close his eyes and crank, crank, crank with only a prayer and a peep to see if aim was still on the struggle below. Dean's eyes opened wide when he saw, not a dead man floating down stream with a smashed canoe trailing behind, but a very sore mariner whipping his boat back into line, safe beyond the rapid, grinning up the cliff with an "I told you so" expression in his eyes, if anyone could have seen it.

Kolb and Loper in new Stone boats

Was Like Tickling Dynamite With a Lighted Match, screamed the headlines. Death Canon of Grand River at Last Conquered by Daring Party led by Kolb and Bert Loper, blared another.

"Snapping their fingers under the very nose of Death itself, taunting gaily with the grim reaper, with their marvelous river skill as their only defense." And the purple prose ran on. "Kolb says that the cataracts excel anything in the Colorado river in fierceness altho of course vastly less extensive in length and number.... Black Canon next week they say."

They had succeeded beyond Kolb's recently subdued dreams. Fortified with success, they returned to Grand Junction and planned a new assault on the Gunnison. But first, an interlude.

Reel No. 2.
Scene No. 1. Camping in a beautiful spot. "Free air and water."
Scene No. 3. The air mattress is inflated by lung-power.
Scene 4.
Kolb: These matches got wet in the last upset. I'll dry them on my hair.
Loper: Well, give them to a man who has some hair.
Scene 7. At rest after a hard days work.
Loper. "You would make less noise if you kept your mouth shut."
Kolb. "So would you."

NAU.PH.568.6012

Kolb Brothers

Kolb caption: "All went well as long as we portaged the boats."

Kolb was not at all happy with his first fiasco on the Gunnison, and Loper wanted to get in as much boating as he could. The Peterborough canoe, furthermore, had more than proven itself rapid-worthy. Loper and Kolb launched back at Cimarron Crossing where the first attempt had begun. Loper was getting into familiar country here, the flanks of the San Juan Mountains. The Gunnison River was first recorded in 1853 by Captain John W. Gunnison, who had found the area wholly unsuitable for railroads. But Otto Mears, the "Pathfinder of the San Juans," with whom Loper had worked in the 1800s, finally pushed a road into this area, followed by General Palmer's Denver & Rio Grande—the railroad that opened the San Juans and lured Benjamin Mettler, and eventually Loper, to the West.

Loper and Kolb launched the canoe and rowed all the way to Gunnison Tunnel—the stretch that had been disastrous to Kolb, Stone, Stern, and Shields—without a mishap, and in less than two days' time. "Much of the success of this trip," wrote Kolb:

> as well as the trip on the Grand River, was due to Loper. He was the most enthusiastic rough-water man I have ever been associated with, not excepting my brother and Mr. Stone, which is saying a good deal. Two trips through Cataract Canyon, on the Colorado River, and boating on the San Juan had given him the experience he needed for this work.

Their next pitch was pure novelty. The workmen agreed to lower the flow and allow them to boat through the five-and-a-half mile Gunnison Tunnel, blasted from the Gunnison through the mountains to irrigate the Uncompahgre Valley. Wrote Kolb:

> I was amazed to learn that a bright pin-point of light somewhere ahead was the sunlight reflecting on the cement at the opposite end of the bore. Walter Tupper, the caretaker, accompanied us. Oars were replaced with paddles. Light was supplied by an oil lantern. A swift current kept us busy; a dead trolley, held by wooden hangers and fastened by drills into the roof gave us some trouble.... There were many weird and peculiar sounds.... 1900 feet inside we heard the roar of a rapid ahead.... The stream had been dammed by something, that was certain, the canoe was bounding and slapping onto the water at a disconcerting rate.

The rapid was insignificant and after sixty-five minutes the three men emerged into broad daylight in the Uncompahgre Valley. Now it was back to work, back into Black Canyon.

Stone had commissioned two new boats for the project—250-pound wooden craft, decked over at either end, much like the Galloway and Kolb boats used for the Colorado. Although Stone was not joining them this time, his gift of new boats was there.

On Friday the 13th of October Loper and Kolb boarded their boats for the eleven-and-a-half-mile run to Red Rock Canyon, during which they would drop more than one thousand feet. They played tag with their retrieved Indestructo bobbing along beside them. Kolb wrote: "Finally it struck a long, clear channel and rounded a turn, floating triumphantly. We followed, expecting to catch it soon but found the Falls instead, and the final end of the trunk is an unsolved mystery." They had reached Flat Rock Falls, a fifteen-foot drop, and had to portage their heavy new boats. Kolb explained:

> The next day, while we were lining my boat through a narrow channel, it slid onto a sloping rock, the bow shot into the air and the stern settled into the water. We had overlooked the fact that most of the water ran under the rocks, and the boat was trying to make a short-cut. A rope

from the bow was hurriedly tied to a tree, to prevent the boat from vanishing as the trunk had. We worked an entire day with a small pulley, with ropes and poles, but failed to recover it. Occasionally we would look at the ledges above and ponder on a climb. The following morning I decided to make an attempt. It was not as bad as it looked and I soon gained the top. By one o'clock I had descended to the tunnel. Tupper supplied me with dynamite, drills, and a hammer and I retraced my steps arriving after dusk.

The following morning Loper went to work. He is a miner and knew what to do with a single-jack. A hole was drilled into the small rock that held the boat, so that it reached a depth of three feet below the water. It was charged with half a stick of powder and was fired. It merely shook and slightly cracked the rock. Two more sticks finished the job and the rock was shattered. It was dark when the boat was rescued. It took another day to replace two boards that were broken near the stern. Canvass, glue and tin completed the repair and we had only lost four days.

We averaged about half a mile per day for the next four days. The rapids were unrunnable; we could scarcely cross the river. Nearly all trees had disappeared, the cliffs seemed to be nearly perpendicular, the rock was granite. Our supplies had dwindled to almost nothing and we had still six miles to go, but miles should hardly be mentioned in this connection. We had reached a place banked with perpendicular walls and a little shore of boulders first on one side, then on the other. This ended with a gorge with cliffs rising sheer from the river, which was only fifty-two feet wide. The approach was over two dangerous rapids and swift water; a twelve-foot fall, among a lot of great boulders, lay at the foot of the gorge. The river above this point had a descent of 100 feet in a fourth of a mile and we were on the right side of the river, away from Montrose; when once past a ledge there was no chance of going back.

A crack in the granite with a talus slope in the bottom appeared to be a possible avenue of escape. I prospected and got half way out before I found that it pinched and was blocked by overhanging rocks, and we returned to our work with the boats, which were at the beginning of the 100 foot descent. While lining Loper's boat it was smashed on the side quite similar to the other break. The granite boulders were slippery as glass and a wet shoe would not hold. Loper fell when pulling on a rope and struck his back on a projecting rock. He was deathly pale and gave no

NAU.PH.568.5971 Kolb Brothers

Pinned at Flat Rock Falls

NAU.PH.568.5911 Kolb Brothers

answer but a groan to my anxious inquiry. I played nurse for two nights; our only remedy was a hot water bottle. Loper improved and helped me repair the boat but he suffered greatly. We were now on half rations.

A flimsy bridge of box elder poles and ropes was thrown across the stream at a point where great polished boulders almost hid the stream. We did not have a great deal of confidence in our engineering ability, but we got ourselves and our boats across.

That night it rained, then snowed. Our last provisions, excepting a half pound of sugar, were eaten that morning. This would seem enough, but we had neither strength nor inclination to make a portage where one was advisable, and lined instead. A boat filled with water, shot into the stream, and overturned. One rope broke, the other was snubbed around a rock and held by Loper. I slid and fell over the icy rocks and wrestled the boat into an eddy when it swung in towards the shore. Then I found that I had wrenched my knee so that I could scarcely stand.

We drained the water from the cameras, and put them under a protecting ledge. The sugar was eaten that noon, our exposed films were divided between us and we turned to the cliffs. When I had climbed

NAU.PH.568.6011 Kolb Brothers

Kolb Brothers NAU.PH.568.9535

Loper drills and blasts

the crack or geological fault on the opposite side I had noticed that the same fault reached across the canyon, with two branches near the top. One of these branches might be an avenue of escape.

One cripple helped the other. The snow grew deeper as we climbed but, fortunately, we had no ledge work until within 300 feet of the top and it was not bad. We were soaking wet from wallowing in the snow but had managed to keep warm.

The plateau was quite flat for a mile or more, and was covered with a growth of scrub oak and sage, with snow hanging thick on the branches. I climbed without a great deal of trouble but could make little headway in the deep snow, and fell frequently. Loper broke the trail, I followed....

A medical examination showed that Loper had broken two ribs, but the injury to his back was much more painful than the ribs. My knee needed a rest. The tendons attached to the knee-cap were loosened or strained. Somehow my good fortune was not holding out this trip. Someone said something about the advisability of starting on Friday the Thirteenth.

Kolb and Loper are in Hospital After Mad Dash in Black Canon, read one paper.

> Mr. Loper says the river is a terror. He says it simply runs down a staircase part of the way and they found ten-foot perpendicular falls, ending in a long millrace rapids hundreds of feet long where the water raced with express train speed.

✣ ✣ ✣

Rachel Loper had sent Bert several letters before the last Gunnison stint, saying she was unwell, begging him to come home. But he had wanted to do this one last bit—he wanted to finish the job. Now a telegram, several days old, awaited him, saying Rachel was not expected to live. Loper caught the next train home. The papers said he would return to the Gunnison as soon as possible to finish the trip, but that was not to be.

Against all odds, Kolb did go back into Black Canyon two weeks later, with William Wright of Montrose. Abandoning one boat they flailed downriver another mile in rain and snow before climbing out. And still Kolb returned. On Thanksgiving day he and three others descended to the river and spent over a week bashing against the river and boulders, finally losing the last boat and climbing out December 8. Defeated? Hell, no. Kolb sat out the winter at home and returned the following spring. With good weather and water, a new canvas boat, and a new, young eighteen-year-old companion named Albert Moore, Kolb finally won through Black Canyon. He dragged the boat out at the Delta Bridge, "and my Black Canyon exploration was no longer a dream, but an accomplishment." An accomplishment. But was it boating?

For Loper, it was back to Glen Canyon.

> Sunday Dec 31-1916
>
> I … was gone nearly two months but had to return on the account of the illness of my wife so I returned home and shortly after I did return my wife underwent an operation and came near loosing her life but at this writing is enjoying good health and is my companion on my trip to do the assessment on California Bar where we arrived about 2 P.M. today and started our assessment for the year of 1916. #

Legend

41 Loper's boats

Bert Loper's boat, the *Grand Canyon*, was battered badly on its way downriver to where it beached. Righted and dragged high on the slope above high water, it looked pretty rough even as Harris's trip rowed away the next day.

Riverman Ken Sleight sensed the historic import of the boat and petitioned the National Park Service to remove and preserve the *Grand Canyon* and its legacy for posterity. His pleas went nowhere and Loper's boat continued its slow disintegration. The pale yellow paint faded and peeled. The plywood, already fractured, began to collapse bit by bit into the hillside. Rain and gully-washes poured over it, filling it with gravel and silt, knocking loose parts inexorably down. As river tourism blossomed, *Grand Canyon* appeared less and less to be a boat, but more a pile of decaying wood becoming one with the Canyon. A cable placed around the wreckage to keep river tourists away soon out-paced the boat in its own disintegration. The stone monument, capped by Rachel Loper's plaque, stands firm, though easy to overlook, being made, as it is, of native stone. Eventually only the monument will remain to tell the tale—and one swift rockslide may someday erase that as well.

Some sixty-six miles farther downstream in Grand Canyon, the *Ross Wheeler*, built but never rowed by Loper, continues its slower demise. More than ninety years have been at work on it, and the bottom of its galvanized hull has rusted through. The oars, pulleys, lifejackets, and other gear Charlie Russell left with it in 1915 have disappeared, carried away by souvenir seekers passing downriver or out the Bass Trail. Twice the hulk has been rolled or moved riverward by vandals or wind, and the *Ross Wheeler*, like its upstream sister, lies just one unfortunate event from memory.

Loper asked to be buried by the river, there to decay. Right or wrong, his boats seem destined for that very fate. To rescue them or not—time may soon enough solve the quandary. #

42 Desert rat

HANKSVILLE UTAH
Mar 19–17
Friend Ed, [Ellsworth Kolb]

I rec'd pictures and appreciate them very much and it made me sick to see the pictures below where I went to think I had not been there....

I have been down on the River ever since the 9th of Dec and may remain some time yet. My Wife is with me and feeling fine. I am not placer mining yet but hope to be soon. It is a little tough on a fellow to be located 90 miles from a Post Office but that is me.

After the Gunnison fiasco, Loper had returned to Torrey where Rachel had been staying with her sister's family. According to notes from Pearl Baker and Dock Marston, Rachel's illness stemmed from a miscarriage.

For a while, Loper went back to freighting. But as winter approached, the Lopers headed down to Glen Canyon. They later referred to their season at California Bar as their honeymoon. It must have been a snuggly one, as years later, when visiting the site with a group of Boy Scouts, one Scout wrote: "We saw what remained of his old house at this place, where he and his wife spent the winter, burning oak brush and willows to keep warm. Bert told us that it was so cold that they almost burned the house down trying to keep warm." Ross Rigby, another Scout, recalled Loper telling them to dig beneath the front door sill as he had buried his tools there. Sure enough, they dug and found a good stash of old implements. A rustic honeymoon.

Sometime the following summer, Loper took a job with steamboater E.T. Wolverton who, according to Elwyn Blake, was doing assessment work for the Cerro Gordo Oil Company on the San Rafael Desert. Blake, a teenager from Green River, had signed on with Wolverton as well. He described part of that summer:

Bert Loper and his wife Rachel, a miner named Tom Keel, and I camped at Lost Spring for a while....

He was forty-two and she twenty years younger. They were a happy-go-lucky pair. He made no end of her Scotch brogue. She kidded him right back, giving as good as she took....

Bert was a very docile man, as I remember it, except for cussing a little when I defended Socialism. Bert was very well informed about the politics of the time....

One morning Bert went out after horses before breakfast. By ten o'clock Rachel and I were worried. I tried to cut sign and find his tracks, but somehow missed where he had gone south, following the horse tracks. By night he still had not returned. As night came on there was nothing to do but go to bed. Rachel must have suffered agonies, though she had unbounded faith in her husband's ability to take care of himself on the desert.

About two o'clock in the morning we heard horseshoes approaching. It was, of course, Bert. He was riding Old Dan and leading the other horse. He had followed the horses all the way to Hanksville. He had caught up with them at the Muddy, but they would not let him catch them, so he had to wade across and follow on to town. He said the ride back hurt him more than the walk through the hot sand.

A short while later Bert and Rachel drove to town after supplies for camp. When they did not arrive back on the day appointed, I thought little of it. Then our supplies arrived with another man driving the rig. We learned that Bert had returned as far as the San Rafael river, where Bert bought some watermelons. He started to lift a sack of the melons into the wagon, when he ruptured his appendix.

Weeks later Bert told me what had happened. "You were at fault," he told me. "I got the melons for you, and so busted my appendix." He also told me that it had been about thirty-six hours after the rupture before he reached a Grand Junction hospital. A week later he was out of bed and walking around.

Bert Silliman, longtime Green River resident, recalled:

Edwin T. Wolverton came to where I was working, and told me that a desert man had just been brought in off the desert, in desperate condi-

> tion and crazed with pain. I went with Wolverton to the hotel room and found him in such agony that he just wanted to be left alone, and was indifferent to be taken to where he could have medical attention. His friends decided that he was in no condition to pay any attention to his wishes to be left alone. He was placed on the first train to Fruita, Colorado, where he had his appendix removed pronto. He was back in a few days, and, of course, the first thing he must do was go down to the river, and see what happened to it during his enforced absence. He fell over a willow stub and tore the incision and had to go back to the hospital for another sew up. Dr. Porter kept him longer this time.

In a later interview with Marston, Silliman added that they hid Loper's clothes the second time.

✣ ✣ ✣

In the spring of 1918, geologist Herbert Gregory began organizing an exploration of the Kaiparowits Plateau region southeast of Torrey, southwest of Hite. Gregory had begun his studies in the area three years earlier. Now, under the auspices of the United States Geological Survey (USGS), he was preparing an in-depth survey. His notes for late April indicate he talked to several prominent men in the area including Loper's boss for the two previous summers, E.T. Wolverton. Wolverton may have recommended Loper as a camp hand—or perhaps Gregory met Loper in Green River, for he lists him as living in that town. Gregory was delighted to find him, writing to his fiancée, "I'm lucky indeed in getting Bert Loper, a second John Wetherill, for packer. He's a dandy. I'm in safe hands." On April 29 he hired Loper as a packer for $5.50 a day.

On May 2 Gregory, Loper, a USGS assistant named Winchell, and cook Willard Drake left Green River for the San Rafael Desert to the south. Three days later they hit Hanksville. "Bert Loper and wife with their wagon leave us to get some stuff from Flat Tops," wrote Gregory. "Will meet us at Hanksville Monday eve … dust and wind terrible."

This was familiar terrain to Loper, who had worked out of Hanksville and Hite for the previous decade and likely knew most of the 105-person population of Hanksville. Gregory planned to work the team south through Halls Creek and the Waterpocket Fold, across the Escalante

River, into the town of Escalante, and out to the Kaiparowits Plateau—all country originally described from the river in 1869 by John Wesley Powell—a hero of Loper's—and by Powell's later land surveys under Almon Harris Thompson, 1872-75. The area was next traversed by the Mormon Hole-in-the-Rock Expedition of 1879-80. Kumen Jones, Loper's landlord in Bluff in 1895, had been a stalwart on that trip.

Even though Loper had much experience as a camp hand, boatman, and freight driver, his skills at trail guiding were untested. Two weeks were enough to transform Gregory's initial confidence into exasperation:

> May 18 1918 - Saturday
>
> Smith's Ranch and vicinity on lower Hoxie (Hall) Creek. The delay at this place is largely due to Loper who after taking a special trip to Cane Springs to get information from Smith about the trail came back with hazy notions about "rim rock," "flats," "rincons" but did not know start or course of trail leading to the lower Escalante. Loper is a good worker, faithful, but slow. Is at his best when on foot or in a boat. With horses and horse trails he is only average.

It wasn't just Loper that wandered. "Loper & Drake failed to find trail," wrote Gregory the next day. "We start over the Water Pocket Fold under the guidance of Clarence Brown." No go: "Failed to find trail continuing to Escalante River and after search & tramps over rocks & in canyons decided to return to Hall Creek." By May 23 they had made it into the town of Escalante where Gregory complained, "Men for guides are also impossible to get—all who know the country are away with cattle or sheep."

From Escalante they marched southeast along the 50-Mile Bench toward Hole-in-the-Rock.

> Camp 27 —50 mile pt. same as 26
>
> Loper came in late and after consultation decided it too risky to go around the point of the mt. with a sure one day & probable two days without water. The guide Mr. Kirchwell did not appear Monday night and tonight. If he does not turn up in the morning early we go back 25 miles to Collett Canyon.

Kirchwell did not turn up. The next day Gregory "learned that Mr. Kirchwell our 'guide' came down to near 50 mile point, could not find us and returned to Escalante. Probably good thing we missed him for a man who does such a fool thing might lead us astray." If Loper was beginning to look better by comparison, he spent the next three days losing ground:

> May 30
>
> Part way up difficult trail Loper discovered that he had forgotten his (survey) camera—
>
> Loper forgot waterbag, camera at 50 mile. . . .
>
> Loper returned from search for camera at 4:00 o'clock. Too late to go on today—
>
> Day lost. . . .
>
> May 31
>
> . . . Loper took us several miles beyond the trail down to Rock Creek. after getting information from sheepherder we returned to the Lakes and went west to a trail I discovered this morning. . . . We were trying to reach Grand Bench but camped at 10 P.M. . . . No water.
>
> June 1
>
> . . . Loper failed to find the trail leading from Grand Bench to Last Chance Creek—although well described [illegible] topog—he thought it best to return.
>
> June 2
>
> . . . Loper & Drake complain of the long & hard days work.

The trip ended without fisticuffs or fatalities, and perhaps even on friendly terms. At least from Loper's side. He always remembered Gregory fondly, writing to Julius Stone in 1936, "In speaking of the good men I have been out with—in 1918 I was out on a pack trip with Professor Herbert E. Gregory and I would go on another trip like it without pay if I could and I will never forget the fireside talks we had in camp at night." Gregory's 1931 seminal report, *The Kaiparowits Region: A Geographic and Geologic Reconnaissance of Parts of Utah and Arizona*, makes no mention of his guides.

Loper's tracks are faint for the next two years. A caption on one family photo suggest he headed for the Mohrland, Utah, coal mines. #

Legend

43 Reilly's bile

As time moved on, the story of Bert Loper's last trip changed for some. P.T. Reilly, who had arrived at Loper's boat with Norman Nevills just days after Loper's death, amplified his distaste for both Loper and his boat. Not only that, but he contributed a novel interpretation of why Loper's trip had come about in the first place. In a 1994 interview with Lew Steiger, he elaborated.

Steiger: Bert Loper? What did you think of him as a boatman?
Reilly: Lousy!
Steiger: Really?!
Reilly: Oh, one of the worst!
Steiger: No kidding?! I'm surprised at that.
Reilly: Why?!
Steiger: Mainly because of Don Harris, who I respect.
Reilly: Oh, Don's a good boatman.
Steiger: Yeah. And you know, he …
Reilly: Oh, let me tell you about that. Don Harris hated Nevills, Harry Aleson hated Nevills, and Bert Loper hated Nevills. That's why they ran three days ahead of us in the 1949 trip, and old Bert got drowned. Harris and Aleson—Aleson had a ten-man, the first ten-man to go through. They'd balonied old Bert into thinking he was going to lead the trip against the hated Nevills. Well, they didn't intend for Loper to lead that trip at all. Every year they'd sandwich old Bert between 'em in his so-called boat, held together with shingle nails. Oh, it was the lousiest boat!

I saw that boat right after it was pulled out of the river. We came by three days later, and the boat was.… I've got pictures of it. He used shingle nails to build it! There was no rock[er] to it at all. God himself couldn't have rowed that boat and made a respectable showing. It was the most terrible, most horrible answer to running a rapid.

> If a man didn't know anything, you would say he did a hell of a lousy job in coming up with this answer.

To Reilly, Loper's last voyage was simply a stunt concocted by Aleson and Harris to show up Nevills.

✣ ✣ ✣

Even in 1969, when Reilly published an article entitled "How Deadly is Big Red?," Reilly was not only ready to condemn Loper's boat, but Loper himself:

> Loper's death is a singular monument to the feuds and intrigues that have occurred on the river because this man, within twenty-three days of being eighty years old, should not have been running ahead of his party; in fact, he should not have been on the river at all.

And this oddity: a footnote in Reilly's *Lee's Ferry*, pertaining to Loper's 1908 visit states, "Clara Russell Davis remembered Loper as being indolent and not as capable as her father in solving problems,"—even though Reilly's notes on his interview with Davis contain no such reference, stating conversely that Davis never met Russell, Monett, or Loper.

NAU.PH.67.46.8.17

P.T. Reilly running a Nevills cataract boat

Why some historians feel the need to go on the attack is not the topic of this book. Suffice it to say that some do, and in the case of Bert Loper, Reilly was more than willing to contribute his share of bile. Thankfully, such aspersions fade with years as the historians' greater work begins to shine. #

life

44 Professional boatman

THE COLORADO RIVER debouches into a great rift formed millions of years ago as Baja California tore away from the mainland, opening the Sea of Cortez. This rift extends well into California, creating a huge depression below sea level: the Salton Sink and its southern extremity, the Imperial Valley. The delta pours into this sink, historically flowing to the south into the Sea of Cortez. However, like any river crossing a delta, the Colorado tended to shift its channel. Prehistorically it would often jump channel and pour northward, filling the Salton Sea to well above sea level until it breached the natural levee separating it from the sea. Then it would flow south again, allowing the Salton Sea to evaporate. Although this was a natural process, it proved unacceptable to white men when they settled the Imperial Valley around the turn of the century. But a little water sounded good. And profitable.

Being innovative, promoters of the Imperial Valley built a gravity ditch along the Colorado delta through Mexico and back into the Imperial Valley. Agriculture boomed. But like many development schemes, the infrastructure failed to keep up with development, and in 1905 the headgates of the canal failed, allowing the entire river to quit the sea and flow directly into the Salton Sea. For nearly two years they fought the river. Finally the Southern Pacific Railroad joined the battle and the river was laboriously redirected back to the Sea of Cortez. From that day forth, controlling the Colorado became an increasing priority for the Southwest. Laguna Dam replaced the old diversion headgate, but remained vulnerable to huge annual floods. In 1907, President Theodore Roosevelt urged a "broad, comprehensive scheme of development for all the irrigable land upon the Colorado River with needed storage at the headwaters, so that none of the waters of this great river which can be put to beneficial use will be allowed to go to waste."

In 1902 the Reclamation Service was formed to look into damming and irrigating the West. As well, the USGS began their own investiga-

Loper with squawfish, Wheeler, Armitage

tions, the 1914 drilling at the confluence of the Green and Grand being one of their inquiries. Geologist Eugene C. La Rue—who later became a player in Loper's career—synthesized the early investigations in his 1916 *Colorado River and its utilization.* He called for dams. Lots of dams.

Only when the Colorado River Basin states met in 1919 and formed the League of the Southwest did grand-scale thinking begin to move forward. Although La Rue felt the first big dam should go above Grand Canyon, forces were aligning against him, pushing for a dam much farther downriver in the jagged black mountains southeast of Las Vegas. In 1920 the Reclamation Service commissioned a reconnaissance of the Colorado River from the mouth of the Virgin River in Nevada to Yuma, Arizona near the Mexican border. Homer Hamlin and his assistant Edgar T. Wheeler were the geologists. The boatmen were Harry Armitage, who had a ranch upstream of the mouth of the Virgin, and Bert Loper. Just how Loper landed the job, or even heard of it, is unclear—perhaps through his 1914 work, perhaps through Gregory, perhaps through the Kolbs.

The four men assembled at Armitage's ranch on the Colorado on April 5, 1920, and loaded their two boats. At the last minute they added a small skiff for a party from Los Angeles—headed by the legendary William Mulholland, water czar of Southern California. Indeed, although stemming the floods of the Colorado was a primary purpose for this first dam, the burgeoning thirst of Southern California drove much of the process. Mulholland's dewatering of the Owens Valley had

Loper and Wheeler at Boulder Canyon damsite

begun in 1913, but it would not be enough. To this day, there is no such thing as enough.

The party moved downriver sixteen miles to camp at Boulder Wash. The following day they escorted Mulholland's group through Boulder Canyon as far as Las Vegas Wash. Dispatching them back to Los Angeles, Hamlin's party returned upriver to the previous night's camp. They spent the next two days investigating damsites in Boulder Canyon. On April 9 they passed the abandoned site of Callville, the former head of steamboat navigation. Here, in 1867, Mormon settlers had pulled an emaciated James White from the river, launching the persistent controversy over his pre-Powell float through Grand Canyon.

For the next two days they evaluated dam sites in Black Canyon. Hamlin felt Boulder Canyon was the superior site, and the eventual project was called Boulder Dam—even though later engineers elected to build the dam in Black Canyon.

On they went, leaving the large canyons and entering broader valleys, passing old steamboat ports at El Dorado, Cottonwood Island, Hardyville, and Needles, noting possible low dam sites along the way. Few whitewater boaters of the Colorado ever saw these undammed lower canyons. Of those preceding Loper, members of the Powell, Stanton, Flavell, Woolley, and Kolb trips continued to tidewater—perhaps a dozen men in all. Loper was the last whitewater man to record a cruise on this stretch.

On April 16 they camped early, tired of beating their way against headwinds. Four days later they approached Yuma. Hamlin:

> April 20. Continued on down the river to Yuma, where we arrived at 4:30 P.M. Very heavy headwinds were encountered in the afternoon. At the Laguna Dam we lined our boats down over the dam and portaged our supplies around. Left the boats, equipment and the balance of the supplies with Mr. Schlecht at Yuma.

The newspapers made no note of the expedition. Homer Hamlin died soon after the voyage. Wheeler submitted his report.

What remains undocumented is the trip's conclusion. When describing this trip in later years Loper always stated that he had gone all the way to "the gulf," meaning the Gulf of California, or Sea of Cortez, more than a hundred miles downstream of Yuma, where the Colorado flows into the sea. In 1936 he wrote to Julius Stone, saying, "After we had the survey completed we continued on down to the Gulf and returned to Yuma." If he did *not* do it, it would be the only claim of his career that he falsified. If he *did* make it to tidewater, he would have to have done it, down and back, on April 21, and caught the train to Los Angeles the next morning—a tight schedule, but possible. A powerboat perhaps? His window of opportunity is bracketed by Hamlin's journal, stating their arrival in Yuma at 4:30 P.M. on the 20th, and a card postmarked April 22 from Los Angeles, reading:

> Dear Rachel—Just a note to let you know I may get home about as soon as you get this or next day anyway. I should get home Sunday so look for me.
> with love
> Bert

It was not a spectacular trip, nor a famous one. But it may well have been the trip that put Loper in the running for the work he loved—boating for bucks. Over the next three years the USGS planned four major expeditions on the Green, San Juan, and Colorado. Each needed a head boatman. Galloway was dead, Stone too old, Russell institutionalized. The choice was between the brothers Kolb and Bert Loper. #

45 Obsolescence

When they pulled away from Loper's boat that next morning, they were rowing into a new era. The old school died with Bert Loper.

—Al Harris, son of Don Harris

In many ways Al Harris is right. Loper's continued presence on the river throughout the 1940s had given the boating community its last solid link to the "old school," dating back into the 1890s. Nevills and Harris were already ushering in a new tourism-for-hire ethic. And just two weeks before Loper's death, Dock Marston had accompanied Ed Hudson on the first motorized descent of Grand Canyon, proclaiming to Elwyn Blake, "Our motor boat run was highly successful and makes obsolete the oar-powered craft in the canyon."

Marston returned in 1950 with an inboard Chris Craft. The Rigg Brothers, with Mexican Hat Expeditions, also built a fleet of Chris Crafts to augment their Nevills-style Cataract boats. In 1951 Rod Sanderson, who got his start working at Bureau of Reclamation dam sites, ran, along with friend Jimmy Jordan, the first outboard motorboats through Grand Canyon. Don Harris and Jack Brennan soon bought outboard skiffs as well, adding powerboat trips to their offerings. But none of these craft were, in a commercial sense, practical. The Nevills Cataracts could carry only two paying passengers per boat, awkwardly at that. The powerboats could do little better. It was a client of Harry Aleson's that ushered the biggest change to Grand Canyon boating.

Georgie White first signed up to hike the lower Grand Canyon with Aleson in 1944. In 1945 and 1946 they swam the lower section of Grand Canyon. In 1947 they rafted Cataract Canyon and in 1948 they tried to raft the Escalante, sometimes floating, often tugging their boat down the tiny stream.

Two years later Georgie parted with Aleson and made her first Grand Canyon raft trip with friend Elgin Pierce. There she found her destiny.

She came back again and again, trying various combinations of rafts lashed together for stability. Finally she bought three thirty-three-foot inflatable bridge pontoons and strapped them together into a huge floating island. This she steered with an outboard motor. Onto this contraption she loaded a dozen or two passengers under her "share-the-expense" plan, offering for the first time, cheap river trips for the masses.

If Marston had made rowboats obsolete with his hard-hulled power-boat trips, Georgie made hard-hulled powerboat trips equally obsolete. The economics of her "G-rig" (G for Georgie) simply made too much sense. Before long, most other river runners followed her lead, patching various bridge pontoons together in a variety of configurations, and motoring great quantities of tourists down the Green and Colorado Rivers. Fortunately for those who wished to travel the river in other ways, obsolescence does have its charm, and a variety of anachronistic techniques survived.

Upstream in Glen Canyon, Scouting groups from Salt Lake City had begun running the river in surplus military rafts. As a guide on their early trips, they had hired Bert Loper. Eventually some Scout leaders began running their own trips: John Cross, Moki Mac Ellingson, and Al Quist. Harry Aleson, too, was offering regular rafting trips through the Glen, and soon, Ken Sleight.

Loper had called Glen Canyon the Colorado Kindergarten, where nearly anyone with a few bucks for a small raft, or even an inner tube, could run the river with ease or safety. But for Glen Canyon boaters, the writing was on the walls: specifically the walls about fifteen miles above Lee's Ferry—the proposed site of Glen Canyon Dam. #

46 Another day older

From Los Angeles Loper made haste to Utah. And for good reason—Rachel was pregnant. A major change loomed, and Bert was looking at serious shifts in his life. It was time to settle down, settle in. In January 1920 he had flirted with buying a place in Grand Junction, writing to Rachel, "Just a line to let you know I am here on my way to see John Scharf to try and buy his place. I borrowed $1500.00 from the Bank in G.R. and we may have a house yet." Apparently that fell through; two days later he was headed home, with no talk of being a homeowner.

Then, on February 9, the Lopers bought a forty acre parcel in Hanksville for one hundred dollars. It was a barren lot on the north edge of the tiny town, one hundred yards from where Muddy Creek and the Fremont River combine to form the Dirty Devil River. What future the Lopers saw in Hanksville—ranching? mining? freight?—is unknown, but presumably a house was in the works.

A small stone monument in the Green River cemetery bears silent witness to the end of that dream.

AMERICA
DAU. OF
BERT & RACHEL
LOPER
BORN
JULY 19, 1920
DIED
JULY 20, 1920

America. Named for her grandmother, who died so young, little America lived only one day. Cause of death was listed as prematurity. In all Loper's accounts of his life, he never mentioned this calamitous turn of

America's stone

Rachel and Bert at graveside, placing roses

fortune. It could not be that it was insignificant—more likely too painful to discuss. Twenty years earlier Loper had lost the first great love of his life, and with her, a child that was likely his son. In 1916 Rachel had miscarried her first pregnancy. Now came the loss of his and Rachel's only child.

The 1920 census, tallied January 17, lists Bert and Rachel living in Hanksville, his occupation: laborer. But after the loss of America, Loper was unemployed again. He had given up placer work in Glen Canyon for good. There was no money in it; there was no way to support a wife. Now, with his future uncertain, he went back to the one thing he knew best: at fifty-one years old, Bert Loper went back underground to mine coal.

✣ ✣ ✣

Some people say a man is made out of mud
A poor man's made out of muscle and blood
Muscle and blood, skin and bones
A mind that's weak and a back that's strong

1920

You load sixteen tons, and what do you get?
another day older and deeper in debt
St. Peter, don't you call me, 'cause I can't go
I owe my soul to the company store

—song by MERLE TRAVIS, popularized by TENNESSEE ERNIE FORD

Seventy-five miles northeast of Green River lies the escarpment locally known as the Coal Cliffs, rising high above the Castle Valley coal mining district. U.S. Fuels owned a good number of the mines, including those at Hiawatha, Black Hawk, Wattis, and Mohrland. Although Loper worked all these mines in the next few years, he first returned to Mohrland, where he had worked as early as 1918.

In the years since Loper had been a hard-rock miner, little had improved. Labor, as always, struggled with management for a fair shake. As remote as it was, Castle Valley was no backwater in the broad picture of labor unrest. Mother Jones had been jailed in Castle Valley in 1904 for her organizational work with the coal miners. A year later in Chicago, Big Bill Haywood had founded the International Workers of the World—the IWW, or "wobblies." A June 1913 IWW shutdown of the Castle Valley mines created enough ruckus that Joe Hill came to Salt Lake City to meet with the workers. A poor idea, as it turned out. Hill was a wanted man—he was arrested there, convicted of murder, and executed in 1915.

By the time Loper signed on at Mohrland in 1920 things were relatively calm. Miners paid a monthly fee to U.S. Fuels for doctor's services, movies, and dances, and had to pay for their own housing, equipment and dynamite. The miners were a cosmopolitan mix of around 275 Finns, Greeks, Italians, Japanese, blacks and miscellaneous whites, living in areas of town called Brotherhood Flat, Gobbler's Knob, Tipple Town, Jap Town, Nigger Town, Greek Town, and for the highbrows, Silk Stocking Row. The question is still posed as to whether such segregation was self-directed or whether the mining companies encouraged it to keep the miners from banding together.

A surviving journal from Loper's time there begins in October 1920, the first activity of note being a trip into town with Rachel to register to vote. For the most part, Loper's days consisted of drilling, blasting,

Mohrland: Bert at work, Rachel at home

and shoveling coal into rail cars, each carload to be credited toward Loper's pay. Three carloads was an average day. Afterward he might head straight home, have a bath, eat, play cards with Rachel or friends, and retire. Other days might find him in town. Although Prohibition had gone into effect January 18, it did not seem to affect the miners' habits: "Went to work at 7:30 and loaded 3 cars by noon and came out to take Rachel down to vote … went up to Watson's and got some wine and by the time I got home I was feeling the wine." Three days later, "I went down to Wine John's and got two drinks of whiskey—1.00."

His monthly paycheck came to $76.40 on November 10. Seventy of it he sent to the bank and spent the evening "writing letters and checks to people I owe." And he owed. What appears to be an undated list of creditors in the front of the diary lists eleven debts ranging from $250 to Dr. R.B. Porter to five dollars to E.A. Bricker—totaling nearly five hundred dollars in all. That's a lot of coal to dig. Loper plugged away.

Nov. 27–20

Had an excellent day in mine to-day and loaded 5 cars which should

> give me 17 tons which is very good and if I only could get as many every day I would soon be out of debt.

That day he topped Tennessee Ernie Ford, but such exceptional days were few. The next week he drew twenty-five dollars against his next check and groused, "I loaded the sum of 67 cars for the month and should have loaded at least 90 but is the best I could get. Put in eve figuring." Then, on December 14, he fell and sprained his back. He was out of work for two weeks.

> Dec 31
>
> Worked to-day and loaded 4 cars and was very tired and so ends another year and I suppose no cause for complaint for while we are not well off there are others in a worse fix so here is hoping we are even with the world and a little better if we can and will try and do unto others as we would be done by.

Loper drilled, blasted, and shoveled some more. He was right, it could have been much worse. Being too old, he had missed World War One. He had side-stepped the Spanish Flu epidemic which killed over half a million Americans in 1918. If nothing else, Loper endured. He corresponded with old friends and family, his brother Jack and cousin C.C. Mettler among them. He bought potatoes by the hundred-pound sack. Loper blew a dollar or two now and then in a solo game, or having a drink with the fellows, but mostly he puttered around their tent-cabin home with Rachel in his off time, beating her at cards. Many was the day, however, when the mine was closed, often due to poor rail connections and no available cars to load. The price of coal was beginning a slow decline. As always, it was felt most acutely by the coal miners themselves. #

47 Bert's whiskey

KEN SLEIGHT was an old-school boatman. He did his first trip with Moki Mac Ellingson and Al Quist and followed them into the Boy Scout boat trip business. After a season or two of hauling scouts through Glen Canyon at fifty dollars a head, Sleight realized he could not make money. He switched to adults, doubled his fare and was able to survive. He would often meet Harry Aleson on the river, sometimes camping together. Sleight would sit around the campfire, hypnotized by Aleson's endless stories. Although technically competitors, they became good friends. When Aleson married in Glen Canyon, Sleight was there. And there began the legend of Bert Loper's whiskey.

Sleight recalls Aleson telling him, over the years, that when they caught up to Loper's boat in 1949, there was a bottle of Loper's whiskey in the hatch:

> They pulled the boat over and he took the whiskey out of the bottom of the boat. Not much is said about it. All I know is what Harry Aleson told me and it's getting further out all the time. But I know that Harry told this story to me a number of times about Bert's whiskey. But I thought I saw that bottle under the seat of Harry's Power Wagon. He says "You know this bottle?" That was the time that I really got part of the story about the Bert Loper thing. And that's when he told me that he was goin' to have it for a special occasion one of these days. He had it for a long time. But it was really an instrumental thing. And it meant a lot to Harry.

It meant a lot to Ken Sleight too. As a boatman, Sleight was in many ways descended from Loper, having learned from Scout leaders who had learned from Loper. Sleight was a romantic with a great fondness for the history, and Loper stood tall in his pantheon. So did whiskey.

In October 1962 Sleight was invited to Harry and Dorothy Aleson's wedding at a magnificent sidecanyon of Glen called Lost Eden. The day before the event, Aleson sent Sleight upriver to Hall's Crossing to pick up Bill Wells, the Flying Bishop of Hanksville, who was to perform the ceremony. Although Sleight planned to return to Lost Eden with Wells that evening, one thing led to another. "I got stopped by Woody Edgell at Hite and we had a few drinks and I didn't get away from there 'til midnight. Me and my dog. It went all night long."

Meanwhile, down at Lost Eden, the party began. Out came Bert Loper's whiskey. Self control was not a factor. "Drank it all," mutters Sleight, "And ended up none for me. I knew as soon as I got there." Although Sleight tells the story with a smile and a laugh, it is clear it outraged him then, and to some extent, still does. He'd been looking forward to the ceremonial sharing of Loper's whiskey his entire river career.

The culprit—the man who drained the bottle—according to Sleight's old trail-mate, poet Vaughn Short, was Dock Marston, noted for his thirst. When Sleight pulled in to the whiskeyless beach, says Short, Sleight's dog went after Marston. He knew his master had been wronged and fingered the villain. As the story goes, that dog would never let Marston near Sleight's boat again. #

NAU.PH.99.3.1.22.42

Tad Nichols

Ken Sleight and Harry Aleson

48 San Juan redux

I HAD BEEN ENGAGED in the coal mines and the mines were very slack so I took a trip to the town of Greenriver, and about the first thing that I bumped into was a Gov't man that was the head of a proposed trip down the San Juan River.... There was also a proposed trip down the Green and Colo. River and I would rather have had that but Mr. Trimble—the boss—seemed to want me with him so I was engaged to pilot the San Juan trip. I signed up and started on the 29th of June.

On May 18, 1921, Congress approved an act "to provide for an examination and report on the conditions and possible irrigation development of the Imperial Valley in California." The implications were grander than the language—in order to safely irrigate the Imperial Valley, the entire Colorado River would need to be harnessed. To do that, ownership of the Colorado's water had to be agreed upon. This led to a second act, authorizing "the states of Arizona, California, Colorado, Nevada, New Mexico, Utah, and Wyoming to negotiate and enter into a compact ... for equitable division and apportionment ... of the water supply of the Colorado." The Colorado River Compact of 1922 soon became the Magna Carta of western water development. But before it was even signed, the USGS began cooperative trips with private power companies, measuring the water, mapping the streams, and searching for dam sites.

The USGS kicked off its survey of the Colorado River basin with two trips at once. Kelly Trimble was chosen to head a survey of the San Juan River, while Will Chenowith headed the survey of the Green and Colorado Rivers from the town of Green River, Utah to the mouth of the San Juan. Loper, with experience on both stretches, could have been head boatman for either. But for his survey, Chenowith chose Loper's friend Ellsworth Kolb, with Ellsworth's brother Emery accompanying them to make photographs. Although Loper's credentials were excellent, the Kolbs had a Grand Canyon trip to their credit, and stood taller in the field of big-water boatmen.

Trimble's survey team began work in Moab, carrying a known elevation point to the San Juan River. Loper joined them on June 29 as they worked southward. Elwyn Blake, the young man Loper had worked with in 1916 and '17, remembered his fortuitous encounter with them as they worked through the county seat of Monticello:

> One day I was sitting at the counter of the old Monticello Drug Store, when in walked several men from a government survey crew.
>
> Out of the corner of my eye, I noticed one man who looked familiar. The group sat down and ordered ice cream. Someone started the phonograph, whereupon the man I had been watching laid his spoon down and listened to the music. I turned around for a better look, for I knew of no man but Bert Loper who would stop eating in order to give his whole attention to a musical rendition.

Blake walked over and clasped Loper's hand. Since he had last seen Loper on the San Rafael Desert, Blake had moved to Moab with his father, who was editing the *San Juan Record.* From there, Blake had gone on to serve the last years of World War One in France and Germany. Returning, he bought a farm outside of Monticello, still working a few days a week at the *Record* to make ends meet.

Loper, delighted to see Blake again, invited him to apply for a position on the river survey. He did, and on Loper's enthusiastic recommendation, Trimble hired Blake as a rodman. At twenty-four, Blake was no newcomer to rivers—when his family had lived at Green River his father had owned a powered boat on which Elwyn had been from Green River to Moab. He had rowed a bit on the fast water above town as well, where the Green River exits Gray Canyon. Now, at twenty-four, he was signing on for his first whitewater trip—five months of it.

Loper returned to Green River to bid farewell to Rachel and accompany Trimble and Miser, the geologist, to the river. Miser gave a portrait of 1921 travel conditions in his journal for July 16. They left Green River at ten in the morning, traveling in the car of a Mr. Douglas, to make the 150-mile trip to Bluff. By 2:30 A.M. the next morning they had progressed less than two-thirds of the way:

En route to San Juan: Blake, Loper, Christensen, Trimble

> We encountered muddy roads several miles south of Lasal and the Ford limped and stopped on such roads until we got to within 2 or 3 miles of Monticello. We left Douglas in the car at that place and walked to town where we slept on bales of alfalfa hay in a barn.

On July 18, the team assembled on the shore of the San Juan four miles downstream of Bluff. This would be only the fourth known descent of the San Juan gorges to the confluence—the first was by E.L. Goodridge; the next two by Loper's mining friend Walter Mendenhall; all three trips having been in the early 1890s.

Although operated by the USGS, the expedition received its funding from Southern California Edison, who would sell the electricity from any hydroelectric dam in the lower Colorado basin. Their representative was newlywed Robert N. Allen, who served as recorder for the expedition. The geologist was portly Hugh D. Miser of Pea Ridge, Arkansas, thirty-seven, whom Blake felt was "utterly unfit for such an expedition," but whose gregarious nature cemented the group during the long, arduous survey. Heber Christensen of Moab was to serve as cook and second boatman. "Hebe was just an ordinary cook," recalled Blake, "but what a story teller he turned out to be. We listened to him for three months, and never heard him repeat himself. He could put us rolling in the sand any time." Hugh Hyde, twenty-one, of Bluff, joined Blake as the second rodman.

The survey work went like this: Trimble set up a survey station while Blake and Hyde moved their stadia rods from point to point. As Trimble sighted them in, Allen recorded the positions. Once the sighting in was done, Trimble and Allen moved their set-up downriver to the next spot and sighted back to the rodmen. This to be repeated ad nauseam from Bluff to Lee's Ferry. Meanwhile Loper and Christensen were to ferry camp downriver with two open, low-sided, sixteen-foot boats, built of redwood in Los Angeles, shipped by rail to Green River, and hauled overland by truck to the San Juan. "So there was seven men and all their duffel, food, and instruments for two small boats," wrote Loper, "so if we did take water once in a while it was not to be wondered at but that only happened a few times."

The first day out Hebe Christensen hit a series of sand waves, panicked, and froze at his oars. Loper chased him down, hollering, towed him ashore, and never let him row again. In effect the trip was, from that point on, a hiking expedition for most of the men. They would hike along the shore from station to station; meanwhile Loper would row the first boat to camp and hike back upriver for the second. So while most of the men essentially walked from Bluff to Lee's Ferry, Loper rowed that same distance twice and walked the full distance upstream, one piece at a time. Often Loper had to ferry men from one side to the other, but largely they spent their time ashore.

> As we drifted down the river from where we launched the boats we pass the Hogan of old Jim Jo, an old Navajo Indian that had passed his four score but he was wise enough to get him self three young wives who kept the Home Fires burning by making Navajo Rugs and tending their little field of corn.... too bad that the law won't let us old ones do like wise.

This was familiar country for Loper, who had been down, and up, this stretch many times in the 1890s. They surveyed the ten miles of flat country below their launch quickly and entered the first gorge of the San Juan. Here they encountered the first glitch in their procedure. Deep in the limestone canyon they came to "the narrows," a point where Loper would not be able to get back upstream for the second boat:

> So it was here that we had to break in another boatman and my choice was reduced to one man for all the rest were out of the running altogether but this one man sure had the courage of his convictions and it

> was a sure shot that he would click and as it happened I sure did not make a mistake in putting Elwyn Blake in as the other boatman—

Blake had impressed Loper from his first work back in the San Rafael Desert, which is why Loper had pushed for him to join this crew. Now he picked Blake for the touchy job of carrying men and equipment through the swiftwater gorge. "I felt a little uneasy as I took the oars," recalled Blake:

> As I approached the big shore rock, I saw a small sand spit below it. I swung the stern of the boat downstream and pulled hard in the swift stream. A few mighty strokes of the oars brought me close. With all my might I pulled toward the rock, barely missing it, as I intended. The prow grated onto the sand with a satisfying sound of a safe landing. It had taken but a few minutes, but what a relief.

For Loper, childless at fifty-one years old, Blake, twenty-four, was on his way to becoming a surrogate son and protégé. "Little did I imagine," continued Blake, "that, within the next few years I would run the rapids of the Grand as well as those of the upper Green."

They worked their way on through the first gorge without further problems and set up camp near the tiny settlement of Goodridge, also known as Mexican Hat. The river was running high; great sand waves were building and breaking in front of camp. "Hugh and I got a thrill from swimming out into mounting sand waves and riding over their humps," wrote Blake:

> Bert, not knowing whether or not we were good swimmers, squatted near the prow of one of the boats, ready to come to the rescue of one of us, should we get into trouble. He seemed to have more concern at this little escapade than he had seeing me off on a sixty-mile trek across the San Rafael desert years before.

Christensen apparently took no offense at his demotion from boatman. "We are seeing great sights and some of the worst country on earth," he wrote to the *Moab Times-Independent.* "It is amusing to see Bert Loper run rapids and sand waves. I never saw a man so skilled with boats as

Elwyn Blake and Bert Loper, San Juan

Hugh Miser

Mr. Loper. We certainly have a good bunch of men, all jolly."

On July 23 they moved downriver to Goodridge Bridge (Mexican Hat Bridge). Wesley Oliver was running a small trading post there and signed on as the expedition supply man. He had driven his truck to the launch a few days earlier and taken all their superfluous gear—evening wear, suitcases, extra supplies—and had them in storage. Trimble and Loper now worked with Oliver to establish supply points where Oliver could bring in food by pack train. The men were unsure just how far it was from Bluff to the Colorado River—one hundred miles? One hundred fifty? They made plans based on their best guesses.

"We sent out our mail by Mr. Neville," wrote Loper. This was William E. "Billy" Nevills, a miner and speculator from California. He had arrived in Mexican Hat a year earlier to keep an eye on some oil claims belonging to a friend. Nevills's thirteen-year-old son Norman would make his first visit to the San Juan in another four years, eventually fall in love with the river, and spend the rest of his life building his career as "America's Number One Fast Water Man"—a title Loper and one or two others would contest. But for now, "Mr. Neville" meant little to Loper or his entourage other than being the gentleman that took care of their mail.

The expedition entered the main gorge of the San Juan, passed

Surveyors' camp; Loper center

Mendenhall Loop—where Loper had spent the long, cold winter of 1894—and camped a mile and a half below. The next day they entered the winding meanders of the San Juan gorge known as the Goosenecks, where Loper was able to place a name on the maps:

> The Tabernacle is another goose neck or loop and is shaped like the Tabernacle in Salt Lake City and it was me that named the Tabernacle in 1894 but it seems as though the name had went out of use in the last 27 years it being that long since I had been away from that part of the river so I told the boss and he rechristened it and so put it on the map.

Given that the geographic names on the San Juan were formalized on this expedition, it is probable that Loper was responsible for many of them, and his memories of Mendenhall's occupation were likely the source for naming Mendenhall Loop.

Loper began trusting Blake to run a boat more often, though the learning curve was sometimes steep. In a set of sand waves Blake, carrying Miser and Hyde, snapped an oarlock and swamped the boat. Jumping into the waist-deep river, they hauled the boat ashore and bailed out.

The summer rains were upon them and floods were rolling down the river with an alarming irregularity. Unfortunately there were no

Heavy loads

river gages on the San Juan in 1921, so we are left only with the descriptions of those on the voyage. "On awakening ... we found that the river was on another rampage," Loper wrote. "—the river raised about six feet in 3 hours and the way it is acting you would think that it was angry about something.... [T]he river being so turbulent spent rest of the P.M. playing rummy."

The next day they camped on Honaker Bar, where Loper had worked for Henry Honaker in the summer of 1894. Ten years after Loper left, gold prospectors had completed—and abandoned—the Honaker Trail. Gone were the precipitous drops and ropework, replaced by an extensive series of switchbacks and stone ramps, taking two-and-one-half miles to climb a mere 1235 feet. The trail, like the San Juan itself, takes a long time to go a short distance—although Honaker Bar is seventeen miles downriver of Mexican Hat, the top of Honaker Trail is less than eight miles by road from the town.

> July-31 and the 52nd. year of my birth but I cannot see any difference in the day but it is just the same old thing as before so after breakfast Mr. Miser and I took a trip to Mexican Hat for the mail. We returned in P.M. by wagon driven by Wesley Oliver we had supplies including beef and Elwyn and I took turns carrying it down the trail which was some job—I think it would have been better to have cut the dam thing

Clubbing fish near Honaker Trail. Left to right: Blake, Hyde, Loper, Christensen, Trimble

> in two but we did not but it was welcome to the bunch in camp just the same—during the night I was awakened by the rising water and had to call for help to move the camp above the water—the river is the highest that it has been since we started and the water is so slimy that the fish by the thousands choked and was easily caught or killed with clubs—had a great time in the sport and we were out in our B*V*Ds and we was never able to get the red out of our garments the river being that slimy—we had to dig a well along side the river where the water would seep in and in that way we could get water for camp purposes and drinking.

Two days later Loper and Allen walked to town again for the mail, but found the pack mule carrying the mail had run off, Oliver having to chase it clear to Bluff. They waited a day for Oliver to return with the mail, then hiked back to camp at Honaker Bar.

On August 5th Loper, towing the second boat, snapped an oarlock and lost control while entering a relatively minor rapid above Johns Canyon. "One of the boats containing two members of the party not only narrowly missed striking the canyon wall," wrote Miser:

> but struck a boulder and was burst on one side from bow to stern. The boat was nearly filled with water by the time a landing place was reached. Then the wet equipment was unloaded, and the boat was dragged ashore and repaired.

Loper rebuilt it as the survey proceeded down the shoreline. At the rapid now known as Government, the men portaged the loads around while Loper rowed each boat through. They rowed out of the gorge on August 10 and camped in an open stretch called Clay Hills Crossing.

Loper and Miser had begun hiking together whenever the schedule allowed, and at Clay Hills Loper suggested they climb the cliffs and walk to Red House, where many years earlier Loper had found a cabin and reservoir during a winter foray from Glen Canyon. It was farther than he remembered.

> AUG-11 Mr. Miser and I started out on our journey and the country sloped to the south and we sure had the full benefit of the sun for the entire day and you will note from the above date that it had a right to get hot and we started out with about 1½ gallons of water but Mr. Miser was a rather fleshy man and the heat worked a hardship on him and by about 10 A.M. the water was gone and it so happened that we did nothing all that long day but walk....
>
> It was getting long to-ward sun down and no water since forenoon and Mr. Miser was in a rather bad way and after having passed several of the aforesaid red points and no water Mr. Miser took it in his head to go to a dry canyon that we had been paralleling and it was then that I got a little anxious and as he left I made a dash up the rise and looked over and sure enough there was the reservoir.

Loper ran back, tracked down the delirious Miser and took him to water. Loper knew over-drinking would make them ill and insisted they drink just six swallows at a time. They spent the night holed up there, over twenty miles from camp. They walked back the next day, weary, but Miser was toughening quickly, enjoying the walks, and relishing the chance to study the barren geology.

The survey was charged with mapping just the river channel until they passed below the 3,900-foot contour—roughly the elevation of a proposed dam near Lee's Ferry. Below that elevation, which they passed five miles below Honaker Trail, they were to map everything. Now instead of passing quickly through open country, they bogged down, mapping every drainage. Below Clay Hills the San Juan opens into a broad valley called Piute Farms, and the survey slowed to a crawl. At the same time the river's gradient lessens, due to a massive delta blocking the river downstream at Piute Creek, and the channel broadens and shallows. When the river was not flooding it was often too shallow to boat. On occasion when drifting sideways the downstream edge of the boat would hit bottom, with the result that the boat's momentum would nearly flip it, dumping the passengers into the river. At other times it was a matter of dragging the boat through the shallows, occasionally extreme enough that Loper inched the heavily loaded boats along, lifting and yanking one end at a time.

They spent days upon days camped in the wide stretches of the river, waiting for the surveyors to map. Loper and Miser hiked and explored, one time boating downriver nine miles to scout upcoming survey work, then spending two days dragging the boat back upriver to camp. A friendship was growing between the uneducated boatman and the college-degreed geologist that endured for decades.

And the floods continued. Where one day the 3,300-foot wide channel was so shallow Loper had to drag the boats, another day saw seven feet of raging torrent and crashing sand waves, collapsing the shorelines and devouring seventy-five feet of riverbank. Flood surges six feet high blasted past camp.

> [It was] while camped at this place that on two different occasions I nearly lost a boat by caving banks and on one occasion the boat was filled and it took the help of Mr. Miser and Hebe to get the boat raised again. After two near mishaps I took both boats out of the river and put them up high and dry—while at this camp we tried about every thing we ever heard of to avoid the mosquitoes but of no avail.

The expedition mapped Copper Canyon and Nokai Canyon and moved downriver past Zahn's Camp, where the five Zahn brothers had scoured the gravel bars for gold. In 1915 the Zahns had driven their Franklin automobile all the way to the river. Also known as Gable Camp, this had been the downstream extent of Loper's longest San Juan venture in 1894. From here on was new territory.

Wesley Oliver packed in more food at Spencer Camp on September 19th. Here the same Charles Spencer, that Loper had met at Lee's Ferry building a steamboat in 1912, had made his first marks on the gravel

Loper running Paiute Rapid

bars of the southwest. Around 1909, with the help of investors, Spencer had built a road into the river from the south and hauled in a gigantic Sampson crusher and a mill, hoping to find gold enough in the bedrock to pay. He didn't.

Increasingly, Loper was letting Blake run the second boat when he could be spared from rodman duty or the canyon configuration demanded. "We had a flood down the river so I had to call on Elwyn again and as the sand waves was running very high Elwyn took a little water but he made the trip in fine style and he sure has the stuff for the making of a real boatman." Meanwhile the hard labor took its toll. Wrote Miser: "Bert Loper has been complaining with lumbago for 2 or 3 days and still has it though he can walk around."

They camped at Piute Creek, at the head of Piute Rapid and carried the gear around the drop. Loper took both boats through empty. Adversity continued. If it was not rain or heat or mosquitoes, it was something else. Miser wrote:

> It began to blow from the south between 9 and 10 A.M. on September 18 and continued without cessation from this direction until 5 P.M. It blew

> in gusts and picked up sand and fine yellow dust, which were carried up into the air hundreds if not thousands of feet. The wind shook Mr. Trimble's plane table so violently and blew so much sand into our eyes that at 11 A.M. we discontinued the descent of the canyon. The beating of the wind against the canyon walls roared like an enormous waterfall or the din of a forest storm.

They waited for Oliver to bring in more supplies. So far he had arrived early at each rendezvous. Now he was several days late. Finally Oliver appeared, worn and hungry, on a lone horse with no supplies. A rockfall in Nokai Canyon had obliterated the trail and he was barely able to get through with his best horse. They needed a new plan. Loper pointed out the only way he knew: he would drag a boat sixteen miles up the swift-flowing river to Spencer Camp and meet Oliver there. This was Loper's specialty—unpowered upstream travel—and although it was not a job he relished, there was no other way.

> I knew that it would be a hard one and as it was I had to take the most of what grub we had to make the trip on for the trip for that distance and under those conditions would take more than one day so I had every thing about ready and had stripped down to my B*V*Ds and when I went up to where the boat was I found Mr. Miser also down to his undies.

In two months on the river the chubby, out-of-shape Miser had lost, according to Blake, thirty pounds, and was now "hardened into a rugged, tough individual"—one who without asking, was willing to share his friend Loper's arduous assignment. The two men marched barefoot up the sand-floored river for the next two days, arriving at Spencer Camp just thirty minutes before Oliver's pack train. "That is what you call a heart breaking trip," recalled Loper. They rested there that night and spent the next day rowing, dragging, and yanking the four hundred pounds of supplies back to Piute Canyon on low water.

The San Juan canyon begins narrowing below Piute Rapid. This was the downstream end of the gold-boom development, and the narrowing gorge made for quicker survey work. Three days brought them to Cha Canyon and the head of the biggest rapid on the San Juan, Thirteen-

San Juan between Spencer Camp and Paiute Rapid; now innundated

Foot. The men surveyed the canyon as the food dwindled. Oliver's work was now done, however, and their next resupply was to be a stash brought up the Colorado by motorboat and left at the San Juan's mouth. This was unmapped terrain; no one knew just how far downstream that was. Not far, they hoped. Loper volunteered to walk downriver and see.

He left early, soon getting ledged out and having to cross and recross the river. He stripped, leaving his clothes under a ledge. Upstream, clouds formed, portending rain and a possible rising river. Loper hurried on. It turned out to be eleven miles to the Colorado.

> There appeared to be a storm up the San Juan and I was in an awful hurry to get back for I knew that if the river raised one foot I could not make it up against the current so I hurried up and got about 15# flour and another item or two and started back and for the fact that I would be in the water and then out of it and the evaporation caused me to become very badly chilled and although I was moving with all the speed that I could muster I was shaking all over
>
> but in getting my little pack I ran across a bottle of vanilla extract which I pushed down in the flour and it happened that the extract was about 60% alcohol so I finally reached down and got the extract and drank about ½ of it, me being that cold and in another place I went in the quicksand completely all over and it was by me floundering around that I finally got out and continued on my way....
>
> There are many times that when a person gets in the quicksand that

Camp after portage of 13-Foot Rapid

> if he just keeps floundering he will get out but if he keeps in a upright position he will perish but I learned lots from a little sorrel horse that I owned many years ago and that horse knew more in lots of ways than many people for it was impossible to trap him in quicksand
>
> but in the course of time I reached the place that I first undressed in the morning and then I drank the balance of the extract and put my clothes on and by the time I reached camp I was perspiring very freely and was any thing but chilled thanks to the extract.

"At dusk I looked down river," wrote Blake. "The indestructible Bert was just coming into sight. His stride was long but far from elastic. He looked up and saw me, and waved a tired greeting. Twenty-two miles of wallowing through the muck and water of the San Juan had not slowed him much." Loper was able to increase the larder by one sack of wet flour. But at least they now knew how far it was to the next food, and knew it really was there.

With the water now at an all-time low for their trip, Loper directed the portage of both boats and all the gear to the bottom of Thirteen-Foot Rapid. This was only the third portage of his career—the first being at Grand Gulch in 1894 and the second near the foot of Cataract in 1907—but it was also his last. Thirteen-foot Rapid remains one of the few rapids in the Colorado drainage that Loper never ran.

Two days later on October 3 they tied up at the mouth of the San Juan. For seventy-seven days they had camped by the shores of the swift San Juan River, never out of earshot of its constant splashing and gurgling. Now, on the shore of the placid Colorado, the river was nearly silent. "Its peaceful nature, in comparison with the swift, noisy, and turbulent San Juan," wrote Miser, "was most impressive."

The men took the next day off from surveying, hiking upriver to visit the Hole-in-the-Rock trail while Loper and the now-seasoned boatman Blake rowed up to ferry them back home.

On October 5, while Loper was patching his overalls with flour sacks, Emery Kolb pulled into camp, followed by his brother Ellsworth and Leigh Lint. On board the three boats were most of the survey crew, including hydrologist E.C. La Rue and Miser's boss, Sidney Paige. As planned, the Chenowith survey had just finished surveying Cataract Canyon. Most of the party was now heading down to Lee's Ferry, leaving behind Chenowith and two surveyors in one boat to finish the line to the San Juan.

They had launched September 10 from Green River and motored three days to the confluence, there to pick up the survey from a previously established benchmark. In 1914, during the flurry of Reclamation activity that employed Loper at the confluence, much of the flatwater of the Colorado Basin had been mapped, including the 120 miles from Green River to the confluence. Like the San Juan survey, Chenowith's party was to map all terrain below 3,900 feet, which began shortly below the confluence. The surveying and boatwork in Cataract Canyon went exceptionally smoothly until the last major rapid, Dark Canyon. There Ellsworth Kolb wedged his boat between two rocks and lodged solidly, water pouring through the cockpit. On board were the maps of the entire summer's work, valued at some ten thousand dollars. After a worrisome night, the crew rescued the boat in the morning. To their relief, the maps had stayed dry.

While Loper was delighted to see his old boating partner Ellsworth, the rest of the party was delighted with the cargo they delivered—a boat and twelve hundred pounds of provisions they had picked up at Hite. The Kolb crowd did not stay long, however, hoping to make it downriver to Aztec Creek that night. Hugh Miser's geologic work now done, he departed with the Kolbs. It was up to Trimble's team to map the remaining miles of Glen Canyon to Lee's Ferry.

The trip changed dramatically for the Trimble Survey. Not only was the rushing of the San Juan silenced, but their favorite crew member, Miser, was gone. Worse, Hebe Christensen, the jolly story-telling cook from Moab, had wrenched his back badly at Piute Creek. Now instead of stories he supplied nothing but ill-tempered grousing. And while Christensen's cooking had been tolerable, Hugh Hyde's—for he had taken over the job—was not.

The survey continued. They had but seventy-eight miles of flat water to Lee's Ferry, but the hardest miles were still ahead of them. They were now 640 feet below the 3900-foot contour, meaning every wide spot and side canyon had to be mapped extensively.

At Oak Creek Loper went hiking with Christensen. In addition to his aching back, Christensen now had a splitting side-ache and nausea. Loper told him that was just how he had felt before his appendix burst. That evening Christensen petitioned Trimble to leave the expedition. When Trimble agreed, Allen asked to go too, having been under the weather for some time and sorely missing his new bride. The following morning Loper loaded the two men aboard and rowed toward Lee's Ferry. Blake took over Allen's position of recorder.

A day and a half later Loper reached Lee's Ferry and luckily found both trip supervisors there—H.W. Dennis of Southern California Edison and T.G. Gerdine of the USGS. All of them piled in an open-backed truck for a long cold drive to Flagstaff. There Loper hired two new men: a cook named Childers, and a rodman, Pat Gallagher (Blake says Pat Powell). Back at Lee's Ferry, expecting to drag his boat back up to the Trimble Survey camp, Loper was pleasantly surprised to have the USGS send him back via William Marrs's sternwheel motorboat, which had been engaged for resupply of the survey trips. They loaded Loper's rowboat, more food, and all three men aboard. Even with motor power, it took them four days to make their way upriver, as they often had to clamber into the river and wade about, hunting deep water. At times they had to drag the boat up riffles with the motor running full bore. They met Trimble's team at Aztec Creek, sixty-eight miles upriver from Lee's Ferry.

While Childers proved to be an excellent and creative cook, Gallagher was but an adequate rodman and a bit of a troublemaker, baiting whomever he could, whenever he could, challenging Hyde to a duel. The survey ground on, as did some teeth. Gallagher and Hyde shot a couple deer, Loper caught a beaver. The surveyors mapped.

One day Loper dropped seventeen miles downriver to visit the Fowler survey—another team working the lower stretch of Glen Canyon. Working for Fowler was a rodman named Frank Dodge, who later became a noted Grand Canyon boatman. Loper was unimpressed with Dodge's personality, "If I had been the boss of the party I would have fired him for he talked very mean to the boss." Dodge had similar opinions of Loper. In October 1949 he wrote to Otis Marston: "He seemed to be an old ill-disposed man—a desert rat who learned to row a boat but would drown if he upset. The older he got, the crabbier he seemed to get."

Also at Fowler's camp, "I met Mr. Tom Wimmer, an old friend from Green River, and after I had payed them my visit I started back, but before I started Tom let me take an outboard motor and I had a very nice trip back to camp." Loper kept the motor for a day. Although he did not elaborate, it may have been his first experience using an outboard and—other than one last trip back to his own camp after returning Wimmer's motor—may have marked his last experience with the activity he was the unrivaled king of: unpowered upstream travel.

On December 15 they finished the survey at Lee's Ferry. Loper had been at work, on land and river, for 170 days—one of the longest trips on record in the Colorado River basin. They drove south to Flagstaff where the trip members splintered off to their various homes. Loper took the train to Los Angeles, spent a few days there and returned home via Salt Lake City, arriving in Torrey to reunite with Rachel on Christmas Eve. #

49 Pearl's Trail

Pearl Baker knew Bert Loper all her life and admired him greatly. Her first article about him was published in the *Utah Humanities Review* in April 1947, while Loper was still living. Dock Marston wrote to Elwyn Blake, "Just when Pearl Baker got into the picture, I don't know but I think Bert gave her a lot of encouragement at first. I think she had access to his files. Later he turned against her and did what he could to discourage her." Just what Marston meant by that is unclear. Equally foggy is the date at which Baker decided to take her Loper profile to book length; apparently she had the idea while Loper was still living. Her son Noel remembers talk of it in the late 1940s:

> My mother and Bert did a lot of visiting. A lot of the visiting included interviews about the proposed book. I believe the friendship was very warm with a lot of mutual respect. The interactions between the two would be beyond my ability to understand at the time. Even after Bert was gone, she would talk a lot about him and what he did.

After Loper's death, Baker worked extensively on the project, transcribing many of his journals throughout the 1950s. She expanded many chapters into story form, fictionalizing discussions and events as they might have unfolded. In the late 1960s she whittled her efforts down to around one hundred pages plus photographs. Baker gave a fair history of Loper's life, with many parts abridged—Loper's climactic 1939 run of Grand Canyon got but a paragraph—and others expanded into pages of imagined dialog and thoughts. She painted in black and white, and Charlie Russell became the villain who abandoned Loper at Lee's Ferry without waiting so much as a day. Although Baker gained much unwritten knowledge from Loper, and her book tells a good tale, it is difficult to tell how much of it is factual, how much fantastic. It is, more than anything, a fond homage to a life-long friend.

Dock Marston read proofs and urged accuracy. "He was an extraordinary River folk but hardly the man of heroic stature that Pearl builds," Marston wrote to Barbara Ekker in 1968. "She is writing a biography and there is no harm in building the plus side. I did take her down on a few details where she got swinging the typewriter rather wildly as those in the know would have ridiculed the yarn."

Marston, however, agreed to write a foreword, in which he tried to fill in a bit more of the historical background and insert a little of his own psychological theorizing, "In 1907 on the Colorado River with Russell and Edwin Reagan Monett, Bert's adoption of his former companion as a father substitute multiplied the shock as he peered into the darkness downriver at Lee's Ferry. . . ."

Baker published *Trail on the Water* through Pruett Publishing in 1969, the centennial of Major Powell's voyage and Bert Loper's hundredth birthday. The only review it received was by P.T. Reilly in the *Utah Historical Quarterly*. He savaged it, primarily due to the fictitionalized parts of the narrative. Marston had little good to say about the final product.

Trail on the Water soon went out of print, Baker buying the remainders and selling them herself. Aside from a few copies drifting about the boating community or libraries, it has faded to obscurity. #

Pearl Baker

Trail on the Water

50 Hell's Half Mile

"YOU MUST WRITE ME," Loper wrote to Miser on March 22, 1922, "and tell me if you have any trips in view for this summer. I have written Trimble and want to write Mr. Gerdine to-night also for I would not mind another trip this summer if I could land one."

The San Juan survey had become a marathon of nearly six months, and all involved had been glad to head home. But by spring Loper was getting the urge to return to the river. The pay was good and constant compared to anything else he might scare up, and the pickings were slim at home. "Greenriver is very quiet just now with all prospects of a continuance of the same for some time. I have been running around on the Desert quite a bit this spring but think it is over for awhile now."

Miser replied in late April, saying he had not heard of any trips for 1922, but that Trimble had assured him that if any were to happen, Loper would be invited as boatman. Loper responded, lamenting the dearth of work locally:

> I would not go to any coal mine just at present not untill the strike is over. I have had a job putting in some cribs above the Bridge here but the job was finished Monday evening so don't know just what I will do. Our trip got just a little tiresome last summer but I wish I had another one just like it and with the same crowd minus the cook.

Loper got most of his wish. In April the USGS, in conjunction with Utah Power & Light (UP&L), announced plans for an imminent survey of the Green River, beginning at Major Powell's launch site of Green River, Wyoming, and continuing all the way down to Green River, Utah, where the Lopers were then living. Kelly Trimble was once again in charge. As promised, Trimble hired Loper as head boatman. Even better, Loper's protégé Elwyn Blake would be a rodman, serving double duty as boatman. Leigh Lint, of Idaho, who had apprenticed rowing on the 1921 Cataract Canyon trip, would serve as a second rodman-cum-boatman.

Hugh Miser would not be on this trip, however. The geologist was to be John Reeside; the hydraulic engineer and recorder, Ralf Woolley; the UP&L representative, Harry Stoner; and the cook, John Clogston—another veteran of the 1921 Cataract trip.

Loper was delighted to have the job, even if the long-term career looked dim. "I really believe this will be my last trip," Loper wrote Miser. "But I said that last year, but my wife does not want me to go any more." Maybe if the expedition did not last six months, things would be better for Rachel.

Loper boarded a westbound train, then transferred in Salt Lake, heading northeast to Green River, Wyoming. He checked into the Stanley Hotel on July 6. The men began assembling the following day. On July 8 they went to the depot and unloaded three new river boats, custom built by Fellows & Stewart of Wilmington, California. They rowed them four miles downriver, ducking beneath cables at the railroad-tie yard. At Scott's Bottom—where Flaming Gorge Reservoir reached its head of inundation in the 1960s—they established camp. It took another five days to gather all the necessary supplies and load nearly a ton into each boat.

Loper and Blake captained the *Utah* and the *Wyoming*, eighteen-foot Galloway-style boats, four-and-one-half feet wide at the oarlocks. They were larger than Loper was used to—so oversized that they toyed with the idea of cutting them down. They crammed the hatches with food, instruments, and camp gear. At 10:00 on July 13 the expedition shoved off for Utah on 3,000 CFS of water.

When not walking along shore, the survey team rode perched on the hatch lids on either end of the boats—Trimble and Woolley with Loper, Stoner and Reeside with Blake. Lint rowed the *Colorado*, a smaller sixteen-footer, carrying the cook, the kitchen, and general cooking supplies.

The purpose of this expedition was to tie together the many pre-existing surveys of the Green, mostly done between 1914 and 1917, and to survey the parts between, which included nearly all the canyoned whitewater sections. The first three days of this expedition, then, involved rowing down the already surveyed Green to its confluence with Henry's Fork, where the unmapped river commenced. Sand bars

The boats, the shorter *Colorado* on left

and mosquitoes were their main foes, young geese and deer their main prey. Loper described digging a great pit, burning a cord of wood down to coals and burying their gigantic dutch oven within, crammed with four young geese. "The next morning when we dug it all out we had a dish fit for a king, the meat was falling off the bones—some feed." Blake described the darker side:

> As the sun began to sink, we saw that our hopes for a mosquito-free campsite were in vain. At first a few of the pests began to come in from across the river. Then we saw clouds of them rising from the opposite shore. It was supper time, both for the vicious pests and for us. We fought them off, piled cowchips on the fire, and tried to eat, while keeping our heads in the smoke. The mosquitoes bored in in spite of the smoke.

At Henry's Fork the surveyors found the old benchmark, tied in, and began the transit downriver. Here the badlands of southern Wyoming end and the Green River abruptly carves into the Uinta Mountains and enters the Colorado Plateau. Here begins the series of slickrock canyons and whitewater gorges that do not end until Grand Canyon debouches the Colorado River into the Mojave Desert some nine hundred miles downriver. First in the great succession of canyons was Flaming Gorge, named, as were most of the canyons, by Major John Wesley Powell on his 1869 exploratory voyage. This brilliant orange scarp leads into the

Loper and his boys; Blake on left, Lint on right

mountainside just downstream of the Henry's Fork, followed quickly by two short canyons: Horseshoe, named for its course into and out of the mountainside; and Kingfisher, named for its residents, still in abundance when Loper passed through. Next came Red Canyon, around thirty miles long, carved deep into the hard, maroon Uinta Mountain Quartzite, home to the first rapids worthy of the name.

It does not take a major rapid to cause problems, as Blake quickly discovered. A momentary attention lapse in fast water perched him firmly on a midstream rock. He gave Reeside, who could not swim, the only life jacket. Looking upstream, he made eye-contact with Loper, who was bearing down upon him, and came to a wordless understanding. Loper rammed the *Wyoming*, shifting it on its perch. As the boats connected, Blake, bowline coiled in his hand, quickly stepped across onto the *Utah* and snubbed the rope around a hatch lid. When the rope snapped tight, the momentum of Loper's boat yanked the *Wyoming* free. "There is no wonder about that happening," grumbled Loper in his log, "for his two passengers positively would do nothing but keep their fat butts planted on that boat, but there was nothing serious at all."

On July 23rd Loper followed Ellsworth Kolb's 1911 footsteps, climbing the far cliff and wandering overland to a cabin. The Swett family was still there, remembered Kolb well, and treated Loper to dinner. He gave them a small packet of letters to mail, and their two daughters decorated Loper in a bouquet of sweet peas. A few miles farther downriver they met the Hermit of Red Canyon. A horrified Ralf Woolley described him:

> The hermit gave his name as Amos Hill. He was 71 years old and has lived in the canyon about 20 years. His house or hovel is a crude tepee over a small hole in the ground. It is hardly big enough for one person, and could be classed as a good sized dog kennel. The sight of it as well as that of the man himself was repulsive. His beard and hair were gray and somewhat matted with dirt. For a head covering he wore a paper sack with the edge turned down to a depth of about 4 inches. His shirt was a piece of dirty canvass with a hole cut in the middle for his head to pass thru, then the two edges were caught together under the arms with cord. His pants were a ragged pair of overalls, and these items with his shoes constituted his entire wardrobe. His shoes were a unique curiosity. The

> soles were two large pieces of cow-hide about 15 inches long with the hair on the bottom side. The uppers were apparently cut from old rubber boots. They were laced to the soles with rawhide strings around the outer edge. To fill the extra space around his feet, or for comfort or some other reason undetermined, he had them stuffed with straw which was sticking out all around the edge of the soles.
>
> He conversed freely with members of the party and willingly answered the questions asked. Among other things he claims to have gone thru the Green River canyons on a raft and taken a horse along with him, a feat which is very highly improbable if not impossible.

The best picture of Hill from the expedition files shows him seated, talking animatedly to fellow hermit Bert Loper—an amateur by comparison.

Ashley Falls was the first serious rapid. Powell named it after seeing the name ASHLEY scrawled on a rock face above the rapid. The inscription marked the passage of General William Ashley, a fur trading magnate from St. Louis, who led an expedition to the Green River in southern Wyoming in 1825. Splitting from his party, he and several men worked their way downriver in bull boats—crude frames of saplings covered with buffalo hides. They made it as far as the Uinta Basin about one hundred miles downriver before returning to Wyoming. There they held the first of many famed trappers' rendezvous.

Powell and most others lined or portaged here, rather than risk wrapping their boats on the huge boulders that choked the stream. Loper saw a way through. Telling Blake and Lint to wait ten minutes between each boat in case of problems, Loper pulled out and vanished into a small slot between boulders on the right side of the river. Blake followed as directed, finding Loper below unscathed. Lint lost his line, bounced off a boulder, but spun through intact.

"About ½ mile below Cart Creek and below another turn in the river," noted Reeside, "is another possible damsite." In fulfilling one of his several responsibilities, Reeside went on to describe in detail the site that later hosted Flaming Gorge Dam, which in turn inundated all the river they had seen since launching. In 1922, however, no one said much about preservation. Progress was the word.

Red Creek Rapid was the second serious obstacle—a long, rocky

Loper in Ashley Falls

Loper in Snap Canyon Rapid

rapid formed by the delta of Red Creek. After a lengthy scout, Loper led the others through. They bumped a few rocks but sustained no damage.

> July 27th—Camp piss ant and of all the camps this one takes the plum for the ants are every where and there is no getting away from them—The boss had some more flat country to work. It rained most all night but that did not bother the ants—

Trimble and team spent the next several days surveying the broad valley known as Brown's Park—a remote basin on the Wyoming-Utah-Colorado border that was once the stronghold of outlaws like Butch Cassidy. It was a hard place to get to, and an easy one from which to escape across state lines. By 1922 few ranchers and no outlaws remained. Stoner borrowed a horse and rode out to the Lodore post office. Loper got "several letters, most of them from Rachel."

Day by day the Uintas loomed higher to the south, until on Loper's fifty-third birthday, July 31, a sharp defile opened. "[The river] seemed as though it was looking for a place to break through the Mountains," wrote Loper, "and when it reached the two bar Ranch it, very suddenly, made a right angle turn and headed direct for the mountain and its entrance to Lodore Canyon is a very spectacular place and seemed to say to a voyager that on entering its narrow opening that he would have to leave all hope behind ..." Indeed, few canyons start with the dramatic punch of Lodore, cutting directly from the flat lowlands of Brown's Park to a three-thousand-foot deep gorge a few miles beyond.

On August 1st the party entered Lodore. The river flow was dropping, but with no gages between Green River, Wyoming, and Green River, Utah, at that time, it is hard to say what water levels they faced in Lodore—with tributaries coming in as they traveled, a rough guess might be a bit over 3,000 CFS—high water by today's post-dam standards, medium for 1922.

The rapid now known as "Winnie's" held, then as now, a major boulder in the very center of the current. Blake, in the lead, pulled hard right, barely missing it and getting a major scolding for trying the stunt without life jackets, non-swimming Reeside clinging to the deck. Loper tried pulling to the left, but with poor results. Unable to clear the boulder he bashed his stern against it, punching the steel portaging handle right through the back of the boat. An hour's work put the *Utah* shipshape once more, patched with rubber cement and canvas, with a 1 x 4 pulled from a food crate nailed over the top. "Our loads are getting very much lighter," wrote Loper optimistically, "so that helped me from getting a worse puncture than I otherwise would have."

The next night they camped at the foot of Upper Disaster Falls—again named by Powell, for here three of his men broke the twenty-two-foot *No Name* in two, losing precious cargo and nearly their lives. In coming through, Loper hung briefly on a rock but washed off quickly and made shore. Blake hung on another and flooded the cockpit. Jumping onto the rock, he lifted the boat loose and jumped back in, only to have an oarlock disintegrate. He washed onto another rock. Replacing the oarlock, Blake yanked his boat loose once again and made shore safely. Lint, in the smaller boat, had a clean run.

Lower Disaster Falls faced them the next morning, with its notorious undercut cliff. Rather than risk getting pulled under it, Loper elected to unload the boats and nose them along the shore—that is, wade along holding the bow, working down through the shallows. "Nosing," unique to Loper, was something he felt was far superior to "lining," or lowering a boat through a rapid with ropes. "Loper simply will not 'line' a boat."

wrote Blake. "He considers anyone who lines past a bad portion of a rapid as a novice. 'Anyone with experience,' Bert asserts, 'knows that it is more dangerous to line a boat than to run a rapid.'" True, few boatmen today line boats, preferring to run the rapid in nearly all instances. But for that matter, even fewer "nose" them. At the time, however, the boatmen nosed their boats past the undercut and, noted Loper "then we had to play jack ass and carry our loads down to the boats."

On August 3 they scouted Triplet Falls, a three-part rapid that has a tendency to slam boats into the nest of boulders that clogs the right half of the river. Loper's team, for they truly had become a team, ran it flawlessly. But beyond lay the steepest prolonged drop in the Colorado River system: Hell's Half Mile. Powell named it and spent days portaging his boats around. No one had ever attempted to run it. Blake recalled:

> "It's going to be a tough job to drag the boats over that hill and around this rapid," I remarked.
>
> "We're not going to take the boats out of the water," Bert informed me. "We're going to run it."
>
> ... Loper donned his life jacket, untied the painter to the *Utah*, took hold of the prow, and shoved off, jumping aboard and quickly grasping the oars.... In a few seconds the *Utah* shot into the midstream swift water. Loper pulled mightily at the oars.... For a moment it seemed that it would go over the top, but with a mighty pull at the oars, and with the help of the piled up water above the big rock, the *Utah* swung by.... Bert was able to land below, where he awaited Lint and I....
>
> Well, if Bert could run it, I could try.

All three made it through the drop, then nosed their boats through a short shallows before reboarding and rowing the remainder of the rapid. Lint, who until now had been having the best runs, piled into the rocks. "Someone threw him a line," wrote Blake, "which he wrapped around the hatch a couple times then, holding one end of the line in his teeth, used an oar as a pry-pole, and with the aid of those pulling from shore, managed to free the boat." Quite a picture.

Then the real work began, portaging over a ton of gear down the brutal route to the foot of the rapid. Stoner described it as being a full three-quarters of a mile, "across a small ridge, down a small red gully

Nosing the *Colorado* through Lower Disaster Falls

to a high-water channel, down that channel to near end, up through cedars to deer trail, along deer trail, 75 ft. above river first with soft red soil and rocks, then firm soil, down to sandbar." Stoner knew the path well, since they carried forty-three loads of about sixty pounds each down that trail. The next morning Stoner was absent from camp, but soon appeared shouldering the last load. "I have made up my mind," wrote Loper, "that the rapid I unload for will have to be a very bad rapid before I unload any more."

The evolution of whitewater boating was unfolding. From portaging boats and gear around rapids, the trend was moving toward lining, nosing, or merely unloading to run through empty. Loper was reaching the acme of his talents as well. To him it was increasingly apparent that even unloading was the hard way to do things. His pioneer run through Hell's Half Mile galvanized his convictions—from that point, for the rest of his life, he ran them all, and he ran them with a full load.

That afternoon many in the party had the scare of their life. During a hike up Rippling Brook, Blake was several hundred feet above the rest of the party when he inadvertently dislodged a boulder. The men below, who were stripping down for a swim in the brook, heard the shouts and looked up to see an avalanche of rock and debris plummeting toward them. They dove beneath a ledge, unscathed but for one man's unoccupied shirt that was run through by a sharp stone.

That night, the scare forgotten, Loper wrote of his ecstasy:

> I find that we have been just three days in Lodore Canyon and have passed hells half mile and when one reads the many hardships and the time the Kolb brothers had and put in in Lodore one will readily realize the unfavorable stage of the river they had ... but it is still a beautiful canyon and what a wonderful world this is to live in where a person can enjoy such wonderful sights and have such wonderful experiences. Who in the hell wants to be a white collar sissy when one can enjoy such grandeur and beauty such as this.

They were through Lodore, having never pulled a boat out of the water—a first. At the confluence of the Yampa River they left a note for the survey team coming down that stream, and moved on, floating around Steamboat Rock and into Whirlpool Canyon. The rapids there were small enough to run without scouting, and the survey team soon entered Island Park—a broad, placid valley making for slow shallow boating and extensive surveying. They spent eight days working through to the head of Split Mountain Canyon, spending much of their free time visiting Hod Ruple's family on their bountiful ranch. "WHAT a garden," wrote Loper, "they had enough to have supplied a whole community and just the three to eat all those nice vegetables. We were in the park 8 days and we sure did plenty to that garden"

The rapids of Split Mountain Canyon were simply fun compared to Lodore. They pulled into Jensen, Utah, on August 23, and the next day shanghaied Joe Dudley's Dodge mail truck for a one-hour muddy ride into Vernal, population 1,200. There they shopped, barbered, played pool, wrote letters, and returned to camp. They were seven weeks out now, with 180 miles to go. Much of what lay ahead had already been surveyed. On August 24 they moved on.

They had sixty-five flat, sluggish miles across the broad, mosquito-infested Uinta Basin, then the first fifty miles of Desolation Canyon to traverse before rapids became common again. For the oarsmen there was, as Loper said, a lot of "stick work." At a camp below Horseshoe Bend they were engulfed in a sandstorm. "Even the cook lost his patience," recalled Stoner, "and the 'descriptives' he used in the telling of what he thought of such a country were not lacking in color and were rivaled only by a former outburst about the makers of can-openers." They spent Sunday, August 27, on a sand bar adjacent to the Ouray

Loper running Chandler Falls, Desolation Canyon

Bridge, watching the Ute Indians that had come into Ouray for their monthly "issue day." The Utes, in turn, watched them.

Below Ouray the gray, shaley cliffs of Desolation Canyon rise slowly to spectacular heights, but the scenery is an acquired taste. "I took a walk to the top of the canyon where I could see the rivers loop below," wrote Loper, "but what I did see was a very uninteresting country—practically no vegetation whatever. About 9-45 the boss had finished his survey of the side canyon and the boats all being loaded we were soon on our way down the river—This is sure Desolation Canyon all right."

The summer rainy season was upon them. They often had to halt work for a few hours in the day, or scramble for shelter in the night. At least it cut the heat. On September 2 they camped at Jack Creek. "We found a rapid, the first in a long time so now we must be approaching the rough water in desolation canyon." Good news. The gray shales gave way to reddish-brown sandstone cliffs, making for more dramatic scenery. On September 7 they camped by the fresh water of Rock Creek and visited with the Seamount family, who were ranching the delta. They gorged on fresh produce, and continued on. Two nights later they camped at McPherson Ranch and once again ate their fill of peaches, melons, and tomatoes. Tora Seamount McPherson baked them four loaves of bread; her husband Jim had brought the mail up from Green River in anticipation of their arrival. Ralf Woolley wrote:

> McPherson's ranch is truly an oasis in a region of desolation. He has everything on it to make a ranch, even such modern conveniences as water piped from a distant spring into the house, a lawn in the front yard, all kinds of farm machinery, and such things as a large steel range in the kitchen and modern bath room equipment. As a matter of fact, one could easily imagine himself in a modern home somewhere in a city. The remarkable thing, however, is the fact that all of these articles that had to be transported into this place were brought up the canyon from Green River, Utah, a distance of about 35 miles, over not a wagon road, but a narrow trail built along the wall of the canyon. Everything is carried in by pack train.

McPherson Ranch was an oasis, and not just for the survey men. It had often been a stopover on the Outlaw Trail. McPherson had little choice but to befriend the rustlers and robbers that passed through this remote country, and the outlaws knew it was best to have friends out here. They treated him well in return.

On leaving McPherson's, all three boats smacked into the rocks of shallow Florence Creek Rapid, Loper and Blake sticking fast. The river was still around 3,000 CFS—a little bony for that stretch of rocky river. They pried loose and floated around the bend into Gray Canyon. Here the rusty cliffs part, only to expose another set of rolling gray escarpments. The river had been falling continuously, making the rapids rockier and tougher to navigate, but Loper and his men continued without any serious difficulty. On September 13 they ran Swaseys Rapid, the last of Gray Canyon, and camped at its foot. Here the surveyors tied into the Warren Survey marker and finished their work.

The next morning they crammed their small stove full of rubbish and firewood and left it on the beach, burning red hot and billowing smoke, as they headed for Green River. At the diversion dam eight miles above town, they called for a truck to haul their gear. The survey team helped Loper, Blake, and Lint lift the boats over the dam, then boarded the truck for town.

The three boatmen, now with empty boats, rowed across the farmland toward Green River. "We stopped at Mr. Brooks ranch and filled up on water melons," wrote Loper. "We tarried rather long eating melons so when I got started I was in a hurry but I had only gone a little way

Lint, Loper, and Blake in rummy game

Rachel and Bert at trip's end

when I saw my wife standing on the bank of the river in company with Mr. and Mrs. Jack Douglas so I landed and Rachel finished up the trip with me."

The trip had taken two months and one day to cover nearly four hundred miles. Loper had added much of Major Powell's route to his résumé, running almost every rapid, nosing around only Lower Disaster Falls and the center shallows of Hell's Half Mile. But there was still one major part missing from his record: Grand Canyon. The USGS survey trip would likely assault the great gorge the next spring. In spite of Rachel's dislike for Bert's extended voyages, his desire for Grand Canyon was running strong. #

51 Dammit Dock

In many of Loper's writings, he mentioned how aggrieved he was that he and his old pal Charlie Russell had become such bitter enemies. He often wrote that he preferred to remember the Russell he knew before, and chose to forget the mentally deranged man Russell later became. In an essay entitled "Thoughts that come to me in the still hours of the night," Loper wrote:

> After we two split up and he got others to take my place and had trouble with them all and he was finally committed to an insane asylum; then I knew I had judged him too hastily, and there were many times when I used harsh language to him. And now that he has been called to go on, and the years have passed, I only remember Charles Russell as he was in those good old days.

After *Trail on the Water*'s 1969 release, Pearl Baker continued to correspond with Marston for a few more years. He finally pushed her just a little too far. By 1971, he was deep into analyzing river runners and wrote:

> There must be a dozen different versions of Bert's THOUGHTS THAT COME TO ME which was an effort to justify his foul treatment of Russell. Imagine what his thoughts were when I told him that I had found Monett! After that, Bert quit this line of sobs. This slobbering was in both the Blake and Hunt files.

"Dammit Dock," fired back Baker:

> knock it off about Bert Loper. We just don't agree. If Bert was wont to justify himself in later years about Monett and Russell, the hell with it. To me Bert was a fine man, and I admired him very much.... I resent

> your trying to make Bert out other than he was—a fine man. What he had done in his youth doesn't interest me, nor does some little derogatory nothing-or-other you are always trying to drag up....
>
> This settles the matter, Dock. I simply don't want to hear any more about it, and if you crowd me on it any further I can only conclude that you not only don't respect my point of view but that you don't want to be friends anymore. I just don't know how to put this matter any stronger.

They did correspond further, but the friendship was permanently damaged. In 1972 Marston wrote to Elwyn Blake:

> She cannot free herself from the drive to put everyone right in the world and she has never been able to get herself properly adjusted. Some time back she threw some bricks at me and told me that my record on Loper had to be adjusted to her picture—or else. So now it is ELSE.

A year later he wrote to Barbara Ekker:

> Re: Pearl: Obviously you know that she is a member of the MAD Club which means Mad At Dock Club. Open membership is available to anyone. They must not expect Dock to respond in kind.
>
> Pearl joined because my research shows that Russell did not betray Bert in 1907 but Bert betrayed Russell. #

52 Retirement

On December 3, 1922, Loper was injured in the coal mines of Mohrland. "The hurt was a very slight one," Loper wrote to Hugh Miser, "but it became infected and Blood Poison set in and I surely suffered for a while, then they shipped me to Salt Lake … I was only in the Hospital for two weeks but it looked for a while as though I might loose my leg …"

After the Green River trip Loper, at fifty-three, had gone back to the coal mines at Mohrland, only to put himself out of commission for nearly a month. "It left me very weak but I am about myself again and working, that is when the mine works, which is not regular by any means."

For most of 1922 the coal mines had been plagued with falling coal prices and worker strikes. Loper was more than ready for another river trip. "The coal mines have nearly stopped, only two days a week and about half of the cars we can load and just after my months layoff makes it bad for me so I have to find something to do." On January 30, Miser wrote that a Grand Canyon trip might be in the works for 1923, and that Loper's name was being talked about for lead boatman. Loper wrote back begging details.

"I have gone and done it again," Loper wrote Miser on February 8, "for while working last Sat. morning a big lump of coal, fully a ton, came down and missed my head about 3 inches and raked me all down the left side and ended up by breaking the small bone in my leg below the knee." While Loper felt the break was not serious, it was "very painful and very disastrous financially."

"Mr. Loper may decide to give up mining," read a note in the Green River section of the *Moab Times Independent*, "as this is his second injury since Dec. 3." Miser wrote back his condolences, but on an upbeat note added that Colonel Claude Birdseye, the head of the upcoming Grand Canyon survey, had just asked for Loper's address.

On March 5 Loper, still on crutches, wrote Miser again, saying Birdseye must have changed his mind, as he never wrote. The reason soon became apparent: Birdseye had chosen Emery Kolb instead. Loper was second choice, should negotiations between Kolb and Birdseye fail. Loper later heard that E.C. La Rue, the trip hydrologist, had told Birdseye that Loper was too old.

There was one consolation. "They will have one good man and that is Blake, and while I likely will not go, I will feel as though I was represented by Blake being on the job, for he comes very near being a pupil of mine and he would be a credit to any man." Both Blake and Loper felt the strong bond between them. Lint, on the other hand, never really bought into Loper. When asked years later what Loper had taught him, Lint simply replied, "Bert was difficult."

La Rue and Birdseye may have come to regret their choice. If avoiding a cantankerous old man was their object, they certainly failed. Kolb gave them cantankerous in spades. Emery, the smaller and younger of the Kolb brothers, had already made a name for himself at Grand Canyon's South Rim, due to his pure feistiness. "Ellsworth was the gentleman," recalled Mike Harrison, who worked there in the 1920s. "Emery was the cocky bantam, always fighting." Initial hiring talks between Emery and Birdseye nearly collapsed when Birdseye forbade Kolb to bring a movie camera. He wanted Kolb focussed on boating, not on his photography business. La Rue was to make movies on the government's behalf. Kolb squawked, calling it "self extermination," but finally gave in. Malevolent feelings grew quickly between Kolb and La Rue.

Feistiness was one problem; overcautiousness another. At Soap Creek Rapid, just twelve miles into the trip, Kolb called for a portage. Blake and Lint were outraged, sorely wishing Bert Loper was their head boatman instead of Kolb—Blake was certain Loper would run it without hesitation. Halfway though the trip ill feelings about photography rights caused Kolb to suddenly quit—but that evening, at his wife's behest, he begged for the job back. He got it, continuing the trip on probation. When they reached the last major rapid, Lava Cliff, Kolb and Freeman lined their boats while Blake and Lint lobbied to run it. Although Kolb agreed to let them try, Birdseye squashed the deal, feeling if Kolb would not run it, no one should. In later years Blake still griped about not being able to run them all, wishing still that his mentor Loper had been in charge.

As for Loper: "My best wishes go with them, but it hurt a little just the same—if I had ever been called on and failed it would have been different but being the oldest Boatman and being left out hurt a little, but it is all over now so I must turn my attention to something else for this summer." With that, Bert Loper basically dropped off the map. There is little written by him or about him for nearly fifteen years.

Occasional notes in the personal sections of regional newspapers mention Bert and Rachel coming to Green River or Moab from Hiawatha or Wattis—coal towns adjacent to Mohrland. A November 15, 1923 item elaborated: "Bert had a nice walk the other morning when floods put the Lizzie in a mud hole, but he is not the only one who has walked."

A Tin Lizzie? Indeed, Loper's notebook for January and February 1924 itemizes such things as food (3 pigs, $11.44), rent ($5.00 a month), mining supplies (pick, $1; cap & powder $5), medical (teeth pulled, $2; Doan's Pills, $.60; truss, $2.79), and monthly payments for a car ($40.60).

An automobile was a supreme luxury for Loper, but Bill Busenbark, born in 1923, recalled Uncle Bert nearly always had a car, and was always inordinately proud of it. He added, however, that Loper's driving skills, like many who had grown up with horses, were often frightening.

On March 1, 1925 Loper wrote Miser from Mohrland, saying he had just returned from Salt Lake City, where Rachel had had an operation, leaving him "about $200 worse than nothing and while I was gone the mine I had been working in closed down so now for another job, but if Rachel comes out with her health restored I will laugh at the world."

He did laugh. Somehow, in spite of his poverty, he managed to quit the mines in 1925. Not only that but he left Utah with Rachel, driving his car all the way to Florida. In February, 1926 Lizzie Mettler wrote them a letter in Tampa, saying her husband, Bert's uncle Benjamin in Durango, had passed away. With roads and cars being what they were in 1926, this implies the Lopers had left Utah by late 1925.

They visited Hugh Miser in Washington, touring the monuments and cemeteries. On September 26, on his way back west, Loper wrote Miser from his old home town of Curryville, Missouri. He described car repairs, long miles, and plans to continue home via Dewey, Oklahoma, where his brother Jack lived, and Durango, where he planned to see his aunt. As it turned out, he was not able to connect with Jack Loper—severe flooding across the Midwest may have rerouted Bert and Rachel, or Jack may have been out on a remote drilling project with the oil company he worked for. No doubt a great disappointment—the Loper brothers had not seen each other for thirty years.

If the number of photographs taken is any indication, the road trip was a high point of the Lopers' marriage. A great stack of snapshots show Bert and Rachel among the palm trees, posing in Washington, always dressed to the nines. How they afforded the trip is unclear.

By 1928 the Lopers resided in the basement of the old Masonic Temple in Salt Lake City, Bert's occupation: custodian. Pearl Baker attributes the career change to a heart attack, but no records exist of such a thing, and Loper never mentions having had one. All that is certain is that Loper, who had lived his entire life in small villages or out-of-doors, always engaged in back-breaking labor, now lived a life of relative leisure, downtown, in a city of a quarter of a million people.

If he was anyone else, one might say he simply retired. But with his dismal and erratic mining employment, his injuries and medical debts, his hit-or-miss river work, he really could not afford to retire. The answer most likely lies in the six months he spent in Chickamauga in 1897, crippled with dysentery. As an honorably discharged veteran, Loper was entitled to a pension, which may well have kicked in around this time—as he was now over fifty-five. In the mid-1930s Loper mentioned in a letter to Elwyn Blake that it was difficult to make ends meet on a pension of sixty dollars a month (in modern terms that would come to about $650). As a miner, his monthly paycheck had been roughly double that in a good month, but good months were few. That fifty-mile walk to Lincoln, Nebraska, to enlist was the best move of Bert Loper's life—for a six-month stint in the army, much of it on furlough or in the infirmary, he drew more than two decades' worth of income. So by pinching his pension, living rent-free as a caretaker, and taking odd jobs when he could, Loper indeed retired. #

53 La Rue

As to the choice of Loper or Emery on the U.S.G.S. trip—I don't know. I first met the former back in the twenties! After he'd had a feud! (fight) with La Rue and Freeman. That was in '21 or '22, upriver from Lee's Ferry.

—Frank Dodge, October 5, 1949

The reasons for Birdseye's choice of Emery Kolb over Bert Loper are unclear and, in river circles, remain controversial. Most accounts point toward E.C. La Rue, the hydraulic engineer for the trip. La Rue, Loper believed, had told Birdseye that Loper was "too old." But USGS rodman and boatman Frank Dodge felt that age was merely an excuse, that La Rue had a grudge against Loper. Dodge's recollection does not hold much water, however, as he states that Lewis Freeman was in on the fight—and Freeman was not there until 1922—at which point Loper was hundred of miles upstream on the Green River. Too, Freeman's writings run long in praise of Loper. Loper and La Rue did cross paths in 1921, however, when their respective survey trips beached together briefly at the mouth of the San Juan.

If indeed Loper and La Rue did come to words, a possible topic could have been La Rue's fixation with Lee's Ferry as the best site for the first great dam on the Colorado. So intent was he on the Lee's Ferry Dam that, when the Boulder Dam site was chosen, his vehement opposition ended his career. Loper, on the other hand, had been with Homer Hamlin when he chose the Boulder Dam site and may have leaned toward that site as the most reasonable—a sure topic to send La Rue into a pique. Yet no journals of either expedition mention any encounter between Loper and La Rue. Nor do La Rue or Loper. La Rue's party was only in Loper's camp together for an hour or two.

Of course, it is possible the problem originated as far back as 1914, when Loper was in Green River building the *Ross Wheeler*. La Rue did a

Moab to Green River survey that September and could have run into a stressed and irritable Loper in town.

Or it could have been in Glen Canyon during Loper's final months at Red Canyon in 1915. La Rue and John Richardson planned a reconnaissance trip downriver from Hite. As Tom Wimmer wrote, "Mr R[ichardson] & L[a Rue] came to Green river to get a boatman by name of Loper to take them down as far as Lee's ferry but L[oper] was at that time down the river somewhare." So La Rue and Richardson bought a rotten old boat at Hite. Wimmer rowed them through. "this v[oy]age was entered with some misgiving as the boat was so bad & neither one of the party had ever been on that part of the river.... So we got in the old leaky thing & started." If Loper had promised to take them through and reneged, with the result that they had to flounder through in the sinking boat, it could certainly have caused a lasting grudge. Perhaps they met near Red Canyon during the voyage and had cross words. Still, Wimmer's account does not say if they had arranged the trip with Loper ahead of time, or simply hoped to find him when they got there.

Or there may never have been a fight at all. As yet, no concrete evidence has emerged to substantiate a quarrel. But the fact remains that many felt that both Loper and La Rue were cantankerous. And it is often true that two cranky people have a hard time getting along. Harry Tasker recalled his own early interactions with La Rue on the 1921 trip: "La Rue was rough. He thought he was important. La Rue started giving orders.... He wanted me to take care of his bed. I'll show you what I'll do with your bed. I threw it overboard." The feelings between La Rue and Loper, at the very least, appear to have been both edgy and mutual.

Perhaps it had to do with Tom Wimmer. Loper had heard a rumor that Wimmer would supervise the 1923 trip. Loper had known him for years only as a flatwater steam-boater on the Green. Loper wrote to Miser in March, 1923, "Mr. Trimble ... proposed to use his influence to get me on but I told him if I could run my own boat in my own way I would be delighted to go but I would not take orders from Wimmer (La Rue Man) for he never done any boating in that kind of water." Then as now, there were factions in the river world, and Loper and La Rue dwelt in different ones.

Maybe the allegation that Loper was afraid of Grand Canyon, widely spread after the 1907 trip, had caught up to him again.

Or this:

The answer may be as simple as the fact that Birdseye had a long-standing acquaintance with Kolb, and chose him regardless of what La Rue or anyone else said. Or he made his choice because by that time Kolb had one Grand Canyon trip and two Cataract Canyon runs under his belt—whereas Loper had not yet seen Grand Canyon.

In the end, it scarcely matters. Loper's great hope of a Grand Canyon run was once again dashed. To the old insult of cowardice was now added the tag of "too old." Kolb took the job, and Loper accepted his fate with some resignation, writing, "That part of the River has long been my Dream, long before lots of the men who will make it ever thought of it, but many a man has gone on with his dreams never come to pass."

Ironically, although Loper was deemed "too old" to run the river (which he certainly was not), he found himself headed back into the mines—something he really *was* too old to do.

Yet 1923 had one ray of light. Lewis Freeman, who had written several books on rivers throughout the country and the world, and who was a boatman on the 1923 expedition, published: *The Colorado River: Yesterday, To-day and Tomorrow.* In it he chronicled the explorers of the river, from the earliest recorded on through the time of his writing. Of Loper's aborted 1907 river efforts, Freeman had nothing but praise:

> The powerful and courageous Loper took most of the work in the rapids of Cataract Canyon off the hands of his still inexperienced companions, but paid the hard penalty of puncturing his own boat.... [Then, after the camera and boat were repaired:] Loper hastened on down Glen Canyon, only to find that his companions had given up on him some days previously and pushed off into Marble Canyon.
>
> Working his boat laboriously back up the river, the bitterly disappointed Loper took up a ranch and claim in the vicinity of Hite, where he makes his home at the present time. He still pulls a strong and skilful oar, and has done notable work in running the boats for some of the recent expeditions of the Geologic Survey on the Green and San Juan. All who have employed or worked with Loper on the river scout the wholly absurd newspaper story that was circulated charging that he deserted his companions through fear of the rapids of Grand Canyon. #

54 No man knows the river

LOPER HAD FRIENDS and family in Salt Lake City. Rachel's mother lived nearby, as did Rachel's younger brother Scotty. Loper and Scotty, recalled Bill Busenbark, loved to put on their finest and squire about the city when they could. "They were trouble," he laughed. But nothing serious. Loper had joined the Masons in 1922, an avocation he took seriously. That connection likely got him his caretaking position in the abandoned old Temple—by then meetings took place in the new temple across town. He took Masonry seriously, doing his best to follow the moral strictures thereof and attributing much of his good character to his abidance in the Masonic codes. Loper's hard-drinking, womanizing youth was long over, his faithfulness to Rachel apparently never challenged or questioned. For Rachel's part, the Mormonism that she had adopted as a young adult had faded, replaced by more traditional Protestantism. The Lopers settled into a content and conservative life in Salt Lake. But even if Loper hoped to forget about river running—and there is no evidence he did—the Colorado River in general and Grand Canyon in particular remained much in the news in 1927 and 1928.

On June 27, 1927, Clyde Eddy, an eccentric pharmaceutical executive from New York launched from Green River, Utah. He conceived the idea of a grand expedition in the style of Major Powell, even going so far as to order oversize replicas of Powell's Whitehall keeled boats. He advertised at colleges for adventurers, never telling them just what he had in store for them. To make his trip more newsworthy he adopted not only a dog, Rags, but a bear cub which he named Cataract. With a dozen unwitting collegians, they launched on floodwaters. Thank heaven Eddy had one good idea to mix in with his bad ones—he hired Parley Galloway, son of the late Nathaniel, as head boatman. The trip was calamitous, but successful. Suffice it to say that Galloway got them through in spite of Eddy's great ideas. Eddy returned to the East to write of his epic voyage.

Lopers in their prime, Salt Lake City

Later that same year the Pathé-Bray film company conceived the idea of a thriller filmed on the river. They hired E.C. La Rue as trip leader and Frank Dodge as one of the boatmen—both acquaintances of Loper. They were hampered not by the heat and floodwaters of mid-summer as Eddy was, but by the low water and freezing temperatures of December. When they were late arriving at Lee's Ferry (possibly an intentional part of the publicity plan) the company called in an "expert" to help search: Clyde Eddy. By the time Eddy arrived, the trip had appeared and Eddy joined them. With ice clogging the river below Phantom Ranch, the expedition abandoned their boats and left the river at Hermit Rapid. The movie never reached fruition.

Lastly, on October 20, 1928, a young honeymooning couple from southern Idaho launched from Green River. The groom, Glen Hyde, had run the Salmon in Idaho and canoed extensively in Canada. His wife Bessie would be the first woman to run Cataract or Grand Canyon. Unfortunately the Hydes brought two things on their trip that were very common on Idaho rivers. The first was their boat, a cumbersome sweep scow, steered but not propelled by huge rudders off bow and stern. The second was the Idaho tradition of not wearing life jackets.

Amazingly they made it through Cataract Canyon and halfway

through Grand Canyon. There they hiked out to visit Emery Kolb, who encouraged them to wear life preservers. They demurred and continued on downriver. When they failed to appear at the other end, Glen Hyde's father asked Emery Kolb to run the lower river in search of them. They discovered the scow empty, but no trace of the Hydes was ever found. The search made headlines across the country.

During the search for the Hydes, the Swing-Johnson Bill passed Congress, authorizing the first great dam on the Colorado, to be built in Black Canyon at a site first described by Homer Hamlin on Loper's 1920 trip. Boulder Dam, as it was initially called, eventually flooded 115 miles of the Colorado, inundating over forty miles of Grand Canyon and several serious rapids.

Utah rivers were getting attention as well. In 1928 Hugh Miser wrote Loper, advising him of a lawsuit in the works between the United States and the State of Utah, regarding the riverbeds of the Green and Colorado. The ownership of these riverbeds, which Utah hoped to exploit, could only be decided by determining whether the streams were "navigable." If they were deemed navigable, Utah had dominion over the bed and could exploit the oil reserves they believed lay beneath them. If the rivers were "unnavigable," the beds belonged to the United States. The case

Bert Loper, Scotty Jamieson

Rachel and Bert

would eventually involve testimony from nearly every living person who had spent time on the rivers, from Major Powell's day until the present. Perhaps, hinted Miser, Loper would get a free trip to Washington.

As the case developed, Loper got a short job as boatman for Lieutenant Colonel Elliot J. Dent, a specialist in river navigation, and Archie Ryan of the General Land Office. Dent's assignment was to examine the Green and Colorado with an eye to navigation. Ryan met Loper in Green River in mid-August. They arranged a small motorboat for use from Hite to Lee's Ferry. Loper then escorted Ryan to Moab, where Ryan and Colonel Dent chartered a trip with the Moab Garage Company's "passenger boat," Virgil Baldwin pilot. The Moab Garage Company had been promoting river travel for some time with a series of often marginally successful boats. This one was propeller-driven and about twenty-seven feet long. Their round trip to the confluence—a distance of just over sixty miles each way—took four days, with Dent making regular soundings and eyeing the layout of sandbars. Several of the bars they got to inspect closely, as they dragged the boat off them.

Returning to Moab, they went to Green River to inspect the river in that vicinity, then, with Loper, they went overland to North Wash, where their motorboat awaited. They headed downriver at 1:30 on September 1. The river was low, and Loper adopted a system of standing in the front of the boat watching the current and signaling to Ryan at the motor which way to steer. Dent bailed almost constantly. It rained. It was a miserable trip, or as Dent termed it, "quite an adventure—When you ship ten gallons of water at one time, in one wave, that is quite a serious proposition. It was a highly uncomfortable trip ... constantly shipping water." In sand waves they would immediately cut the motor and drift sideways—a peculiar but not uncommon technique to prevent sand waves from breaking over the bow of a boat.

They made eighteen miles the first day, stopping to visit Loper's old cabin at Red Canyon, and another fifty-six the next day. Demoralized by the weather and an inadequate boat, Dent made few notes or soundings. They spent the majority of the third day hiking to Rainbow Bridge, and motored in to Lee's Ferry shortly after noon on the fourth day. Leaving the boat at Lee's Ferry, they drove north to Salt Lake City. Two weeks later, Loper was in Los Angeles.

The court sessions were beginning for what came to be known as the

Riverbed Case. The list of witnesses formed a veritable Who's Who of the Colorado River: Dellenbaugh from the 1871-72 Powell expedition; McDonald, Nims, Edwards, and Kane from the Stanton Expedition; Julius Stone; Ellsworth Kolb; Bill Reeder from Charlie Russell's last trip; Walter Mendenhall of San Juan fame; Miser, Hyde, Allen, and Trimble from the San Juan survey; Lint and Reeside from the Green River survey; John and Homer Hite, Ben Harshberger, Frank Bennett, Arth Chaffin and a host of other Glen Canyon miners; Wimmer, Yokey, Baldwin, Marrs, and Wolverton from the steamboat crowd; John Richardson of the 1914 drilling project; Clyde Eddy; Parley and John Galloway; Daily, Clark, and Woodbury from the Pathé-Bray trip; Loper's 1895 hosts from Bluff, Kumen Jones and one of his wives; Lee's Ferryman Jeremiah Johnson; archaeological explorers John and Louisa Wetherill; Glen Canyon boater Dave Rust; Colonel Dent—the list went on and on and on, with over 170 witnesses in all. They collected over 5,500 pages of testimony.

Loper testified on September 26th, stating his occupation as "practical miner." He was recalled for the Salt Lake City hearings in December, his combined testimony filling nearly 140 pages. "Bert Loper was put on and made a fine witness," wrote Frederick Dellenbaugh in Los Angeles, "very clear and strong in his descriptions and answers." Loper told of his early trips on the San Juan, his times in Cataract and Glen Canyons, his upruns, his trip with Ellsworth Kolb, his survey work, his love for the river. "I lived with that river so much," he said, "it pretty near became a part of me."

Sometimes Loper would run astray, at one point giving a full account of his aborted 1914 trip and hike out of Cataract with Russell. And, as with many witnesses, he ran long pontificating on the theories of boating and the ways of the river. The *Los Angeles Times* described Loper's testimony:

> River Inquiry Hears Boatman
>
> "No man knows the Colorado River."
>
> That is the opinion of Bert Loper, old-time placer miner and boatman on the stream.
>
> "For years it was about my only companion," he said yesterday, testifying for the Government before Special Master Warren in the case

> relating to the river's navigability.
>
> Tears came to his eyes. "I used to sit on the bank and watch it," he went on, "and it was always changing. Every stage of the water—and there are many stages—makes a different river."
>
> The Colorado is a capricious creature. It is mysterious. You might say it is the "most human" of all rivers, for men who have lived much of their lives along its course get sentimental about it.
>
> That was the way with Loper. In his narrative he portrayed characteristics of this old, ever changing "associate" of his in terms that made the subject throb with romance and feeling in the murky courtroom.
>
> When it came to the heart of the matter—that is, whether the Colorado is navigable—he gave it a very bad name. He loves the river but not to the point where he will praise it as a transportation utility.
>
> In the several boat trips he made up the stream at various points, "it was 90 per cent tow and 10 per cent row," is the way he put it.

The after-hours boatmen's rendezvous must have been spectacular. One day's line-up in Los Angeles, for instance, included Harry McDonald, Fred Dellenbaugh, Robert Allen, Dave Rust, Dean Daily, and Bert Loper. In fact, that day may have been serendipitous for Loper, for within the year he became involved with both Dellenbaugh and Rust, seminal figures in river history and river guiding respectively.

In between the Los Angeles and Salt Lake sessions came Black Tuesday, October 29, and the formal beginning of America's plunge into the Great Depression. For Loper, already well established at the bottom of the economy, it probably made little difference. In the basement of the old Masonic Temple, Bert and Rachel were better set than many to weather the storm. #

55 Dams

Captain Jacobus Loper, a Dutchman, was in the New World by 1647 when he married Cornelia Melyn in New Amsterdam (now New York). Their son James settled in East Hampton and was the first of several generations of prominent Long Island whalers. Another local whaling family was the Dominy clan. As decades and centuries passed, members and lineages of both families drifted west. Around 1820 they met again, when William Loper married Frances Dominy in Lycoming County, Pennsylvania. Their son Jehail eventually spawned Bert Loper.

The Dominys continued west as far as Wyoming, where—as Bert Loper shoveled away at the placer gravels of Glen Canyon—Floyd Elgin Dominy was born in 1909. Dominy grew up in the ranchlands of Wyoming, building irrigation dams, working for the newly-founded Bureau of Reclamation, eventually rising to the post of Commissioner.

Boulder Dam filled in 1938, before Loper made it through Grand Canyon, drowning a half-dozen rapids that Loper would never get to run. Eight years after Loper died, the first dynamite blasts ripped into the walls at the Glen Canyon damsite. This was a galvanizing moment amid several years of struggle between the nascent environmental movement—often led by the Sierra Club's Executive Director, David Brower—and Floyd Dominy's dam builders. The battle lines had formed upstream on the Green and Yampa Rivers, where the proposed Echo Park Dam threatened Lodore Canyon, Echo Park, and the canyon of the Yampa River—all within Dinosaur National Monument. The environmentalists won the fight at Echo Park, but in saving the sanctity of the Monument, many unprotected canyons were passed by and went under: Flaming Gorge, Kingfisher Canyon, Horseshoe Canyon, much of Red Canyon and Cataract Canyon, all of Narrow Canyon, three sections of the Black Canyon of the Gunnison, and the biggest and most glorious of all, Glen Canyon.

Floyd Dominy was at the helm of the agency that, between 1957 and 1963, built Glen Canyon Dam, drowning Loper's beloved Glen Canyon. Dominy next began a fierce campaign to dam and inundate much of Grand Canyon as well. In this, he was beaten by the newly energized environmental movement.

In Bert Loper's many writings, he never comments about his feelings toward dams, reservoirs, and inundation. Certainly he took pride in his work as a guide for engineers on the Lower Colorado, San Juan, and Green Rivers. Those trips had one primary purpose: to locate damsites and establish reservoir capacities. Loper grew up in the era where progress was still unquestioned, where people were raised with such hardships that nature for its own sake represented simply more hardship. And although Loper loved his rivers and canyons more than life itself, it never seemed to occur to him that they, too, would fall victim to progress. In the great battles between Dominy and Brower, it is hard to say where Loper's allegiance would have fallen. But in January, 1959, as the construction of Glen Canyon Dam plodded forward, foreshadowing the inundation of Loper's Red Canyon homestead and countless other places, Rachel Loper wrote to Harry Aleson:

> It would have been nice if Bert could have lived to have seen the Dam at Glen Canyon, he always said they should have one there, also Hell Roaring Canyon Dam. I hope he can see it. I know that he will be proud of them. #

56 Rivermen

In 1871, at the age of seventeen, Frederick Dellenbaugh joined Major Powell's second expedition down the Green and Colorado Rivers. Halting at Lee's Ferry for the winter, they worked on overland surveys until the following summer. In August, 1872, they finished their river work, leaving Grand Canyon at Kanab Creek. Fred Dellenbaugh worked the following winter with Powell's survey, returning to his home in the east in February, 1873, a changed man. From that point Dellenbaugh split his energies between producing art, exploring the world, and writing the history of the West. His 1902 *Romance of the Colorado River*, published shortly after Powell died, recounted Anglo exploration of the region from the Spaniards in the 1500s, through the fur trappers of the 1800s, then focussed on the river work of both Powell trips and the Stanton expedition. The 1909 edition gave brief descriptions of later expeditions, including the 1907 descent of Russell and Monett. He did not take sides, stating simply, "Loper and one damaged boat were left at Hite," but did point out that "their boats of steel were the most unsuitable of any ever put on the river."

Dellenbaugh's 1908 *A Canyon Voyage* paid book-length homage to the 1871-2 Powell Expedition. Many early river travelers used Dellenbaugh's books as guides.

If one can fault Dellenbaugh's river history, it is primarily in his uncritical evaluation of Powell. John Wesley Powell, like any human, had his faults and failings—but not in Dellenbaugh's books. His inordinate praise of Powell backfired, however, leading others—Stanton in particular—to devote great effort into highlighting Powell's shortcomings. But Dellenbaugh's work saw far wider distribution, and by the 1930s he was the unquestioned authority on the history of the Colorado and unabashed champion of his mentor, Major Powell.

In October 1929, Dellenbaugh went to Salt Lake City to help with research for the United States council in the Riverbed Case. In addition to burying himself in old records and files, he had a chance to visit with locals and tour the area. In his diary for October 12 he wrote:

> This morning Bert Loper came for me with Dave Rust to go down to Springville where Loper knew a man who had been one of the earliest settlers in Moab. Bert had his car down at the old Masonic building where he is living now rent free as a sort of caretaker—with his wife—till they sell it I suppose—till the owners sell it. His car has had hard usage down south and now has 3 disc wheels and one wooden spoke wheel and if the engine stops it is hard work to get it going again. I walked down to the yard alongside of his home where the car is parked. We got in there. The engine started rather easily when cranked cold but when heated up the bearings clamp and it is a hard job. The car ran well otherwise and we bowled along an excellent highway southward.

After dropping Rust at his home in Provo to prepare lunch, they went to see Loper's old Moab friend, Crip Taylor, who as they came to find out, was not expected to live through the day. Abandoning the visit, they traveled farther south to Spanish Fork to see a landmark on Father Escalante's 1776 route, then returned for lunch at Rust's.

Afterward they stopped to interview another Moab old-timer, Rust and Dellenbaugh going indoors to visit. "Bert L. remained with the car," wrote Dellenbaugh, "as he did not want to stop the engine it being so hard to get it going again." That evening Loper dropped Dellenbaugh at the Hotel Utah:

> Loper's car got something wrong with the clutch and he could not come to a dead stop so he slid away without my being able to get my coat and camera from the back seat. He forgot they were there. When I got upstairs and he had had time to get home I telephoned him. He had not noticed the coat and camera but immediately went out, got them, and walked up to my hotel and my room with them.

Dellenbaugh was being paid to research Mormon river history. Sometime that fall Loper, too, joined the staff, apparently to peruse published river books in search of evidence. On March 3, 1930, he wrote to Dellenbaugh:

Frederick Dellenbaugh and Emery Kolb

NAU.PH.568.11184

Kolb Brothers

Dave Rust on the Fourth of July, Glen Canyon, 1930

Fraser

Mr. Collins gave me a job in the office so have been very busy ever since, did I say very busy perhaps I should have said busy but I am putting in the time and incidentally I have read my Colo River books in the Office which are *Romance of the Colo River, A Canyon Voyage.* I forget the exact title of Eddy's Book. Also read Freeman's book....

Mr. Collins has about 12 or 14 girls, Mr. Ryan, Mr. Bywater and myself and they are going until 10 or 11 every night and my job has surely opened my eyes in regard to what it requires to put a case before the Supreme Court. Mr. Collins sure has been true blue to me which, and as the small boy said, "I sure need the Money."

✣ ✣ ✣

David Dexter Rust, five years Loper's junior, and a staunch Utah Mormon, had a river background reminiscent of Loper's. He and his brother Will worked two seasons in Glen Canyon as placer miners, meeting early river travelers as they passed through. The Rusts were among the few witnesses to Flavell and Montez's 1896 passage. Rust also had a lasting friendship with Nathaniel Galloway, whom he met rowing and towing his way up into Glen Canyon from Lee's Ferry, searching for gold and furs.

In 1906–7 Rust worked for his father-in-law, Dee Woolley, improving a route into Grand Canyon from the north along Bright Angel Creek, establishing "Rust's Camp" at the bottom of the Canyon near the river (later called Phantom Ranch), and pioneering a cable crossing to connect to the South Rim. While based there in 1908–9, Rust did a bit of boating up and down the Colorado near his camp, sometimes taking passengers. He later exported this practice to Glen Canyon.

Early boaters always had some goal in mind—exploration, railroads, prospecting, trapping, photographing. The 1909 Stone/Galloway trip was the first to float just for the sport of it, and Galloway the first boatman to receive compensation for guiding such a trip, even though Stone rowed his own boat. Loper, in 1911-12, was paid to take Seaboldt from Hite to Lee's Ferry and back, but that was purely for mining investigation. Loper had, as well, boated for scientific work for the USGS, and for camera work with Ellsworth Kolb, likewise for pay.

But it was Dave Rust who initially invented commercial boating on the Colorado in the truest sense, bringing the concept of "passenger" to the river. "My purpose has been to conduct travelers who wish to take an unusual trip in that wild country, in connection with horseback trips, automobile trips, in the scenery lands of Utah.... It is an unusual tour which I take with sportsmen who desire that sort of thing." Beginning around 1923, Rust brought one or two groups a year to Hite and guided them through Glen Canyon to Lee's Ferry. He used fourteen- and sixteen-foot collapsible canvas-and-steel King rowboats, carrying one passenger with himself. Passengers, if he felt them capable, might row other two-man Kings, or it he felt them inept, he would hire a boatman—occasionally his sons. Rust typically ran his trips in spring or fall, with around five days of river travel and another three or four days of hiking to places like Rainbow Bridge. Rust prided himself on the safety of his trips. Only once, on a 1926 trip with Utah Governor Dern, had another boat, disregarding Rust's cautioning, plowed head-on into a sand wave and flipped end-over-end backward. Even so, there was no harm done.

For several years one of Rust's best customers was an avid outdoorsman named George Corning Fraser—a Princeton-educated Wall Street lawyer. For more than a decade Fraser had spent his vacations exploring the wild expanses of Southeastern Utah and the Navajo Reservation, often hiring Dave Rust as his guide. In 1930 Fraser chartered Rust for a trip through Glen Canyon, bringing his eighteen-year-old daughter

Fraser

Fraser

Loper at Hermitage

Loper and Sarah Fraser in Aztec Rapid

Sarah along. Rust in turn employed a second boatman: Bert Loper.

Loper and Rust got along well. "It would be hard to get two 'ROUGH NECKS' closer to-gether than Dave and I," Loper wrote to Julius Stone.

In early July—a hot choice of times—the Fraser party spent two days struggling down North Wash from Hanksville by horse-drawn wagon and a half-day assembling and loading their boats. At launch, Rust took Fraser; Loper took Sarah. "Bert was a wonderful man," recalled Sarah in 2000. "He and I were in one boat … he lived on the river. He was a fascinating person, he remembered everything … he talked continuously."

"We drifted slowly downstream," she wrote in 1953, "stopping off to see almost everything of interest mentioned by Major Powell."

Loper was impressed with the maneuverability of the light boats, and took easily to his duties as tour guide. He told Sarah of his years in Glen Canyon, his trials and travails, his honeymoon with Rachel, saying he finally left Glen Canyon with five dollars less than he came in with. When they hiked up Hole-in-the-Rock trail Sarah was felled by heat exhaustion. "Bert Loper stayed with me, he was very nice. He was the nicest man." They hiked up Forbidding Canyon to Rainbow Bridge.

Fraser

Fraser

Loper

Sarah Fraser and Loper at Kane Creek

And Sarah remembered one side-trip she was not invited on:

> I never did meet the hermit because I wasn't allowed to meet him because he never wore any clothes! And then Mr. Rust couldn't persuade him to put anything on, so they said it was better if I just stayed in camp they'd go see him. And they had a wonderful time with him, spent all afternoon there, I had a very dull time. I guess he was quite a guy.

Just who the hermit was is unclear. Prohibition was in force then—perhaps the hermit lived in a bottle.

They ate well, had ham on the Fourth of July, caught catfish, camped in the open without tents, and talked geology incessantly.

> He was a marvelous man, Mr. Rust.... Dad and Mr. Rust had a very pleasant relationship. They told each other jokes, and they always included me. They never went off by themselves to study geology, they went off and took me to teach me.... If they had an argument, it was a perfectly happy discussion of what was what and they came to the right conclusion. They got along very well. Mr. Rust was very amusing.

George Fraser, Bert Loper, Sarah Fraser, Dave Rust

Fraser

After the trip Loper returned home, as did the Frasers, who went the long way via Salt Lake City and California. On what must have been a slow news day, the voyage made the Salt Lake newspaper:

> N.Y. WOMAN SWIMS RIVER COLORADO
>
> Explorer Here After a Thrilling Trip Down Canyon
>
> Enthusiastic over her first trip into the untamed country of southeastern Utah, Miss Sarah Fraser of New York City arrived in Salt Lake Monday and told of one of her most thrilling experiences—swimming the Colorado river.…
>
> Mr. Loper thinks Miss Fraser is probably the only person who has ever swam the river at Crossing of the Fathers, with the exception of some early-day travelers who may have performed the feat by hanging onto a horse's tail. The river at this point is nearly a quarter of a mile wide and negotiating the stream is declared a noteworthy accomplishment because of the swift currents.…

In August Sarah sent Loper a packet of photos, saying, "Everything is so quiet here that I wish I was back on the river swimming on it and across it.… Your story about *who goin' to shoot which apple off'n whose haid* makes the biggest hit always."

Loper had boated for gold, he had boated for adventure, he had boated for science. Now he could add to his résumé the titles of river historian and commercial guide. #

57 One last dance

FROM BEFORE the time of written record, men have been riven between women and the sea—tugged and torn by two tremendous female forces, each demanding their attention, their time, their devotion. For more than a century that same struggle has played out on the Colorado, from Major Powell and Emma Dean to the modern-day boatman trying to make a living on the river while keeping a relationship at home. Loper was no different, caught between his love for Rachel and the irresistible draw back to the Colorado. A modern musical captures that schism in a way factual prose cannot:

One last dance with the river
One last wild embrace
One last rush down the rapids
The roar of the canyon
The rain in my face

One last run down the river
One fine fare thee well
One last heart-stopping voyage
The crash of the water
The rhythm and swell

The light at river's end
The still before the falls
The way the sunrise paints the
canyon walls

A doe beside the stream
A kingbird's morning song
If you had seen what I've seen
You'd want to go along
You'd have to go along

One last dance with the river
Bessie, come with me
One last pass through the thunder
The chaos, the wonder
The flood running free

One last search for adventure
One last daredevil ride
And then with all my heart I swear
I'll gladly spend eternity
By your side

— from *RIVER'S END*
a musical by CHERYL COONS
and CHUCK LARKIN

#

58 Salmon

"I WAS NEVER SO SICK of a place in my life as I am of this place," Loper wrote Miser in December 1931:

> and if I could get an auto to the river at the mouth of North Wash I would go back down there and stay awhile. I thought I was going to get to go on another trip last summer but it never materialized, so it was just another disappointment for me, but I get so awful tired of the city.

Loper had run into complications with his Riverbed Case employer, Randolph Collins. Loper loaned Collins $227, a substantial sum for that time, Collins promising to pay it back in increments. One after another, the checks bounced. Eventually Loper enlisted Hugh Miser in Washington. Miser, in turn, enlisted the U.S. Solicitor General. Collins paid the debt.

Three years in Salt Lake City were more than enough for Loper. He kept busy with his Spanish American War Veterans group, taking on the position of Commander in 1931, and officiating at meetings every Tuesday evening.

> It has been a wonderful year to me; it has taught me so many things that I never knew, taught me to live more for others and less for myself, and now I can get up and address an audience, and I have had some wonderful compliments paid me on my years work as Commander.

When Loper was not working with the Veterans, he was often busy with the Masons. He wrote Miser in 1932 to borrow a set of slides to give shows to both groups. Occasionally he got work out of town; on January 20, 1933, he wrote Miser:

> I made a trip down in Glen Canyon and just got back last Friday and

> may go again in Feb. but my vetran work I am going to have to give up for I am not financial able to continue any longer.... It seems as though the more one does the more that is expected of him....
>
> I do not believe that I am one day older than I was in 1921, and all my friends tell me that I am getting younger every day, and surely feel it, and on my trip down to Glen Canyon I had to do a hundred mile by pack outfit and had not been on a horse for years and our trip was over the roughest part of a rough country, and I came through fine and am ready for more of the same.

An unsigned travel story in the June 1, 1933, *Milliard County Chronicle* mentions meeting Loper in Hanksville, calling him, "an old river rat at home with the bucking rapids and side currents." Mostly, though, Loper escaped notice. For the next two years he shows up nowhere. In July 1935, the Lopers sold their forty acres in Hanksville to Louisa Johnson for forty dollars. It was the only real estate Loper had ever owned, and he lost sixty dollars on the deal.

Bill Busenbark, the youngest son of Rachel's sister Maggie, remembered Loper's Salt Lake years, as he would occasionally travel north from Wayne County to visit his grandmother, brother Tom, and the Lopers. "Bert did a lot of jobs, whatever he could pick up," Busenbark recalled. "I remember there was a church house there, I don't remember whether it was Presbyterian or whose it was, but it was right there behind the Masonic Temple. It burned down." Loper got the job of tearing the ruins down, returning home each night covered with soot and grime to hop in the bath.

> He wasn't a drinker but he's sweatin' in the old summer heat, you know, all dirty. He'd get in that old bathtub and soak, and scour up and Rachel would have a sandwich and a cold beer for him, ice cold beer. If she didn't have a cold beer for him, she'd send me out and get one. Bert really loved that beer.

Occasionally the Lopers made the long drive down to Grover to visit Maggie's family. Bill Busenbark remembered those visits as well.

> I can remember Bert and Rachel coming down to Grover several different

Motorman

Pianist

times and in a Buick each time but a different Buick. I think he had at least two Buicks, two different Buicks.

Bert was quite a politician. In fact he got in a few scrapes over that. And he'd like to take Mother on. Mother was a strong person and well educated. And knew of what she spoke. And that was in the Roosevelt era when they was getting all these programs going. And I think Bert was puttin' 'em down, you know. And Mother took him on. And I don't recall what Rachel's reaction was, if she run and hid or what, but there was no problem you know, after they got it all settled. Mother wouldn't have him back down for a while maybe. And neither would he. He was a tough old son-of-a-bitch, you might say, when it come to politics. Cause he'd been through it.

But he was always courteous and kind with Mother and he always loved her, loved our family, and we always loved him, and liked him. I don't know as I ever heard Mother complain about Rachel going off with an old river rat or anything like that you know. It just seem like that's just part of the family, that's how it was supposed to be.

Keeper of the legend: Bill Busenbark with Uncle Bert's valise of writings, 2004

> But he did like to come and visit us, and like I say, he'd take me under his wing, and he liked to teach you things, he was a master at teaching. But he'd just walk up to me, slap me in the belly, and say, "Belly in and chest out, and straighten your shoulders," and he'd say, "When you talk to anybody, see, you look 'em right in the eye. They'll know whether or not you're lying to them."
>
> Then he'd probably want to know where the best looking ant hills were that were around. He'd like to go out there and he'd pick and choose the nice gravels off the ant hills and he'd swallow 'em. That's for his digestion, like a chicken, digest his food. I think that would—he never had ulcers. Funny he didn't have other things, though.
>
> But I liked Bert's voice, he had a commanding voice, and I would call it a deep baritone. Bert would like to get me and we'd go to the old piano and he'd chord the piano and sing these ballads, and no one was home and sing those words to just rattle the walls.
>
> He was a convincing guy to talk to, cause he was so sincere. He'd just speak from his heart. And he was so sincere, that's what I loved about him so much—if he said it, it's gotta be true. Or he wouldn't say it. I never heard him ever press anyone hard with his own beliefs. He didn't need to. All you had to do was talk with him and you'd develop respect for him.

Driving, though, was a big part of those visits. "Bert was an exciting driver," Busenbark laughed:

> Bert was an enthusiastic guy.
>
> One thing you could be proud of was the least amount of flat tires you'd have. Jeez these tires'd just go flat for no reason at all. So he and Tom [Busenbark] had come down and the trip had been quite uneventful, and Bert was driving, this was coming back [to Salt Lake City]. And Bert's drivin' and they come back there, and Bert came to a rest there at the intersection, and slapped old Tom on the knee, "Why Tom," he says, "It's been a great trip. We haven't had a single hardship." And he jumped on the gas feed, I guess he thought it was the brake, but he jumped on the gas feed, rolled across the street and plunged right into the hospital.... four more blocks east and a half a block north and they'd have been home.

✣ ✣ ✣

Whitewater boating was slowly gaining popularity during Loper's absence from the river. In Vernal, Utah a loose group formed, calling themselves the Colorado River Club. Their genesis led back to none other than Parley Galloway, son of Nathaniel, who in 1930 was locked in the Vernal jail. The jailer and his cousin, Frank Swain and Bus Hatch, listened to enough of his stories that they decided they wanted to try it. Agreeing to bail Galloway out of jail in return for whitewater instruction, Swain and Hatch quickly found they were on their own—Galloway skipped bail.

That did not slow them down. Together with a few more in-laws and friends, they built boats and learned to run them on the upper Green, gaining enough confidence that in 1934 they tackled Grand Canyon. Since they had few funds, they joined forces with Swain's friend Dr. Russell Frazier who had money. Their exploits were characterized by their love of a good time, and their boat names reflected their attitude: *What Next, Don't Know, Who Cares.* They survived their Grand Canyon trip in spite of extreme low water, hungry for more rivers.

Dr. Frazier, who lived just south of Salt Lake, was hooked. He befriended every riverman he could find, and that included Loper.

✣ ✣ ✣

In the summer of 1936 the call of the river grew too insistent for Loper. When the July issue of *National Geographic* ran a story called "Down

Idaho's River of No Return," Loper was ready to go. Together with his friend Charlie Snell, Loper quickly planned a trip on the Salmon. First, however, they had to build a boat.

At almost the same time Loper received a surprising package in the mail—a signed copy of Julius Stone's *Canyon Country: The Romance of a Drop of Water and a Grain of Sand.* Stone had published this account of his 1909 trip with Galloway in 1932, but a trip to Salt Lake City had jarred his memory of Loper: "I stopped over a little while to see Dr. Frazier," wrote Stone. "He was good enough to … take us to the Masonic Temple so hopefully I might have a chance to shake hands and swap talk with you, but unfortunately you were out."

Loper was thrilled to receive Stone's book. He wrote Stone, expressing his thanks and surprise and telling of his plans:

> If I finish this month I will be 67 years old and, as the saying goes, still going strong, for I am going to try the Salmon River this month, that is, my buddy and I are going to start this month, but we do not know how long we will be, for we want to try to see if there is any of the, as Cass used to say, little yaller fellers [gold], so we may be gone the rest of the summer and again we may be back soon.

He went on to tell Stone that his new boat was nearly complete but they were having a difficult time finding decent eight-foot oars. Were they available in Ohio?

"Dear Bert," wrote Stone a week later. "A letter from my old friend, Andrew Lorimer, advises me that he has arranged for the shipment of two pairs of oars to you by express. Please accept them with my compliments. I wish I could be with you."

Loper responded, overflowing with thanks, enthusing about Stone's book, and telling more of his plans for the Salmon:

> I will try and describe to you my partner—He and I punched cows together more than 50 years ago in the four corners country and then we lost sight of each other for many years, and finally met again in Salt Lake.… He is not a placer miner but a prospector for anything and he heard that I had, some time in the past, crossed the river in a boat so conceived the idea that I might be able to steer one down the Salmon …

> I will admit that we both are no spring chickens—he being two years older than I.... The last trip I made down glen canyon I was in the company of a couple of youngsters and I did not have to take their dust at any time, but I suppose that I will have to, at some time, step aside.
>
> My partner wants to quit at Riggins but I am going to try and go to the Columbia ... just to see if I could run the big falls on the Columbia.

River fever. Loper and Snell finished the boat, loaded it on a trailer, tuned up Loper's jalopy, and left Salt Lake City the evening of July 20. They drove at night, presumably to keep the car from boiling over. They rebuilt the trailer hitch in Moore, Idaho, and ground over Willow Creek Summit on the 22nd. They camped that night on the shore of the Salmon at Challis. They could have driven another sixty miles down the river to launch at the more traditional site—Salmon, Idaho—but that meant a longer car shuttle. They preferred to do any extra mileage by boat.

They set their pace from the start, laying over four days to rest, tune the boat, drink beer, dodge rain, celebrate Snell's sixty-ninth birthday, and swat mosquitoes. Of the boat, which they named *Old Betsy,* Loper wrote, "We are more than proud of it for it leaked practically nothing.... I suppose that the cause of our pride in our boat is from the fact that we made it ourselves, and it should be a source of greater satisfaction to do a thing and do it well."

They walked into town once or twice a day to have another beer, send letters, and stock up on provisions—more beans, more bacon. Loper had added an unusual piece of equipment to his river gear: a typewriter. "I went and got me a 'Portable' and with my one finger I will do the best I can." Loper had gotten it in his mind that he wanted to write, to document his trips, to tell his story. His scant education did not slow him down. He typed, page upon page, often prattling in circles when he could not come up with anything of importance to say.

> I have about three days all under the heading of the 20th. and as I have a very bad head-ache I will let it go at that and will try and straighten it up to-morrow. This is the 23rd. of July and as I have stated in the above writing I will try and get this thing straight; Of course we got the first three days all to-gether and now I am trying to get straightened out and

> this is under the date of July 23—so I will have to get last night's doings in on this date.

They hired a Mr. Kelly to shuttle their car over the Sawtooths to Riggins, where they planned to end the trip. Finally, on the morning of July 27, they launched, rumbling across a few gravel bars and bumping an occasional rock. Opening a hatch at noon, they found it flooded, with Loper's bedroll soaked. They camped, hung things up to dry, and caulked. "My hands are a little sore, but I put my gloves on before I made any blisters and I am very much in hopes that my hands will harden before we reach the bad water."

With the boat patched they put in eight hours the next day—"My hands are plenty sore to-night, blisters as large as quarters."—and by noon on their third day, pulled into Salmon, Idaho. They laid over another three days, doing much the same as at the last town—drinking beer, writing and receiving letters—Bert was getting about one a day from Rachel—caulking the boat, getting new oarlocks welded, and visiting. While searching for historical information to put in his journal, Loper made friends with Lois Guemlick, a correspondent from the *Salt Lake Tribune,* "and a very nice appearing lady too." One more person to type letters to. On August 1 they breakfasted with Captain Harry Guleke, the senior boatman of the Salmon River.

Guleke came to the Salmon River in the 1890s, initially working river trips with the Sandiland brothers, George and Dave. They ran ponderous wooden barges down the "River of No Return," carrying supplies to and from miners, trappers, homesteaders, and hermits on the three-hundred mile voyage to Lewiston. Their boats, called sweepboats, were often over thirty feet long, eight feet wide and three feet high. They steered them with huge, long rudders, or "sweeps," out the fore and aft. "Cap" Guleke, as he was called, had taken over their business by 1900, and made something like two hundred trips down the river. At seventy-four, he was still boating, still manning the sweeps. "A most interesting character," Loper wrote of Guleke, "and has been some man in his day and even now is a well preserved man both mentally and physacally." Seven years older than Loper and still running sweeps—he could not help but inspire Loper.

Always before, Loper had run muddy desert water. Now he floated in thick conifers on a clear, sparkling river. "What a wonderful river this is and it seems as though the farther we go the more wonderful it becomes." Loper and Snell cast off from Salmon on August 1, running several small rapids. The following afternoon they camped across from the small settlement of Shoup. Along the way they stopped to talk to everyone they saw, and pan occasionally for gold, with poor results. At Shoup they did the usual—laid over for six days, drank beer, loafed around, caulked the boat, and wrote letters. To Hugh Miser, Loper wrote:

> I have my typewriter and am trying to do a little writing, but my education is not good enough to do very good writing, but I thought that I might get someone to re-write it for me.... Tell Colonel Birdseye that I am still going strong as a boatman (I hope). This may be my last trip on rough water, but I hate to think that it will be.

Snell and Loper took turns feeling "very bum," but on August 8 they were ready to move on. Five miles downriver, Loper remembered he left his camera behind (What was it with Loper and cameras?). "Am feeling a little worse for the day on account of having to do that 10 mile walk.... We have had some nice big waves but it kept us very busy dodging the big rocks." They camped at an old Civilian Conservation Corps (CCC) camp and Loper bummed a generous supply of aspirin for his headaches, backaches, arthritis, and rheumatism. The CCC crew was building a road that, had it been completed, would have traversed the entire Salmon gorge.

The next day Loper and Snell pressed on, running several small rapids, bumping a few rocks, and giving the CCC boys a show. In camp Loper wrote, "I shaved, and when I tried to shave the back of my neck it made me think of my barber in Salt Lake City. I also thought of my Wife and how I loved her when she washed some dirty shirts and sox." That's true love.

On August 10 they ran Long Tom Rapid "and it was a very thrilling ride, and I got slapped around some, but for that I do not care if they just leave the rocks out.... the wildest water we have seen so far...." Passing the Middle Fork of the Salmon, they camped and, with dark clouds heading up the canyon, set up tarps for rain. "Charlie is up the river a little ways fishing and I do hope that he gets a big one for I am

Old Betsy

getting just a little tired of fat sow belly."

It rained for days. They laid over. "It brought forth plenty, for it seemed to just try and see how hard it could rain, and there must have been a cloud burst up the country somewhere for the river is running heavy drift and is very muddy and it raised about a foot or more." They laid over another day and helped Mr. Davis, a miner camped nearby, give aid and shelter to three people whose camp had been washed away. The storm eventually broke, and on August 14 they cast off again.

> We, after breakfast, broke camp and started down the river, and, when we least expected it, got slapped around like a couple of step children, for the rapid below camp had changed its appearance with a two foot raise and in fact had made another rapid of it, and we took quite a bit of water in our open compartment....
>
> The river is beginning to take its drop in bunches now, and that is all in the rapids, and where we were having the fall of the river cover most of a mile it now takes more like the Colo. river.

That afternoon they camped with Mr. Cunningham, one of the sweep-boat drivers Loper had read about in *National Geographic.* Nearly all boatmen on the Salmon, in fact, ran sweepboats, and few felt comfortable with rowboats. Cunningham was an exception, being the "only boatman on this river who has seen any merit in our boat."

The rapids were getting tougher. "It takes all my river skill in maneuvering the boat through where the water is running in gigantic waves and white caps, but it surely makes one feel good to do those things and do them well and if they are not done well it is very bad."

It was definitely time to lay over again. Snell fished, Loper climbed the ridges. "I am wonderfully well pleased with these old legs of mine for I find that they are not entirely through yet." Snell brought in twelve fish, and for the remainder of the trip, fish constituted their main fare.

August 16. "Charlie and I decided to try to make another mile today...." They made a mile and a half, before camping with Jack Killum and family. Killum, another prospector, wrote poetry, and Loper spent the afternoon transcribing poems into his growing sheaf of typescript. The next day they inched down the river another mile. "It is getting so the biggest part of our days work is packing and unpacking but we are having a glorious trip just the same." Snell caught another slew of fish. The Forest Service pack-train was plodding upriver, and Loper took the opportunity to send a letter to Rachel.

> It is nice to get this chance to send her a letter but I do wish she could send me one for I am getting a wee bit lonesom—I think I will have to make another trip next summer and bring her with me, for I would sure like for her to enjoy this beautiful River of no return with me.

They laid over for three nights. Loper had a headache for two mornings, but still climbed a nearby mountain. "Charlie has his sour dough working and we will have sour dough bread for supper and I do hope that it is better than his baking powder bread."

August 21, day twenty-six of the expedition:

> We sure had a wonderful day, just one Foamy rapid after another and then long stretches of beautiful water.... We came to Little Squaw Rapid and was it a rapid? I'll say it was and it was fun to see the way that "old betsy" get knocked around, but that is what makes boating a pleasure—that is what gives it a thrill.

Time for a layover day. Make that a double. Then off downriver again on the 24th.

> We had it fast and furious and that included the famous Devils Teeth Rapid.... Charlie proposed lining the boat but I have seen so many boats injured by lining that I decided to run it and we fared very much better in this than in the Little Squaw....
>
> We reached the mouth of Chamberlain Creek just as the wind was beginning to blow up stream so I refuse to pull against a strong head wind so we went into camp ... and how the wind did blow the balance of the day and that is what makes me feel miserable, so I put in the balance of the day just being miserable.

Layover.

On August 26 Loper and Snell entered the Idaho Batholith, the heart of the Salmon River gorge. They scouted Salmon Falls, and "it took us just one minute to run it—It sure was exciting for we got handled rather rough in that minute but it was rare sport." Quadruple layover.

September 1, day thirty-seven. "We were on our way and OBOY! what a way. We had the roughest water of the entire trip and we hit one rock rather hard—harder than any other so far and I hope that it will be the hardest for the entire trip." September 2 brought them to Big Mallard, a notorious drop.

> It looked very serious for a minute for we were held just above a huge rock with the nose of the boat backed into a huge roller and when I looked around it looked like Charlie was trying to put the entire Salmon River in his hip pocket, but when I stepped on the lower end of the boat it floated away.

Quadruple layover. Weather rolled in on them again. They wandered about the canyon, checking again for decent gold panning.

> But it all looks very "lean" to me—and to think that Charlie and I thought we were coming to a place that was too hard for people to get into but find that it is all prospected and you might say inhabited....
>
> It is getting rather monotonous having to lay over three or four for

> every mile or two, and when the weather clears up I am going to try to do a little traveling, for if there is nothing here for us we had just as well be at home as here.

They broke camp on September 6 and rowed as far as Ludwig Rapid before camp. The next morning Loper was feeling a bit bilious, so they laid over, then laid over again. So much for the traveling. September 9: "I got up this morning with the intention of moving but when I started to tear down Charlie objected and we had our first few words, for it seems as though he does not want to get through at all." It was day forty-six and Loper was ready to go home. Charlie wasn't. The next day, "… we made our whole mile to what is known as Lone Pine Bar where we proceeded to unload and, I suppose, will stay here untill the spirit moves Charlie." Layover.

> Last night was the coldest one of the trip and was well represented with rain and of course I had to get a little wet—I think that I will have to wear all the clothes I have—that is if I do not get Charlie to move—We are just 38 miles from Riggins and, as the hills are well capped with snow, I am getting in a hurry for it is getting very disagreeable in the cold water.

On September 12 Loper pried Snell into the boat, and they made nearly ten miles before camping at the Bemis Ranch. There Loper found a telephone to see if Kelly had delivered Loper's car to Riggins. He had. Layover. Things got crankier around camp.

> Got up nearly froze this morning and my bones ached and it was very stormy and of course we did not move and it looks like that we will not move for another day or two—I sat around Charlie's two-bit fire and did not thaw out very quick.

Another layover. "I returned to camp for our grumpy little meal.… It is becoming very disagreeable weather now and we stand around the fire and freeze on one side and burn up on the other." A third layover.

September 16, day fifty-two:

> We have had frost the last two mornings, so this morning when I got out of bed I made the proposition to Charlie that we would finish the trip so he agreed so we loaded up and started on our way and it turned out to be the best day that we have had so far and did we have some water—the wildest of the trip and it was out of one foamy into another and it continued all day....

The next morning they were on the river early again.

> The outfit that made the rapids sure kept a dandy out for the last for it was the only one that we have gone on and looked over before running for a long time, and it was sure some rough. But the real nightmare came after that for we had dead water the most of the way on to Riggins and a strong head wind and my hands was good and sore when we arrived at our destination—Riggins.

Loper's patience had run out—with the weather, with the diet, with Charlie, and with his journal. All talk of continuing on downriver to the Columbia, or even to the Snake, had long ago evaporated. At the bottom of his fifty-third and final page he, for the first time, went from double-spaced to single-spaced in order to cram the last few lines on the page:

> We landed about 3-30 P.M. and walked into the city and found the car and 4 letters for me—I could tell a lot about the car but time and space will not premit so ends our water part of the trip and I do hate to stop before we finish the entire trip but I do hope to do that some day

The end. He never described their drive home. #

59 Centennial

As the concrete plug in Glen Canyon grew higher, Dock Marston snatched the last opportunity to uprun the river. In 1960 he acted as guide for a group headed by Jon Hamilton, a New Zealander whose father had invented the jet boat. They thundered down the canyon in June on one of the last floods to make it past the damsite. Turning around, they fought their way back up to Lee's Ferry.

The dam gates soon closed. Marston and photographer Bill Belknap rowed tiny plastic SportYaks through on the trickle as the dam filled, setting records for the first post-dam run, the smallest boats ever used, and the lowest flows navigated. Marston not only chronicled and cross-examined river history—he made it.

By the time of Bert Loper's one hundredth birthday in 1969, river running in Grand Canyon was exploding. Well publicized fights against dams on the Green and Colorado had brought attention to the sport. Glen Canyon Dam had somewhat stabilized the flow of the Colorado, producing what many felt to be a longer, more predictable river season. The idea of running commercial trips through Grand Canyon spread like wildfire.

Jack Brennan had retired by then, leaving Don Harris and his new wife Mary in charge of Harris River Tours. Scout leaders who had their river beginnings in Glen Canyon with Loper had formed their own companies.

Nevills's outfit still existed as Mexican Hat Expeditions, run by his daughter Joan and her husband. For the Powell Centennial they ran one final commercial trip in the old Nevills Cataract boats, from Wyoming through Grand Canyon, before transitioning to motorized tours.

Bus Hatch's sons were running Hatch River Expeditions. Harry Aleson's protégé, Georgie White, was running her own commercial tour company in large motor rigs, and Martin Litton, who got his start with P.T. Reilly, was running wooden dories through the Canyon. Other outfits appeared, spawned from within these companies, and more yet appeared from California. Thus was born the modern river business. In 1972 the number of Grand Canyon outfitters was frozen at twenty-one companies—a number that dwindled by one-third as companies gobbled each other up. Usage, too, was frozen at that point. The Colorado River through Grand Canyon was officially deemed "full."

Hundreds of young men and several bold young women rushed or stumbled into the profession of river guide, with few senior guides to teach them the ways of the river. Boating skills were raw and being learned the very hard way. Equipment, too, was primitive. Sanitation was bleak, the beaches strewn with litter, charcoal, and toilet paper. Facts of river history were sparse, and myth was rife. Over the next few decades this rag-tag collection of river folk evolved into a highly professional, highly regulated trade. Usage inched up along with the Canyon's "capacity," as determined by the National Park Service.

Demand for private river trips—those who wished to run the Canyon on their own without the services of a guide—began growing rapidly, quickly outpacing the designated quota.

According to Dock Marston's body count, exactly one hundred different people had passed through Grand Canyon at the time of Loper's death (Loper, in 1939, having been number sixty-seven). By the early 1970s, some fifteen thousand a year were making the trip. Just two decades after Loper's lonely death at 24½-Mile Rapid, the once-rarely boated Grand Canyon had become an industry.

With the passing of the old guard, the bickering between river runners like Marston, Nevills, Reilly, Aleson, Loper, Larabee, and Frazier largely faded. In its place grew a new rivalry that at times grew equally shrill. As the allotment for boaters passing through Grand Canyon filled, various factions jockeyed for their share. Commercial outfitters had, and hoped to keep, the lion's share. Private river runners fought for more trips. Oar-powered and motor-powered factions sparred over the right to be there. Even the scientists who worked along the river corridor took their share of broadsides.

Loper, in his day, had the luxury not to worry about these new spats. In fact, he had *been* a commercial boater, a private boater, an oarsman, a motorman, and one of the original science boatmen. It didn't much matter to Loper, as long as he could be on the river. #

60 Call of the river

"I THINK THAT this is the hardest letter to get started that I have ever written," wrote Loper to Stone after his Salmon trip:

> for I have wanted to write it different from all the rest. You know that I took your book along with me so I could get an idea of just how to write but I have given up all hope of ever becoming a writer—the first obsticle is the lack of an education and the other is my inability to handle the english language in a proper manner. I have read your introduction to your book several times and the beautiful language in that makes me despair.

"Please don't bewail your lack of education or of redundancy in the use of words," Stone replied, "because you have a forthright way—even though it might sometimes seem crude to highbrows—of expressing yourself. The whole essence of any narrative, whether fanciful or factual, is to have something to say, and then to say it."

Stone need not have worried. Loper did not give up writing any more than he gave up boating. The Salmon, in fact, had given him his second wind on rivers, and his letters ran long. Nor did Loper sit at home: "When I got home Mr. Miser of the USGS called for me and we went down to the Henry Mountain country and after returning we took another trip down to Green River, and then I went down to Boulder Mountain on my deer hunt."

The marathon landed him square in bed. "I have not been so sick in 20 years having been in bed for more than two weeks and for a while I was afraid that I was going to have the pneumonia for my right side was very sore and even now I have a rattleing in those wonderful lungs that I have spoken of before."

Loper's dream of a Grand Canyon trip had never died. Now, with the success of the Salmon trip, it was shimmering before him once more—as were the Snake River and others:

> [I] still hope to do that before I quit and that is about the best way to stay young that I know of and I hope to stay in the game for awhile yet and if I can raise the money to get me a boat made of doroaluminum I think that I would have a boat that would do all the canyons of the pacific slope.

Loper was proud of *Old Betsy*, but had found her heavy and a "little sluggish." Duralumin, an alloy used for airframes, would make for a lighter, stronger boat. By reducing weight, "it would mean that I could run just that much more difficult rapids." Loper researched the Snake, looked for ways to join a Grand Canyon trip, and kept dreaming.

A month behind Loper, rowing down the Salmon, was a young loner named Buzz Holmstrom, who began solo river running on Oregon's Rogue River in 1934. He had repeated the Rogue in 1935 before soloing the Salmon in 1936. There he visited Jack Killum, the poet Loper had met, and obtained Loper's address. In early November Loper received a note from the young boater, asking how the Salmon compared with the Colorado. He mentioned that Frank Dodge was preparing to lead a Grand Canyon survey. Holmstrom had tried unsuccessfully to get on Dodge's crew and was now planning to go alone.

About that time, Dr. Russ Frazier told Loper about his and Julius Stone's plan to place a plaque in Grand Canyon. They wished to install it at Separation Rapid, in memory of the three members of the Powell Expedition who had left the trip at that point and vanished into the wilderness. Some subsequent rivermen—Dellenbaugh in particular—had branded the men "deserters" and lobbied successfully to have their names left off a monument at Grand Canyon commemorating the Powell Expedition. Frazier was outraged, as was Stone, and their plaque-placing ceremony aimed to help right that wrong.

Loper wrote Miser, asking for information on Dodge's upcoming trip, telling of Holmstrom's plans, as well as his own. "It is rumored that there is to be a reunion of river men at Separation rapid next summer some time so I might get in with this man [Holmstrom] and make the trip so I could be in at the reunion—I understand the party will come up from the dam so I think it would be rather nice if I could come from above and meet them."

On October 1, 1937, a ragged young man knocked on Loper's door. It was Buzz Holmstrom, on his way to Wyoming to launch his solo journey. Holmstrom, expecting a decrepit old man, was surprised to find "a big strong man appearing to be about 50." They had much in common. Poverty: Holmstrom came from a poor logging family in coastal Oregon, and had been working to support his family since halfway through high school. Boatbuilding: Like Loper, Holmstrom had of necessity built his own boats and taught himself to row. Solitude: Holmstrom, sometimes by choice, sometimes by chance, had spent much of his river time alone. And big dreams: Holmstrom fixed his sights on the Colorado, and was not going to be dissuaded. The two men formed an instant bond.

Although Loper toyed with the idea of joining Holmstrom, it was not to be. In their respective writings, neither man elaborates as to just why, Holmstrom simply saying Loper "is 69 years old now and thought he'd better not." Holmstrom launched alone on October 5 in Green River, Wyoming. He rowed nearly every daylight hour for the next fifty days, thunking his boat into Boulder Dam on Thanksgiving Day. With that, the quiet, humble Holmstrom had become the first to solo the Colorado.

Five days before finishing, Holmstrom had caught up to, and passed, Frank Dodge—the first time two river parties had met in Grand Canyon. Dodge's was a geology trip sponsored by Carnegie Institute and the California Institute of Technology, and of the seven young geologists on the expedition, each went on to become a leader in his field. Dodge, having now made two and one half trips through Grand Canyon, was the most experienced Grand Canyon boatman to date.

That soon changed. Norman Davies Nevills, whose father had met Loper back on the San Juan in 1921, had come of age and was in the process of inventing commercial boating for not only the San Juan River, but Grand Canyon as well—a development that would have profound impact on Loper. Profound enough that a detailed recounting is necessary.

Hack Miller

Holmstrom on his boat, Salt Lake City

Norm Nevills on a San Juan punt

Norman and his mother had joined Billy Nevills in Mexican Hat in 1928 and opened the Nevills Lodge. In 1933 Norman served on a map-making team with the Rainbow Bridge-Monument Valley Expedition—a group of academics exploring the great wilds of Navajo Country. For river work they used collapsible Wilson Fold-Flat boats, and Nevills inherited one after the trip. He used it to boat the swift San Juan near Mexican Hat and quickly got hooked on whitewater. That same year he met and married Doris Drown.

Planning a river honeymoon, Nevills and friend Jack Frost built a wooden boat. For a test run he rowed it, with Doris, as far as Honaker Trail in December, 1933. They had planned to go farther, but low water persuaded them to hike out.

The next March, Nevills and Frost built a second boat. Norm and Doris ran it as far as Honaker Trail, where Frost and his wife joined them in the second boat. Historian and boatman Gaylord Staveley describes the evolution of their boating technique:

> As Frost ... told it later, both men had been handling the boats in the conventional way, pulling downstream, until he got turned backwards by one of the rapids and discovered that floating stern-first was better because he could see where he was going. Norm, he said, resisted the idea initially, but then began trying it.

As was likely the case in Loper's earliest boating, the San Juan's shallows contrived to teach them the "Galloway technique."

In March 1936 Nevills rowed Ernest "Husky" Hunt down the San Juan to Lee's Ferry for pay, sparking in him the idea of commercial guiding. In September he rowed two couples from Iowa down the same stretch. In 1937, botanist Dr. Elzada Clover stopped at the Nevills Lodge. Between Clover's interest in cacti and Nevills's interest in boating they concocted a grand scheme—a botanical expedition down the Colorado River. That winter Nevills set about designing and building a fleet of boats suitable to the task.

A perhaps apocryphal story has the design of the new boats coming from craft Nevills's father had seen while prospecting on the Yukon. Like a Galloway boat, they were flat from side to side, upturned at the ends, bow and stern decked in, with a large cockpit for the boatman. Like Loper's *Old Betsy*, it was made of the new wonder material, plywood. What was quite different was the extreme width, making the boat shaped more like a sagging flat-iron.

To help finance and build three new boats, Nevills enlisted the local USGS water gager, Laphene "Don" Harris, a small, wiry young man from Soda Springs, Idaho. Nevills had given Harris a ride through the sand waves near Mexican Hat. That was all it took. Recalled Harris, "My blood started to boil over about that time." Intrigued by the whitewater, Harris signed on to row one of the new boats on the expedition. In trade for his construction and rowing services, he would own his boat, the *Mexican Hat*, at the end of the trip. Nevills named his own boat the *WEN* after his father's initials. The third, in honor of the trip theme, they named *Botany*.

As it came time to launch, Dr. Clover had enlisted two students: Lois Jotter and Gene Atkinson. Nevills invited Wilbur "Bill" Gibson, a commercial artist who had stayed at Nevills Lodge, to row the *Botany* and help document the trip. They launched at Green River, Utah on June 20, 1938 amid a media fanfare. The last woman who had tried this—Bessie Hyde—had vanished on the river ten years earlier.

They drifted the first 120 miles, with Nevills still completing the deckwork. Cataract Canyon, still running high and furious, gave them incredible difficulties—an escaped boat, a flipped boat, and days upon days sweating, dragging and hauling when Nevills called for a portage.

When they were late arriving at Lee's Ferry, the media frenzied. A Salt Lake City reporter interviewed Bert Loper.

"He Thinks They'll Make It" read the headline. Beneath it was a large photo of Loper in a suit, pointing at a map. Loper, level-headed, tried to assuage the newsmen. He knew Cataract Canyon, and he knew high water:

> I'd be willing to start after them if I could get a boat and supplies, but I wouldn't want to start for at least a week, because I think it will take them that long to get down.... I understand [the river level] was over 70,000 feet last week. That means they'll have to make some long portages over rocks 15 or more feet high and scrambled together like eggs, in order to skip the worst rapids. That takes time.

The Nevills party, he said, would be doing very well to reach Lee's Ferry by July 12th.

Loper was right; they were fine. They drifted around the bend to Lee's Ferry on July 8. Things were not going smoothly on the trip, however. The portage work had been brutal, the temperatures extreme. Nevills, trying to launch a career in extremely perilous circumstances, was nervous, cautious, controlling. He rubbed the younger members of the group wrong. Nevills and Clover in the *WEN* floated ahead. The other four drifted far behind muttering. When they arrived at Lee's Ferry, Atkinson left the expedition. So did Don Harris. "I was nearly out of leave," he recalled, "although I could have gotten an extension on my leave, I think. But I left the party there anyway. Kind of regretted it ever since."

Nevills replaced the men with Lorin Bell and Del Reid, and continued. At the Bright Angel Trail, Emery Kolb hiked down and joined them. The tribulations in Cataract had knocked most of the bugs out of the operation, and Grand Canyon went relatively smoothly. Since 1937, when Buzz Holmstrom and Frank Dodge's trips had come through, the waters of Lake Mead had backed up over the last two major rapids. Neither Nevills, nor anyone else, would again get the chance to run Separation or Lava Cliff Rapids.

The year 1938 was a turning point in the history of the Colorado. As late

Bad hair

Bad tie

He Thinks They'll Make It

Bert Loper, veteran Colorado river boatman, who thinks expedition now running rapids will be "doing very well" if they reach Lee's Ferry by July 12.

as 1937 every river trip had been a major expedition. Not that Nevills's wasn't—but he was at the head of a flood that soon took river trips from the newspaper headlines and put them in tour brochures. Soon after Nevills came Holmstrom again, this time with a photographer, Amos Burg. Burg was rowing an entirely new craft: an inflatable rubber raft, custom made for the trip by B.F. Goodrich. Burg strapped a wooden frame to the rubber oval to steady his oarlocks, and rowed it through. Or tried to. The *Charlie*, as he named it, proved too floppy for the biggest waves, and he portaged or lined most major rapids—but tougher rafts soon replaced *Charlie*. Holmstrom, meanwhile, set another record. In 1937 he'd lined three rapids and portaged two. This time he ran them all, from Green River, Wyoming to Lake Mead—no one had ever done it before.

When Holmstrom and Burg came through Green River, Loper was there. Burg recalled Loper "ridiculed my rubber craft as a new fangled contraption." They picked up a helper in town, Willis Johnson, who thought a river trip sounded far better than his job picking watermelons. Johnson remembered:

> Some old guy with a red shirt, he was looking over our equipment, and he was telling some other old guy there on the riverbank, "Next time we read about these guys, it'll be in the obituary." So I asked one of the natives, "Who's that old guy?" He said, "Well, that's old Lying Bert Loper."
>
> But he's really not a liar, you know. He saved a lot of lives. He would tell such horrible stories that them young guys in Green River stayed home. They didn't build a raft and go down the river.... He was telling it for their own safety.... He done them guys a favor.

And still more: behind Holmstrom and Burg came three French kayakers—two men and a woman. They cast off in Green River, Wyoming, making it as far as Lee's Ferry before winter stopped them.

Bert Loper could not avoid the constant reminders of the trip he still longed to make. One news story in particular got under his skin. In August Julius Stone and plaque-meister Russell Frazier launched a Glen Canyon expedition. Frazier claimed to have discovered the very spot where Fathers Escalante and Domiguez crossed the Colorado back in 1776—*El Vado de los Padres*, Crossing of the Fathers. He had to plaque it. Loper, who had visited the crossing spot for years, blew a cork. "There is only one man that I take issue with," he wrote to Elwyn Blake,

> and that is Dr. Frazier for I still think that he is a grabber of un-earned notoriety for he is now posing as being the man that DISCOVERED the crossing of the Fathers and I have known it for more than twenty years, so have many others and it was in 1930 that Dave Rust and I took a Wall Street Lawyer and his daughter through the Glen and the girl swam the river at that particular place and then along comes a moocher of notoriety and claims the discovery of that that was known by many."

Hugh Miser was still overseeing USGS work in the San Rafael Desert in the fall of '38 and was able to hook Loper up with a bit of work. Charles Hunt, head geologist on the survey, was finishing several years' work and orchestrated a field conference in the Henry Mountains. Miser came out for it, as did Herbert E. Gregory, who Loper had guided (or tried to) through the area back in 1918. Loper came down to help with camp logistics and to see old friends.

The conference was a disaster. "The first day out Gregory's horse fell," wrote Hunt:

> and Gregory had to be returned to town with cracked ribs. The second day Loughlin's horse fell and Loughlin had to be taken to Price with a dislocated shoulder. The third day, Miser's horse fell and he had to lead it off the mountain. It was decided to terminate the field conference.

The good news was that Loper met Charlie Hunt, and the two began cooking up a river trip.

Back in Salt Lake, the Lopers moved from the Masonic Temple to the KDYL Playhouse, where Bert again served as custodian. In early October, Loper took Rachel on a drive to Durango, Colorado to visit Blake. Soon after their return, Loper checked into the Veterans Hospital with severe shoulder pain. On November 11, Loper wrote Blake:

> This will just be a little hurry-up note for I am just out of the Hospital for to-day—been in ever since I arrived in Salt Lake and if the doctors know what they are talking about I may be there a long time yet for my

Bert Loper, far left. Charlie Hunt, foreground

> hurt has got worse ever since I came back and it is some problem to get any sleep at all, and it is some problem to keep peace at home for Rachel wants me to come home and stay but I had just as well stay at the hospital untill I am well as to come home—I am getting electrical treatments and while my shoulder is getting sorer it may be on the way to recovery at that.... I have to be back to-morrow morning in time to get my treatment.

Two weeks later he wrote Miser:

> I have both arthritis and nuritis and they have my arm and my shoulder in a cast so I cannot move my arm around so much and I am getting about four hours sleep a night and before the cast I was making a very poor cut out of sleeping at all.

In all, Loper spent nearly five months in the Veterans Hospital that winter. That is where Don Harris found him.

Don Harris was greatly disappointed not to have made the trip through Grand Canyon with Nevills. Even so, Nevills, good to his word, had given Harris the *Mexican Hat.* Now, with a boat, a thirst for whitewater, and a summer vacation looming, Harris was looking for a trip. In corresponding with movie-maker Bill Gibson, who had continued on through Grand Canyon with Nevills, the two hatched a plan. They would run the upper Green through Lodore; Harris would row, Gibson would film, and Gibson's friend Chet Klevin would cook. With the Green River in mind, Harris looked up the head boatman from the 1922 Green River survey, Bert Loper. The response from the old man in the hospital was not what Harris expected. Loper was not interested in talking of the upper Green. Instead he recounted his lifetime of foiled plans for running Grand Canyon, and said, "So I'd like to go through Grand Canyon and if you'd like to go, maybe we could organize a trip." #

61 Passing on

As early as 1948 Dock Marston was planning to have his comprehensive river history out "next year." P.T. Reilly, too, had a book in the works—a magnum opus on the history of Lee's Ferry. Both men continued their research year after year, amassing phenomenal collections of fact, opinion, and folklore; journals, photographs, correspondence, and interviews.

But Reilly and Marston, similar in their brusque characterizations of other boaters, inevitably had a falling out with each other. When Reilly wrote a savage review of Pearl Baker's *Trail on the Water,* Marston wrote her in consolation:

> By one group he [Reilly] is known as the GREAT EGO. In turn, he applies the appellation THE SWOONERS to that group. He is very difficult and few get along with him but I did for 16 years and we exchanged very extensively. In 1965 he got MAD at me and our communication is now virtually limited to exchange of Xmas cards.

And each Christmas card carried a terse query: "Hope you are well and giving your work its final polish," "Since this job was so near some months back, it must be near the print stage at the moment. What is the schedule?" "It was a slight disappointment, when opening the envelope, that your Lees Ferry opus didn't appear."

Sadly, neither man lived to see their life work published. Marston never finished writing, and Reilly wrote so extensively he could not find anyone willing to publish his uncut manuscript. Meanwhile their acerbic opinions, increasingly freely dispensed, tended to color their own legacies as much or more than any others'.

Reilly's great work, *Lee's Ferry, From Mormon Crossing to National Park,* was edited posthumously by Robert Webb and published in 1999.

It stands as the seminal work in its field. Marston's manuscript, never completed, may never be published. His collection, however—some 432 file boxes of notes, 251 volumes of photographs, 163 reels of movie film, 60 boxes of slides, and more—form the mecca of Colorado River history to this day. David Lavender's 1984 *River Runners of the Grand Canyon* was largely mined from Marston's material, as were significant portions of many other authors' subsequent works. In this sense, both men's river legacies run strong. Had Marston and Reilly not shown such obsessive devotion to historical research, much of the history of Lee's Ferry, river running, and the Colorado River would be forever lost. For this, posterity owes these men a tremendous debt.

And really, it was primarily in their correspondence and writings that the two men waxed so contrary. Those who ran rivers with them remember them fondly as good boatmen and great mentors. Too, many researchers recall generous assistance from both Reilly and Marston. As time passed, both men's dyspeptic assessments of other river folk slowly faded as comprehensive studies of individual boaters appeared.

Each man died unpublished at eighty-five years of age; Marston in 1979, Reilly in 1996, each going out with a whimper. For grand exits, Bert Loper, upon whom they heaped so much scorn, had them beaten hands down.

Don Harris outlived them all, passing on quietly in 2004 at the age of ninety-two. The few cutting remarks Nevills sent Harris's way in the 1940s had been long since forgotten. Harris's commercial boating career—encompassing the wooden Cataract boats of the 1930s and '40s, the hard-hulled motorboats of the 1950s and '60s, and the inflatable pontoon boats of the 1970s—ended quietly in 1973 after an auto accident crippled his left arm. He ran many private trips after that, his last being the San Juan in 1992. Between Loper and Harris, they covered a full one hundred years on the rivers of the Southwest, beginning and ending on that muddy little stream in southern Utah. Harris, more than any of the others, ended with the legacy of a truly great boatman and a gentleman absolute. #

62 We ARE GOING THROUGH

River talk was in the air the winter of 1938–39. In January, on one of his days out of the hospital, Loper looked up Don Harris. "He mentioned Norm [Nevills] had asked him to go along on the Green River, Wyo. to Utah trip next summer," wrote Harris. "Wanted to know what I thot of Nevills and if I would advise him to go. I told him that if he didn't mind someone else being boss, that he probably would get along O.K." That was enough for Loper.

In early March Loper checked himself out of the hospital. "I was just going along without any change," he wrote Blake, "so I thought I could doctor myself at home.... My shoulder is not well by a long ways, but it is a lot better than it was." During his convalescence, he had secured a job for the coming summer. On and off for twenty-five years now, Loper had engaged in government science support work—now he had lined up a position taking geologist Charlie Hunt through Glen Canyon. Although Hunt would have preferred an open rowboat for the trip, Loper was able to convince Hunt's boss, Hugh Miser, to let him build a new Grand Canyon whitewater boat for the job.

Don Harris had not made up his mind. Loper had: Grand Canyon. He wrote Blake, asking if he wanted to go, saying "there is no one I would rather go with as much as I would you.... I may make the trip alone for it is now or never and I know of no other way I could celebrate my 70th birthday any better."

Loper wrote to the Harbor Lumber Company, who in 1934 had developed Super Harbord, the first marine-grade plywood. Nevills had used it for his boats. Loper asked for prices. On March 27 Loper wrote Miser, saying, "My arm is not well but it is so much better that I would not hesitate to start on a boating trip right now."

Meanwhile Harris, Gibson, and Klevin tried to decide what trip to do. "For heaven sakes just speak up if you would rather go thru the big canyon with Bert," wrote Gibson in April:

Don Harris

Bill Gibson

> Speaking of the Big Canyon, won't the water be higher than all hell down there around the middle of June? I suppose Bert has forgotten more about the conditions of the river than I will ever know, but the way I heard it, was that the water ran *pertty* high there at that time.... I don't know, I am just askin, and if you want to go I for one am game. At least we will be in for some WILD riden'.

Charlie Hunt wrote Loper in April, confirming an early June launch and offering a paycheck of three hundred dollars for boat and boatman. Loper, safely out of the hospital's clutches, ordered plywood and began building his boat. It looked much like *Old Betsy*—a crude Galloway-style boat. Just what became of *Old Betsy* Loper never said—most likely the beating it took on the Salmon had proven lethal. He did, however, still have the oars Julius Stone had sent him.

On May 7 Gibson pushed Harris for an answer, "Is everything okay to go down the Green?... Gosh, Don, we don't want to let our own enthusiasm run away with us and high pressure you into doing something you don't want to do." In the end, Harris opted wholeheartedly for Grand Canyon. Gibson and Klevin followed suit.

Visiting Rust: Dodge Freemen, Hunt, Loper, Miller

Dave Rust

Loper finished his boat in late May. Since Hunt wanted Loper for overland work prior to the river trip, Bert, Rachel, and their grand-nephew Blaine Busenbark headed for the Colorado to deliver the boat. Twenty miles from the river they got bogged down in the sands of North Wash. Loper was able to get Arth Chaffin, then operating Hite Ferry, to come up and gather the boat, while the Lopers retreated to Salt Lake.

Charlie Hunt and his assistant Ralph Miller left Salt Lake City with Loper on June 5, 1939. As with Herbert Gregory and Hugh Miser, Loper was once again allying himself with giants of Western geology. And once again making lifelong friends. Traveling through Green River, Hanksville, and Notom, they spent five days getting to the river, Loper "loafing" while Hunt and Miller geologized. They spent another four days investigating the Hite area while Loper tinkered with his boat. They launched on the afternoon of June 15, making four miles downriver. The plan was for Loper to deliver Hunt and Miller to Lee's Ferry around July 5 and rendezvous with Harris, Gibson, and Klevin.

On June 18, they stopped at Red Canyon, where "We visited the old workings that I used to work and then returned to the old cabin and the utter desolation of the place made me feel rather blue" At Tickaboo, someone had burned Cass Hite's cabin to the ground. Loper's shoulder was working fine, but "my knee is causing me lots of pain and it is with difficulty that I walk at all."

While camped at Smith Fork on June 24, Dave Rust and his geologist client Dodge Freeman stopped in. They camped together that night. Loper typed. Or tried to. "It seems like every time that I get this old typewriter out to do some work the wind starts to blow so hard I have to quit."

At Hall Creek they ran into Arth Chaffin chugging upriver in one of his cobbled-together floating contraptions, looking like a cross between a garbage scow and a Model-T. He gave them a ride.

✣ ✣ ✣

On June 26 Harris, Gibson, and Klevin launched at North Wash and began pursuit. With no geologists along they had plenty of time to visit side canyons, Hole-in-the-Rock, and make the hike to Rainbow Bridge. On July 2 Harris wrote: "Toward dark the wind receded some and how relieved we were. To our great surprise we heard a husky 'Ship Ahoy' from the R. bank at mile 24½. We found this to be Bert Loper's Party and camped with them tonite." While Loper and Harris's new team introduced themselves, Hunt cooked dinner.

The next morning Harris and company rowed on to Lee's Ferry. Loper, Hunt, and Miller spent another day and a half doing geology, arriving at the Ferry on July 4. Hunt and Miller, their work done, left with Charlie Hanks. It was a bittersweet finale to Loper's career as a government boatman—upon reaching seventy years of age, he would no longer be eligible for the job. But as one door closed, another was opening. Loper was embarking on a decade of pure pleasure trips.

For the next two days Loper, Harris, Gibson, and Klevin wrote letters, did final carpentry on Loper's boat, and painted it. At 10:30 on the morning of July 6, they pushed off into Grand Canyon.

> I will say here and now that if it had not been for Mr. Harris I would not have made the trip.... I had been planning this trip long before Don was born but there seemed to be a jinx that would head me off at Lee's Ferry every time that I tried to go through, and all he knew of me was what he had heard, and I knew nothing of him, but in the laying of plans for the trip he would brook no interference and it was always we ARE GOING THROUGH.

In February 1908, as stories of Russell and Monett's success scorched

Loper, he had written, "I surely expect to show the world that I have the nerve to finish the trip." Now, finally, after three decades and three foiled attempts, Loper was rowing downstream from Lee's Ferry. In four miles they passed beneath Navajo Bridge, which had bypassed Lee's Ferry in 1928. With sheer limestone cliffs rising five hundred feet on either side, they were committed. Recalled Harris:

> We stopped at the first big rapid, which is Badger Creek, and pulled into shore and walked down to take a look. Make an inspection on it. I said to Bert, "You think we can run it?" He says, "Sure we can *run* it! It's just a matter of *how* we're going to run it!" Picked out a course. And [Bert] says: "From then on Don Harris never asked '*Can* we run it?' he just asked, '*How're* we going to run it?'"

The next rapid was the ill-famed Soap Creek, known as the last rapid in Grand Canyon to be successfully run. The first attempt was in 1911 when Ellsworth Kolb washed out of his own boat. He climbed back aboard and rowed ashore. Making a second attempt, he flipped his brother's boat, while Emery cranked the moving picture camera. Blake and Lint wanted to run it in 1923, but Kolb forbade it. In 1927, Clyde Eddy vowed to portage Soap Creek. But he got mixed up and portaged Badger Creek Rapid, believing it to be Soap Creek. Riding with boatman Parley Galloway, Eddy then bounded through Soap Creek not knowing where he was. He figured it out later, his chest swelling with pride. Most subsequent trips elected to run it. When Loper and Harris pulled over to scout, Harris asked *how* they were going to run it.

Soap Creek, wrote Bert, "was much worse so [Don] seemed very dubious about running it but I told him it was made to order, and I will always believe that the foundation for the successful completion of the trip was laid right there." Confidence and certitude, believed Loper, trumped doubt and fear.

That night, eighteen miles into the trip, Loper mused:

> Nothing serious so far and even Soap Creek Rapid which has a rather noted reputation, there is nothing so far that has Cataract tied—I notice that the most of those [boatmen] that have made Grand Canyon, they seem to discredit Cataract, but if the rapids below are much worse than

How're we going to run it, Bert?

> Gypsum or Dark Canyon Rapids, in Cataract Canyon, then we will be in for some hard work.
>
> There sure is a thrill in running rough water and I hope that the sense of elation never leaves me, but there is so much more to a trip of this kind than the rapids, for the wonders of the majestic walls—the grandeur and stupendiousness of the mighty chasms through which the Colo wends its way is sure an awe inspiring sight and I would sure feel sorry for the one who fails to appreciate it.

Gibson's fears of high water had proved needless. The river peaked in late May at around 50,000 CFS. By the time they launched it had dropped to a meager 10,000 CFS—low water for a wooden boat—and it continued to drop all trip. In fact, it is good they went as early as they did—by August 3 it had dropped to 3,500.

The next day at mile 24½ Bill Gibson was swept from Harris's deck by a side-curling wave. He grabbed the safety rope as he slid off, and climbed back aboard. Not far beyond, Harris dropped over a pour-over and filled his cockpit to the gunwales. For ten miles beginning at mile 20, the rapids come fast and thick. Although Harris was a quick study, he had much to learn. Exiting the "roaring twenties," they paused nearly an hour at the verdant waterfall Powell named Vasey's Paradise, then pushed off for camp.

Klevin took to the kitchen work splendidly. Gibson strove to get the best pictures possible. But something about him was a little off. Loper later wrote of it, but was infuriatingly vague as to the problem or its cause:

> There were times that I did not know just how to take him until Chet told me something and then I looked at it in another light. There were times that he seemed morose but after I learned then I knew better and it also brought home to me the fact that we are oft times prone to pass snap judgment and I will say that I have never seen anyone that performed his duties more thorough or complete.

At noon on the third day they lunched at the confluence of the Little Colorado River. It was at this point that Powell said Marble Canyon ended and Grand Canyon began. (By modern usage, Marble Canyon is

Loper emerging from hatch, Bright Angel beach

considered a subset of Grand Canyon.) The men were making terrific time. They ran rapids of increasing difficulty all day and camped at the head of one of the toughest in the canyon, Hance Rapid—a long rocky channel, especially tough at low water.

"It was the worst looking one I had seen on the trip to date," journaled Harris:

> Rocks were scattered everywhere in the channel. Bert ran thru first and hit a big rock right at the head of the rapid. No serious harm was done except that this bump threw him off his course and he went way over to the R. Side in a mess of rocks and pours—came thru some of the way prow downstream and hit a couple more rocks.
>
> Take it from me I was plenty nervous about going back to my boat and trying to run it after I had seen what Bert did. Regardless, I went back and shoved off. Luck & God's blessings were with me. I was able to keep in the channel I had chosen and come thru in fine shape without hitting one rock. However, to do this took every ounce of strength I could put into pulling the oars on 2 or 3 different maneuvers to prevent hitting rocks.

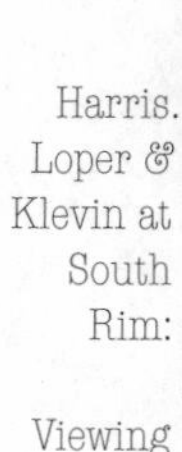

NAU.PH.96.3.35.9
Bert Lauzon

NAU.PH.96.3.35.12
Bert Lauzon

Harris. Loper & Klevin at South Rim:

Viewing Kolb's boat

Returning to river

Below Hance the Colorado enters the Granite Gorge, with ominous black schist cliffs rising steeply over a thousand feet on either side. The rapids run bank to bank, often making a portage impossible. Since Powell first described it, the Granite Gorge has given boatmen heebie-jeebies and no end of boating crises. Not Loper and Harris. They ran Sockdolager without a problem. In Grapevine Loper hit a few rocks but without damage. They landed at Bright Angel Creek at 2 P.M. on their fourth day. That's fast, especially for such low water.

Loper was pleased and awed. "I have read so much about it all that it seems as though I had been here before." He noted that the Colorado through Grand Canyon, with a paltry drop of about seven feet per mile—far gentler than many easier rivers—had such huge rapids. "The solution to that is that about 99% of the fall happens in the rapids and not between—The hazard of a rapid is not always in the amount of fall but how it falls." He also saw how rapids that were rocky and difficult at one stage of river flow, might wash out entirely at a higher flow, and that every trip encounters a different river. "I find it is sure a silly thing to criticize another for it is seldom that we know the stage of water he was on."

The next morning, July 10, they rose at 6 A.M. for the hike to South Rim, and reached the top before noon, Loper in the lead. So much for the bad knee. Although neither Kolb brother was there, Emery Kolb's

Boats at rest, Elves Chasm

daughter Edith showed their movie and had Loper give a short talk afterward. Loper even signed some of Ellsworth's books for tourists. Edith made a long distance call to Los Angeles where Emery was in the hospital. Ellsworth was there visiting, so Loper got to talk to both. They hiked back to the river that same day, reaching the beach in the dark. That night Gibson woke up screaming, dreaming he was drifting into Lava Falls on his air mattress.

With the water dropping, they were off early on the morning of July 11. The rapids below Bright Angel are an all-star line-up including many of the biggest rapids in Grand Canyon: Horn Creek, Granite Falls, Hermit. They ran them without incident. But Crystal, which only later became a major rapid in a 1966 flash flood, managed to be the big problem. Harris had not yet learned to see a pour-over from upstream, and slid directly into another. "The prow dropped down as the stern started out," wrote Harris, "and we settled back into this terrible place about half sidewise. In this position enough of the boat was facing the water above to push us on out. However, in the mishap Bill was washed off twice, hanging on to his rope each time and climbing back on." They made it another four miles and four rapids before camping.

The next day they finished the rapids of the Upper Granite Gorge, but not without problems. Loper wrote:

Harris in camp. Loper's boat on edge

> In walking down along one of the rapids I slipped on a slick granite boulder and hurt my leg quite severely and I also hurt my bad knee but all in all I am doing fine.... I struck a couple of rocks and came near turning over about 3 times so when I made camp I took the boat out of the river and examined the bottom and everything is O.K. and with a lame shoulder and a bum knee we call it a day.

That same day they had come across the old *Ross Wheeler*—the boat Loper had built in 1914 and Russell had tried unsuccessfully to run through Grand Canyon. "I found that boat tied up above high water where Russell went to pieces and I think I could, with a little work, make another trip with that same boat."

Another day put them through the rapids of the Middle Granite Gorge without problems. They lunched at Deer Creek Falls, where a sidestream pours out of a high cliff to the river, and continued nine more miles. They camped below Kanab Creek, where Powell had ended his 1872 expedition.

The next morning they scouted Upset Rapid, named in 1923 when Emery Kolb flipped. They picked out a bouncy run down the left side of

Gibson, Loper, and Harris at the *Ross Wheeler*

the rapid and ran it. Seven miles later they pulled into a crevice in the left wall and lunched where Havasu Creek pours its blue-green waters into the Colorado. "I must have taken on too much Rye Krisp or something because I was in rather a bad way the balance of the day." They camped that night at Stairway Canyon, just a few hundred yards above a minor rapid named Gateway. Loper described the next morning:

> We got a fine start and the first rapid was Gate-way canyon rapid which was so unimportant that we never stopped to look it over but as we dropped in I told Chet that we were going to miss a picture and as we dove down—nearly straight and came up like-wise we were caught by a side twister and went up-side down. But we climbed on the overturned boat and caught hold of the edge and gave a pull and she righted beautifully and all oars was in place but we lost our bucket and the grate that we had for to cook on but other-wise every thing was fine. And while I have been doing this—off and on—for more than fifty years that is my first capsize so I should not feel bad and it makes me feel a little proud of the old boat. But while Don was following me he never knew—until I told him—that I had been up-side-down.

Harris made a small note on the edge of his own journal: "As we started on from Gateway Rapid Bert yelled back to it, 'Kiss my ass.'"

An hour later they were on shore, scouting Lava Falls. As far as they knew it had only been run once, by Buzz Holmstrom the year before. (Later research concluded that Flavell probably ran it in 1896, Glen and Bessie Hyde ran it in their sweep scow in 1928, and Bob Francy ran it later that fall on his search for the Hydes—but Loper and Harris had no way of knowing this.) "After looking it over from both sides we decided that we could run it," stated Loper, "and did so." As it turned out, that was a good year to run Lava Falls. Less than two months later a gigantic debris flow thundered down Prospect Canyon, choking the rapid into a steeper and more difficult cataract.

"Although I had my first up-set of my whole career," journaled Loper that evening, "after running lava falls I feel very well satisfied—so ends the day—"

By the latter half of the trip—as so often happens with a good teacher and a great pupil—Harris was having better runs than Loper. "I learned

Harris caption: "Bert in the snorrin' zone".

more about the tricks of the river and studying the currents and things from Bert Loper than I did from anybody else," recalled Harris. "Norm knew the river well and was a good oarsman, but he hadn't the experience in whitewater that Bert had.... He had a knack with oars that I've seldom seen equalled."

They bucked wind and groused for the next two days. "It seems we all have had a siege of the belly ache and I can't understand why rye crisp and to-mato juice should do that to us." Finally they entered the Lower Granite Gorge. On July 17, Loper rowed into 231-Mile Rapid and got clobbered. "The boat came near capsizing," wrote Harris:

> and during the tilt Chet was tipped overboard. When the boat come out from under the wave Chet was trying to get back on. Seeing his difficulty he gave up and went on all the way thru the rapid staying from 30 to 50 feet ahead of the boat all the time. Bert picked him up below as if nothing had happened.

Five miles later they hit the slack water of upper Lake Mead. They stopped at the mouth of Separation Canyon to look for Dr. Frazier's

1934 plaque—the one he planned to replace in 1939—to no avail. Here three of Powell's men left in 1869, hiking out to their death at the hands of ... maybe Shivwits Indians, maybe Mormons, maybe exposure. Loper and Harris rowed another three miles on the slow, placid lake-water and camped.

They had done it. Loper, in his seventieth year, had finally made it through Grand Canyon. He had shown the world, and had a damned fine time doing it.

For the next two days they rowed the calm water that had recently inundated the final forty miles of Grand Canyon. Loper: "I am too nervous to let Chet row so I do all of that." Harris: "Chet swears to hell he'll never eat RYE KRISP again this side of eternity." Loper: "After watching Chet do a little rowing I became rather wormy so I took the oars."

On the evening of July 19 they rowed out of the Grand Wash Cliffs, where Grand Canyon and the Colorado Plateau formally end, and into the Basin-and-Range country of the Mojave Desert. They rowed a few more miles to the small, remote marina at Pierce's Ferry and camped. They had arranged for a tour boat to pull them the seventy miles to the

NAU.PH.96.4.114.10 Bill Belknap

Klevin, Loper, Gibson, and Harris, end of trip, Hemenway Wash

dam the next day, so declared their trip officially over. Although they never stated any goals, they had tied George Flavell's 1896 record for fastest trip through Grand Canyon, and were the first trip to have run all their boats through every rapid. In the seventy years since Powell's first voyage, theirs was the sixteenth trip to complete Grand Canyon.

> It was then that I expressed—to the boys—my appreciation of the most wonderful trip but their kind consideration shown me for I always tried to remember that I was the old man of the expedition and the only [time] that I was reminded of the difference was their kindness to me and I will say that I was waited on more on this trip than about all the rest of my life.... [T]here was never a cross or harsh word spoken and me being the leader of the trip I often wonder if there ever was a leader that had the whole hearted support that I had.
>
> ... and to think of the many years that I have wended my lonely way along some part of the Colorado water shed and with my blankets unrolled on some sand bar with the starry canopy of heaven over me have I dreamed not only of making this trip but of making it as we did make it with every one of those ferocious rapids conquered, and

> to think I had to wait untill I had rounded out my three score and ten before the dream came true, so after my little talk of appreciation to them we made our beds down on lake mead for the last time.

Harris was equally enthusiastic, writing, "We all felt the trip was indeed a great success and beyond all doubt the most enjoyed of any ever taken on the Colorado River, regardless of who made the trip or when it was taken." Gibson's movie of the expedition, *Canyon Caravan*, shows them throughout the trip having fun—good, solid fun—and perhaps this was the first trip where people really did. And although their boating skills by modern standards do not appear that great, they were plenty good for 1939.

The following afternoon the launch arrived from Boulder City. Tying the rowboats single file behind, they motored the four hours across Lake Mead to Boulder Dam. There Loper ran into Frank Dodge, now a retired boatman, and spent the night on Dodge's houseboat. After a day or two of royal treatment—by the tour company, Dodge, and others—Klevin and Gibson left for California and Loper and Harris returned to Salt Lake City. Of the trip finale, Don Harris recalled:

> When we were being towed across Lake Mead after running the Grand successfully, Bert got to thinking. He says: "This has been a wonderful trip; ideal. There has never been any friction or contention. And the age of you three young fellows combined about equals my age. That's an old man with three young fellows and there hasn't been any friction. So let's plan to go when I'm eighty, ten years hence."
>
> I said, "Oh, that sounds agreeable to me," not even imagining that he might still be alive ten years later. #

63 Alone

The Healer

When my mind feels soiled by cities,
And my ears are deaf with din;
When I've had too much of people
And my nerves are drawn too thin;

I seek the desert's silence
Where the mighty mesas stand
Like the ruins of old cathedrals
In a vast impressive land.

I bathe my heart in stillness
As cool as a mountain lake.
I ease my mind's hot tension
And end its fevered ache.

The desert is old in wisdom
That the ancient gods have known
And a man may know its healing
If he goes to its heart … alone.

—Don Blanding

one of two Blanding poems
oft recited by Bert Loper
#

64 Thoughts that come

Loper was ecstatic. "It has been said that one could not work for Uncle Sam after he was 70 years old," Loper wrote Miser, "but that would not fit in my case for I took off 15 years on that trip this summer so that makes me 55 now." If he could conjure up a trip for 1940, Loper added, "just think how young I would be.... Ponce de Leon would have nothing on me."

Loper felt rejuvenated enough write to Blake, "I am thinking of going to Greenriver and try and get a job in the cantaloupes and I might make a hundred...." Melon picking. Back-breaking labor even for a young man. "Do you remember that it was 16 years ago that my friend (?) E.C. La Rue said I was too old?"

To Julius Stone, who had rowed his own boat through Grand Canyon thirty years prior at the comparatively young age of fifty-four, Loper wrote:

> I am taking this opportunity to make my report on those Oars—They have done the Salmon-Glen-Marble-and Grand Canyons and never a portage or a line down—I do hope you will forgive me for being a little boastful but the incentive is very great for, with all respect and consideration for all other trips through the Grand I do believe that the last trip was the most smooth and successful of any trip that was ever made for we ran every one and hardly scratched our boats.

For some time Loper's correspondents—Miser, Blake, Hunt, Stone—had been encouraging Loper to write down his life story. That fall Blake wrote, saying he'd been out of work for a while and was writing and submitting stories for publication. He mentioned he would like to write about rivers and about Loper, and began asking specific questions about Loper's youth. Charlie Hunt, back in Washington, D.C., appears to have offered to proof Loper's writings as well—or perhaps even craft them into a biography. Loper's typewriter soon began to overflow with rendition after rendition of his life and times and trips and friends and boats and rivers.

"I never reached the 6th grade in school so therefore I know nothing about punctuation," Loper apologized to Blake, "and that makes my writing rather poor but I am going to try anyway." Loper set about transcribing his diaries. As it turned out, he set about expanding them: "The writing takes so much more writing than is in the diary for there are so many things that I am reminded of so therefore I write nearly twice as much as in the diary." Sadly, Loper's original diaries, with the exception of one small fragment, no longer exist. Hence Loper's accounts of his trips are at least one "filter" from spontaneous, and must be judged so.

Adding from memory many years later is a dangerous thing as far as facts are concerned. Yet there is no indication that Loper fabricated any of his history. Rachel Loper once wrote to Dock Marston, "I know everything Bert has ever written has been the true thing for he never exaggerated, any of his trips, that is why some of his writings are dry, compaired to some I have read." Dry, often rambling, but true as far as Loper could remember. For the most part, Loper stuck to plain, unemotional facts. But every so often he would just start to pontificate. "I got to thinking the other morning (I usely wake about four in the morning and then is when I do my thinking) and I got to thinking ..." And he wrote:

THOUGHTS THAT COME TO ME IN THE STILL OF THE NIGHT
(Of men that have travelled with me on many trips)

It would be most impossible for another person to realize, or understand, just what it meant to me to take the trip through the Grand Canyon, for the days, weeks, months, and years that I have put in on that river and in those Canyons seem to have made me part of the whole grand set up. There have, without doubt, been better boatmen than I who have traversed that mighty Canyon, but there have never been any that have given the time to the study of it that I have, for as I said, I seem to be a part of it, for I have lived in it, on it, with it, and in an instance or two, under it. I have after days work, layed on the bank and listened to it—I have listened to the grinding of Mush Ice—I have listened to it when it

> hardly made enough sound to hear at all. Then there would come a time when there would be a gentle murmur which told me that it had begun to awake, then from that, there would come a swish as though it were becoming peeved at something. Then from that there would be boils, swirls, eddies, and whirls, and then I knew that the river had started house cleaning. But it always seemed that it got mad about it all, for it always acted angry at those times. I have listened to it from its very lowest to its very highest and there would be a time when I would go out some morning and miss that angry sound, and although it would still be high and angry the sound would be gone, and I would know that its house cleaning was done.
>
> I have noticed the difference in the river on the rise and on down. I have noticed the difference in high water and floodwater—
>
> but I started out to tell what it meant to me to make this trip through the Grand. I had been disappointed many times. So many times that I had started out with the expectation of going through and something would happen to keep me from the trip. So when it did come, well, I can never explain just how I feel or just what it means to me, and although I have made the most wonderful trip through, I still want to go again. Instead of breaking a record on time I would like to take just twice the time of before and try to grasp all the wonders of the mighty chasm—try to see all that there was to see. I do, in a way, feel glad that the other trips never materialized, for if they had, I would never have had the pleasure of this trip. Never was there another one like it.

Thoughts That Come … rambled on for another seven pages, enumerating dozens of men Loper had worked with, wandering into events and places as the mood struck.

In another letter to Blake, Loper spent a page ranting about Dr. Frazier, who was now claiming to have rediscovered the alcove in Glen Canyon that Major Powell named Music Temple. Loper had visited it years earlier, leaving a note with his name in a can there:

> When we visited the temple this summer we did not find our names but they had been replaced with those of the Frazier out fit, and besides there had been very few miners that had not visited it … such is vain gloriousness. but there is no use to howl against the general order of

> things for Frazier has always had all the money he needed and I have had just the opposite.
>
> But I am a very fortunate GUY for I still have good health and some of the most wonderful friends in the world and I would rather go up to a drift and get what I could for a trip than to give up that which I have—I love the old muddy stream and if I could get an extension on time I would agree to put it in on the river—there are so many that always tell me that I will get mine there, but I know of no better place to finish up than there.

Loper had been thinking a lot about boats as well. From the primitive plank boats he had run on the San Juan, to the steel Whitehalls he had run with Russell, to his homemade Galloway style boats, Loper had a broad experience. To Blake he proposed the next stage in boat evolution—a boat that would begin to resemble the modern Grand Canyon dory—a boat Loper would not live to see:

> When I did capsize, Klevin and I got on the upturned bottom and gave a little pull and it righted itself … and when I build again the top will have the same rake that the bottom has for what I cut off the bottom to make the rake I will put it on the top and you can figure it out for yourself that it will nearly right itself.
>
> … if Don's boat ever turns over it will take all hands and the cook to right it.

Somehow Loper had been able to keep house and home together in downtown Salt Lake City for several years without steady employment, and still take time out to build boats and run rivers. In 1939 they were living with Rachel's nephew, Tom Busenbark. By 1941 they had moved to 519 3rd East. How the Lopers managed financially is a mystery. They barely did.

> I have had a job picking ducks [plucking feathers] but I ran a splintered bone under my fingernail so I am off for a day or two—the "sledding" for the Lopers is rather bad this fall—the worst since I came to S[alt] L[ake] but Rachel is Department President of the Auxiliary to the United Spanish War Vetrans and her time will be up next June so that

> will mark the exodus of the Lopers from Salt Lake City.
>
> I do not know just where we will go but some-where away from here—there are places that we can live on $60 per month but not in a city—did I say City? Why we are in the biggest Village in the whole world and it is dominated by a very inferior bunch at that, but the cost of living is beyond the means of the Lopers.

In January Loper wrote Blake again. The exodus from Salt Lake would be delayed:

> I am always pulling a bone-head and I have just done that very thing—I have gone and let the Vetrans put me in as the Chairman of the United Vetrans Council.... There is always a question that comes to me and that is just why do I, or have I, lived in this place all this time when I am not a City man and I am not or have I ever been....
>
> I have in mind a trip for this summer just for you and me—it would be just a trip to do our writing and it would, at the same time, connect you up on the river—why couldn't you and I put in at Greenriver and float down as far as Lee's Ferry—or farther and write as we went along just travel as we pleased and then we could get under a ledge and write for a day and when we got tired of writing we could load up and make another go down—and besides just think of a trip of this kind from all its angles I will admit that I am a little selfish for I do believe that I would be the big gainer from the trip but I know that it would be another wonderful trip and if we had time to go on through the Grand I know that we could write stuff that never has been written and besides I have the boat all ready and every thing except the picture end of it all—
>
> sometimes I think that I spend too much time "dreaming" and this may be just another dream but since I have finished the Grand I am beginning to believe in dreams for you know that my dream came true from two ways for I had dreamed that I would make the Grand but that I would run every rapid—do you blame for believing in dreams? #

65 Late bloomer

Bert Loper spent most of his life wanting to run Grand Canyon. In part it may have been to prove himself, to combat the allegations of cowardice pinned on him in 1908. In part it may have been to follow one of his great heroes, Major John Wesley Powell. But largely it had to be that he had become a whitewater man, and in the world of whitewater, Grand Canyon was the Big One. Yet by mid-life he often expressed resignation that it might never happen.

Was it a lack of resolve? Not really. More likely it was a combination of two things: circumstance and poverty. Circumstance had squelched his 1907, 1914, and 1923 trips. Poverty had prevented him from launching an expedition of his own.

Yet in his late sixties—an age where average men have let dreams of derring-do slip away—Loper's resolve grew stronger. His 1936 Salmon trip catalyzed that determination, and when Don Harris wandered into Loper's life he seized the opportunity.

Just weeks shy of seventy, Loper achieved his dream, and achieved it in a most spectacular and successful manner. Anyone else could relax, sit back in the glow, and know his own victory.

Not Loper.

To Loper it was more of a great awakening. No longer would he sit back and watch others—Eddy, Holmstrom, Nevills, Hatch, and more—while he was denied. The 1940s saw Loper's second youth, a new determination to run every river he could manage, to pass on his skills and stories, even as his own body began to conspire against him. #

66 Partners

LOPER WAS BOILING over with plans for another Grand Canyon trip, another Salmon trip, the Snake, the Columbia—the entire Pacific slope. By spring, however, he had narrowed his sights to a trip he conceived even before his Grand Canyon trip. Piece by piece, Loper was checking off the entire Colorado River drainage. Perhaps he had gotten the idea when running with Ellsworth Kolb, who tried to run all the forks of the Colorado. The largest unrun stretch in Loper's résumé was now the upper Green River, from its source in Wyoming's Wind River Mountains to Green River, Wyoming. For 1940, Loper planned to run that, then continue on downriver, retracing his 1922 trip to Green River, Utah. In 1922 he had "nosed" around parts of a few rapids. This time he would run them fair and square. Don Harris signed on.

In June, Loper, Harris, and Harris's brother Blaine trailered their two boats north, across the sage flats of central Wyoming, to the shore of Lower Green River Lake, just a few miles from the very source of the Green. Surrounded by snow capped peaks, the three men cast off for Utah. For a few miles the river runs gently through a sagebrush valley as it heads north out of the lakes. As it curves west, then south, it drops through a hellacious non-stop series of rapids where the river carves steeply through boulder-studded glacial moraines. Oddly, neither Loper nor the Harris brothers kept journals for this trip. No time perhaps. They had six hundred miles to make in two weeks, so Don could get back to his job.

They survived the rapids of Big Bend, then affixed a small motor to the *Mexican Hat* to speed their journey across the long flat heart of Wyoming. Loper, according to the *Salt Lake Tribune*, "took one ducking when his boat, being towed by that of Harris, was thrown against a bank and a willow tree swept him from the deck." In a week they made Green River, Wyoming. Taking on more supplies, they continued.

They had more water than Loper had had in 1922, making for easier

The Salt L

They Will Brave Treacherous Water

The three members of the second river expedition to leave Green River, Wyo., within a week . . . Left to right, Blaine Harris of Soda Springs, Idaho; Don Harris of Green-river, Utah, and Bert Loper of Salt Lake City. They left Green River, traveling in two boats, Tuesday morning, five days behind the Nevills 1940 expedition.

Veteran S. L. Boat Runner Starts Green River Trip

News clipping of 1940 trip

Towing Loper across Wyoming

boating. "Lodore was different," Loper wrote Julius Stone:

> for at Lower Disaster there was three channels and even Hell's Half Mile has changed, but we were just 4 hours from the head of Lodore to the foot of Hell's Half—We ran up to the head of Hell's and tied up, and looked it over, went back and got in our boats and was at the bottom in 30 minutes.

As Loper had sworn to do eighteen years earlier, they ran them all and ran them with full loads.

On June 28 at Echo Park, just below Lodore where the Yampa joins the Green, they found Buzz Holmstrom. He was working for the Bureau of Reclamation on a survey of the Echo Park dam site. With Boulder Dam now full, the beaver-like Bureau-folk were ready for a new project. Holmstrom was building boats for them, and running crew from the camp to the damsite and motor by motorboat. After a visit, Loper and the Harris brothers shoved off. "As I pushed off [Holmstrom] asked me if I was ever going to wear out—I asked him if he meant me or the boat—It would be hard to make anything out of Buzz but Buzz, but he always seems to be happy." Holmstrom wrote a letter to Julius Stone recounting Loper's trip and describing the fate of the oars Stone had sent Loper back in 1936. "He finally broke one. Below the head of Hell's Half Mile the river divides into three parts and he went to the right and got tangled up in some rocks and it wasn't the oar's fault."

The next morning, having made it through Split Mountain Canyon unfazed, they remounted their motor for the long flat Uinta Basin. Rounding a bend, they caught Norm Nevills's 1940 expedition, on their way from Green River, Wyoming to Boulder Dam. Nevills was missing, however, having caught a ride into town to begin their resupply. In his place was Bus Hatch, who had driven out to the river from Vernal to meet Nevills. Harris and Loper tossed them a line and towed them the remaining miles into Jensen.

By 1940 Hatch had developed a reputation as a river runner. Between himself, his brothers, his double cousin Frank Swain (Bus's mother was a Swain, Frank's mother was a Hatch), Swain's brothers, and their occasional financiers, Dr. Frazier and his merchant friend Bill Fahrni, they had run most of the rivers in the West: the Green from Wyoming to the confluence, the Colorado from there to Boulder Dam, the Middle Fork of the Salmon, the Yampa, and others. As yet, though, the spark for commercial operation had not kindled with Hatch as it had with Nevills. Still, any river runner that came through Vernal looked up Bus Hatch. And that night, with Nevills, Loper, and Harris all in town, was one of those nights. Hatch, the gregarious boatman, and Nevills, the publicity-minded boatman, threw a party in Vernal. Loper and Harris parked their boats at the bridge and joined the festivities.

They were on their way at dawn, however, motoring another hundred miles across the barren Uinta Basin to Desolation Canyon. There they dismounted the motor and rowed the final hundred miles of rapids into Green River, having traversed something like seven hundred miles in fourteen days. It was a record, if only for the fact that no one had ever tried that trip before. And apparently no one else ever did before the dams of the 1960s made it impossible.

"We proved it could be done in plywood boats," stated Harris years afterward. "But you have to go when the water's right on the peak, or you'd have them beat to pieces, it's so rocky in places. We proved it could be done, but we also proved it wasn't practical at all."

Loper's river map was nearly complete. There was one more stretch he needed to fill in and it was mostly flatwater. In 1916 he and Ellsworth Kolb had finished their run of Westwater at Cisco, Utah, some hundred and ten miles above the confluence of the Green and Colorado. Kolb never got around to filling in the final stretch on his checklist. Loper made it a priority. The *Salt Lake Tribune* explained:

> LOPER TO COMPLETE COLORADO RIVER CRUSADE
>
> Bert Loper, whitewater addict at 71 years, just completed a boat trip from Green River Lake, Wyo. to Green River, Utah, at which time he completed a chain of river trips which is the longest in Colorado River history.
>
> But this wasn't enough for Bert, who will put in at the Colorado at Cisco tomorrow morning at sunup and ride downstream to the junction of the Green River at the head of Cataract Canyon. This portion of the canyon is the only part of the expansive Colorado River watershed the veteran Loper hasn't negotiated.

Loper planned to take his motor along and return upriver to Moab after the float. To Julius Stone, Loper elaborated:

> This is to be my vacation and I will go alone and I intend to do as I please and if I want to fish, that is what I will do and if I do not want to get up before noon I will "LIE THERE."
>
> But my trip though Grand last summer was a hurry up affair and the same this summer so now I am going to do as I please and take all the time I want and I expect to spend my 71st birthday at the head of Cataract Canyon.

"Still enjoying what others might call hard work," read a story in the *Salt Lake Telegram*, "Mr. Loper considers he's just getting his 'second wind.'" Off he went. Twenty-five miles of flatwater gave way to about ten miles of small rapids and another ten or so of flatwater into Moab. From there it was another sixty-five miles to the confluence. His goal completed, he clamped his 4½ horsepower motor on the back of his boat and motored back upstream to Moab. On August 9, 1940, he wrote to Elwyn Blake:

> I finished the Colorado River Water shed and the idea of being all alone is not what it was years ago and after Laying around the Junction for two days I pulled up and started on my way back.... As it was my first trip De Lux I sure enjoyed it very much, that is while I was moving, but when I stopped it was rather uninteresting—I do not like the Grand River Canyon as much as I do the canyons of the Green; one minute we have a canyon and then we have a broken up mess.

Loper's record of consecutive miles run in the Colorado drainage can never be equalled, due to subsequent damming of many of the streams. It has precious few holes in it. Loper was a scant two years too late in Grand Canyon to run the ill-famed Separation and Lava Cliff Rapids before they were inundated. He portaged 13-Foot Rapid on the San Juan and Shoshone Falls on the Colorado. He missed the lower Gunnison on his run with Ellsworth Kolb. And the mountain-bound stretch of the Grand (Colorado) from its source at Grand Lake to Shoshone Falls, from what Loper had seen, looked like no place for a wooden boat.

But Bert Loper racked up more miles in more reaches of the Colorado than anyone. And even though modern kayakers can check off many more miles on the capillary streams, Loper laid claim to the arteries.

For Loper, that final segment was an anticlimax. But there were more rivers and more boats still to come. Don Harris was not about to quit; Loper would be his main boating partner for some time. Even though, as Loper admitted, at seventy-one, boating wasn't quite the breeze it had always been. To Miser he wrote, "I had a very hard trip last summer for it seemed that it took me so long to get in to the hard work and step into hard work from a life of idleness for a youngster like me."

Still, Loper was not your normal man in his seventies. "He was a powerful oarsman for his age," recalled Don Harris. "When Bert was in Salt Lake City he entered a rowing contest in Liberty Park. He competed against young fellas, and he won the prize." His strength was not merely physical—he was a man of great will power.

"He smoked 'til he was fifty years old, so he told me," said Harris:

> And then he quit; made up his mind he was going to quit. And he quit smoking to where he was a real crank about anybody smoking. He just

couldn't stand to see anybody smoke. He was a great guy!

Back in Salt Lake City, Loper kept churning out autobiographical treatises, mailing them to Elwyn Blake, Hugh Miser, and Charlie Hunt. During the fall and winter of 1940, Loper produced most of his detailed accounts of his childhood and early love life, in addition to expanding most of his diaries. He continued his work with the Veterans and Masons, and as it was an election year, he politicked. "We had to try to keep Bill King off the Democratic ticket—which we did." King, a long-time prominent Utah politician, was soundly defeated that fall by the liberal wing of the party. Loper, a long-time laborer, was decidedly liberal. "I have been interested in politics along other channels besides King so I have kept busy."

Financially, as always, life was a struggle. Rachel's mother was failing, could no longer live alone, and was boarding with Bert and Rachel. For money that winter, Loper plucked ducks at Bratten's Fish Market. At home he wrote. To Blake:

> I do not remember if I told you of how I became an avowed atheist in my early twenties and that frame of mind continued for several years untill I awoke and found that I was trying to tear down without trying to build up or trying to put something better in its place and while I am not a church member I have very different ideas to day to what I did have in those days …
>
> I have just looked up the word RELIGION and part of the definition was CONSCIENTIOUS and that may be all the claim on religion that I can take and I read a little tract once that left an impression on me and that was—In order to attain immortality is to so live during this life that after death you will continue to live in the hearts of your fellow man … and it always seemed to me that it would be so nice to be remembered for the good deeds that I have done.

Some of Loper's "religion" came from his work with the Masons, whose ethics followed traditional Christian belief. Much of their creed Loper could recite by heart. "Bert was very much interested in his Masonic work," Rachel wrote to Marston, "for that was his religion, and he did try to live up to it, but none of us are perfect."

Loper had other touchstones as well—songs and poems espousing his loves and beliefs. His youthful atheism had given way to a homegrown form of reverence.

> There is one thing that I wish to impress on your mind and that is—with all the hard ships that I have went through—this is just about the very best world I ever lived in—you know that we live our lives in cycles and there was a time that I felt sorry for my self ... but I would not trade my past life for no millionaires son life and I am still glad to be in this perticular world.

On August 24, 1941, Loper took a different sort of river trip, joining Claud Asher and A.W. Farnsworth for a motorboat trip 120 miles down the Green from Green River, then up the Colorado sixty miles to Moab. To Blake he wrote:

> That is five times that I have been through labyrinth and I never got half as much out of all the other trips as I did this one for I let the other fellows do the steering and I just sat and faced the direction we were going and took in all the beauty and grandeur of those canyons and now I want to take Rachel and go down and stay all summer and explore ...
>
> We had a high speed motor and we could make 30 miles an hour up stream but that is too fast if you want to see anything.

Two-thirds of the way up to Moab from the confluence, in the flat water beneath Dead Horse Point, Loper, repeating his act on the upper Green, fell overboard.

The last few trips had been tiring. Loper, now approaching seventy-two, decided it was time to take a little better care of himself:

> I am taking a course in the Deseret Gym so I can keep partly fit and BELIEVE IT OR NOT I do not drink any more—for I figure God has given me a wonderful house in which to live and I have been doing nothing to keep that house in repairs so I will give nature an even brake now that I have reached the AGE OF REASON....
>
> My job was not very big but it enabled me to get out of debt and now I am trying to keep ahead instead of behind—in other words I am

> trying to pay as I go instead of having my check all spent before I get it and it is running me rather short just before Xmas.

Sometime that winter the Lopers finally pulled out of Salt Lake City and migrated to Green River, finding lodging in Millie Biddlecome's tiny garage apartment. Biddlecome had known Loper for decades, since his visits to Hanksville in the 1910s.

In a third house, sandwiched between the Lopers and Biddlecome, lived her daughter, early Loper biographer Pearl Baker. As a child in Hanksville she had known and admired Loper. Later, as a young widow, she had managed the vast Robbers Roost Ranch, west of Canyonlands. Eventually selling that and remarrying, Baker had left Utah for Oregon in the 1930s. Now separated, she and her son Noel were back in Green River.

Noel Baker still recollects his neighbor:

> I remember him as being pretty serious. He obviously had a sense of humor, but a teenager would not appreciate it. I don't believe Bert had much education but he read quite a bit and he remembered what he read. He enjoyed talking, especially about the river. I don't remember any pets, either a cat or a dog, but he did like animals. My brother's horse was in a pasture behind the houses and Bert would occasionally feed him for Jack. Whenever Bert would go near the hay, the horse would whinny and run up to the fence. He didn't always get hay but he did get a good patting.
>
> I think Bert enjoyed being a little bit of an instructor. I played cribbage with him. While I don't think he ever threw a game, he gave me lots of pointers on playing. He had lots of people, river rats and such, who visited him. He seemed interested in all their plans and would give them advice as needed about the river. Bert didn't smoke and if he drank it was very seldom.
>
> Rachel was just like another grandmother to me. She made me feel welcome any time I went over to their home. She always had a slight Scottish burr when she talked.

Green River, with a population under one thousand, was far more Bert Loper's speed, although Rachel missed the big city. Bert picked up the occasional odd job and continued his Masonic career, beginning a slow rise to leadership of the lodge, while Rachel did the same with the Eastern Star.

Don Harris meanwhile had risen above the differences he'd had with Nevills and joined him for a 1941 trip down the San Juan and Colorado. But the friction was still there, and this was the last trip the two men shared. Loper, too, felt little desire to run with Nevills. When Harris hinted he might do a 1942 trip with Nevills, Loper wrote Blake, "that would let he and I out."

Although Nevills and Loper were on cordial terms, sharing the same Masonic Lodge, Nevills's unrelenting self-promotion rankled Loper. Nevills was a genius at getting publicity, but to Loper and many others he was a noisy newcomer. Loper in particular had a hard time bearing the boasts of men whose river achievements were so much slimmer than his own.

The 1940 Nevills trip that Loper had encountered on the Green River, had continued, taking the second pair of women though Grand Canyon as well as a man that would spend the rest of his life making Arizona famous: Barry Goldwater. In 1941 Nevills ran a third successful trip through Grand Canyon, accompanied this time by Alexander "Zee" Grant, paddling the first kayak through. As he arranged yet another trip for 1942, he signed on two people that would make resounding splashes in the river world. One was Ed Hudson, who dreamed of powering upstream through Grand Canyon. The other was a stockbroker from Berkeley, Otis "Dock" Marston. Marston fell head over heels for the river and with Nevills's operation, becoming a promoter for Nevills and soon, a boatman.

In the late spring of 1942, Don Harris and Loper teamed up again. The two men began a series of six annual trips, none of which they wrote logs of, nor even dates for, nor a list of those who went with them. The two men had a relationship centered on their love for boating. Although Harris is rumored to have said that the way to get along with Loper was to "do it his way," they worked well together and had a strong friendship. "There was no generation gap between Don and Bert, " says Harris's daughter Melanie, "They were the same."

For the first trip they chose the Yampa. They had passed its mouth in Echo Park in 1940. Now they drove to Lily Park, some fifty miles up the Yampa, to launch. Its beautiful winding sandstone canyon at that time had no rapids of note. (Later, in 1965, a debris flow at Warm Springs formed a man-killing rapid.) They hit Echo Park and retraced their 1940 trip down through Split Mountain Canyon, across the Uinta Basin and down through Desolation and Gray Canyons to Loper's new home in Green River.

In 1943 the two men rendezvoused for a trip from Green River to Hite, through Cataract Canyon. They each brought a passenger: Richard Bedier, a Green River neighbor of Loper's, and Jules Conrath, one of Harris's fellow USGS gaging men from Mexican Hat. Although Grand Canyon has long been famous for its rapids, Cataract, especially before Lake Powell drowned out Gypsum and Dark Canyon Rapids, was in many river stages a tougher, if shorter, run. Loper was then seventy-four. They made a lightning trip—four days, motoring the flatwater and rowing the rapids.

In 1944 they planned another trip. "We wanted to go through Cataract Canyon," recalled Harris:

Glen Canyon 1944: Jack Brennan, Arth Chaffin, Bert Loper, Don Harris, E.T. Eliason

> We each wanted to row our own boat. We didn't particularly like to ride alone. So we put an ad in the Salt Lake Tribune to try to recruit a couple passengers to go with us to help defray expenses and to give us company riding in the boats. Jack Brennan was one of the fellows that answered the ad and went with us. Jack was a postal clerk in Salt Lake City. There was another fellow too [E.T. Eliason, a co-worker of Brennan's], but he didn't take to the river like Jack did. The river got in Jack's blood.

This time they ran all the way through Glen Canyon to Lee's Ferry. Hite ferryman Arth Chaffin joined them for the float through Glen Canyon. Somewhere in Cataract—Don Harris said it was in the Big Drops—Loper had his second flip. Unlike his first flip, there are few more violent stretches of whitewater to swim in the Colorado River. Being seventy-five could not have helped. A set of handwritten notes in the Pearl Baker collection record Loper's comments: "Under water, seemed a mile under. Got to thinking helluva time to lose head. Popped up, big wave, got breath, and went down—about 3 times. Didn't lose head."

In 1945, they repeated the Yampa trip, again running all the way down the Green to Green River. Jack Brennan by now was a regular participant.

Oddly, through this four-year period, Loper's correspondence dries up almost entirely. It may simply be that one stack of papers has been lost, much as Loper's original journals have disappeared. Whatever the reason, there is little record of his doings. World War Two was on and he had an occasional job as a bridge guard for national security. His Masonic records show he became Senior Deacon in 1943, Senior Warden in 1944, and Worshipful Master in 1945—the highest position within his lodge.

One beam of light is shed, however, by a man from Cattoosa, Oklahoma named Paul Jackson "Jack" Watkins. On June 1, 1944, sixteen-year-old Jack Watkins knocked on Bert Loper's door.

> Rachel answered the door and invited me in and called Bert to come and we began talking about the river. Bert was continuing to talk about the river, with me trying to tell him that I was his brother's grandson. Finally Rachel and I was able to get him to listen and he began asking questions about his brother and his family.

The visitor was indeed Jack Loper's grandson. Watkins's mother, Edna Loper Watkins, had died young. His father, a bootlegger who had spent time in prison, "was not much of a father." Watkins had spent much of his youth, therefore, with his grandfather. Remembering a parcel of Bert's photographs of the Colorado that had arrived eight years earlier, Watkins always longed to meet "uncle" Bert. "I decided to go see Bert and knowing that I would never get permission to go, I boarded a bus in Dewey, Oklahoma." Two days later he was in Green River.

> Bert and Rachel accepted me into their home, with Bert finding me a job and Rachel mothering me as if I were her son. It was a happy time for me to see them and be a part of their everyday life.
>
> After I was at Bert's for a couple of weeks Bert received a letter from my Granddad asking if I was there with him and Rachel. Bert told me to write and tell him that I was there and I did what he told me to do and nothing was ever said again about the letter. Whatever Bert's thoughts were he never asked me any questions and did not mention it either.
>
> Bert was going to town and hanging out and at home. He would write letters and do odds and ends that Rachel wanted done. Bert did not have a Social Security check coming in every month but he did get money from serving in the Spanish American War. It was not a lot of money but it was money he received each month and he supplemented with doing guide work on the river and odd jobs. He was seventy-five years old when I was there. Rachel and Bert truly loved each other and their life style was very layed back.

Jack Watkins returned home in August, but always felt his visit forged Bert Loper's resolve to come back and visit his brother in Oklahoma one more time. #

Paul Jackson Watkins 1947

67 I'll sue you

AUTHOR CHARLES KELLY managed to get on a lot of people's bad side with his bold opinions. He was forced to buy back his first book due to allegations of slander. He was for many years the volunteer custodian of Capitol Reef National Monument, and later ascended to the role of its first Superintendent.

"Charles Kelly was regarded by most as a difficult man," reads the Utah History Research Center's introduction to the Kelly Collection. "His ideas about people and history were definite. He conceived distinct and vocal dislikes.... This misanthropic tendency was probably his most identifiable trait."

In addition to managing Capitol Reef, he wrote—mostly history, mostly about Mormons and outlaws—and occasionally ranged beyond fact. He also aspired to be a Colorado River historian, and hence ran afoul of Loper.

As early as 1943 Kelly had some definite opinions about Bert Loper. To Julius Stone he wrote:

> Bert Loper, who claims to own the Colorado River, just finished a trip through Cataract Canyon. Says he ran Green River, Utah to Hite in four days, and went through Cataract in one day, without getting out of his boat. Knowing Loper I take that for what it may be worth. He is 72 now, and is claiming to be the oldest man ever to ride a boat down the Big Creek. Apparently he never reads the *Saturday Evening Post.* [Kelly was referring to an article about a flatwater float through Glen Canyon by Frazier and Stone, when Stone was eighty.] When I last talked to him he seemed quite peeved because you hadn't asked his permission to use his river. How do they get that way?...
>
> Possibly he has had a slight nip from the same bug that bit Major Powell who bitterly resented anyone else going down what he claimed to be his river. However, it is barely possible that Bert might have had a for-

> tunate period of high water and went down the crest of the flood, which might enable him to do exactly what he claims, but, like the Scotchman, "I hae me douts."

Of course four days was an almost unheard-of speed for that run. Unheard-of, that is, until the advent of outboard motors. Three years earlier, Loper had been on a one-day motor trip from Green River to Moab: more than 180 river miles, with one-third of it upstream. Green River to Hite is some ten miles shorter and all downriver. Although no records exist of the date of Loper and Harris's 1943 Cataract trip, it was likely in July, after the peak flood, making for relatively easy boating in Cataract. Two days to the confluence, a day in the rapids, and a day to motor out—quite easy, actually.

What Kelly's communiqué illustrates, better than an argument about river running, are the ill will and proprietary feelings that existed between Colorado River boaters with strong egos. Loper and Kelly both had them, and they just did not get along. Their particular friction may have started when Kelly joined Frazier and Stone in claiming rediscovery of Crossing of the Fathers. Loper was adamant that many had been visiting the site in the decades before the "rediscovery." Frazier and Kelly took offense. And so forth.

In later life, Loper was furious with Kelly, claiming he had loaned him an irreplaceable photograph of Cass Hite, and Kelly had lost it. Although Kelly denied it, he later hemmed and hawed that perhaps the picture had disappeared, but it was not his fault.

Loper passed his feelings on. Shortly after Loper's death, Kelly told of receiving a hot letter from Rachel:

> The opening paragraph was: "If you ever write anything about Bert Loper, good or bad, I will sue you." I replied that thousands of men, women and children were now going down the river and it was no longer news. I also listed the things Bert claimed I had stolen from him, reminding her I had never visited him but once and talked to him in her presence. I told her the stories Bert had spread about me had injured no one but himself. So I guess that chapter is ended. #

68 My sweetheart

WITH WORLD WAR Two in full swing and her husband working as a bridge guard in Green River, Rachel Loper went to Salt Lake City to find a way to do her part. On November 13, 1944, she took a job packing boxes at Hill Field, the Army Air Corps base north of town engaged in round-the-clock maintenance and supply operations. For the next six months Rachel punched the clock for eight hours a day, six days a week, living in a dormitory at Hill Field. She shared quarters with her landlady from Green River, Millie Biddlecome. Rachel's only known diary dates from this period and sheds a wonderful light on the state of the Lopers' twenty-eight-year-old marriage. Rachel was then fifty-two, Bert seventy-five.

The diary chiefly records the humdrum activities of the day—breakfast, going to work, coming home, taking evening typing classes, having a bath, going to bed, and the day's letters. Rare was the day that Rachel did not record sending or receiving a letter to or from Bert—often both. But once in a while she mentioned how she felt:

November 23, 1944—Thanksgiving day we worked but I am thankful I can work also that I have a wonderful husband.

November 24, 1944— … had a letter from Bert tonight and I am happy to hear from him I sure am.

November 30, 1944—up at 5-30 A.M. same thing over and over went to breakfast.… Rec a letter from Bert and it always peps me up to hear from him.

December 1, 1944—Rec a letter from Bert and was it a blue one I'll say it was but he sent me $10 to come home on so tomorrow Millie and I will be off for Green River. [The bus to Green River arrived at 2:30 A.M. Sunday morning, and Rachel had to catch the 2:00 P.M. bus home back to Salt Lake that afternoon.]

December 13, 1944—Rec. my first Pay day $54.94 was I thrilled I'll say I

> was, had a letter from Bert and am I proud of him this was my first letter this week and I could just hug it to ribbons for I love that guy.
>
> December 18, 1944— ... just think one day closer to Bert & will be glad when it is Sat. so I can be with Bert. [Bert took the bus to Salt Lake City for the holidays, but Rachel only got a few days off to be with him. Even though they were apart for just a few days at a time that week, they still wrote.]
>
> December 26, 1944— ... wrote a letter to ... my Darling Husband Bert Loper.
>
> January 1, 1945—went to work today but hated to I wanted to be with Bert but could not so New Year came in, Bert in Green River me in Hill Field hope this is the last New Year we will be apart.
>
> January 5, 1945—rec. a letter from my Husband Bert and it sure makes you feel good after a hard day.
>
> January 8, 1945—had two letters from Bert and he was really disappointed no mail for him for two days.
>
> January 9, 1945—read a letter from Bert and it makes me feel very good to know he got 3 letters at once and I guess he was happy and I am happy for him to.
>
> January 12, 1945—rec 2 letters from Bert and am I happy for 2 & I would like to quit and be with Bert. Now home writing letter to Bert, Millie is typing, one week from tomorrow I will see my Sweetheart.

The lovebirds made the pilgrimage to see each other a couple times a month, even though they got precious few hours together for their efforts. "Oh hell, I'm tellin' ya," recalled Bill Busenbark. "They were just like a couple of young lovers, yesterday, today, tomorrow, just always the same." In Salt Lake they stayed with Rachel's nephew Tom. Tom's son Blaine was especially close to the Lopers. He had often stayed at Bert and Rachel's before they moved to Green River. Blaine was usually a part of their Salt Lake City visits, going to shows, meeting the bus, and so forth.

Daily letters continued into the springtime.

> April 10, 1945—I am a little worried about Bert he is going to see Dr. Orr for an examination so I am very nervous till I know just what happens here I am.

April 11, 1945—Today is the 12 April and our Dear President Roosevelt Died of a hemridge in the Head. Rest weary wanderer Rest we have lost a great man an Nobleman I feel so blue tonight no letter from Bert and our Pres. passing away makes me feel bad

April 16, 1945—Bert is supposed to be Xrayed today and spinal test and I am worried.

April 19, 1945—rec a letter from Bert and am happy he don't think he will have to have an operation but he has gall stone and will be treated for it. I will go to Green River Sat if he is home

May 14, 1945—read a letter from Bert then he called me on the phone but it almost knocked me out I was scared stiff, then I came up and wrote Bert a few lines

May 15, 1945—I wish Bert would call tonight since I have come to.

The war was drawing to a close. Germany surrendered in May, and three months later America bombed Japan into submission. With the war finally over, Rachel returned home to Bert. #

Rachel and Bert in Salt Lake City

69 Bert's ghost

Like a planet forming from the coalesced dust of the universe, the Colorado River culture formed from hundreds of different boaters, pulled together by the gravity of Grand Canyon. In the vacuum of the late 1960s and early '70s grew Bert Loper's legacy. Although many knew first, second, or third-hand the tale of Loper's death in 1949, and the wreckage of his boat was still plainly visible where Harris and friends had dragged it, few knew many details of Loper's life. Some had the good fortune to find Pearl Baker's *Trail on the Water.* Others made up the story as they went along. But it was Loper's post-mortem adventures that sprouted the most interesting variations. As early as 1972, Edna Evans wrote in the *Arizona Republic* [and later published in *Tales from the Grand Canyon; Some True, Some Tall* (1985)]:

> As for Bert Loper, the [boatmen] say that his ghost still plies the Colorado and he resents the new-fangled unsinkable neoprene pontoon rafts, the outboard motors and the ever-increasing number of tourist types running the river. If a coffee pot tips over, if an outboard motor chokes and expires, if some equipment turns up missing, Bert Loper is blamed.
>
> At night, a noise can be heard above the roar of the river. "Creak-thump, creak-thump, creak-thump!" It is the sound of wooden oars against metal oarlocks. Loper is out rowing his boat, annoying campers and collecting equipment.

The myth continues, twisting this way and that. Nowadays in addition to Loper stealing things from river trips—"I guess Bert needed my socket wrench!"—he leaves them behind. In the bushes near camp a boatman may find Bert's shovel or Bert's screwdriver. One thing that has yet to show up, although it was present when Harris's trip first found Loper's boat in 1949: Bert's typewriter. Perhaps that's responsible for a few mysteriously dinged propellers. #

70 Infirmity

WITH THE END of World War Two in August, 1945, river running began to re-emerge as a pastime. Norm Nevills had passed the war years doing San Juan trips and one Cataract Canyon trip, but now he began laying forth plans for the Salmon, and Snake, and Grand Canyon. Hatch, Swain, Frazier, et al continued to do an occasional trip, but had not considered taking it into the commercial realm. But a few new faces had emerged in the small pond of river running.

Jack Brennan was steadily transforming from passenger to boatman. Another convert was a co-worker of Brennan's from the Post Office, an ambitious Salt Lake filmmaker named Al Morton. Something about him—it might have been the importance he placed on his film work over and above other trip dynamics—chafed Loper.

A third emerging character on the river was Harry Aleson. Most river folk arrive on the Colorado somewhere in the upper reaches, whereupon they launch and float downstream, falling in love with the place as they go. Not Aleson. Little about the man was not eccentric. He appeared first on Lake Mead, at the foot of Grand Canyon, and spent the early years of his involvement with the Colorado trying to go *up* the river. Aleson had been gassed in World War One and had intermittent stomach problems for the rest of his life. Based for a while in Los Angeles, he began exploring the desert country around Lake Mead and found it to be the most captivating landscape he had ever seen. He began to spend much of his time hiking and boating in the area, conceiving the idea of driving a motorboat up the rapids of Grand Canyon.

There he met Norman Nevills, and entered into an agreement to tow Nevills's annual Grand Canyon expeditions across the lake with his motorboat. There too he gained employment as a boatman with a federal dam investigation in the lower gorge, getting fired when he flipped their boat on one of his unauthorized spawning runs. And there he found a cave, called it MY HOME, ARIZONA, and moved in, living there intermittently for years. Words like peculiar or idiosyncratic didn't quite fit Harry Aleson. He was downright bizarre.

Sometime in the mid-1940s, Aleson joined forces with a disaffected passenger of Nevills named Charles Larabee. For reasons not entirely clear, Larabee took a visceral dislike to Nevills. In truth, a hatred. As a way to attack Nevills, he financed Harry Aleson's attempts, initially to uprun Grand Canyon, then later, to run commercial float trips on the Green, Colorado, and San Juan in competition with Nevills. Throughout the 1940s Aleson hiked, boated, and researched the history of the Colorado.

A steady stream of correspondence began suddenly on November 15, 1945, with Loper writing Aleson, who was in the Veterans Hospital in Salt Lake City, perhaps suffering from his stomach troubles. Loper could empathize, having been struggling all year with gall stones. The doctor had told Loper to stay at home and rest, and put him on a strict regimen, which seemed to help as long as he followed it.

> My gall stones have not bothered me any but I think I feel just a little pain in the region of the former pain to night so I will live my diet a little more closely.... It is very tiresom having to stay in the house all the time but such is the Doctors orders.

Pearl Baker described another facet of that winter:

> Theoretically Bert spent the winter in bed, but his pajamaed figure was a familiar sight to the neighborhood. Rachel wouldn't let him dress because he was supposed to stay in bed. Bert's boundless energy led him not only all over the house all the time but from one end of the yard to the other. He didn't build a boat that winter, but that is about the only deviation from normal that he allowed Rachel and the doctor to put over on him.

"I am feeling very well," he wrote Aleson a few days later:

> but I do get tired rather easy but I think I will be in shape in 1949 to finish my river work—I see in the papers that Brennan and Harris are mapping a trip for next april but I do not know where but they did mention the Grand but next year is not my year so I will not be included

Pajamaed Loper at large

> in their trip but I am not going to cry about not being in on their trips untill 1947 and then I will go in training for that.

Loper seemed content to ride out his health issues, viewing them as temporary setbacks rather than irreversible handicaps. At least on his good days. On November 20 he wrote to Aleson—still in the Veterans Hospital—with more resignation:

> They say that I have just about reached the end of the road but at that there is much satisfaction in the life I have lived so there-fore I have very few regrets and in looking back over the river trail of mine and I get to thinking what I would do if I had it to do over again I think I would do the very same thing only—prehaps—more so.
>
> The trail I have traversed has all been the very hard way and more than once I have gone up to a drift with a saw-hammer and a wrecking bar and come away with a boat and even in my mountain climbing I never belonged to an alpine club and the deserts I have plodded over was with blistered feet and a parched tongue and everything I have done in my 60 years in the west have been the very hard way but I still love it

> all—There is many things I would like to do but there must be an end to all things so I guess that will include me—

By January 4, 1946, Loper showed little improvement: "I am just about the same only my gall stone is a constant reminder that it is still there—I am still on the same diet as in the hospital but I eat much more here than I got there so that might not be so good for me.... The Missus is fine and just as tyranical as ever." By February two doctors had recommended an operation. He finally gave in, going to Fruita, Colorado, where he was operated on March 21. From his descriptions, it sounds as if he had his gall bladder removed—entailing a week or two in the hospital and about a six-week recovery.

Over the winter Loper had corresponded with Jack Brennan and planned to join him and Harris for a river trip in the summer. "But there is one thing, mister," Brennan had cautioned him, "I am not going to let you sit and kill yourself like you almost did last year. [Loper had been ill on the Yampa trip.] I will always feel sort of guilty about that, even if I do know that I would have to hit you over the head with the spare oar before you would give up." He added details about a boat he was building—modeled after Don Harris's *Mexican Hat*, to be named, in honor of his mentor, the *Loper*.

Loper was still recuperating in the hospital in early April when he wrote Aleson that he had already had some incisions tear open again, so figured he would have to lay low and cancel his river plans for 1946. Brennan wrote hoping he would change his mind—this was to be his inaugural trip rowing the *Loper* and he dearly wished for Bert's coaching. By April 20 things had so improved that he wrote Aleson again, saying, "It nearly breaks my heart to have to pay all this money for my operation but I am feeling so good it ill behooves me to complain.... I called my river off this year but I have re-considered and it is my in tentions now to go about July."

They went in June, repeating their 1945 Yampa and Green River journey from Lily Park in Colorado all the way down to Green River. Loper claimed to have gained a pound on the trip, and Brennan was officially now a boatman, causing Loper to wonder if he had trained his replacement. Still, he felt the gall stone problem was behind him.

Don Harris, Jack Brennan, Bert Loper

"People here thought that when I went to Fruita Hospital that I would never come back," Loper wrote to Blake, "and when I made this trip so soon after they thought that I would never finish it and it seems strange to me for I never felt better, all but my legs are rather slow about coming back to normal."

During June and July Nevills went north to run the Salmon and Snake Rivers, trumpeting his success to friends in the press, hoping always to further his success and notoriety. The old-timers groused, of course. "My many friends seem to get all worked up over some of the things that Nevills contend," Loper wrote to Aleson in August:

> but it makes no difference to me. Nevills says that he has demonstrated the possibility of navigating the Salmon in small boats and it has been navigated in small boats many times before he ever thought of boating it—and the Snake was boated by open boats on the survey through Hell's Canyon.

Meanwhile problems with the Green River bridge once again led to the hiring of a guard. Loper took the job, calling his pay through that winter

"Pennies from Heaven," enabling him to recoup the money he'd spent on his operation. He continued to correspond with Aleson, whose frequent letters told of his past trips and future plans. In January Loper responded with his yearnings and fears, "About all I will be able to do from now on is to DREAM for I am afraid that Don has a new partner now besides I can't expect to keep on forever but I am still in the hopes that I will traverse the Grand again."

On March 1 he laid out his feelings to Brennan:

> You spoke of inviting me on another trip but I have never got entirely over the one last summer—Now I do not want you to think that I did not enjoy that trip for it was wonderful ... and while there are no two men that I would rather go on a river trip than you and Don, I still would rather have my own boat—of course there is—or should be—a stopping place for every one especially me but while I will have to give up my leadership for such trips there is no one that I would like to take my place like Don for he has every thing that goes to do such things but Jack I am thinking that it will be you and Don from now on and—I am sure—that I could not pick a better man for Don than you and in the years to come I am sure that you will think of me some-times but I have had a wonderful life for I have done so many things that I wanted to do if I did every thing the hard way and have seen so much of MY WONDERFUL WEST and it has always been a fairy land to me and still is but there will never be one that can see this west like me except Don for he and I see the same things and as we go along and see a little rivulet we think as how that which has been washed away has passed through OUR GRAND CANYON
>
> If I had you here I know that I could talk all night and I am hoping that you will write me before next fall—In August it will be 50 years since I have seen my brother and he and I are all that is left of the Lopers as far as we are concerned so I think I will try to go see him this summer and if I can get back in time I want to make a boat trip to Moab and back so I will try to get me a 16 H-P- out board and if we do we will take a whole month for it—My two Doctors have warned me to slow on account of my heart but—I don't Know—Love to you and the Missus
>
> Bert #

71 Ancient mariners

BERT LOPER is now 78 and we must admit his spirit is magnificent. He is no feeble old man but full of fight.

MARSTON to FRANK DODGE, 1947

The idea of running a boat through Grand Canyon at eighty continued to be thought outlandish for more than forty years. Loper held the record for oldest to attempt it, at just three weeks shy of eighty. But in 1991, Georgie White, who turned eighty the previous autumn, motored her own G-rig full of passengers through the Canyon, not once, but repeatedly for the entire boating season.

In 1999, fifty years and one month after Loper died, Martin Litton, founder and former owner of Grand Canyon Dories, rowed his own dory through Grand Canyon at the age of eighty-two. In true Loper fashion, he refused to let anyone touch his oars for the entire trip. "Old" was not in his vocabulary. "I'm sorry I'm not deteriorating at the rate people expect me to," he muttered.

Loper had always seemed younger than he was. At sixty-eight, Buzz Holmstrom described him as "a big strong man appearing to be about 50." Much of Loper's great boating took place between his seventieth year and his death, including all three boat-flips.

Looking back across the decades from the twenty-first century, attempting Grand Canyon at eighty still seems remarkable, but no longer suicidal. Attitude, health, and fitness are key. The number of years is, to a large degree, irrelevant. As Loper often said, and Don Harris repeated in his later years, "I'm not old. I've just been around for a hell of a long time." #

72 The Great Maestro

When the Salt Lake Boy Scouts asked Harry Aleson about guiding a group of their Scouts through Glen Canyon, he hit the ground running. He typed up page upon page of ideas, schedules, lists, plans, and guidelines. And he named his price: one hundred dollars a day—a fee that, in 1947, was so outlandish that the Scouts did not even respond. Aleson was undaunted. He wrote to the head of the Mormon Church, insinuating that it would be irresponsible for the Boy Scouts to attempt Glen Canyon without his expert guidance, going so far as to suggest that the Church pay his stated salary. Under pressure from the Church, the Boy Scouts hired, not Aleson, but Kent Frost, who had rowed for Nevills and knew his way through Glen Canyon. As the Scouts bussed through Green River on their way to launch at Hite, John Cross, one of the leaders, ran into Bert Loper and made an agreement for Loper to lead the second Scout group, due to launch a few weeks hence. Loper's only stipulation was that he be allowed to bring along his Coleman stove to cook on. His salary: Eighty dollars for the whole trip.

In an indirect way, the Scout trips came about as a result of Loper and friends. One of the fellows who had joined Don Harris on the river in the 1940s was Harris's neighbor Wayne Nichol. Nichol later showed his movies of Glen Canyon in Salt Lake. In the audience was John L. Cross, who was high in the Scouting organization. Cross, inspired by what he saw, suggested the Scouts do a Glen Canyon float. Two other Scout leaders, Al Quist and Malcolm "Moki Mac" Ellingson, collaborated with Cross to design the river trip.

It had been nine years since Amos Burg ran the Colorado in his pioneer raft. Since that time no one else had tried it—primarily because there were no rafts available. Now, in the wake of World War Two, thousands of surplus rafts were pouring onto the market. Cross, as it happened, worked for the War Assets Administration and was privy to the release of surplus gear. When he saw one-man rafts coming on the market for one dollar apiece, he and the other Scout leaders nearly jumped on the deal—until they visualized the nightmare of herding fifty separate boats down a swift river. The next bargain that showed up was a ten-boat parcel of ten-man rafts for $350. Here was a craft that showed promise. A raft big enough to row or paddle, tough enough to withstand the rigors of rapid, rocky rivers, convenient to roll up for transport and stowage, and dirt cheap. For ease of use and storage, and for pure economy, the wooden river boat could not hold a candle to this craft.

This time they went for it. Buying canoe paddles, life jackets, and primitive camp gear, they were ready. Kent Frost was an ideal guide for the minimalist adventure, having made many extended outings in the wilds with nothing more than a rifle and a sack of salt. He and his cousin, in fact, had once walked across central Utah to the Colorado and floated through Glen Canyon to Lee's Ferry in a homemade plank boat. For Frost, the Scout trip was a piece of cake.

The second Scout trip left Salt Lake City on May 24, picking up Loper in Green River. It took a half-day to push, tow, and wallow down sandy North Wash, but they were rigged, ready, and floating by noon. Loper, initially skeptical of the inflatable rubber craft, quickly adapted. John Cross recalled:

> Bert picked himself out a spot in the front end of the boat where he could kind of lean up and sit on some duffels and lean back up against an inflated seat, and put his feet up on the bow of the boat. And everybody else did the work and all he had to do is sit there and take in the scenery and relax and tell us stories about his adventures on the river.... We learned firsthand much of that river history as he had lived it and relived it over the years.

The Colorado was booming along at 50,000 CFS, the spring run-off energizing the normally placid river. "It was exciting to go down the river!" recalls John Huefner, a Scout on that trip. "And oh, not more than a hundred feet in front of you, the raft in front of you would just disappear in the sand swells. And so then you go, 'Oh, look what we got

Loper and the Scouts preparing to launch

to look forward to!' and all of a sudden whoop, we're down in the rolling sand swells." Each morning Loper would gather the captains of each raft, brief them on plans and expectations, then pick a raft to ride on.

Loper had no end of stories. When they asked him why he slept on a cot instead of in the soft sand, he told them of waking up on the beach one morning with a rattlesnake coiled on his chest. That cured him. He gave them a full tour of his Hermitage at Red Canyon, and at Cass Hite's grave Loper told the long saga of Hosteen Pish-La-Kai. The Scouts climbed out the Hole-in-the-Rock trail and made the long walk to Rainbow Bridge, camping overnight beneath its stone span.

"And Bert was, of course, so informative," says Huefner:

> He told us about the history of the river and told us about the currents and the boats that they went down, and how many times he had been down the river. He told us that on his eightieth birthday he was going to go down the river for the last time. And he did. But a grand old man. I feel very fortunate that we were able to have him as our river guide.

On May 28th Don Harris and Jack Brennan passed them. Loper's prediction was partially true—the two men were a team, and had begun running trips for hire. They had seven tourists piled into the *Mexican Hat* and the *Loper.*

On the sixth night the Scouts camped at Lee's Ferry and packed for the two-day drive back to Salt Lake City, via the North Rim of Grand Canyon and Bryce Canyon. Bert Loper was a great fit—he loved the kids and they loved him. They dedicated their mimeographed trip log to Loper, John Cross's verse ending:

Go, lead the rest who may follow
Through deserts of cacti and sand,
But stay in the hearts of your comrades
Bert, you're a part of this land.

"The trip with the Scouts was one of the most wonderful that I have ever taken," Loper wrote Aleson. "33 in the party—not a swear word—not a cigarett—not a cross word—or an argument and in addition to that there were four denominations represented Baptist—Prebresterian–Catholic and Mormons and still no argument."

In thirty-one years of marriage, Rachel had never been on a river trip. She had poked around a bit in upper Glen Canyon with Bert on their honeymoon, but she had never seen first-hand what it was that had captured the other half of her husband. Bert was finally ready to remedy that. Equipped with a new 16-horsepower motor, he planned a 360-mile round trip from Green River to Moab and back. They launched in July, taking Blaine Busenbark, then fourteen, along. According to the newspaper, they planned to be gone a month. They made it to the confluence of the Green and Colorado without trouble, but for reasons unrecorded they chose not to go up the Colorado side, but instead to return to Green River. A little over halfway back, a minor problem soon turned into more than they could handle: Loper's motor quit. As the boat drifted near the shore, Rachel stepped out with the rope to tie up. But she slipped, took a dramatic fall, and broke her shoulder. They were on the east shore of the Green, more than fifty miles below town, with no motor. The next morning, leaving Blaine to care for Rachel, Bert began an arduous hike for rescue. His attempt to share his love of the river with Rachel had gone horribly awry.

To Rachel the prospects of Bert not making it out may have loomed large. "That old desert was pretty wild and wicked," opined Bill Busenbark. "But if she had Bert on her arm she wasn't afraid of God, man or Devil. So as long as Bert was there, but as soon as Bert walked off, well all the good was gone and there's nothing but evil left there. And it might have been pretty tough. He might have got out there and perished."

But later that morning, by pure luck, Harry Aleson pulled into camp in his new Glidecraft motorboat with passenger Ralph Badger. They were on a pleasure trip from Green River to Moab, and saw Loper's boat. Aleson wrote in his log:

> That grand old river man (78), Bert Loper had left to hike overland, on plateau, East side of Green River and strike mouth of San Rafael by swimming Green at 10,000 second feet. (With a weak heart, he may never have made it, on possibly a three or four day hike.)
>
> Mr. Badger stayed with Mrs. Loper. I took nephew with me, up a side canyon on East end of Bow Knot Bend. Bert had an hour and a half start at 8:20 AM—We caught him—some 6 miles up at 10:08.

Saviors Aleson and Badger on an undated rafting trip

Aleson ran back to the river and rebuilt Loper's motor while Bert and Blaine walked back down. Then, taking just Rachel with him and leaving the three men to camp overnight, Aleson, using both motors, powered upriver twenty-eight miles to the San Rafael. He hiked one mile out to the Chaffin Ranch and was back at the boat an hour later with a truck. He had Rachel safely in Green River that night, to be taken to the hospital in Fruita the next day. He was back at Loper's camp late that morning. Giving Loper his repaired motor, Aleson and Badger went on their way to Moab.

Whether Loper would have survived the hike out is anyone's guess. But his gratitude to Harry Aleson was boundless. The eccentric Aleson had been a true hero in a bad situation, and had performed selflessly and flawlessly. If Loper could somehow pay him back, he would.

✣ ✣ ✣

In October, with Rachel's arm still in a sling, the Lopers boarded the Greyhound for Oklahoma. According to the *Washington Countian* of Dewey, Oklahoma, the Loper brothers had not seen each other in fifty-one years. "Bert had notified Jack that he was coming to visit about three days before they arrived," recalled Jack Watkins. "Jack had a neighbor to pick them up at the bus station and bring them to his home. Georgia and I drove up and Jack and Bert was walking back from being down town and Jack was laughing at something Bert had said."

Since Bert had last seen him in Ardmore, Oklahoma, in 1896, Jack had married Edna Abston and had two children, Virginia and Cled Dempsey Loper. They had moved to Louisiana, then Texas, then back

Jack Loper

Jack, Edna, Virginia, Cled

to Oklahoma following the oil business, settling in Dewey in 1914. Jack often worked in remote camps as a pump tender, finally retiring in Dewey. After Virginia died in 1939 of the family curse, tuberculosis, her son Paul "Jack" Watkins—who had summered with Bert in 1944—often stayed with Jack and Edna. Cled Loper had married, had a daughter, Cleda Ann, and followed petroleum work to New Mexico and on to Texas. They drove up to Dewey for the occasion.

Both Cleda and Jack revere their grandfather as a kind, if silent, man. "Grandpa, he was a very quiet-spoken man," recalls Cleda Loper. "He was very quiet. He loved animals. He loved to play cards, and he'd play solitaire for hours. But I just loved him."

"That ol' man Jack Loper was my idol," recalled Jack Watkins. "I wanted to be just like him."

"The reunion was a happy one," said Watkins. "They would go off by themselves and talk, and Rachel and Edna visited at the house. Being separated for fifty years but keeping in touch, knowing where each other was at, was a sign of two brothers who loved each other. Their formative years sure prepared them to live in a cruel world, and they were both survivors."

Jack and Edna Loper ready to go. Jack Watkins: "He was buried in that hat!"

"You've got to look at the life they led," adds Cleda. "They didn't live an easy life—there was no easy life back in those days. You had to work for everything you got. If you got anything at all. But they didn't know any different. Really. And as long as they could eat and have a roof over their heads, they were happy."

Jack Watkins had a special treat for the family. That week he wed Georgia Cowan and all the Lopers were able to attend.

After two weeks, Bert and Rachel caught the bus back to Green River.

✣ ✣ ✣

That same fall Dock Marston first appeared in Bert Loper's life. After beginning as a passenger on Norm Nevills's 1942 Grand Canyon voyage, Marston had become a tremendous fan of Nevills, the river, and its history. In 1947, Marston decided that the "true facts" of earlier river runners needed to be collected and published, and he began writing to every river runner he could find (and their relatives, and their acquaintances); searching out and copying journals, letters, and logs; and motoring around the West to visit and interview boaters and those

Bert and Rachel

Veterans of four wars. Commander Loper on left

who had known them. Since he had inherited substantial real estate from his father, Marston was able to abandon a career in stocks and bonds to focus entirely on river running. He initially figured it would take him six months, but the concise history he hoped to collect almost immediately overwhelmed him, mushrooming from an interest to an obsession.

The correspondence files of every living boatman soon clogged with long letters from Marston, bristling with interminable questions, usually brusque and to the point. While some correspondents were put off by Marston's manner and wrote little if anything in return, others rose to the challenge. Julius Stone, Norman Nevills, Harry Aleson, and Frank Dodge—to name a few—responded in like volume.

So did Bert Loper—he had plenty to say. Loper's file in the Marston collection is a goldmine of information, much like Loper's correspondence with Elwyn Blake, Hugh Miser, and Charlie Hunt. These latter three, by 1948, had largely given up any serious interest in editing Loper's work or writing his story. It was not that they lost their admiration for him—more that their own lives were too busy and Loper's prose too difficult to work with. Now, in Marston, Loper found a new audience. Initially, Marston was head over heels about Loper's helpfulness. He logged his interaction with Loper to Harry Aleson:

> September 16, 1947: Bert doesn't trust me completely yet but I hope he gets around to it soon as I need his help.
>
> December 23, 1947: I had a fine letter from Loper. That man is one of the greats.
>
> January 7, 1948: Bert has been wonderful. I have grand letters from Dodge. Blake is most helpful. Emery squeezes in some help but I realize he is busy.... Of course there are a few skunks but I think they just need educating. That is the way with skunks.
>
> January 13, 1948: Bert Loper is amazingly helpful. Harris was more than fine and so was Tadje. It is tough digging it out of Eddy and Nevills. You are not as helpful as Loper but you are better than Nevills.... I cannot repay Loper for the help he has given me.

Loper overflowed, loaning Marston manuscripts and journals, typing letters to Marston, regurgitating much of the prose he had written in years previous. His opinions had aged and solidified as well:

> There are boatmen that have traversed that turbulent stream that are better boat-men than I but I do lay claim to the fact that there have never been any one that have made the study of the river any more than I for I have watched it from extreme low to extreme high—I have listened to the different sounds it has made in those rising and fallings and there are many things that I could tell that is too much to write about.

Loper waxed vehement about what sort of behavior was unacceptable in historians:

> There are those of river fame that I do hate and invariably they are the ones that have tried to belittle the doings of better men than they and also have waited until after death to besmirch the record of a good man and of all the dirty things that have sprung from the mind of a diseased man is the book called the *Controversies of the Colorado* River by Robert Brewster Stanton.

And about his inevitable demise:

> If I knew that on a certain day I was to pass on I would get in my boat and would land in Grand Canyon on that day for it seems to me that it would be such a nice place to pass on to one that loves the whole set up as I do.

Marston soon developed another angle: who was the best boatman? At the same time, his focus began to drift from a person's feats to that same person's faults. To Aleson he wrote:

> January 11, 1948: Harry: In your letter of the 4th you say "Loper is right on TOP." Now you have found one of my weak spots. I am interested in getting a line on the relative abilities of the boatmen who have piloted boats down thru the Canyon.... Do you think Loper rates above Holmstrom and Emery Stone [sic]?

Loper opined on several boatmen, putting Blake, Lint, Holmstrom and

Harris at the top in no particular order. About others he ticked of a few faults: "Frank Dodge ... may be the very best but he spoiled it all in being so hard to get along with." The Kolbs: "Emery is of the Brass collar type and Ed [Ellsworth] was about the very best to be out with that I ever was out with. Emery ... is a high hat and Ed is the opposite."

About Charlie Russell, Loper groused about one of Russell's newspaper claims: "He spoke of how the art of running rapids was discovered by himself, which was wrong for I was running rapids in that manner before Russell was ever born and Nate Galloway was doing the very same thing."

Don Harris weighed in:

> At the time I first boated with Bert Loper (1939) there is no question in my mind but what he would be at the top of the list. I might rate him, Nevills & Buzz 100%—each being graded slightly different points on different items, but the total to add up to about the same. Of course, now, Bert's years are too many for him to rank at the top, but as far as knowledge of the Colorado is concerned, to me he is still the Great Maestro....
>
> I don't know to what degree Bert Loper has been praising me to you, but I probably know him much better than you do, and know that when he gets started on a topic involving River travel he really carries on. He doesn't know when to quit. At times he definitely "pours it on" too heavy. I think one reason why Bert regards me a very close friend and speaks of me highly, is the fact that I was the one who made it possible for him to make the Grand Canyon run in '39, a trip which, I believe I'd be safe in saying he enjoyed as much & possibly more than any other made before or since. And this run hangs in his mind as one of the bright spots. It is maybe this, and not necessarily my aptness as an oarsman, that gives Bert his regard for me.

Frank Dodge had only this to say: "Bert Loper is terrible old and of course living in the past. A good boatman is all I know of him."

The winter passed in correspondence. Loper and Marston talked about getting together for a river trip on the Yampa or Glen Canyon to talk and write. Marston asked Loper to come up with a figure whereby he could make a little money putting the Yampa trip together. Loper replied, "I believe I have told you the story of the kid and the horse—the kid said that 'Dad wanted $10.00 for the horse but if you would not give 10 he would take 5.'" Like the kid, Loper just did not know how to ask for a fair wage. He couldn't. "Norman Nevills is a wonderful river man and I sure do take my hat off to him in being able to tell them just how much he wants to take them through any place."

The Boy Scouts wrote to Loper as well, asking about trips for the spring. Was he available? What about the San Juan? Loper wrote back that he would do Glen Canyon for eighty dollars, the same as last year, but that he would want one hundred for the San Juan as that would be tougher. He mentioned the high figure Aleson wanted for similar work and said, "The difference is that he commercialized the business and I do it for the love of it all—He and Nevills may think I am a piker for asking so little but I am a little ashamed to take even what I did get when one considers the CAUSE in which the trip is made." The Scouts went ahead and told him they'd give him one hundred regardless of which trip they picked.

Meanwhile, the decade since Loper and Harris's 1939 Grand Canyon trip was nearly past. Although neither man was actively planning the ten-year reunion, neither had forgotten the commitment. "Don Harris was down to see me," Loper wrote Marston in February, 1948, "and reminded me that next year was our year so if I am as good then as now I will surely make it or at least try even if I am planted on the way." #

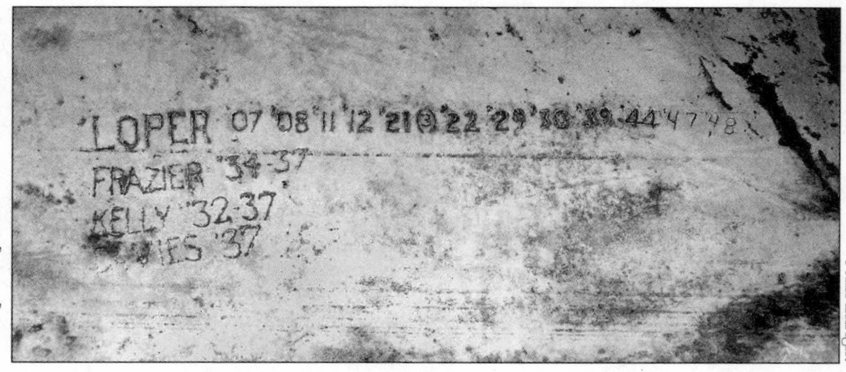

Loper's sign-in inscription, Sentinel Rock, Glen Canyon

John Enright

Legend

73 I can't set around

Realism and impressionism are two different ways to portray a vision, a truth. Impressionism may use different colors, shapes, and settings to create an image that is in many ways "truer," or more insightful, than a photograph could ever be—exposing feelings in a way that simple facts cannot.

Loper's story grew, passing along the river from one boater to the next, even into a few books and documentaries. Balladeer Tom Russell got wind of the tale in the early 1970s, read a bit about Loper, and was inspired to write a song. In *Beneath Canyon Walls*, Russell takes poetic license with Loper's actual situation but evokes Loper's spirit in an astonishingly powerful way.

Beneath Canyon Walls

Old Bert Loper was a whitewater man
For years he ran the rivers up and down
In the Arizona canyons where the Colorado ran
Bert was the best damned river man around.
But one day his years caught up with him
And the sawbones told old Bert to pack it in.

And Bert said:

Chorus: *I can't set around just waitin' on the Lord*
While that woman's out there runnin' wild and free
Cause I belong in that old Colorado
The river's been a mistress to me
Guess I'll up and try her one more time
Though I know I'm way beyond my prime
I've gotta have one more boat to row
Lord I love to ride her rollin' flow

Livin' in a rest home for many a long year
Starin' at the lonely willow shade
Dreamin' 'bout the mountains with her canyons far beyond
Thinkin' about all the runs he made
And wonderin' does she ever think of me
While she's out there rollin' to the sea

Chorus

Then one day in the spring of 1949
Bert he couldn't stand it anymore
He up and walked away, left that willow glade behind
Headin' for the Colorado shore
And they said that he ran the rapids in the night
Gave that old harsh mistress one last fight
Just a pile of broken splinters in the light

Chorus

—Tom Russell #

74 Curmudgeondom

This drive of his towards the Canyon is the strongest that I have seen in any man.

Dock Marston, on Loper, to Dave Rust

Loper took a job in the spring of 1948 at Crystal Geyser. Billed as the world's largest coldwater geyser, it was a short drive on a twisting dirt road to a point on the river just a couple miles downstream of Green River. It was not an old geyser or a natural one—it had been formed accidentally twelve years earlier when local oil drillers missed the oil and hit water and carbon dioxide instead. Its carbonated waters produced spectacular eruptions and soon formed a series of rusty, crenelated, Yellowstone-like terraces. Making lemonade from the lemon, Green River boosters began promoting it as a tourist attraction. Loper, as the old man of the river, was the perfect tour guide. As geyser geezer, he told visitors of the history and geology, and likely rambled on to tales of rivers and adventures as they waited for the periodic eruptions.

The Boy Scouts hired Bert Loper to guide their June Glen Canyon trip. This time he had them deduct part of his fee in trade for trip fare for his grand-nephew Blaine Busenbark. Picking Loper up in Green River, they went for a tour of Crystal Geyser, then headed down the east approach to Glen Canyon, passing through Monticello and Blanding. Kent Frost recalled seeing Loper pontificating in the center of a group in the park in Blanding. Frost, who never met Loper formally, thought Loper was giving off a lot more hot air than information. Heading west from Blanding, they visited Natural Bridges before winding down White Canyon to Hite. The road was so brutal, recalled one Scout, that Loper said he had to put his false teeth in his pocket to keep from losing them.

The water was peaking at 80,000 cfs—pretty high and swirly for a

Geyser Geezer

bunch of kids. The arrangements were similar to the year before, with the exception that the lead boat had a motor for corralling the spinning rafts. Loper again took on the job of guide and story-teller. He apparently threw in a bit of moral leadership as well. "Take it from Bert that tobacco is not good for man," read the trip log. "He knows from experience (not a L.D.S. [Mormon})." Clark Christiansen, one of the Scouts, recalls that Loper neither smoked nor drank, and had no use for drinkers. Like so many cured of vices, Loper had begun to proselytize. Although Loper skipped many of the big hikes, he continued to instruct and tell tales. They finished the trip—not without incident: one boat flipped—and began the long bus ride home. They spent the night at Marble Canyon, where the trip log notes, without elaborating, why Loper does not stand out in too many memories of that trip. "Bert has been sick the whole trip, so he sleeps inside."

The Lopers often traveled, by car or train, to Salt Lake City to visit friends and relatives. While there, Loper could usually get work plucking ducks at Bratten's Fish Market. River runner Dee Holladay, whose father worked at Bratten's for decades, remembers seeing an old man every now and then in the back room, "in there with an apron on and feathers a foot deep. That old guy was Bert Loper."

Back in Green River, he puttered. Not everyone thought highly of Loper. "Bert was considered by most as a tinkerer," recalls Ted Ekker. "He messed around with the river instead of going and getting a good job or developing himself and taking care of Rachel and things like that. And money. How did he survive without money?"

Loper's barber, Alma Scoville, says Loper was genial and loved every kid in Green River, but echoes Ekker in pointing out that some adults felt he was a bit of a ne'er do well, goofing off and running boats when he should be earning money to lift Rachel and himself above the poverty level. Perhaps Loper's apparent youth worked against him—in his late seventies he was, by almost any measure, of an age deserving retirement—he just didn't look it. But as longtime Green River resident and riverman Bob Quist points out, "Around here, if you could *possibly* work, you *worked*. Age didn't matter." Hence the disapproval.

Others felt even worse. Jack Rigg of Mexican Hat Expeditions recalled meeting one of the McPherson girls. She had lived much of her life on the family ranch in Desolation Canyon, and later lived in Green River: "She was also the neighbor to Bert Loper and considered him a mean, cranky old S.O.B. from way back."

In 1955 Dock Marston jotted down notes from an interview with Frank Lawler, an old Glen Canyon acquaintance of Loper's living in Hanksville: "Loper was biggest publicity hound—biggest bragger—he was such a farce—I never did like him—he would sneak away from Scout trips and drink beer—he made that last trip only for publicity"

Norman Nevills had taken a particular dislike to Loper. In March, 1949 Nevills wrote to P.W. Tompkins, one of his regular passengers: "Too, did I tell you a party of Boy Scouts led by Bert Loper called in at Music Temple and wrote their names all over those of Powell and Dellenbaugh? I always claimed that Bert Loper was a pretty ignorant version of a would be riverman, and now I know it!"

Tompkins wrote back: "If you have 'court proof' that he was present and knew of it at the time it took place, I certainly would go to the limit and give him all the adverse publicity he deserves.... I can't imagine anyone so devoid of pride and self respect ever to have permitted defacing those names and Loper should get what he deserves providing you have the undisputed facts in the case."

Nevills responded: "We got a record, photographs and all, of Bert

Loper and his defacement of the Music Temple. Believe I will release it this coming month. Have hesitated to do so as there is always, then, the usual cry of my trying to discredit another riverman."

Oddly, there is no other record of this defacement by subsequent travelers. What, if anything, took place, must have been either very impermanent, overstated, or imagined. The 1948 Scout trip recorded signing in at the register, and both 1949 trips commented on the Powell inscriptions with no mention of graffiti.

But there were far more good impressions floating about than bad ones. Other than the gossip of his indigence, Ted Ekker recalls Loper as "quiet, never bragged, never spoke ill of anyone that I can remember." And when work was available, Loper was ready: "Someone was always lookin' for someone to come and help, even in the haying business. Haying, there was no machine, so it took a good, sturdy, stout man, and that was one thing that Bert was, was a very strong man, he could physically do anything."

Beyond local opinion, Loper was increasingly the subject of newspaper stories. Ever since his 1939 trip, his expeditions usually made the papers. As his age and exploits became increasingly less plausible, he began to command wider attention.

The June 6, 1948 *Rocky Mountain Empire Magazine* ran the second of a series on rivermen called "Kings of the White Water" (the first piece was on Nevills). The story, largely lifted from an homage to Loper in the *Utah Humanities Review* that Pearl Baker had published that April, was a full feature story of Bert Loper and Don Harris, detailing their long whitewater careers. Loper was portrayed as the "Leathery Master," Harris as his heir apparent. "Once whitewater gets into a man's blood," Berta Harris was quoted, "there's nothing you can do about it." Bert agreed: "A river makes me feel like a boy again. There's a thrill in it, a sense of elation I hope never leaves me." Rachel summed it up: "If Bert tells you he's going to run the rapids when he's 80, don't worry—he will." #

75 Rachel

Ah, Rachel. Would that there was more to say. What did she do all those years while Bert was gone on the river? What did she think about, what were her wishes? She never said. Relatives remember that she usually stayed with either her sister Maggie or her nephew Tom. That's it.

Although it has a chauvinistic ring in today's world, it seems she was simply a homemaker and devoted wife. Bert was the center of her world. Wayne Nichol's daughter Irene remembers Bert and Rachel visiting one evening shortly before Bert's last voyage. She recalls feeling put off by Bert because he dominated Rachel so. But seems both Bert and Rachel consented to such a structure of their relationship.

And then the center of her world vanished.

After Bert's death she made the news a few times when visiting the Grand Canyon or dedicating a memorial. But after a few years she faded from view. Rachel remained a single widow, living in Salt Lake City. She soon took a job at the Ordnance Depot in Tooele, thirty miles to the west of Salt Lake City, carpooling out each day. For a time she lived with Tom Busenbark before taking her own apartment in downtown Salt Lake.

She never returned to the Mormon faith her family had immigrated to practice. She had become a Presbyterian by convenience—"their church was closer," said Bill Busenbark. The rest of the family held firm. "I think Mother was a little disappointed in her that she didn't strive harder for the faith she had been converted to. But Mother wasn't one to be bossy or tellin' people what they should do."

Rachel Loper retired in 1958 and spent the rest of her life uneventfully, outliving Bert by more than twenty-five years. Never much of a writer, her thoughts went unrecorded. As old age approached, she bought a burial plot in Sandy, Utah, south of Salt Lake. In explaining why she picked such an out of the way place, Bill Busenbark said, "Well, it was a new cemetery and plots were cheap." She died at the age of eighty-one. On her tombstone, below her name and dates, her epitaph—the statement of who she was and what she was about—reads simply, "Wife of Bert Loper." #

Rachel Loper 1960

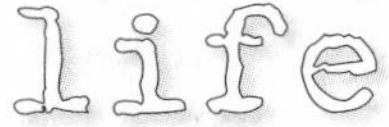

76 One more boat to row

He could no more keep off the river than an alcoholic from drink
—Bert Silliman, February 19, 1953

"I do not know just who Don will have on the trip," Loper wrote Marston in September 1948, "and there is one that wants to go that has never done me a wrong still I do not like him so I would rather pass the trip up." Al Morton, the photographer, was pressuring Harris for a spot on the trip. Harris had made no commitment, and Loper had such a visceral reaction to Morton—although he never stated why—that he would rather skip his long planned trip than have Morton along. "Mr. Morton was through here a day or two ago," Loper had written Aleson that summer, "and was very anxious to have me say he could go along, but I refrained from such a thing."

Morton wrote Aleson to see if he might be planning a trip. Sensing a customer, Aleson wrote back quoting a high figure to guide Morton through. Morton declined. Aleson, meanwhile was hoping he and a particular female client of his could join Loper. A woman named Louise Fetzner had signed on for one of Aleson's 1948 Glen Canyon trips. In spite of the fact that Mrs. Fetzner was married, sparks flew between them. That winter, although Fetzner was ostensibly acting as Aleson's secretary, their letters waxed torrid.

Aleson wrote Harris and Loper asking if he and Fetzner might tag along with the trip in Aleson's raft. Loper, forever grateful for Aleson's rescue of Rachel two years earlier, said yes. So did Harris.

Meanwhile, the river was rising and it was time for Boy Scout trips. Loper signed on for two, the first launching April 16. "We could have given greater rein to our imaginary fears," read the trip log, "had it not been for our guide, Bert Loper, the original and only River-Rat. Bert was as calm as the river between rapids.... His muscular frame belied his age, and it was due to his experience alone that any proof of his fourscore years could be believed."

Loper was back in fine form, his upcoming Grand Canyon trip looming and perhaps giving him more energy than he had shown in years. Yet his emotions were running strong too. Clarke Lium, a Scout, recalled that as they pulled in to Red Canyon to visit the Hermitage, he asked Loper if he were coming up to see it. "No, I'm not," replied Loper. Lium could see that he had tears in his eyes. There were just too many memories up there, he told Lium. He could not relive them again. He stayed down at the boats.

For the most part, though, he was his jovial self. "This guy was really interesting, this Bert Loper," recalls Scout Allen Proctor:

> They would assign him to a different raft each day, and he would sit in the middle and be a rider. The Scouts would be the ones that'd paddle the rafts, but he would tell his stories and point out different things along the route as we went down. And he would sit around the campfire and talk about it.
>
> The kids loved him. Of course there was nothing else to do and the kids would sit around the fire and listen to his stories.
>
> I remember him complaining because he had to take all these pills. He was showin' us one: "That one's so big I can hardly swallow it." I don't know what they were, but he was a fun guy, just fascinating to listen to. I remember him telling us when he was in the raft one day, that when he died he wanted to die on the river.

"Well he was kinda like a grandfather figure to us all," says Lamont Jacobs, another Scout.

> And he seemed to know everything about the river, when we'd get in, in the evenings, why he'd go and tell us stories about the river.
>
> He seemed like a tough individual and things didn't bother him, you know. We'd kinda be cold, and he wouldn't have much on or just a little vest or something, and it didn't bother him like it did us.
>
> I remember him eating. We were all kinda getting our fires ready and so forth, why he got out a little can like a soup can, maybe it was bigger than Campbells soup, maybe like a stew can, and anyway, he put

Back in the snorrin' zone

some things in that can and boiled it up and that was his supper. And I remember it took him about a third of the time it took us to get his dinner ready.

Alden Lewis was with a group of Scouts he called outlaws. "We had kind of motorcycle clothes and didn't act like the rest of the Scouts. Bert kind of liked us though. He thought there were too many rules." On the last day the outlaws decided to quit paddling and drift. When they arrived hours late at Lee's Ferry they were soundly chewed out, and ended up camping up the beach from everyone else with their own campfire. "After a while Bert came up and sat by our fire. He seemed to sympathize, felt a lot of people have too many stories, too many rules. He understood that outlaw attitude. After a while the other Scouts started drifting up to our fire. Bert bridged the gap."

Back in Salt Lake City, the Scouts organized a rendezvous one night. Lewis remembers looking for the building when he saw an old man in overalls shuffling around in the street, confused. Then he saw it was Bert. "Boy am I glad to see you!" Loper said, glad to have someone to help him find the meeting. Loper was the guest of honor, and the Scouts presented him with an award for his services.

Loper wrote to the Harbor Plywood Company in Washington about wood for a new boat. According to the *Moab Times-Independent*, Loper mailed the receipts for wood from his 1939 boat in asking for more of the same. Something in his letter impressed M.S. Munson at Harbor, and he offered the wood for the new boat for free if Loper would pay the freight. Upon his return from Glen Canyon, Loper began the new boat, making it larger and broader than any before. Although this gave it increased stability, it would also prove tougher to handle.

In Millie Biddlecome's shaded yard in Green River, Bert and Rachel sawed, hammered, screwed, and painted. It is a testament to her devotion that Rachel continued to help—bringing him things, helping paint, feeding him, and ushering him inside for a rest when he grew weary—in spite of the project causing her deep concern. Loper's health was far from good, and doctors were advising nothing but rest and relaxation. But Loper was as hard-headed as ever. He'd planned this trip for ten years, and nothing was going to get in the way. Nothing. "That's all he talked about," recalls Alma Scoville, "He was going to go back down that river if it was the last thing he did."

"When constructing the boat," recalls Noel Baker, "he insisted on doing all the work himself. He obviously had some help in moving the

boat, but I believe all the work was his." Ted Ekker, a teenager at the time, and son of a close friend of Loper's, concurs, adding, "As I recall, he was meticulous about the way that he built the boat. He knew that was his life that he was puttin' in to that boat. That he might not make it if the boat didn't go, see? So naturally he would have to build it as good as it could be built."

"Hardly a close friend Bert knew but gave him some little thing for his boat," stated the *Times Independent:*

> screws, nails, glue, lumber—and finally Bill Jones, a very close friend, painted the signs, '*Grand Canyon*.' Hardly a day went by but that some friend called to take pictures and gab about the boat. Bert had Tex Reid haul it to the river one Sunday for a tryout.

But as a boatbuilder, Loper was, shall we say, primitive. Although the first boat he built, the 1914 steel *Ross Wheeler* was a beauty, his later boats, made of plywood, were increasingly cumbersome. His 1939 boat appears stern-heavy in Bill Gibson's movie footage. With his rowing seat and oarlocks well behind the center of gravity, the large stern is at the mercy of the river, often getting the best of Loper in the big waves. His

Test run, May 1949

Grand Canyon may have been the least inspired of all. With its gigantic stern compartment carrying the heavy outboard motor at the extreme end, it had to have been extremely difficult to pivot. Howard Welty, who was on Loper's last voyage, said, "His boat was much harder to row than ours—it was eighteen feet and had less rake than others. When he was in the boat, both bow and stern were in [the water]." Although the basic structure was screwed together, much of the paneling was attached with shingle nails. The gunwales lacked any structure at all, the oarlocks simply bolted to the unsupported plywood. But it was a boat, nonetheless. It rowed, it motored, it floated, and it was his own. It was what he was used to.

On June 10, the Boy Scout truck arrived in Green River to pick up Loper for another trip. They had renamed their group in his honor, *The River Lopers.* Somehow he coaxed them into loading his new boat atop the truck, along with his outboard motor. Movie footage shows Loper stepping spryly into his open boat—he had removed the decks for this flatwater trip. It was a different trip, with Loper alone in his boat. "Bert was always buzzing up and down, telling us where to paddle," recalls Harold Okubo. Paul Kimball recalls him as "a strong-shouldered man for his age, sometimes rowing, sometimes motoring." But he was quieter this trip, perhaps weighed down with the gravity of his upcoming Grand Canyon trip. "He was a quiet guy," says Scout Bill Wardle. "You could tell he knew a lot, and he didn't say a whole bunch, he wasn't too talkative. You know usually a lot of the times people that know a lot don't say a lot and the other way around. But he knew a lot, he knew where to find a spring by walking in the middle of nowhere and things like that. He was a smart old guy."

Scout truck with *Grand Canyon*

Loper at Hermitage one last time

One of the few stories about Loper from that trip comes from Jim Smedley:

> There was a stretch we went through that was called Bullfrog Rapids. I remember we were kind of anticipating it a bit, and when we got through one of the Scouts said, "That was more bull than frog." And that upset Bert Loper. And the reason, it was very obvious, he knew the danger of those rapids. He knew his responsibility to those Scouts. And he knew that from time to time, depending on the water levels or whatever, that that could be a very dangerous stretch of the river. And I think he perceived that the Scouts were, or that Scout, was a little flippant with respect to what dangers that river held. But his response was an indication that he was taking those Scouts on a pretty good adventure, which ran some risks.
>
> Well, he was a good man, I know that. And I know that he was respected. He was mindful of the risks of that river, and he cared about us. #

77 Grand old man

I do not know much about gods; but I think that the river
Is a strong brown god—sullen, untamed and intractable

— T.S. Eliot

Throughout the Colorado River drainage, many early boaters stand tall in history. Major Powell remains the most prominent—his journal still being the most-read of any. Others pop up in river histories and boatmen's tales. Stanton's railroad surveys, the Kolb brothers' wild ride, the mysterious fate of Glen and Bessie Hyde, Buzz Holmstrom's solo run, Georgie White's outrageous career—all these and more form the basis of many campfire tales. But on most stretches of the Colorado River system, Loper holds a low profile. His exploits on the San Juan in the 1890s and 1921 have faded from the memories of all but the most serious devotees of San Juan history. His 1922 and 1940s trips on the upper Green River, too, have dropped from most accounts. His Cataract Canyon trips are a footnote to most who work in that area, and tales of his years in Glen Canyon, along with his Red Canyon Hermitage, have drowned beneath the muck of Lake Powell.

In Grand Canyon, however, Loper's legacy runs strong. Why? What keeps his reputation alive here, where he made but one full trip and the bare beginnings of another? What about this man made him *The Grand Old Man of the Colorado*? And why is most of his career, which took place on the rivers of Utah, so obscure?

Certainly his spectacular death in Grand Canyon makes for a dramatic tale. And the crumbling remains of his boat, high on the river bank, are marked on every river map. But Loper is just one of many who lost their lives on the Colorado.

In Grand Canyon, it is Loper's life, not his death, that continues to draw admiration from boatmen. Although few can articulate it, they admire him as someone who was strong, independent, stubborn, and devoted to the river. A man who did what he wanted, built his own boats, ran it his own way. Loper was not the world's greatest boatman, but he was more than adequate, better than most. Nor was he a saint—he had his share of flaws, missteps, and shortcomings—and detractors eager to point them out. But he stands in stark contrast to other river characters as the man who had no family, no education, and no money, but still found his way to the river in larger and more enduring ways than anyone. And he was doing it before almost anyone thought it was fun.

There is definitely something about Loper's self-sufficiency that appeals to many modern guides who live from season to season working out of the back of their battered pick-up truck, wondering if the summer's wages will tide them through until the next job. The contrast between Loper and most other boatmen is stark—the well-heeled boaters could take a Grand Canyon trip when they wished, how they wished, and retire to their comfortable home in the city afterward to pass judgment on others. Not Loper. To be on the river, Loper had to *want it*—to an unparalleled degree.

The things that shine through a half-century after his passing are his love for the river and his sheer determination, in spite of health, poverty, or inconvenience. His drive to be on the water superseded all else, even to the point of twice rowing upriver through a wintery Glen Canyon.

Jack Brennan

And in the end he escaped the horror of a lingering, bedridden demise by doing what many men dream of: he died making love to his mistress, immersed in his lifelong dream. #

78 Heading out

ON JUNE 19 the Boy Scouts delivered Loper and his boat to Salt Lake City, where Rachel had been in his absence. He and Rachel stayed with Tom Busenbark while Bert tinkered with boat details. His long-planned Grand Canyon trip was now less than three weeks away. Bill Busenbark remembered one of Loper's last great driving adventures:

> He'd pulled up in front of the house there on Redondo Avenue in front of Tom's place. And he had his boat on the trailer, and had to have something done, I don't know what it was, whether it was for the hitch or whatever it was, but he took it up to a shop and left it overnight or something.... In the meantime the city come in and excavated right in front of Tom's place, go down to the water meter or something, and they dug a hole there, oh Jeez it must have been eight or ten feet long. And deep, five feet deep. So Bert goes up and picks up his boat and ... old Bert come a-wheeling up there and first thing you know he and the car and trailer and everything is hanging right over the top of that old ditch.
>
> But apparently he didn't do too Hell of a lot of harm to it, 'cause as far as I know, I never heard of any mention of damage. Probably one thing, he didn't see it, even though there was a pile of dirt heaped up there. Another thing was "Hell, there was a road there when I was here yesterday." So maybe you might say he wasn't too keen on his lookout.

Loper's Grand Canyon trip had taken final form. In addition to Loper, Harris, Aleson, and Fetzner, Jack Brennan would be along. As well, they had booked two paying passengers. Salt Lake stockbroker Ralph Badger—who had been with Aleson when they rescued Rachel Loper on the Green River—signed on for the whole trip, and Howard Welty, an Oakland, California school teacher, amateur filmmaker, and friend

Loper's rig in Salt Lake

A last outing

of Dock Marston's, planned to join the first half. In addition, Harris had invited his neighbor and fellow boater D. Wayne Nichol to come along as Loper's passenger. It was Harris's supreme hope that Loper's pride would subside enough to let Nichol row when Loper was not feeling up to the task. "Doctors advised him not to engage in any strenuous exercise," recalled Harris decades later. "His heart was a little abnormal. But other than that he seemed to be in good physical condition."

"We dropt in on Bert and Rachel at Green River," Marston wrote Elwyn Blake:

> and found them about ready to take off for Salt Lake. There Rachel was to stay while Bert went to Lee's Ferry to start down the river. I wish them all the luck in the world but I must admit that Bert looked rather feeble in carrying his 80 years around. His new boat is adequate for the job and I believe he can do the job with luck with him.

To Nevills, Marston was slightly more complimentary of Loper's handiwork:

> Checked in with Bert Loper. Saw his new boat and he has done quite a remarkable job of construction on it. He was very tired and the 80 years were hanging heavy on him. We went along as far as Provo. We wish him all the luck but must admit that he is crazier than either Nevills or Marston.

✣ ✣ ✣

The year 1949 remains a landmark in Grand Canyon river history. It saw the first trips for P.T. Reilly, Jack Brennan, and Harry Aleson, as well as the last trips for Bert Loper and Norm Nevills. In June the one hundredth person made the complete voyage through Grand Canyon.

Most significant, perhaps, was Ed Hudson's trip that launched June 12. A year earlier, Hudson built a wooden inboard motorboat, the *Esmeralda II*, with plans for uprunning the Colorado through Grand Canyon. Underpowered, he had failed.

For his 1949 attempt, Dock Marston convinced him to run downriver first and stash gasoline for the uprun. Although Hudson's second uprun failed as well, his motorized downriver run—a first—made history, Marston claiming to have ended the era of rowboats.

Now, with the *Esmeralda II*'s exhaust still hanging in the Grand Canyon air, Bert Loper—born during the Powell expedition—made final preparations for one more trip. #

79 Destiny

"EVERYONE went hiking up to Hole-in-the-Rock," recalls Alden Lewis of his 1949 Glen Canyon trip.

> Bert stayed back. So did I. After a while he came over and asked if I didn't want to do a little hike. I did. We climbed up a ways and sat on a ledge and talked as we looked out over the river.
>
> Bert was his own man. He had high expectations, and could be judgmental about those who did not live up to them. He had a great compassion for the earth. Had a bit of outlaw in his eyes. He looked like an old eagle looking out over his lair.
>
> He talked of the two great loves of his life, his wife, and the river.

In the end Loper had to choose between those two loves. As death approached, would he go to Rachel, or to the Colorado? In the mythic sense there was little choice. Rachel could be his adoring wife, his lover, his partner in life. But the Colorado was lover, sister, mother, god, and goddess. Through her he had his only "sons," Elwyn Blake and Don Harris. The River could give him both life and death—indeed, the archtypical goddess often consumes her child. Loper made the only choice he could.

No accounts exist of that final parting of Bert and Rachel in Salt Lake City. Bill Busenbark felt Rachel never doubted he would return from his river trips, that he was essentially immortal, that he could do anything. Jack Watkins, Loper's grand-nephew, disagrees. "She knew on that last trip," he says gravely, "She knew he was not coming back."

Did Loper plan to die that way? Did he know this was the end? Wayne Nichol's family felt he did, and in fact were a bit resentful that Loper was taking Wayne with him on his crossing of the River Styx.

Certainly Loper *planned* the trip—but that was ten years earlier. And for that final decade, as his health deteriorated, the trip was always in his mind. His heart was on its own schedule, however. As early as 1947 he wrote that if he knew he would die on a given day, he would get in a boat and row into Grand Canyon. But was that really a plan? Probably not.

When interviewed in Salt Lake City before he left, he claimed to have several more trips in mind. But by that final night on the river, with his heart paining him, the doctors' warnings ringing in his ears, he finally seemed to realize that the end might well be near. Even so, he felt he would rather die than relinquish the oars on his long-planned expedition. In the end, Loper left it to fate. If this be the end, so be it. Take me.

Few are so lucky. #

80 Casting off

Nothing in his life
Became him like the leaving it; he died
As one that had been studied in his death,
To throw away the dearest thing he ow'd,
As 'twere a careless trifle.
— SHAKESPEARE, Macbeth

BERT LOPER left Rachel in Salt Lake City and headed south to meet Harris. Of course, he took his typewriter:

> July 6
>
> Our Colo. River Expedition left Salt Lake about 9-39-A.M. and it fell to me to haul my boat to Richfield with my car and in as much as my car can do nothing but boil, the trip was a very unsatisfactorial one for about all the Dam Motor did was to BOIL and I used 7 gallons of water from S Lake and that is not what we call pleasant motoring but we—in time reached Richfield where we transferred to Don's Trailer and Motor so from there we continued on to Jacob's Lake where we holed up for the night which passed very nicely
>
> July 7—we were up in good time and we loaded up and had breakfast at Marble Canyon Lodge—after which we went on to Lee's Canyon Lodge for our mid day lunch. It was here that there was about the first adverse feelings—between Don Harris and I.

For the ten years that Loper and Harris had known each other, Loper repeatedly commented on how they had never had a cross word between them. Finally, on the day of their final launch, they did. Harris elaborated in a 1950 letter to riverman Frank Masland:

> Early last spring (1949) when Bert's 80th year was at hand, and I realized

that he was still determined to run the Grand again, I tried to convince him to refrain from spending money to build his own boat for just this proposed trip, but instead to go as a passenger with me or one of the other boatmen. He would not listen to such a thing. He was, at nearly 80 years of age, rigidly determined to pilot his own boat and go in lead on this trip.

I realized Bert's physical condition and keenly knew that he was in no shape at his age to be bucking the rough water of the Grand Canyon, and especially not to be piloting his own boat. I knew the responsibility for his safety, in the main, rested with me, but I decided to take a long chance, against many odds, and go thru with the planned trip, rather than tell Bert he could not go. I knew that if I told him that, it would bring an end to a long, cherished friendship for Bert. It is needless to say, that right up until the time we shoved off from Lee's Ferry at 4:00 PM July 7, I was continually hoping that something would arise, beyond my control, to prevent Bert from starting the trip.

The afternoon of July 7 was mostly spent in launching the boats at Lee's Ferry and stowing away dunnage in the hatches, to which Bert contributed very little because he complained of being tired and so we insisted he go lie in the shade and rest. When everything was in readiness for the shove-off Bert wanted to wait and start the next day, while I suggested we shove off then and drift down for just a few miles, stating that we could just drift and be at the head of Badger Cr. Rapid in little over an hour.

At this time I said something, very unintentional, but which apparently changed Bert's whole attitude toward the trip and everyone concerned. It was merely that I suggested he let Wayne, his passenger, take the oars while we drifted down for a few miles, then he (Bert) could just sit and rest till we pulled in for camp.

I also added, "That is one of the reasons for Wayne riding with you—to relieve you at the oars whenever you need him."

Bert apparently regarded this statement as an inference that he was no longer capable of staying at the oars all day, every day, for the entire trip, for after that he had an attitude of "I'll show you—I'm not letting anyone help me."

We immediately shoved off that afternoon and during the remainder of that day and until noon on July 8 Wayne offered on several occasions to 'spell' Bert at the oars. Bert would not even let Wayne touch an oar—just ignored his suggestions. I tried to persuade Bert to let me run thru the rapids first, so in the event he got into trouble, there would be a boat below to lend him aid.

Bert replied, "I led the party and went through the rapids first in 1939 and I intend to lead this trip and go through first."

He kept rowing all the time between rapids when it was so needless to do so. He would not 'hold up' so the boats following could not all keep in sight of him. Badger and Soap Cr. Rapids are the only ones where we pulled ashore to inspect from the bank before running. From every angle on the river he was so unlike himself. He used very little precaution and would not listen to any suggestions which I or any other member of our party had to offer. Had I known beforehand how his actions and attitude were going to be I never would have agreed to going thru with the proposed trip.

Howard Welty's river journal gives a more in-depth view of Bert and one of the only real clues that Loper sensed the end was finally near. On that first night on the river, Welty wrote of Loper:

After chores were done he came over and sat down by me to get acquainted. He told me of his life and experiences in the mines and on the river and recited from memory a long poem of Don Blanding's that expressed great love of the outdoors, nature, etc. He then told me that four doctors had advised him not to make this trip and that if he did he would never come out of it alive, on account of a bad heart condition. (He says he will be 80 yrs. old the 31st of this month!) He said he wanted me not to let him be taken out of the canyon or away from the river if anything should happen to him, but to bury him above high water and put some stones over him so that when anyone "comes down the river they will say 'there lies Bert Loper who loved this canyon and the river'." I told him we would try to carry out his wishes if anything happened to him, but I urged him to let his boatmate, Wayne Nichol, row most of the time so he wouldn't have to strain his heart, but he replied that another boatman wouldn't do as he would want it done (in bad water) and he couldn't just sit there, "Couldn't stand it!" and he would rather die at his oars than sit by and let another man handle his boat. He also requested

> that we make and all sign an affidavit concerning his death, should it occur, so his wife could draw his Spanish-American War veteran's pension, the only asset he would be leaving her. I promised.

In a phone interview with Dock Marston nine days afterward on July 18, Welty added a significant detail absent from his journal, saying Loper "told him he was tired and had pains around his heart." When Marston interviewed Welty in person a month later on August 14, he reiterated, "Bert said he was tired—talked of having pain by heart."

Jack Brennan's journal told a similar story, but with other significant details:

> Bert had his 16 horsepower motor, and considerable gas, which made him quite a heavy load so I took all of the packaged goods I had allotted to Bert, and divided them between Don and myself, leaving Bert a few cans. It took us two hours, under a boiling sun, to get everything ready, and we then dropped the boats down below Paria rapids, to a point where the road comes close to the river....
>
> Then Bert decided, for some reason that has never been clear, that he wanted to stay at the lodge for the rest of the day, and leave the next morning. All of the rest were anxious to get started, and could see no reason for not doing so, and so we appointed Don a committee of one to see if he could change Bert's mind.
>
> He finally consented rather reluctantly to go as far as Badger Creek, and the first rapid. So we finally shoved off at a little after three in the afternoon. Berta drove to the bridge, and waved to us as we passed under, and the big trip was off to a good start.
>
> Bert pulled on the oars all the way down, while the rest of us drifted lazily along, and so Bert had already beached at the head of the rapid, eight miles down river from Lee's Ferry ...
>
> We decided it could be run easily down the tongue, or smooth "V" at the top of the drop. There was a good camping spot directly opposite the middle of the rapid, and we planned to pull out into the eddy, and camp there. Bert merely agreed, and went back to his boat, while the rest of us were discussing the possibility of a movie, and Ralph wanted to film it, I imagine since it had the same name. We all made the run without incident, Bert, however, failed to make the eddy, and went down

some distance before he pulled in....

Don had pulled out to pick Ralph up, and Harry and I drifted down to where Bert had stopped, and found he had landed at a good spot for the night. Bert complained of a headache, and after sitting around for awhile, he dug out his old typewriter, and started pecking away....

We stacked the dishes in the pan, since it was dark when we finished eating, and sat up for an hour or more, "shooting the breeze." Bert had dozed off, and snored pretty lively for awhile. After he woke up, he joined in the conversation for awhile. The first opening he got, he told us that four doctors had advised him against undertaking the trip. He told us if he didn't, all he wanted was for us to bury him by the river, and protect his grave from the animals etc., with a cover of stones, and to sign an affidavit so Rachel could get her share of his Spanish American War pension. He was quite moved, and very impressive, but Bert was always inclined to be somewhat melodramatic, and I don't think anyone was too much put out at that time. I was looking directly at him while he was talking, and I could see he had tears in his eyes, and it bothered me to some extent, however I was still of the opinion that he would play out and let Wayne take over part of the time. I should have known him better, I guess.

Welty's journal continued:

July 8

Started out about 8:00 o'clock, Bert leading out. I protested to Don that he should lead, both for organization and for safety, so we would have a strong and expert boatman at the foot of every rapid to act in case of accident or necessity. Don agreed, but spoke of Bert's apparent unwillingness to take anything but first place since he had heretofore always been the leader of the parties he accompanied and he just couldn't follow someone else.

Soap Creek Rapid, about 2½ miles down river was a powerful and impressive flood. We looked it over very carefully before putting the boats in. On my way back to get the camera to film the run Bert misinterpreted my gesture and made the run before I got my camera set up. He did an expert job of it however. Don followed and the boat seemed to run like a roller coaster, high on hills of water for 8 or 10 seconds at

> a time. I missed getting movies of Harry's rubber boat, but he made a fine run.
>
> Lunch—at Mile 21 Rapid, before running it. Bert seemed tired and lay down after eating. About two o'clock we all scanned the rapid carefully and decided on the course to run. Bert remarked very earnestly that our boats must keep closer together because of the danger of leaving some without help in case of trouble. He doesn't realize that he is the chap who barges off ahead of the leader and gets away ahead. He got into the "*Grand Canyon*" before the other boats were fully ready, and cast off. He stood up in his boat to scan the tongue of Rapid 21, and in spite of his age looked every inch the rugged veteran leader.

As is so often the case, the romance of a great moment, when examined closely, has warts. Loper's end, dramatic as it was—mythic, even—was utterly exasperating for those accompanying him. But at that point he was oblivious to the effect of his behavior on others. His speech around the fire the night before leaves little doubt he felt the end closing in. With the last of his strength he held steady to his dream, to run them all, to run them first. With the rest of the group still scrambling, Loper and Nichol were off, and none of them save Nichol would ever see Loper again. "Bert started," Said Welty a week later, remembering his last sight of Loper. "He stood up like a king." #

- end -

1949

epilogue

Si monumentum requiris, circumspice
(If you seek my monument, look around you.)

— Christopher Wren

On April Fools Day 1975, Curtis Verploegh, nineteen, was on a solo hike in Grand Canyon. He had descended the Grandview Trail and was working his way upstream along the Colorado River to the Tanner Trail. He had just passed the mouth of Cardenas Creek when something caught his eye. Bones. Human bones. A human skull. Although initially startled, the thought came to him that "Hey, it happens to all of us. They're just bones." He sat down. The skull and parts of a skeleton were weathering out of the windblown sand, back in the driftwood, many yards above the shoreline. There was no skin, no tissue, no clothing. Just bones. His thought that they might be prehistoric Indian remains was quickly displaced by the realization, when he lay next to them, that this person was too tall, maybe over six feet. Whoever this was lay on his back, head pointing east.

"It is hard to describe how I felt at the time," Verploegh wrote 28 years later:

> A mixture of sadness for this person, their family and friends, a pointed reminder of our own mortality.... I don't remember exactly, but under the circumstances I probably carried on some sort of necessarily one-sided conversation on the possibilities and had enough manners to share a nip from my flask.

Verploegh spent the night nearby and hiked to the Rim the following day. The Visitor's Center was closing as he arrived, but he got the ranger to open the door long enough to take a report—sufficient for them to find the skeleton. "She didn't even get my name," he recalled, and was thus conscripted to history as "an unidentified hiker from Socorro, New Mexico."

Two days later Coconino County Sheriff Joe Richards helicoptered into the canyon with Park Rangers. Richards thought the skeleton appeared to be that of an older person with a large nose, and began to suspect it might be Loper. Ranger Carroll L. Nichols recorded finding the skull, leg bones, and several other bones. Richards was quoted in Arizona newspapers as finding "the skull and a few arm bones." Four days later the *Arizona Daily Sun* of Flagstaff said Northern Arizona University anthropologists identified the skull "as that of an old, Caucasian male who had lost his teeth."

While Richards inquired of Loper's relatives and searched for dental records, the Museum of Northern Arizona's Barton A. Wright drew a facial impression from the skull. "It's not specific details of the face that an average person uses to recognize another individual," Wright was quoted as saying in the *Arizona Republic*, "It's a broad impression.... Don't make me out as an expert. All I draw is my impression of a skull to help in identification. Most of the work is done by the sheriff's office." Yet the picture Wright drew bore a striking resemblance to Bert Loper.

"After a great deal of investigation and analysis of the remains found in the Grand Canyon," Richards wrote to Tom Busenbark, "I believe we are in a position to state that they are probably the remains of your uncle, Mr. Bert Loper." Richards went on to inquire what the family wished to do with the remains.

"Initially we thought they should just put him back where they found him," recalled Bill Busenbark. "That's where he wanted to be." But word got to Loper's comrades at the Veterans of the Spanish American War. "They were outraged," said Busenbark. "They said, 'The family won't even give their relative a decent burial! *We'll* do it!'" Rather than make a public scene, the family agreed to have the remains sent to Sandy, Utah, where they were buried in a small box next to Rachel. Her grave was fresh—Rachel had died just fifty-two days before Curtis Verploegh stumbled across the bones.

A few doubt they were Bert Loper's bones. And truthfully, no conclusive proof exists. The NPS files end with the line "not positive ID." But Bill Busenbark recalled that the authorities in Arizona claimed, from looking at the skull ossification, that the man was deaf in the left ear.

Pete Nichols

Skull and assorted parts at Cardenas Creek

Barton Wright facial impression

"Bert was," said Busenbark. That was enough to convince him. The fact that anthropologists claimed it was an old man who had lost his teeth certainly fit Loper, and seems to rule out another likely identification: C. Boyd Moore who drowned in 1955, just a few miles above where Verploegh found the bones. But Moore was only twenty-two. Sheriff Richards said the bones were near "old high water line." Loper died in the 1949 flood at around 50,000 CFS, which corresponds to the common pre-dam high water line marked by the lowest mesquite trees. Photographs taken during the retrieval concur, showing mature mesquite trunks near the bones. Water was dropping fast, running approximately 48,000 CFS when it might first have deposited Loper at Cardenas—and falling water does deposit more drift than it picks up. Moore drowned in 27,000 CFS, which would have put his skeleton near the 1975 high-water line—and water levels peaked that summer just barely over 30,000. Although both skeletons would have been subject to redeposition in the high flood of 1957, peaking over 120,000 CFS, both skeletons were likely without flesh by then. Neither were likely to float away from their initial deposition site.

A photograph of the skull shows a toothless head with a jutting chin, reminiscent of Loper. In all probability the bones were his. He likely floated the forty-six miles from where he was last seen in less than a day, and could easily have been concealed in the driftwood and mesquite

Bill Busenbark

Barton Wright facial impression

Twin graves at Sandy, Utah

when Don Harris floated by two mornings later.

Perhaps it was wrong to remove Loper's remains from the river where he spent so much of his life, where he had brought himself at the end knowing he might well die doing so. So many times, in so many ways, he had expressed a willingness, even a desire, to die in Grand Canyon. And he had been quite explicit about wishing to remain there if he did. Even Rachel, when she visited Loper's boat in 1952, said, "Here's where he wanted to be. I wouldn't have it otherwise."

On the other hand, he got his wish to die in Grand Canyon and perhaps it is only fitting that he—or some part of him—is now back with Rachel with whom he shared, in the words of nephew Bill Busenbark, "One of the world's greatest love stories."

In the end, Loper got both. A few dried bones rest with Rachel in a cemetery in Sandy, Utah. But the majority of Bert Loper, literally and figuratively, mind and body, heart and soul, will forever reside in and along the muddy Colorado. #

sources

J. Willard Marriott Library, University of Utah

ALBERT LOPER PAPERS: Bert Loper's nephew, Bill Busenbark, long held most of Loper's papers and writings. From 2001–2004 he allowed me to be the first to work with this massive collection. Shortly before he died in 2004, Busenbark donated the collection to Marriott Library.

RICHARD WESTWOOD PAPERS: Richard Westwood is the nephew and biographer of Elwyn Blake. Included in this collection are Blake's manuscripts: *As I Remember; Dean of Rivermen; Boating the Wild Rivers.*

NORMAN DAVIES NEVILLS PAPERS: This vast collection contains a massive amount of correspondence illuminating early river running.

CHARLES KELLY PAPERS: Another collection with much material pertaining to Colorado River running, and biographical material on Cass Hite.

COLORADO RIVERBED CASE TESTIMONY. In an effort to determine ownership of the Riverbeds of Utah's Colorado, San Juan and Green Rivers, thousands of pages of testimony were gathered from hundreds of witnesses in 1929. The tales of many boatmen are told here that are preserved in no other place. Much of this is available online. Search: Colorado Riverbed Case.

UTAH DIGITAL NEWSPAPERS: (UDN) University of Utah, through a series of grants, has digitized thousands of pages of old Utah newspapers. Without it I would have missed much. Search online: Utah Digital Newspapers

The Huntington Library

OTIS R. "DOCK" MARSTON COLLECTION A gold mine of material on Loper and all other river folk. Files particularly useful regarding the life of Bert Loper include: Harry Aleson, Pearl Baker, Millie Biddlecome, Elwyn Blake, Jack Brennan, Harold Bryant, Arthur Chaffin, Francis Dodge, Barbara Ekker, Louise Fetzner, George Fraser, Nathaniel Galloway, Wilbur Gibson, Laphene Harris, John Hite, Charles Kelly, Ellsworth Kolb, Emery Kolb, Chester Klevin, Eugene La Rue, Frank Lawler, Leigh Lint, Albert Loper, Rachel Loper, Hugh Miser, Edwin Monett, Al Morton, Norman Nevills, Goddard Quist, William Reeder, P.T. Reilly, Charles Russell, David Rust, Archie Ryan, Bert Seaboldt, Bert Silliman, Julius Stone, H.L. Stoner, August Tadje, Howard Welty, Tom Wimmer; Chronological files, 1893–1950.

University of Arizona Library

PAPERS OF FREDERICK SAMUEL DELLENBAUGH: Correspondence and journals. Some of these have been placed at Arizona Historical Society.

Cline Library, Northern Arizona University

Emery Kolb Collection: Extensive correspondence files including Loper, Russell and others.

P.T. Reilly Collection: Extensive correspondence with Dock Marston and others. Tremendous amounts of material on Lee's Ferry area.

Ohio State University Archives

Julius F. Stone Papers: A treasure trove of early boating correspondence.

Utah History Research Center

Harry LeRoy Aleson Papers: Aleson's vast correspondence with early river runners, including Loper. A tremendous resource.

Pearl Biddlecome Baker *Trail on the Water* Papers: Contains a great deal of Loper material and journals found nowhere else.

Laphene "Don" Harris Papers: A partial selection of Harris's material. The rest still resides with the Harris family (Harris Family Collection).

National Archives and Records Administration (NARA)

Military service and pension records, Bert and Jehail Loper, Phillip Mettler; 1920 Hamlin & Wheeler report.

United States Geological Survey Library

Papers, reports, and field notes of Hugh Miser, John Reeside, Ralf Woolley.

Other libraries consulted

Local histories, city directories, genealogical material, newspaper files, etc., in public libraries in: **Arizona**: Bisbee, Grand Canyon National Park, Sharlot Hall Museum Library (Prescott); **California**: San Diego Historical Society Research Library; **Colorado**: Cortez, Cripple Creek, Durango, Telluride; **Iowa**: Burlington; **Kansas**: Mulvane; **Missouri**: Pike County; **Nevada**: Boulder City, Bureau of Reclamation Library in Boulder City, Las Vegas, Central Nevada Museum (Tonopah); **Oklahoma**: Ardmore, Bartlesville, Dewey; **Utah**: College of Eastern Utah, Green River, Moab, Salt Lake City.

Public Records

Land, marriage, mining, and probate records: **Colorado**: La Plata and Montezuma Counties; **Indiana**: Putnam County; **Iowa**: Des Moines County; **Missouri**: Pike County; **Nevada**: Esmeralda and Nye Counties; **Texas**: Grayson County; **Utah**: Garfield, San Juan, and Wayne Counties.

Bert Loper journals

Sometime in the 1940s Bert Loper and others began transcribing the journals of his early river years. Unfortunately Loper's original diaries prior to 1920 have not surfaced. The 1907 – 1917 transcriptions come from three sources:

First, the Albert Loper Papers. Journals from 1907 through 1909 appear to have been transcribed by Loper himself. Occasionally he added (with no overt clue to the reader) hindsight observations, comments and short essays, obviously written with the benefit of many years' perspective. However, most of the writing appears to be honest transcription.

Transcriptions from 1910 through 1912 come from a separate file, laid out in a sort of "book" format, beginning with Book 1, Chapter 4, Page 1 (Sept 21, 1907) and ending Book 2, Chapter 5, Page 38 (Dec 31, 1912). This file has occasional comments and questions to Loper, and occasional insertions of dialog reminiscent of Pearl Baker's *Trail on the Water*. For this reason I believe Baker did this work. Where I have copies from both files, the latter shows some grammatical changes throughout the work. For the most part, the major emendations and editings are in the 1907-08 chapters. Hence I have used the former file for 1907 through 1909, and trust the remainder is fairly true to Loper. Just what Book 1, Chapters 1–3 were remains a mystery.

The second source is the Pearl Baker *Trail on the Water* Collection. This includes the first half of 1911, all of 1913, and most of 1914. Baker apparently transcribed these and may have done some editing. She occasionally inserted an "Author's Comment."

The third and final source, for June 24, 1914 – January 1, 1917, is the Otis Marston Collection. This short transcription claims to be transcribed from the original diary.

Missing are all the original diaries. Also missing are transcriptions of:

- many dates between January 1 and May 15, 1911. These may not have existed or been edited out by Baker.
- April 27 – May 6, 1913. This page is missing from the Pearl Baker papers.
- February 25 – March 4, 1914. This page is missing between two of the Baker folders.
- May 16 – June 23, 1914. This gap is between the end of the Baker files and the beginning of the Marston file.
- From January 2, 1917 onward. The Marston file implies the original diary continued after the transcription ends.

Other journals and memoirs

1893–95 San Juan memoirs exist in several versions in the Albert Loper Papers and the Marston Collection

The original 1920 Mohrland diary is in the Albert Loper Papers

The 1921 San Juan journal and 1922 Green River journal were transcribed and edited from the originals by Loper, and exist in the Albert Loper Papers and the Otis Marston Collection. The originals are unaccounted for.

The 1936 Salmon River journal may well be the original typescript. It is in the Albert Loper Papers.

The 1939 Grand Canyon journal is a typescript, apparently edited by Loper, and exists in the Albert Loper and Marston Collections. Copies of a few pages of the original 1939 journal are in the Marston Collection.

The short 1949 journal is from the original typescript by Loper and exists in the Loper, Marston, Aleson, Harris, and other collections.

Rachel Loper's original 1944–45 diary is in the Albert Loper Papers.

Bert Loper Correspondence

Between 1930 and his death Bert Loper corresponded at length with many people. Copies of much of this correspondence exists in one or more collections.

Most of Loper's expository writing was in letters to Elwyn Blake, Hugh Miser, and Dock Marston. Loper apparently made great use of carbon paper copies when typing, so that often more than one copy exists. Moreover, Marston, in a diligent effort to preserve the record, made re-typings and photocopies of many of the letters, often sending them to others to keep. Consequently, many of the letters between Loper and Miser, Marston, and Blake exist in many places: The Albert Loper Collection, the Otis Marston Collection, the Richard Westwood Collection, and The Pearl Baker *Trail on the Water* Collection. As well, they often exist in several different files within the Marston Collection.

Letters to Julius Stone are from the Julius Stone Collection. Many of them also exist in the Marston Collection.

Letters to Ellsworth Kolb are from the Kolb Collection, but may also exist in the Marston Collection. Letters between Kolb and Stone are in the Kolb, Stone, and Marston Collections. What a tangled web it is.

Letters between Harry Aleson and Loper are from the Harry LeRoy Aleson Papers.

Some of Don Harris's correspondence is in the Laphene Harris Collection. Other material, including Gibson's letters to Harris in preparation for the 1939 trip, still resides with the family.

bibliography

A COMPLETE BIBLIOGRAPHY for works relating to this story would fill a book. In fact, two such books are in print and are excellent resources for Colorado River history: *The Books of The Colorado River & The Grand Canyon,* by Francis P. Farquhar. Originally published in 1953 it details the 125 most significant Colorado River books published until that time. *The Books of The Grand Canyon, The Colorado River, The Green River & The Colorado Plateau,* by Mike S. Ford, continues that work from 1953–2003. Both are available from Fretwater Press.

Although I did research in literally hundreds of books, the works below were critical to the production of this book or are quoted from.

✣ ✣ ✣

Avery, Valeen: *Free Running,* 1981

Baker, Pearl: *Trail on the Water,* 1969

Blanding, Don: *The Rest of the Road,* 1937

Boyer, Diane & Webb, Robert: *Damming Grand Canyon: The U.S. Geological Survey's 1923 Colorado River Expedition,* 2007

Conley & Carrey: *River of No Return,* 1978

Crampton, Gregory: [1]*The Hoskininni Papers,* 1961
also: Glen Canyon Series *Historical Site Reports*

Dimock, Brad: [1]*Sunk Without a Sound: the Tragic Colorado River Honeymoon of Glen and Bessie Hyde,* 2001
[2]editor: *Every Rapid Speaks Plainly: River Journals of Buzz Holmstrom,* 2003

Evans, Edna: *Tales From Grand Canyon, Some True, Some Tall,* 1985

Freeman, Lewis: *The Colorado River: Yesterday, To-day and To-morrow,* 1923

Ghiglieri, Michael: *First Through Grand Canyon,* 2003

Goldwater, Barry: *Delightful Journey,* 1970

Hamlin and Wheeler: *Report of the Reconnaissance of the Colorado River from Virgin River to Yuma,* 1920

Kolb, Ellsworth: *Through the Grand Canyon from Wyoming to Mexico,* 1914

Kelsey, Michael: *River Guide to Canyonlands National Park,* 1991

La Rue, E.C.: *Colorado River and its utilization,* 1916

Lavender, David: *River Runners of the Grand Canyon,* 1984

Miller, David: *Hole-in-the-Rock,* 1959

Milligan, Mike: *Westwater Lost and Found,* 2004

Miser, Hugh: *The San Juan Canyon,* 1924

Pyne, Stephen: *How the Grand Canyon Became Grand,* 1998

Reilly, P.T.: *Lee's Ferry: From Mormon Crossing to National Park,* 1999

Suran, William: *The Brave Ones,* 2003

Topping, Gary: *Glen Canyon and the San Juan Country,* 1997

Swanson, Fred, editor: Fraser, George: [1]*Journeys in the Canyon Lands....*
[2]Unpublished biography of David Dexter Rust

Tanguichi, Nancy: *Castle Valley, America: Hard Land, Hard-won Home,* 2004

Webb, Roy: [1]*Riverman, The Story of Bus Hatch,* 1989
[2] (editor) *High, Wide & Handsome, The River Journals of Norman D. Nevills,* 2005

Welch, Conley & Dimock: *The Doing of the Thing: the Brief, Brilliant Whitewater Career of Buzz Holmstrom,* 1998

Westwood: *Woman of the River: Georgie White Clark, White-water Pioneer,* 1997

chapter notes

Sources are listed below for each chapter. References are as follows:

Marston: This typeface refers to the collections on pages 436 and 437—in this case, the Otis Marston Collection.

Loper Journals: See explanation of page 438–439.

Loper Correspondence: See explanation on page 439.

Miser[1]: Names with ordinal numbers refer to the bibliography on page 440—in this case, Miser's *The San Juan Canyon.*

✣ ✣ ✣

1 Oral tradition with details from Nichol, Brennan, and Welty accounts. Loper journal. Marston: Rust file.

2 Sumner and Bradley quotes from most recent transcription in Ghiglieri[1].

3 Original letter in possession of Ivan and Irene Nichol Munsun. Nichol history from interview with the Munsuns.

4 Loper Correspondence; U.S. military and pension records for Jehail Loper and Phillip Mettler; U.S. Censuses, 1820–1880; Putnam County, Indiana, land records; Des Moines County, Iowa, land records; Kirk Loper genealogy files; Internet genealogy sites (Ancestry.com, Genealogy.com, RootsWeb.com) Pike County, Missouri, land, probate, marriage and cemetery records; actual tombstones; local library; Loper family bible in possession of Cleda Loper; Loper family reminiscences from Cleda Loper and Jack Watkins.

5 Don Harris interviews, Loper Papers, Marston Brennan trip log.

6 Loper Correspondence, Durango Public Library for local history, Interview with Vaughn Short on mining, Montezuma County, Colorado, land records; U.S. Census.

7 Howard Welty Jr. interview, San Diego Historical Society; Marston: Welty file.

8 McPherson and Kitchen, "Much ado About Nothing: The San Juan River Gold Rush, 1892-93," *Utah Historical Quarterly*; Topping[1]; *Durango Herald* January 11, 1893; Miser[1]; Pyne[1]; San Juan County, Utah, mining records; UDN.

Loper told of his San Juan experiences many times in many ways. In this I have sutured together with ellipses a somewhat coherent telling of his tale that can be found in no single account. Ingredients: Loper letters to Marston, Blake, Miser; Loper's San Juan write-ups for 1890s and 1922; Loper's Riverbed Case testimony.

9 Harris: Don Harris journal; Marston: Don Harris file; Aleson: Jack Brennan journal; Louise Fetzner journal.

10 Miller[1] *Writings of Kumen Jones*; Marston: Elwyn Blake file; Loper Correspondence.

11 Marston Collection: Welty file; Nevills; Reilly: 1949 journal.

12 Alden Lewis interview; Pike County, Missouri, records; Cleda Loper and Jack Watkins interviews; Jack Loper

obituary, *Bartlesville Enterprise*, June 8, 1953; Frame: *A History of Ardmore;* Ardmore Public Library; Kirk Loper private collection; Mulvane Public Library; Sarah Truly Loper relatives: Jeanne Truly Davis, Priscilla Wilt and her sister Robbie; Whitesboro Public Library newspaper collection; Grayson County, Texas, probate records, cemetery; NPS: *Chickamauga and Chattanooga: Administrative History*, NARA: Bert Loper military records (oddly, only his military records survive. Although Loper referred to his pension for decades, no records of the pension have turned up after three separate requests.)

13 LOPER PAPERS; MARSTON: David Rust, Don Harris, and Rachel Loper files.

14 LOPER PAPERS.

15 LOPER: Clippings file.

16 Telluride Public Library; Cripple Creek Public Library: *Victor Daily Record*; U.S. Census, 1900; BAKER PAPERS; Copper Queen Mine tour; Bisbee Mining and Historical Museum; Bisbee Public Library; Cochise County voting records; Museo Histórico de Mexicana de Cananea; Loper Correspondence.

17 MARSTON: Nevills, Loper, Aleson, Bryant files. ALESON: correspondence, LOPER.

18 Loper Correspondence; MARSTON: Russell and Monett files; Sharlot Hall Museum: newspaper files and city directories; Central Nevada Museum: Goldfield newspaper files; REILLY: Sanger files.

19 MARSTON: Monett and Loper files.

20 Loper Correspondence; Loper Journals; RIVERBED CASE; UDN; *Salt Lake Tribune*: Russell stories; MARSTON: Russell, Monett, and Loper files.

21 Blanding[1].

22 Loper Correspondence; Loper Journals; UDN; Topping[1]; Crampton[1]; *Salt Lake Tribune*: Russell stories, KELLY PAPERS.

23 Marston: Monett, Russell, and Loper files.

24 Loper Journals, MARSTON: Loper file.

25 MARSTON: Fraser, Monett, and Loper files; LOPER PAPERS.

26 *Salt Lake Tribune*: Russell stories; MARSTON: Monett and Russell files. University of Arizona Library: *Arizona Mining Review*, LOPER: clipping file.

27 Baker[1]; UDN; Marston lecture, Grand Canyon, mid-1970s.

28 Loper Journals

29 LOPER; MARSTON: Rachel Loper file.

30 Loper Journals; Baker[1]; Barbara Ekker, personal communication; U.S. Census; Stone[1]; MARSTON: Baker, Dubendorff, and John Hite files; James[1].

31 MARSTON: Baker file; BAKER PAPERS.

32 Loper Journals; Kolb[1]; Suran[1];Topping[1]; Avery[1]; BAKER: Hunt notes; LOPER: correspondence from Hite relatives; MARSTON: Loper files.

33 MARSTON: Bryant file; REILLY: Marston Interviews 1964, 1976, Reilly's commentary.

34 Loper Correspondence; Loper Journals; MARSTON, Russell and Loper files; KOLB: correspondence; UDN; STONE: Kolb.

35 MARSTON: Dodge and Loper files; LOPER; Barbara Ekker files.

36 Loper Correspondence; Loper Journals; LOPER: clipping file; Mullins Pressed Steel Boat catalog, 1914; RIVERBED CASE: Loper, Wimmer; WESTWOOD: Blake, *As I Remember*, STONE; KOLB; UDN; Kelsey[1]; MARSTON: Blake, Tadje, Quist, Reeder, Russell, Loper files.

37 MARSTON: Russell file.

38 Loper Journals, Bill Busenbark interviews; Gary George, personal conversation; LOPER: Rachel Loper obituary.

39 LOPER: clipping file; ALESON; MARSTON; Rachel Loper file.

40 LOPER: clipping file, postcards; Loper Journals; KOLB: Ellsworth: *The Long Water Trail*; *Grand Junction Daily Sentinel*; Milligan[1].

41 Ken Sleight, personal communication

42 KOLB: correspondence; BAKER; Dimock: Scout interviews; WESTWOOD: Blake: *As I Remember*, MARSTON: Blake, Silliman, Loper files; USGS: Gregory, field notes 1918; STONE: Loper file; Marriott Library: Ross Rigby interview; Museum of Northern Arizona: Gregory, correspondence.

43 Grand Canyon River Guides Oral History Collection, P.T. Reilly, 1994; BAKER, correspondence; Reilly, "How Deadly is Big red?", *Utah Historical Quarterly*, 1969, Reilly[1].

44 La Rue[1]; Hamlin and Wheeler[1]; LOPER: postcard.

45 Al Harris, personal conversation; MARSTON: Blake file; Westwood[1].

46 LOPER: postcard; Barbara Ekker, land records; Utah Vital Statistics; U.S. Census; Taniguchi[1]; Loper Journals.

47 Ken Sleight interview; Vaughn Short interview.

48 Loper Journals; Loper Correspondence; WESTWOOD: Blake: *As I Remember, Dean of Rivermen, Boating the Wild Rivers*; USGS: Miser, field notes, 1921; Staveley, "Norm Nevills," in *Boatman's Quarterly Review*, 2004; MARSTON: Loper, Dodge, La Rue, Kolb files.

49 Baker, Pearl: *Utah Humanities Review*, 1947; Noel Baker, email; MARSTON: Blake, Baker, and Ekker files; Baker[1].

50 MARSTON: Loper file , Loper Journals; Loper Correspondence; WESTWOOD: Blake, *As I Remember, Dean of Rivermen, Boating the Wild Rivers*; Stoner, "Snapped on Green River Trip," *UP&L Synchronizer*, 1922; USGS: Woolley, *Narratives of Boat Trips Down the Green River*; (Special thanks to Jim Aton for sharing many of these.)

51 MARSTON: Baker and Blake files. BAKER; Barbara Ekker correspondence; LOPER; ALESON.

52 Loper Correspondence, UDN; Boyer & Webb[1]; MARSTON: Blake, Loper, Lint files; LOPER; UHRC: City Directories

53 MARSTON: Dodge, La Rue, Wimmer, Tasker, Miser files. Freeman[1].

54 Bill Busenbark interviews; Loper Correspondence; RIVERBED CASE: Dent, Loper; DELLENBAUGH: correspondence; LOPER: clipping file.

55 Kirk Loper genealogy files, internet genealogy charts; Floyd Dominy, personal communication; ALESON.

56 Arizona Historical Society: Dellenbaugh diaries for Riverbed Case; LOPER; Swanson[1,2]; Fred Swanson personal communication, Fraser interviews and correspondence; MARSTON: Fraser file; UDN; LOPER: correspondence, clippings file.

57 Coons & Larkin, *River's End*, unpublished, performed 2005, 2006. Printed with permission.

58 Loper Correspondence; UDN; Bill Busenbark interviews; STONE: Loper file; LOPER; Conley & Carrey[1]; Loper Journals.

59 Goldwater[1]: First One Hundred list.

60 STONE: Loper file; LOPER: letters, clippings; Loper Correspondence; Welch,

Conley & Dimock[1]; Staveley: "Norm Nevills"; Willis Johnson interview; Hunt, "Around the Henry Mountains with Charlie Hanks," *Utah Geology*; UHRC, City Directories; Don Harris interview; Webb, Roy[1]; Harris Family Collection.

62 MARSTON: Harris file. HARRIS: Don Harris Journal, UHRC, Harris family, Loper Correspondence; Loper Journals; Don Harris Interview, Gibson: *Canyon Caravan.*

63 Blanding[1]

64 LOPER; Loper Correspondence; MARSTON: Rachel Loper file; UHRC: City Directories, STONE.

66 Don Harris interview; Loper Correspondence; LOPER: clippings; Webb, Roy[1], 1940 journal; STONE, Loper and Holmstrom files; Noel Baker email; Melanie Harris Blair interview; MARSTON: Harris file, chronological files 1940–49; Masonic records, courtesy of Bill Baker, BAKER; Jack Watkins interview and correspondence.

67 STONE, Charles Kelly file; MARSTON: Kelly and Loper files; KELLY.

68 LOPER: Rachel Loper diary; Bill Busenbark interviews.

69 Evans[1].

70 ALESON; LOPER; Loper Correspondence, MARSTON: Brennan, Loper files.

71 Martin Litton, Don Harris: personal conversations.

72 ALESON; John Cross, Essay: *The Way it Was;* John Cross interview; John Huefner interview; LOPER: Glen Canyon log; Blaine Busenbark interview; Bill Busenbark interview; Cleda Loper interview, Jack Watkins interview and correspondence; MARSTON: Loper, Aleson, Harris, Dodge files.

73 *Beneath Canyon Walls*, by Tom Russell, as sung by Katie Lee. (Katie calls it "*Bert Loper.*")Printed with permission.

74 LOPER: story on Crystal Geyser, Scout trip log, 1948, clippings; Dee Holladay interview; Ted Ekker interview; Alma Scoville interview; Bob Quist conversation; Kent Frost interview; Clark Christiansen interview; MARSTON: Loper, Rust, Nevills files; NEVILLS, correspondence with P.W. Tompkins.

75 Bill Busenbark interviews; Irene Munsun interview; MARSTON: Rachel Loper file.

76 MARSTON: Loper and Welty files; ALESON; HARRIS; LOPER: Scout logs, 1949; Clarke Lium interview and correspondence; Allen Proctor interview; Lamont Jacobs interview; Alden Lewis interview; Alma Scoville interview; Ted Ekker interview; LOPER: clippings; Harold Okubo, correspondence; Paul Kimball, interview; Bill Wardle, interview; Jim Smedley, interview.

78 Bill Busenbark, interviews; MARSTON: Harris, Loper, and Nevills files; NEVILLS; Don Harris interview.

79 Alden Lewis interview.

80 Loper Journals; MARSTON: Loper, Harris, Welty, and Brennan files.

EPILOGUE Curtis Verploegh: personal correspondence, interview, and: "Bert Reluctantly Catches a Flight for SLC," Grand Canyon Historical Society, *The Bulletin*, April 2003; LOPER: correspondence relating to bones; clipping files; Bill Busenbark interviews; Grand Canyon National Park incident files; Dr. Tom Myers, email.

photo credits

Photographers, when known, are credited on the edge of each photograph. The collections in which the photographs reside are listed below. I have made every attempt to secure permission where the photographer's identity is known.

The Huntington Library, San Marino, California

Otis R. "Dock" Marston Collection: vii, 88b, 95b, 96, 124, 149a, 162, 259a, 386a, 422a&b, 424

Cline Library, Northern Arizona University, Flagstaff, Arizona:

Emery Kolb Collection: 130, 137, 149b, 160, 163, 218, 220, 221, 222, 223a&b, 226, 227, 230a&b, 231a&b, 308a

Tad Nichols Collection 253

Martin Litton Collection: 201b

Bill Belknap Collection: 2, 176, 357

Lauzon Family Collection: xii, 350a&b

P.T. Reilly Collection: 61, 240

J. Willard Marriott Library, University of Utah, Salt Lake City, Utah: 36, 43 , 45, 201a, 333b, 367b,

Albert Loper Collection, now at Marriott Library: iv, v, xi, xiv, 52, 71, 88a, 111, 113a&b, 135, 142, 213, 214, 224, 248 a&b, 250a&b, 256, 259b, 260, 261, 262, 265, 267, 268, 276, 277, 280a&b, 283, 285, 287a&b, 292 a&b, 293a&b, 299a&b, 300a&b, 308b, 310a&b, 311 a&b, 312, 316a&b, 232, 336a&b, 338, 367a, 375, 382, 386b, 393, 396a&b 397, 398a&b, 406a&b, 410, 413, 414a&b, 415a&b, 416a&b, 417b, 421a&b

Grand Canyon National Park records: 434a

National Archives and Records Administration: 242, 243

San Miguel Historical Society: 30a

Noel Baker: 273a

Bill Busenbark: 435b

Brad Dimock Collection: viii, 8, 21b, 24, 79a&b, 81, 95a, 103, 131, 135, 183, 203, 273b, 317, 333a, 344, 359, 395

David Edwards Photography: 457

Don Fowler: 147, 161

Don Harris Family: 26, 54, 343a&b, 347, 349, 351, 352, 353, 354, 355, 356, 388, 431

Cleda Loper: 19, 20a&b, 21a, 30b

Kirk Loper: 64

Calvin K. McDonald and the Kumen Jones Family, 56, 57a&b

Ivin and Irene Munsun, 11a&b

W.L. Rusho; 402

Wendell Turnbow: 417a

Jack Watkins: 377, 419

acknowledgments

It is preposterous to suppose I could properly acknowledge the many, many people and institutions that have made this book a reality. Among those thanks, the hardest are to those who did not live to see the book. Bill Busenbark passed in 2004. He and his wife Beth opened their home to me on more than one occasion and let me be the first outside the family to pore though Bert Loper's bulging valise of papers and boxes of photographs. Jack Watkins passed in 2006, having been of great help over the years and, along with his wife Georgia, inviting me into their home. Don Harris passed in 2005, having granted me interviews and friendship over several years, even before I was working on the Loper project, and access to his photographs and files. Wherever these men are, I thank them and hope the book embodies what they envisioned.

Thanks to:

Cleda Loper, who granted me an interview and lunch, and shared with me her memories, the Loper family Bible, and photographs of her grandfather Jack and her great-grandmother, America Loper.

Ivin and Irene Nichol Munson for stories and photographs of Irene's father, Wayne Nichol, and a copy of Nichol's letter from Phantom Ranch.

Barbara Ekker, for endless help with the background and history of Hanksville characters.

Kirk Loper of Mulvane, Kansas, who collected and posted pieces of the history of the Mulvane Lopers, and who, when I showed up in Mulvane, set aside most of a day to go through his genealogical files.

Fred Swanson, for help with the story of Dave Rust and the Frasers; Sean Stewart at the San Diego Historical Society Research Library for information on Howard Welty. Bill Baker, who helped with the outline of Loper's Masonic career; Mike Milligan for help with Westwater history. Dave Spillman and Brad Ilg for steering me to Curtis Verploegh, the unknown hiker who found Bert's bones.

Bert Loper's river scouts for their letters, emails, and interviews: John Huefner, Don Ensign, Clarke Lium, Gordon Woodbury, Bill Wardle, John Cushing, Vaughn Wonnagut, Vere Barrett, Allen Proctor, Earl Hansen, Wendell Turnbow, Stanley Spotz, James Smedley, Karl Swan, Clark Christiansen, Harold Okubo, Cleese Hilton, Alden Lewis, Lamont Jacobs, Allan Nelson, Gene

Bramhall, Don Winward, Dennis Temple, and Paul Kimball.

For granting me their time, interviews, and correspondence: Blaine Busenbark, Al Harris, Melanie Harris Blair, Kent Frost, Alma Scoville, Ted Ekker, Gary George, Noel Baker, Darlene Morton Phillips, Mrs. Howard C. Badger, Curtis Verploegh, Bob Quist.

Among the more far-flung thanks are to many I met via internet genealogy chat-rooms and list serves and wild-hunch Google searches: Gloria Lester, for help tacking down Jehail P. Loper's records; Jeanne Truly Davis, Priscilla Wilt and her sister Robbie, descendants of Sarah Truly Loper, for help piecing together the later life of Jehail P. Loper; Linda Lowe, descendant of Marcellus "Pete" Mettler, for help with the Mettler ancestry.

My incredibly helpful friends in the online river history world, who answered many inane questions and pointed me in new directions: Jim Aton, Alfred Holland, Don Fowler, Katie Lee, Gus Scott, Ken Sleight, Bob Webb, Roy Webb, Drifter Smith, John O'Brien, Earl Perry, Richard Quartaroli, W.L. "Bud" Rusho, Mike Anderson, John Weisheit, Jim Knipmeyer, Gaylord Staveley, Barry Scholl, Dan Cassidy, Ellen Meloy, Eleanor Inskip, Earle Spamer, Dove Menkes, Dave Mortenson, Diane Boyer, Tom Myers, Don Lago, George Sibley, Amil Quayle, Bego Gerhart, Dave Lyle, Matt Kaplinski, Cort Conley, Vince Welch, Steve "T-Berry" Young.

Stalwarts at institutions who have gone above and beyond: Dr. William Frank at The Huntington Library, curator and wizard of the incomparable Marston Collection; Roy Webb at Marriott Library at University of Utah; Richard Quartaroli at Cline Library; Mike Quinn, Kim Besom and Colleen Hyde at Grand Canyon National Park, Bill Garrett at the Boulder City Bureau of Reclamation Library, who tracked down a photocopy of the report of Loper's 1920 voyage, which even Dock Marston failed to find—and Marene Baker at National Archives who against all odds found the original report.

My patient and hard-working manuscript reviewers, whose advice I usually followed, but occasionally overrode at my own peril: Bob Webb, Al Holland, Jim Aton, Earl Perry, Roy Webb, Drifter Smith, John O'Brien, Kevin Dee, Christophe Magny, Achim Gottwald. All errors are mine alone.

Jeri Ledbetter for patience, diligence, and swiftness in the tedious job of indexing this beast. And much, much more. Dave Edwards for the killer author shot. Tom Russell and Cheryl Coons for use of their brilliant lyrics.

Apologies to all I missed, and a huge thanks to all my friends and compatriots in the river community, for whom this book was written.

index

D

E

F

G

H

I

J

K

L

M

N

O

P

Q

R

S

T

U

David Edwards Photography

the author

BRAD DIMOCK was born in Ithaca, New York and received a Bachelor of Arts from Prescott College in 1971. He has spent much of his time since then as a boatman in Grand Canyon and rivers throughout the world. Fearful of real work, he began writing in the mid-1990s. His 2001 *Sunk Without a Sound: the Tragic Colorado River Honeymoon of Glen and Bessie Hyde*, received the National Outdoor Book Award and the Arizona Highways Nonfiction Book Award. He lives and writes in Flagstaff, Arizona.

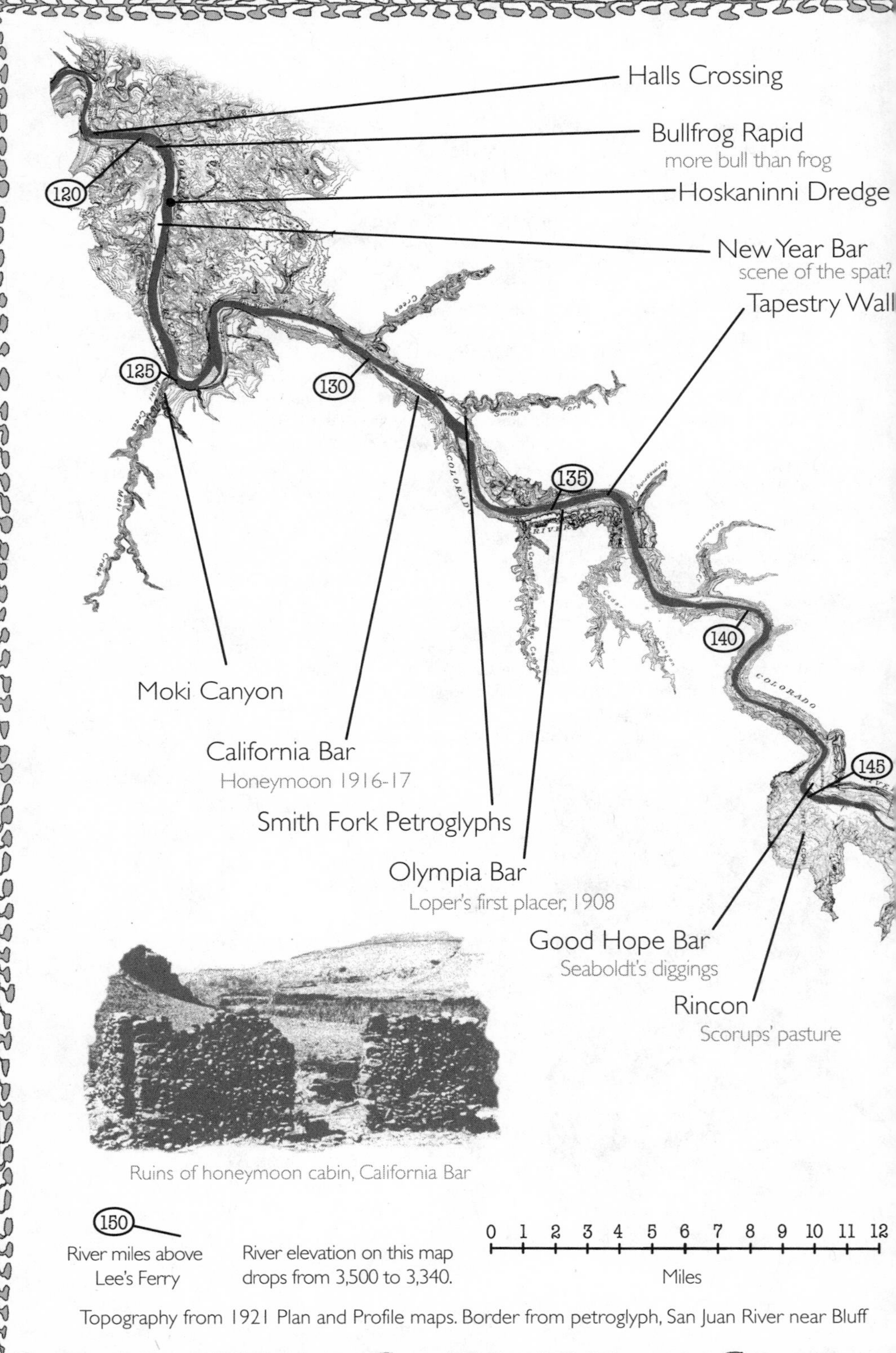

Ruins of honeymoon cabin, California Bar

Topography from 1921 Plan and Profile maps. Border from petroglyph, San Juan River near Bluff